Arctogea

The North Polar Garden of Eden and the Celestial People

Volume I

Summer 7531

(2022 A.D.)

Adam Volynets

…..For more than 2000 years this place is recognized as a center - a place of the beginnings of three major Asiatic religions: Hinduism (Brahmanism), Buddhism, and Jainism. This place is the world center by definition in that:

CHATURDVĪPĀ VASUMATĪ

(THE FOUR-CONTINENT EARTH)

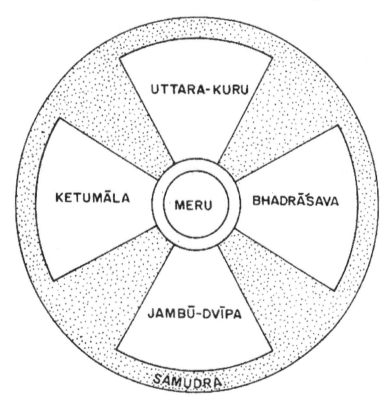

Adapted from Siracar 1967

1. *It establishes order in Chaos.*
2. *It communicates with other cosmic levels – heaven, earth, and the netherworld.*
3. *It is a navel that spreads nutrients over the four cardinal directions covering the entire creation.*
4. *It is a place where the sacred manifests.*

Content

Introduction

"The man of the future is the man who has the longest memory" -
Friedrich Nietzsche

A tree whose roots are cut off is doomed, and it will surely die sooner or later. Man, who has lost his ancient tradition, loses his nature and essential sustenance, then his soul becomes an easy target for the subterranean gravitational forces which would tend to drag him into the abyss itself. That is why it is necessary to try to relight the lamp in our inner altar, which will shed even a small light so that the ghosts of oblivion do not swallow us. The Trinity is also intertwined in a temporal sense, so knowing the past enables us to understand the present from where we consciously act and create a new future. It's time to remember. The further we manage to go back, the easier it will be to be ahead of time. Today, history science, thanks to many forgotten, old, but also new researchers, is gaining more and more intensity and curiosity, where subsequently the thick layer of fog is rising more and more, and with that our horizon is clearing. Following the scientific discoveries of the past centuries in step with the mythological traces and remains, this adventure of ours will take us precisely to one archaic and magical land that is undoubtedly the inspiration for every fairy tale. However, this book is not the work of a fantasist, nor is it the product of a love of learned paradox, nor is it a cunningly contrived story aimed at certain tendencies in current science, philosophy, or religion, but rather it is a thoroughly serious and sincere scholarly attempt to present the true and final solution to one of the greatest and most fascinating problems connected with the history of mankind, as to where his native nucleus, his terrestrial paradise, known from the Bible as the Garden of Eden, was located.

The suggestion that the primordial paradise homeland was at the Arctic Pole seems, at first sight, the most incredible of all crazy and deliberate paradoxes. But the progress of geological discoveries of recent centuries has freed the hypothesis from fatal improbability. Moreover, when one considers the vast variety and breadth of fields from which the evidence of truth must be drawn; when one remembers how current those comparative sciences on whose results the argument must mainly depend; the most striking alleged evidence will be noted, both in the physical and anthropological domains, and practically they represent the very most modern conclusions of science. The interest which has been invested in our problem for so long and which has stimulated so many attempts to solve it; has never been greater than today. The passage of centuries has made many other questions obsolete, but not this one. On the contrary, the more the modern world advanced in new knowledge, the more the necessity of finding a valid solution grew. People feel it as never before, while at the same time the starting point of human history cannot be determined, the historian, the archaeologist, and the paleontological anthropologist all work together in the dark. It is seen that without this desire the ethnologist, the philologist, the mythographer, the theologian, the sociologist, none of them could have constructed anything which was not subject to profound modifications, if not complete overthrow, now when any new light was thrown on the parent region of the prehistoric movement of humanity. Every anthropological science, therefore, and every science connected with anthropology, seems now to stand in a state of doubtful anticipation, ready to work a little tentatively, but conscious of its lack of the necessary original data, and conscious of its consequent lack of valid structural law. To the believer of the Revelation, or even in the most ancient and venerable folk traditions here presented, they will be found to possess a singular interest. For many years the public mind has been schooled in a narrow naturalism, which in its worldview has as little room for the unusual as it has for the supernatural. Decade after decade the representatives of this teaching have measured the natural phenomena of each age and place with the fine measuring rod of their own local and temporary experience. So long and so successfully have they dogmatized the constancy of the laws of nature and the uniformity of her forces that in recent times no small degree of courage has been required to enable an intelligent man to stand before his generation and confess his personal belief in the early existence of men of gigantic stature and almost incredible longevity. I also venture to say about this antediluvian episode of history into the existence of this race who are mentioned in the mythologies of almost every nation, even the Bible itself mentions these men of gigantic stature, where, according to my opinion, they were also significant part of this pre-flood civilization: *"**There were giants in the** *earth in those days; and also after that, when the sons of God came in unto the daughters of men, and they bare children to them, the same became mighty men which were of old, men of renown".* - Bible, Old Testament, Genesis 6:4.

Especially the clergy and Christian teachers and writers of biblical history were embarrassed by the popular distrust of these subjects, and not infrequently by the awareness that this distrust was in some measure shared by themselves. However, these questions are much more complicated and indeed sometimes difficult to answer precisely, I will still leave space for the following volumes to weave our hypothesis. This proposed hypothesis will be comprehensively and rigorously examined and analyzed and according to the evidence presented, the reader will be free to draw his conclusion. Hypotheses, although promising, still must face science. Our hypothesis must be rejected if the hard facts of any of the following sciences show that it is impermissible:

1. ***General Geogony*** or the science of the origin of the earth;

2. ***Mathematical or Astronomical Geography***, especially its teachings about the settlement or non-settlement of the circumpolar region with respect to light;

3. ***Physiographic Geology***, especially its teachings on the probability or improbability of the former existence and subsequent submergence of the polar earth;

4. ***Prehistoric Climatology***, especially about the temperature of the Pole at the time of the beginning of human history;

5. ***Paleontological botany;***

6. ***Paleontological zoology;***

7. ***Paleontological anthropology and ethnology;***

8. ***Comparative mythology***, viewed from the aspect of science from the oldest traditional beliefs and memories of mankind.

On the contrary, if the hypothesis is capable of meeting especially this eightfold test, especially if we can show, it not only to be acceptable; but also, to a greater or lesser degree to be supported by the positive evidence of the facts in almost all these fields of knowledge, we shall allow ourselves a much fuller and more conclusive verification than is usual in prehistoric researches. Although I'm an artist by profession and not a graduate archaeologist, geologist or historian, I still try my best to keep the rational dimension and to be grounded, not resorting to any imagination, personal sentiments, or romantic fantasies.

If we go back to our ancient past especially here in the Balkans, we gradually arrive at the prehistoric Neolithic epoch of the culture known today as Vinča (5700-4500 BC), where many scientists in recent years agree that it was a highly developed civilization. Going even further, we arrive at the Starčevo culture (6200-4500 BC) and up to the Mesolithic age of the Lepenski Vir complex in today's Serbia, where radiocarbon analysis estimated this culture at 9500-7200 BC.; which is perhaps justifiably considered as the first center of Old Europe. But is this where our prehistoric story begins or just ends an old cycle? Could it be that there was also an older antediluvian age of human civilization, echoed in various legends and ancient writings, including the Holy Scriptures? Can we at least for a moment break the classic historical taboos and embark on an unusual scientific expedition and search for the ancestral home? The presented analyzes show that there are many arguments for the formation of a different image of ancient Europe (the one that preceded the Roman and Greek civilizations) than the image of today's conventional history, as well as the many arguments that indicate that the Vinča civilization must have had continuity to historical times and after that. The culture of Vinča is part of the general cultural heritage of today's civilization, and analyzes of continuity indicate that its share must have been dominant, given that it covered a large territory and spread its influence over much larger areas through metallurgy and literacy. However, there is no doubt that the Vinča civilization was Indo-European. The analyzes of numerous researchers fit into such an approach, showing that the kinship of the Slavic people with the natives was in a sphere that far exceeded the area of Vinča culture (as defined in archaeology). These analyzes also show that this kinship between peoples and tribes was preserved until the period of the collapse of the Roman Empire; and that numerous traces can be found among all European peoples to this day. If we consider that the previous analyzes have largely satisfied the need to determine the origin of today's European civilization and the homeland of the Indo-Europeans in the late Neolithic and early Metal Age, we now come to a logical question that naturally arises: where were the ancient Indo-Europeans and can we find traces of them based on the available data? Archaeological findings confirm the existence of developed Neolithic civilizations in the Danube region in the last ten millennia.

Votive Carts from Dupljaja. Belong to the Dubovac-Žuto Brdo culture, which was represented in the southern Banat, the Danube region, and Eastern Serbia during the Middle and Late Bronze Age. approximately 3,500 years old, were discovered at the beginning of the 20th century in the Banat town Dupljaja.

According to the logic of continuity analysis, it would be easy to conclude that a population with similar anthropological characteristics could have existed in those areas many millennia ago. However, the facts of anthropological studies indicate that the Indo-Europeans in the Mediterranean area were preceded by different peoples (most often determined to be Negroids). [1] The reason for such changes should be sought primarily in the climatic and geological changes in Europe, the Mediterranean, Asia Minor and the Middle East during the past 20 millennia. The last Ice Age in Europe is known to have frozen most of the land north of the Alps and the Danube, and warming began about 20 millennia ago. It is also known that there were several mini-cycles of climatic variation in these processes. Ocean levels are known to have varied by more than 100 meters in these processes, and large areas of present-day Europe have changed their shape. *L.N. Gumileev* cites the results of ***Brooks'****(Alison S. Brooks)* research (according to *Vere Gordon Childe*), according to which, during the *Würm ice age*, Atlantic cyclones passed over the Sahara, Lebanon, Mesopotamia, Iran and India, which created lush steppes in today's desert zones of the Sahara, Asia Minor, and the Middle East. At the end of the 4th millennium BC, cyclones extended to the north, the steppes dried up and favorable conditions for the population concentrated in the Nile valley. Similarly confirmed by *E. Le Danois* [2], according to which around 5,000 years before Christ, Calabria, Sicily and Tunisia were connected by a land bridge; The Black Sea and the Caspian and Aral lakes formed one common depression; Lake Chad was the size of today's Black Sea and there was a slightly smaller Lake Niger; The Red Sea was a lake, and the Nile flowed into Lake Chad (he made the delta only around 3300-3200 BC); The Western European Atlantic coast stretched beyond the Canary and Azores Islands, and the Aegean Sea was the mainland and connected the Balkans and Asia Minor. According to astronomical calculations, the key moments of climate change occurred around 4,800. and 2,000. years before Christ.

1. Niko Županih: *"Trojans and Aryans"*, LXXXVI book. "Voice" Serbian Kraljevsk Academy, Belgrade, 1911.

2. Ed. Le Danois: *"Le Rythme des Climats"*, p. 109-119, Payot, Paris, 1950.

The question is: where could the so-called Indo-European people live more than ten millennia ago and how did their migration proceed in the Danubian region of the Balkans, Asia Minor, and north of the Black Sea? The migration wave was from the far North and this is how the great migration of Indo-Europeans took place and the period coincides with the appearance of Neolithic Danube cultures, which would then be a completely logical continuation of this civilization. With his research on climate change, the Serbian mathematician, astronomer, climatologist, geophysicist, civil engineer, doctor of technical sciences, as well as a popularizer of science and physics *Milutin Milanković* (*Милутин Миланковић 1879 -1958*) established a very precise model, which found general acceptance in the last decades, as it has proven to be extremely accurate. In one of his analyzes he very precisely locates the period when there could have been a phase of the mild climate in the arctic zone:

"During the thousand years ending in 9,500 BC, a mild heat wave swept over Northern Europe. During that millennium, summers were unusually warm in the northernmost parts of Europe, so that herbs could grow there that now cannot..." [3].

3. Milutin Milanković: *"Calendar of the Earth's Past",* p. 7, From the 117th book "Voice" of the Serbian Royal Academy, Graphic Institute "Makarije" a.d., Belgrade-Zemun, 1926.

On the other hand, myths about the global flood are widespread among many peoples outside of Europe, so this logically points to a collective memory of very old events, most likely caused by climatic and tectonic disturbances of certain lands. The Russian scientist *Lev Nikolayevich Gumilev* (*Лев Николаевич Гумилёв 1912- 1992*) [3] came to similar conclusions, although in completely different ways, analyzing the traditions of the steppe peoples of Eurasia. Thus, in his works *"Ethnosphere - History of Humanity"* and *"History of Nature"*, he concludes that, sometimes at the end of the last Ice Age (20,000-12,000 BC), there was a very lush steppe around Northern Siberia, and today's cold taiga did not exist. This climatic feature was conditioned by the existence of a stable anticyclone which, in turn, resulted in a very small amount of precipitation. Enough amounts of water ensured that the surrounding glaciers melted, creating numerous rivers and lakes, full of fish and birds. Herds of cattle, deer, mammoths, and gazelles grazed the steppes. It is the setting in which the race of Indo-Europeans was created, cultivating the cult of the Sun.

3. L.N. Gumilev: *Ethnosphere - The history of people and the history of nature",* Ekopros, Moscow, 1993.

With the complete end of the Ice Age, cyclones penetrate northern Siberia, northern Russia, and Scandinavia, bringing cold and moisture. The climate changes drastically, fertile steppes turn into cold taiga, ice and snow come from everywhere; the animals, huge herds from the steppes and followed by masses of hunters, move south. Isn't that the same glaciation that the ancient Iranian Avesta (sacred book collection) remembers? This is how the great anabasis of the Indo-Europeans occurs. However, **Gumileev** nowhere claims that the inhabitants of that ancient steppe were only Indo-Europeans; their fate could have been shared by the ancestors of many other races and ethnic groups that we know today. But the memory of it is most vividly preserved in the tradition and culture of the Indo-European peoples. **Gumileev** was probably right, because a long time ago in the northern part of Eurasia there was racial mixing, primarily between Indo-Europeans and Turanian tribes, probably creating the Alpine racial type and the Finno-Ugric peoples as one of their products. Indigenous tribes in the northernmost parts of the world such as the Inuit in Greenland, the Samoyeds from Siberia, the Sami people in Finland, the Eskimos that are present to this day are a clear indication of this thesis.

The German famous philologist, orientalist, and professor **Friedrich Max Müller** (*1823 - 1900*); noted that all impartial scientists felt that **"none of the systems of interpretation was satisfactory"** [4]. The flourishing and study of mythology, he adds, was caused by the flourishing of comparative philology. The discovery of the ancient languages and sacred books of India, and the discovery of the close affinity between Sanskrit and Zend on the one hand, and the language of the principal European nations on the other; is a profound revolution that has, called into question the generally accepted ideas of the ancient history of the world.

4. Max Müller, *Lecture of Science of Language,* volume II, p. 445-446

It turned out that the languages of the main European nations, both ancient and modern, bore a great resemblance to the languages of the Asiatic elite, that is, to the Brahmins of India and the followers of Zoroaster (Mazdeans) in Persia; and from that affinity for the Indo-European languages, it inevitably follows that all these languages had to be continuations or dialects of an original language, perhaps extinct today, and through that, consequently, the existence of an original people and cultural matrix. Likewise, today's historical science still refers to a common Proto-Indo-European culture of the past. Even according to the Bible, itself in the chapter *Genesis 11: 1-9*, for the pre-flood, it is shown that the human society represented one people, who spoke one language, and the biblical episode *"confusion linguarum"* (the mixing of languages) shows us that after the Tower of Babel, different languages arose, where people could understand each other less and less. However, the biblical myth about the ancient unity of the language as well as the mention of the "chosen people", or by others the "people of God" or the "heavenly people" should probably be viewed from the perspective of the Indo-European theory. Although these modern and scientific terms like this of the so-called "Indo-Europeans" will be used in this book, even a personally consider it a somewhat inappropriate coinage, perhaps for some a confusing term, which requires additional explanation. The study of Vedic literature and classical Sanskrit taken up by Western scholars has confused their ideas about the history and culture of man in the past. ***Dr. Otto Schrader*** (*1855 -1919*) in his work ***Prehistoric Antiquities of the Aryan People***, from 1890, gives exhaustive answers about the original culture of the Indo-European peoples, based on comparative philology. In that context, the author does not use the term "Aryan" exclusively for the people who brought those basic Vedic or Avestan books and science to India and ancient Persia, he does not use this term only for the Indo-Iranian peoples, but also for the Indo-Europeans in whole, otherwise, the author himself often alternates the term "Aryan" with the term Indo-European peoples. The simplest comparative ethnological analysis of Indo-European peoples, especially with ***Veltman's*** illumination *(Александр Фомич Вельтман 1800 - 1870)*, shows the great role of epic poetry, which served as a transmitter of all types of knowledge, and the great role of the cult of the Sun and light. Epic poetry embedded with such deep and extensive knowledge and philosophical principles could not possibly have been the result of the meditations of individuals over a period of several centuries. It is quite logical that such a grandiose result of spirituality could be formed only after thousands of years of living in stable conditions, with the great role of the Sun and its cycle. In his conclusion, *Tilak (Bal Gangadhar Tilak 1856 - 1920)* uses the results of astronomical studies of the Earth's movement around the Sun and the theory of insolation as an explanation for the ice age cycles. At the time of *Tilak's* analysis, *Milanković's* theory did not yet exist, which fully confirmed this and gave very precise parameters of ice age cycles in the last hundreds of thousands of years. By combining *Milankovic's* facts *Tilak's* Artic theory and accompanying *Lev Gumiljev's* analysis of the area of Northern Siberia, the picture of the Indo-European polar prehistory began to take on a completely realistic outline. Newer results of paleogeological and paleoclimatic research have encouraged Russian scientists to pay more attention to this and to come to new facts in their research that support the Hyperborean theory of Indo-European origin. These theories also show the deep common roots of the Indo-European peoples and reveal a huge amount of information about the ancient history of the Slavic people preserved in Russian mythology, stories *(skazki),* fairy tales in verse *(bilinas),* and many preserved material and written traces. *Aleksandar Fomich Veltman* understood this 150 years ago. His analysis based on connecting facts from historical writings and folk poetry gave an incredibly good conclusion. New evidence shows how much *Veltman* was ahead of his time and how much his conclusions are still a valuable guide for further research. *Gumilev* with his theory about Siberia provides a realistic basis for the existence of a wide spatial zone with a stable favorable climate over a long period of time. *Tilak's* theory moves it all further to the north, and the agreement with *Milanković's* calculations indicates the possibility that such a period existed around 10,000. - 9,000. years before Christ. *Tilak* calculates that the maximum of cold winters in the northern hemisphere occurred around 9250 BC. and that the postglacial period occurred no later than 8000 BC. (he considers that the ice age ended about 10 millennia before Christ). Based on the results of scientific research that I have provided so far, he starts from the assumption that at the very beginning Neolithic Europe was inhabited by races, whose descendants are the present-day peoples of Europe who speak Indo-European languages, excluding the possibility that they were brought from somewhere in Asia in the post-glacial period, but emphasizing that it still does not mean that it is about the autochthonous population of Europe. *Tilak* also believes that there are good reasons for assuming that the use of metal was brought to Europe by foreign peoples. It also starts from the fact that man existed before the ice ages, and that during the change of the ice ages, the forms of the continent were changed. He considers that there are sufficient reasons to consider that a mild climate reigned in the Arctic region during the interglacial ages. *Tilak* also emphasizes that new scientific discoveries do not disprove the claims made in the Vedas, which indicate that their creators once lived in arctic regions. The continuation of that period could extend over the next few millennia, with the population moving south. More recent research by *Valery Nikitich Demin (Валéрий Никúтич Дёмин (1942 - 2006)* completes the theories. [5]. *Demin* cites the results of recent international research in the north of Scotland, which confirm that even 4000 years ago the climate in the North was far more hospitable than today. Studying the Vedas, Hindu *Lokamanya Maharaj Bal Gangadhar Tilak (1856 – 1 August 1920)* discovers a series of data, which normally cannot be logically explained, but become completely clear and logically connected if it is assumed that the creators of the Vedas at the time of their creation (according to Tilak, at least 4,500 years before Christ) lived in the polar zone and that they had great knowledge of astronomy. Only then do descriptions of long dawns, the Sun's circling on the horizon, and days and nights of six months each become comprehensible. *Tilak* builds a theory according to which Indo-Europeans lived for a long period in the Arctic region before the last major climatic changes in Eurasia. Before embarking on the exposition of the facts of *Tilak's* theory, let us note that such a theory has a deep logical basis.

5. Valery Nikitich Demin: *"Mysteries of the Russian North"*, Veche, Moscow, 2000. - Valery Nikitich Demin: *"Hyperborea – The Historical Roots of the Russian People"*, ITD Grand Fair-Press, Moscow, 2001. - Valery Nikitich Demin: *"Rus Hyperborean"*, Veche, Moscow, 2002.

Demin also cites data from earlier research by Russian oceanographers and paleontologists, who determined that during the 30-15 millennia before Christ, the climate of the Arctic was milder and that the Arctic Ocean was warm, no matter the presence of glaciers on the continent. *Demin* states that American and Canadian scientists have reached similar results. They determined that at the time of the Wisconsin glaciation, there was a zone of temperate climate in the center of the Arctic Ocean in which there could be flora and fauna that could not survive in the polar and subpolar zones of North America. This conclusion is even more favorable for the viability of the Hyperborean theory than *Tilak's* theory and *Milankovic's* climate change calculations allow. New results of palaeogeographers and paleo climatologists, available on numerous Internet sites, bring numerous confirmations to theories about a warm period at the end of the Ice Age in the Arctic zone and about the existence of a large number of lakes in Siberia around 10,000 years BC, the largest of which covered most of northwestern Siberia. It was also established that there were steppes and that many mammoths lived (eg on Wrangel Island until 3,500 BC) [6]. Thus, in his analyzes of the Arctic climate at the end of the Ice Age, the Canadian archaeologist **Robert McGhee** determined that the climate in the Arctic zone 7,000 years before Christ. was significantly warmer than today and that it lasted for the next 3,500 years. [7] *Valery Demin* organized two expeditions in 1997 and 1998 (under the names of *Hyperborea 97* and *Hyperborea 98)* following the path of the first systematic research of the area where Hyperborea could be located, conducted in Russia in 1922 by **Alexander Barchenko** and his associate *Alexander Kondjain* on the Kola Peninsula in Russian Lapland, on the shores of the old water sanctuary of the Sami people - Lake Sejdozera. The results of this expedition, along with the data that inspired the research, disappeared into the archives of the KGB, and the researchers themselves lost their lives in purges over the following years until 1938.

6. T.R.Holme: *"The Mammoth Riders"*

7. Robert McGhee: *"Climate and People in the Prehistoric Arctic"*

For our hypothesis a huge contribution has been received by the great cartographers, especially *Gerardus Mercator (1512 –1594)* who introduced Arctogea on his maps as a large land around the North Pole, with a cruciform shape of four rivers or sea straits. The mystery of *Mercator's* map is joined by the fact of the existence of several geographical maps that show parts of the land that could not be known at the time of their creation (for example, the famous map of the Turkish admiral *Piri Reis*, on which the contours of the American land were extremely precisely drawn several decades before they were officially discovered by *Amerigo Vespucci*, and analyzes of that map show unusual features of the drawings that would normally have been created on the basis of high-altitude photography).

Also, the collective unconscious, which according to *Carl Gustav Jung* (*1875 – 1961*), is the oldest, deepest, and the most influential layer of the psyche, represents the spiritual treasury of the inherited experience of the ancestors, given in the form of a predisposition for a certain way of human experience and reaction to the environment. The collective unconscious is universally transcendent, because all people, regardless of historical epoch or culture, have approximately the same collective unconscious, which is the basis for the overall superstructure of the personality. This superconscious unconscious can be irrational and destructive if it is neglected and misunderstood, but it also contains the highest values, spiritual experience, and wisdom of generations of ancestors that have accumulated over centuries. The structure of the collective unconscious consists of its elements known as archetypes. By activating and penetrating those dormant and subconscious chambers, we can retrieve certain memory fragments and recall them. We all carry within ourselves that primordial record of Eden that is tirelessly waiting for us to activate it. Each of us has a deep inner urge, consciously or unconsciously, to find our paradise that provides peace and well-being. Today we strongly feel the pressure from the chaotic and hypersonic modern civilization, so exhausted we dream of flawless freedom and rebirth. We dream of our garden of paradise, which is located somewhere far from the worldly ecumene, it is our garden in the center of which grows the tree that is impatiently waiting for us to taste the fruits of joy and happiness. I sincerely hope that this work will also be a motive and an incentive for the reader to find his Garden of Eden. This book would not have been realized without the significant contribution of numerous genius minds and famous names from various scientific fields who will be mentioned here in certain circumstances. To all these authors, whose names you will have the opportunity to hear on the following pages, I give them deep respect and affection for the overall contribution and development of this polar hypothesis. I dedicate this work to all souls who are tirelessly searching for the truth, those souls who are impatiently waiting to quench their thirst and fatigue from the fountain of youth!

• *The Return of the Myth*

"As above, so below, as below so above!" – Hermes Trismegistus

The return of the myth represents a sincere attempt to recall and resurrect the ancient traditions and legends, where this time their seriousness and endurance will be tested by modern scientific research methods. The very Hellenic term "μῦθος" (*mythos*) literally translates as storytelling. If we start to follow the course of the history of almost any nation, we reach an archaic stage, a zero point of myths and traditions that slowly fade into darkness and oblivion. Somewhere in the middle of the XIX century for the study of prehistoric man, various attempts were made to systematize myths, how they would be rationally explained and how the ancient history of man would be illuminated. A myth represents the culture of a people or a society, it is a set of one or more symbols, put into a form to express a story. Mythology is a collection of multiple myths of a culture. According to the authorship, the myth generally belongs to the anonymous oral creation. Among primitive people the mind of one generation accurately repeats the minds of all former generations; the construction of the intellectual nature no longer varies, is not transmitted from generation to generation only the shape of the body or the color of the skin; rather, generations feel the same emotions, think the same thoughts, and use the same expressions of their ancestors. And this is to be expected, since the brain is as much a part of the hereditary, material organization as the color of the eyes or the shape of the nose. In order to penetrate the essence of myths and resurrect them again, to see where modern interpreters have gone wrong, we must carefully and meticulously study them, where it is necessary to rely not only on the comparability between the stories themselves but also on modern scientific discoveries, to feel what the possibilities are of their being valid in relation to our arctic hypothesis. Myth, apart from being a story, turns out to have a much deeper dimension, a spark of life and a covenant that maintains long continuity. What is important for us is that the myth sometimes exists on a collective level, that is, as a global phenomenon, where we literally find the same myth (monomyth) among many ancient civilizations and peoples at the same time, even if they were separated even on different continents. A myth often refers to a wisdom lesson in the form of a story that has deep explanatory or symbolic resonance for pre-literate cultures that preserve and celebrate the history of their ancestors through the oral traditions of skilled storytellers. A myth is generally a short epic work, it is a work in the form of a story, where we certainly should not adhere strictly and literally, because, as we know, the ancient poets themselves had a sense for artistic expressions, followed by symbolism, where quite it would be normal for various hyperbolized and stylized ornaments to be present. Literature very often borrows themes and motifs from myth and folklore. In fact, literature first arose as a myth, then the myth became a fairy tale, a folk tale, so through the long process it penetrated deeply into the blood vessels of society and became an arch-impulse for human behavior. Over time, history becomes legend and legend becomes myth. But sometimes reverse processes occur, where myths become real historical events until something is discovered and proved that it was a real or partially correct historical event. Take for example the case of the ancient city of Dwarka [1], which seems to me worth mentioning briefly. The mythical city of Dwaraka was recently found in the Indian Ocean. During 1983-1990, the *Marine Archeology Unit of the Indian National Institute of Oceanography* (NIO) carried out underwater excavations at Dwarka and Bet Dwarka. According to Indian archaeologist *S.R.Rao*: ***"Available archaeological evidence from land and coastal excavations confirms the existence of this city-state with several satellite cities in 1500 BCE."*** (Many researchers believe that this city is much older). He felt it reasonable to conclude that this sunken city is Dwaraka as described in the epic *Mahabharata*. It is the holy historical city mentioned in the myths of

Hinduism, Jainism and Buddhism. Thus, the mythical or legendary city of Dwaraka today has a completely different status, which gives it a positive credibility.

1. Dwarka is an ancient city also known as Dvāravatī (द्वारका) "The Gated City", where the name of the city according to the Sanskrit word "dvara" (doors, gates,) definitely corresponds to the Serbian word for doors "двери / dveri", It is believed that Dwarka was the first capital of Gujarat. Dwarka has also been called throughout its history as 'Mokshapuri', 'Dwarkamati' and 'Dwarkavati'. It is mentioned in the ancient prehistoric epic period of the Mahabharata. According to legend, Krishna settled here after defeating and killing his uncle Kansa at Mathura. This mythological account of Krishna's migration to Dwarka from Mathura is closely related to Gujarati culture. Krishna is also said to have drawn 12 yojanas or 96 square kilometers (37 sq mi) of land from the sea to create Dwarka. Dwarka was founded as the capital of Saurashtra by the Vedic Indians during the Puranic period. During this period the city underwent reconstruction and received the name Dwarka. The friendly native population also induced Krishna to settle in Dwarka when he decided, after the fight against Jarasanda, king of Magadha, to retire from Mathura. Krishna is said to have ruled his kingdom from Dwarka while living with his family at Beth Dwarka.

By being passed down from generation to generation, myths became the basis for numerous literary reworkings and through such a long-term transition, they sometimes lose their originality, and new additional, fictitious or free interpretations from newer generations can be added to them, where sometimes they really are it loses or obscures the original meaning. As sacred stories, myths always refer to some crucial, crisis, transformational moments of human destiny. Myth is a kind of archetype of human experience with the world. It is interesting that we can look at the myth through several levels, that is, through several dimensional perceptions, from which several schools of interpretation arose in the past. We can conclude that the myth also has its own three-layered division. Myth seems to name its spiritual or astral, inner or psychological and of course material or terrestrial level of existence. Here I want to point out that we do not know the thin line, at least not that crucial moment about when ancient poets or historians talk about a myth as fantasy story, and when about a real historical event. The ancient historians themselves used this term to tell an ancient story and did not mention that it was something invented or unreal. That division and classification was made by modern historians. Sometimes some heroes or events are also defined as "semi-mythical", where the boundaries become even thinner, while the uncertainty in fiction or reality is even greater. The ancient transmitters themselves made no such distinction. They simply left information where they themselves experienced it as if it were some played out historical events from the past, but with scarce data. We can also speculate that the ancient texts were also with errors in the translations by the later medieval copyists, but many key works that should fill the picture are unfortunately lost today. So, modern historians where **Plato** *(Πλάτων Plátōn; 428/427 or 424/423 – 348/347 BC)* himself singled him out as one of the most meritorious authorities for laying the foundations of Western philosophy and science, where many of his works were systematically adopted, on the other hand, in the case where he talks about the past and history of Atlantis **[2],** as in the dialogues "**Timaeus**" (*Τίμαιος*) and "**Critias**" (*Κριτίας*), then modern scientists and philosophers decided immediately to place this information in the folder called "myth", i.e. in a story that has not yet been proven , although myth for the general public is often perceived as synonymous with fiction or fantasy.

2. Atlantis (in ancient Greek: Ἀτλαντὶς νῆσος, "Island of Atlas") - a legendary island, which is first mentioned in Plato's dialogues Timaeus and Critias. According to Plato's account, Atlantis lay "behind the Pillars of Heracles" and it was a naval power that conquered much of Western Europe and Africa as early as 9,000 years before the time of Solon or approximately 9500 BC. Plato's story is simple, and it gains weight because of the great reputation of the people involved: Solon, one of the Seven Sages of the Old World, who left his unfinished manuscript with the translation of the temple tablets of Neith, Egypt, on which the history of Atlantis was recorded. Critias, orator, statesman, poet, philosopher, hardy man who inherited the manuscript of Solon as a family heirloom. Strabo, the chief chronicler of the Roman Empire, did not doubt the existence and sinking of Atlantis. Crantor, a follower of Plato and a distinguished scholar in the Great Library of Alexandria, which was the center of the sciences of the classical world, and where the minds of the time regarded the story of Atlantis as an event of history. Krantor in 260 BC personally traveled to the Egyptian temple and found the tablets with inscriptions that confirmed the story.

Myths and legends can certainly be explained and interpreted in different ways. Thus **Yāska [3]** mentions three or four different schools of interpretation, each explaining in its own way the character and nature of the Vedic deities. One of those schools wanted to assure us that most of the deities represent historical figures, who were later deified because of their properties and supernatural works. Other theologians have divided the deities into two categories: *Karma-devatas* or those who have been raised to the rank of deities by their own works; and the *Ajana-devatas* or those who were of divine origin. On the contrary, the *Nairuktas* (or adverbs, etymologists) hold that the Vedic deities represent certain cosmic and physical phenomena, such as the appearance of the Dawn or the shedding of storm clouds with lightning, the rising of the Sun, and similar. The school of *Adhyatmikas*, however, interpret the Vedic hymns in their philosophical sense; and there are those who interpret the myths in many other ways. For our story, from our own point of view and north position, we can trace the myth through the prism of the hermetic maxim, so that each school in its own way, at a certain moment, could be functional and correct in every sense. Remember the ancient quote of wisdom: "*As above, so below*".

3. Yāska was an early Sanskrit grammarian (7th - 5th century BC). The predecessor of Pāṇini (7th - 4th century BCE) he is traditionally identified as the author of the Nirukta, the school of "etymology" (explanation of words) within the Sanskrit grammatical tradition.

In this context, it is of crucial importance to note that we must first understand that the translations of ancient epics and myths are translated from languages that are no longer in use, where many words are unclear, where many of the experts have different views and misunderstandings about translations and interpretation of meaning, and most importantly, even one wrong word could completely change the picture, either on purpose or accidentally. In that way, some famous interpreters of the Vedic scriptures, due to the misunderstanding of the Sacred Geography and the polar laws of nature there, encountered difficulties in the translations. Also, many original ancient works have disappeared, leaving only parts or modest fragments. Let's not forget the fact that many ancient libraries were also destroyed along with the entire literary treasury and priceless wealth, so the libraries of Alexandria, Persepolis, Athens, and Constantinople, together with the Etruscan library in Rome, were burned almost simultaneously. All the originals were burned or disappeared, while the copies that were made of them "in time" were kept and cared for. The library of **Yaroslav I the Wise** *(978-1054)* or **Ivan IV the Terrible**

(1530-1584) also disappeared without a trace. On the other hand, we can assume that even the ancient authors themselves sometimes did not have full knowledge and understanding and even a suitable vocabulary for them to convey the events in full light, because not only were they not living witnesses, but between them and those events as is the case with Atlantis and *Plato*, thousands of years had already passed. And those millennia are a much larger timeline than the one between us and the ancient poets themselves. It is important for us to be open for critical thinking and to make an analysis ourselves, not to believe everything that is offered to us, but to check, to doubt and at the same time to think and research openly. Mythologists focused their research on the era when man's origin was believed to be post-glacial and it was assumed that his physical and geographical environment was not different from what it is today.

All ancient myths were interpreted from the assumption that they were created and developed in areas whose climatic and other conditions differed insignificantly from those we know today. Thus, all Vedic myths and legends were interpreted with naturalistic theories. That method was first put forward by Indian etymologists, and then developed by Western scientists, but its spirit has remained practically unchanged, although the researchers of the last hundred years try to break the ice. It is still believed to this day that the origin of the Indo-Europeans is to be sought somewhere in Central Asia, and that the Vedic hymns, supposed to have been composed after the separation of the Hindus from the common Indo-European stock, contain exceptional notions peculiar only to that of the Indo-Iranian branch that lived near the tropical belt. Under the guidance of doubt, it remains for us to make an analysis with all the possible modern methods at our disposal, how to set up a newer hypothesis that may not be as new or as surprising as it appears at first glance.

The myths of Atlantis and Hyperborea are deeply woven into the mythology of many European nations, so they should not be ignored. Both lands are unsolved mysteries. In the first place, we should mention the French astronomer, otherwise the astronomer of the last French king: *Jean Sylvain Bailly (1736-1793 - the year when Bailly was guillotined)*. Like *Tilak*, who was stimulated to research by information about the position of the constellations that he could find in ancient Vedic literature – *Bailly's* curiosity was stimulated by ancient astronomical maps brought to him by missionaries and travelers from India. According to *Bailly*, they could only have been created by precise observations from the area between the 50th and 60th degrees of north latitude. He assumed that they were observations of *"some unknown people" - Bailly* calls them Atlanteans - who migrated from the extreme north to the south. The author also found numerous confirmations for his assumptions, researching many mythologies. Here is his main conclusion: *"when we unite those traditions, often cloudy and confused, we notice with astonishment that they all strive for the same goal, which places their origins in the North."* [4]

4. Jean Sylvain Bailly: *"Lettres sur l'Atlantide de Platon et sur l'ancienne historie de l'Asie pour servir de suite aux lettres sur l'origine des science, adressées à M. de Voltaire par M. Bailly"*, Londres-Paris, 1779.

Bailly called these "unknown people" "Atlanteans": but we will identify them with the Hyperboreans, since their homeland is located "between the 50th and 60th degrees of north latitude", that is, in the circumpolar regions (the mythical Atlantis reported by *Plato* was located somewhere in the northwestern Atlantic). For authors like *René Guénon (René Jean-Marie-Joseph Guénon (1886 –1951)*, Atlantis it is closely related to Hyperborea, but still as a secondary center of the polar tradition, and it is wrong, and even dangerous, to equate them. The location of Atlantis has been searched to this day in countless studies in all areas of the Atlantic and Mediterranean, and the situation with Hyperborea is somewhat simpler; because only a limited area in the north of Eurasia is available for its closer location. Many scholars have already expressed their opinion that the geographical origin of the Indo-Europeans is to be sought in the Arctic regions; and *Dr. William Fairfield Warren (1833 –1929)* himself, president of Boston University, published a work entitled *"Paradise Found or the Cradle of the Human Race at the North Pole"* in 1885. In this work, *Warren* places Atlantis at the North Pole, as well as the Garden of Eden, Mount Meru, etc. *Warren* believed that all these mythical lands were folk memories of the once inhabited far northern seat where the man was originally created. The identification of Atlantis with the North Pole was maintained by the positioning of Atlas in the far north by mapping ancient Greek cosmology. *Warren* equated the primordial titan Atlas (Ἄτλας) of Greek mythology who supported the heavens on his shoulders (or the pillar of the earth) with the Atlas described in *Plato's* dialogue *Critias* as the first ruler of Atlantis (Κριτίας, *114a*). Thus, the *Axis Mundi* or cosmic axis of the ancient legends (*Yggdrasil, Irminsul, the World Tree or the Pillar of Atlas*) had to be in the far north *"at the top of the world"*. *Homer* (Ὅμηρος *c. 8th century BC*), *Virgil (Publius Vergilius, c. 70 – 19 BC)*, and *Hesiod, (Ἡσίοδος, between 750 - 650 BC)* all placed the *Atlas* or world-pillar at the *"End of the Earth"*, where, as we shall see in this volume, they denoted the far northern Arctic regions, while *Euripides* (Εὐριπίδης, *c. 480 – c. 406 BC)* he connected Atlas with the North Star. Therefore, Atlantis appears to be synonymous with Hyperborea which was once in the far north, at the North Pole, at the top of the North Atlantic Ocean since Atlas in his ancient Greek cosmological mapping stood exactly at the far northern zenith, below *Stella Polaris* or the North Star. Paleoclimatic and geological analyzes provide a chance for such research. Myths about the flood are widespread in many peoples and outside of Europe, so this logically indicates the memory of very old real events, most likely caused by climatic and tectonic disturbances. Unfortunately, the general knowledge of climatology spoke against such possibilities for a long time. And yet, some recent results of paleoclimatology and paleoceanography point to the possibility that this was not always the case and that myths reflect real events. We will attempt now to go further into an entirely deeper layer of our collective memory, into an older pre-cataclysmic cycle. This book also aims to answer whether there may have been a pre-glacial or ante-diluvian epoch and proto-civilization that exerted an influence globally on all post-flood civilizations and cultures. Our specific mission in this book is to try once again to unfreeze the myths and legends, that are mainly associated with the *Arctic Paradise* and with the help of comparative research and modern discoveries to check whether this hypothesis and theory can gain new light, credibility, and verification. If the ancestors of the Vedic bards lived in the polar regions at all, the cosmic or meteorological local conditions must have influenced the mythology of that people, and if our polar theory is correct, a closer examination of the ancient myths must disclose facts that cannot be explained by no other theory.

Chapter I
Polus Arcticus

Anthropology, in the person of some of its most authoritative representatives, is today teaching, with a positiveness of conviction hitherto unequaled, that the real cradleland of the whole human family, and the center of its original dispersion, "must be sought in 'Arktogäa' a north-polar country which no foot of man shall ever again tread, a land covered with everlasting ice, or submerged beneath the billows of the ocean." - Ludwig Wilser (1850 – 1923) Menschwerdung, Stuttgart, 1907, pp. 11, 13, 15, 72, 107ff. German anthropologist, racial theorist, archaeologist, prehistorian, and author.

First of all, if we etymologically start researching and look at the word "*pole*" itself, we will see that its meaning is closely related to the Greek πόλος (*pólos*, which translates as "axis of rotation"), but it is also more related to the Slavic word *"пол" (pol),* from where also derives the word "*половина" (polovina)* – "half", which is analogous to the Greek word ἡμισφαίριον – "hemisphere". It seems to many scientists and researchers that almost any imaginable place on Earth could be suggested by them for the Eden of the Biblical book of *Genesis*. However, there remains a region of the rarest interest in astronomical, physical and historical geography, the natural center of the only historical hemisphere. Considering the fascination of the subject and the inexhaustible ingenuity which has been expended upon it, it seems incredible that it should have been left to the recent years of the nineteenth century to bring forward and seriously test the proposition that the cradle of the Indo-Europeans, The Garden of Eden, according to biblical tradition, was located at the North Pole, during the flood. It is evident that on reflection our hypothesis immediately and materially modifies the whole problem of the location of heaven on earth. In view of the proposed prehistoric circumpolar continent of the North Pole as the cradle of the Indo-Europeans, the memorable features of that primeval habitat would have to be marked as well. If a person is at the North Pole, the first thing he will notice will be the movement of the sky above him. In the temperate tropical zones, we see how the stars rise in the

East and set in the West. But for the observer who is at the North Pole, the picture is completely different. At the Pole, the fixed center of the heavens is directly above it, and it naturally appears to be the summit of the world, the true heaven, the immutable seat of the supreme and all-ruling God. And therefore, during the whole long life of the antediluvian world, the circumpolar sky was to human thought the true seat of the Most High, and the most ancient post-flood nations, though scattered on the sides of the whole globe, half or two-thirds of the distance to the equator, it seems that they could not so easily forget that in the center and true top of the rotating sky was the *"Throne of the Creator"*, and that there, in the far north, was their heavenly and promised land.

If therefore, primeval Eden was at the Pole, the descendants of the first man, going away from such an original country, could hardly have failed to remember it as the center of all lands, the *omphalos* of the whole earth.

Standing at the Pole of the earth, an observer would be not only directly under the center of the celestial hemisphere, but also directly on the center of the surface of the terrestrial hemisphere. There, and there alone, the heavenly bodies would move, in horizontal planes, round and round him everywhere at an apparently equal distance, and he would seem to himself to stand on the one precise center-point of the entire earth. Every departure of a few miles in any direction from this polar position would at once confirm this first impression. If, therefore, primeval Eden was at the Pole, the descendants of the first man, going away from such an original country - *"Heaven on Earth"*, it would be hard for them to forget it so easily that this was the center of all countries, the world center, i.e., *omphalos* - the navel of the whole world. Supposing the first man to have been located in the central and most elevated portion of the hypothetical Eden-land, the streams there originating and flowing seaward would have flowed, not in one but in various opposite directions toward all the cardinal points of the horizon. Moreover, all of these streams being obviously fed, not by each other, but by the rain from heaven, it would not have required a very powerful imagination to conceive of them as parts of a finer and more celestial stream whose head-springs were in the sky. [1] [2] [3]

1. Compare the poetic depiction of God's river in Psalms 65. 9-10.

2. You visit the earth and cause it to overflow; You greatly enrich it; God's stream is full of water; You prepare their grain, for thus you prepare the earth. You abundantly water its ridges, you calm its furrows, you soften them with rains, you bless its source."

3. Likewise, Aristotle, in his *Meteors (Μετεωρολογική; Meteorologica or Meteora)*, speaking of the flow of vapors, says, "there is a river in the air, which constantly flows between the Heavens and the Earth, created by ascending and descending vapors. - Burnet, *Sacred Theory of the Earth*, p. 226.

If finally, the streams flowing in opposite directions grow into four rivers of opposite currents, *flumina principalia*, as many old theologians called them, dividing the circumpolar earth into four nearly equal quarters, it will definitely be a feature of the "*Heavenly Earth*" which will forever be remembered. In the following chapters, we shall expose the fundamental fallacy of the popular impression that at the Pole six months out of all twelve of the year are spent in darkness, and we shall show that, on the contrary, less than one-fifth of the year is thus spent, while more than four-fifths are spent in light. This being true, a primitive dwelling in that part of the world would be remembered by the descendants of the first man chiefly as a land of beauty and the supreme home of the sun. Moreover, it is impossible for Arctic explorers to describe in full illustration the nocturnal splendor of the *Aurora Borealis* in those regions, where the whole top of the globe often seems to be covered with flickering curtains, draperies, and currents of living spreading flame; therefore it is easy to believe that, after mankind had been banished from such a home, it would be memorialized as an abode of unearthly and supernatural splendor, fit for the habitation of the gods and holy immortals.

Finally, assuming the prevalence of a uniform tropical temperature, we find the biological conditions of the region such as the extraordinary prevalence of daylight, the more intense terrestrial magnetism, and the incomparable electrical forces which feed the northern lights, all combine to increase the probability that if there ever existed such earth as we supposed, it must have represented forms of life exceeding those with which we are acquainted; flora and fauna of almost unimaginable energy and luxuriant development. Under such conditions, men themselves might have attained a greater stature, power, strength, and longevity than had ever been attained since the Deluge, which destroyed "the world that then was"; and immediately or eventually caused the movement of the seed of our new post-flood humanity into the cold and desolate regions of the northern temperate zone. Alleging that the first men were of tall stature, strength, and longevity, surely that fact would have remained in the memory and traditions of mankind long after his exile from his former and happier home! Looking back now at these various points, it is at once perceived that they represent conditions of human existence which were totally different from the conditions of life as we know them today, or as they were once known in what is called a historical age. They necessarily change in the most profound way the whole problem of the location of the biblical paradise known as Gan-Eden. No solution has ever been presented in the refutation of so many points. No one has ever postulated that here we have such an extraordinary adjustment of both heaven and earth. No one had ever before sought, in order to formulate, the incredibly wide overlap of testimonies. If it is false, then it requires from human tradition dark memories of the world - conditions that have never existed in human experience. It is crucial to our further investigation to show the scientifically proven geographical features and natural laws that govern the Arctic and the Circumpolar Circle.

Polar features:

1. The sun rises in the south.

2. The stars do not rise or set, but they circle in horizontal planes, completing an orbit in 24 hours.

3. The year consists of one long day and one long night of 6 months each.

4. There is only one morning and one evening, that is, the sun rises and sets once a year. dawn and dusk last for 2 whole months, or 60 24-hour periods. The reddish morning and evening light is not localized to one particular place on the horizon in the East and West, as with us, but moves like the stars, circling the entire horizon like a wheel, completing its orbit in 24 hours. That orbiting of the morning light since dawn continues until the sun appears above the horizon, then the sun follows the same path for 6 months, that is, it moves without setting, completing a full circle or orbit every 24 hours.

Circumpolar features (Arctic Circle):

1. The sun is still south of the observational zenith, but this is the same case for the observer in the temperate regions, however, we cannot take it as a special feature.

2. A large number of stars are circumpolar, that is, they are above the horizon during their entire orbit, and therefore they are visible from here. Other stars rise and set as in the temperate zone, but they orbit along oblique circles.

3. The year consists of three parts: a) A Long and uninterrupted night, at the moment of the Winter Solstice, which lasts more than 24 hours and less than 6 months, depending on the local latitude, b) the uninterrupted long day, at the moment of the Summer Solstice and c) the change of ordinary days and nights during the rest of the year, whereby a day and a night together do not exceed the duration of 24 hours. The day that follows the long uninterrupted nights is at first shorter than the night, but it continues until there is a long and uninterrupted day. At the end of the year, the night is first shorter than the day, then it begins to increase until the beginning of the long sleepless nights that will end the year.

4. The dawn at the end of long and sleepless nights lasts for several days, but its duration and its brightness become less and less as we move away from the Pole, the appearance of the circling of the morning glow will be even less noticeable during the greater part of the duration of the dawn. Other dawns, that is, those that separate ordinary days and nights, will last the same as dawns in the temperate zone, only a few hours. The sun, when it is above the horizon during the continuous day, will move without setting around the observer as at the Pole, but along oblique and uneven circles, and during the long nights it will be below the horizon, while during the rest of the year it will it rises and sets remaining above the horizon during a portion of a variable day depending on the sun's position on the ecliptic.

A hypothesis so unusually difficult must surely fall apart if it is not true. The reader is therefore not promised any new *ignis-fatuus* challenge, but at least the satisfaction of a definite result in regard to a theory, where we cordially invite his critical and patient attention to the facts which will be presented in the chapters that follow.

• *Scientific Geogony*

Les lois générales de la géogénie favorisent d'une façon remarquable l'hypothèse dont nous venons d'ebaucher les traits – Count Saporta

"The general laws of geogenesis remarkably favor the hypothesis we have just stated."

Geogony is a scientific field for the study of the earth. Could it once be proved that the Arctic extremity of the earth has always been the ice-bound region that it is now and has been for thousands of years, it would certainly be useless for a moment to hypothesize that the cradle of the human race was ever located there. Probably the popular impression that since the beginning of the world the far north has been a region of unbearable and unsustainable cold is one of the main reasons why our hypothesis has been so late in attracting attention. At the present time, however, as far as this difficulty is concerned, scientific studies have amply prepared the way for a new theory. That the earth is a slowly cooling body is a doctrine now universally accepted. When we say this, we say nothing for or against the so-called nebular hypothesis of the origin of the world, because both friends and enemies of this unproven hypothesis believe in what is called secular cooling or cooling of the earth. All authorities in this field consider and teach a time when the slowly solid planet was too hot to support any form of life, and that it was only during a period of cooling that a temperature adapted to the needs of living beings was reached. On what part of the Earth's surface would this temperature be reached first? Or could it be reached everywhere at the same time? These are the most interesting questions, and the writer has often been surprised that in the scientific treatises on the frozen sphere he could nowhere find them formally discussed. Granting, however, a uniform internal heat, and an even loss of it in the mode of surface radiation in all directions into space, it is certain that if these were the only factors in the problem, the cooling process would affect every part of the surface in a uniform manner, and we can safely conclude that the temperature compatible with organic life would have been reached at the same time at all points on the Earth's surface. But the mentioned factors are not the only ones of the problem. In those distant geological times, the heat received from the great central furnace of our system, the sun, could not have been less than at the present time. Some astronomers and geologists claim that it was bigger. [1] In any case, therefore, already at the time when the Earth's atmosphere became penetrated by the sun's rays, local temperature differences must have been created at the base of the atmosphere, regardless of whether the body of the globe was still covered with a crust or not. And then, as now, apart from air and water currents, every particular point on the surface of the globe must have had a definite temperature, first from the fixed and uniform heat of the earth's mass, and secondly from the varying amount of heat received from the sun.

1. Winchell, *World-Life, p. 484-490*. Alexander Winchell (December 31, 1824, in North East, New York – February 19, 1891, in Ann Arbor, Michigan) was a geologist from the United States who contributed to the field mainly as an educator and popular lecturer, and author. In 1875, he worked as a Professor of Geology and Zoology at Vanderbilt University. There, his views on evolution, as expressed in his book *Adamites and Pre-Adamites: or, A Popular Discussion* (1878), were not acceptable to the University administration because they departed from the biblical learning. Today, views on the "inferiority of the Negroes" (a quote from his 1878 book) would probably be the focus of controversy. In any case, he was obliged to resign in 1878. He then returned to the University of Michigan, where he was a professor of geology and paleontology. His work in geology was not as significant as his teaching and popular lectures and writing in this field. last. He was very concerned with reconciling science and religion. He was an advocate of theistic evolution.

But the difference between the solar heat obtained at a point below the Equator and that obtained at a point at the Pole could not have been less in those times than at the present time; and this continual increase of the earth's equatorial heat from the direct rays of the sun immediately suggests the parts of the globe to which we must look, if we would discover the regions which first became sufficiently cold to sustain organic life. Then, as now, the polar regions must have been colder than the equatorial, and hence, as far as the teachings of theoretical geogony may be trusted, the conclusion is inevitable that there, in the polar regions, life first became possible. The implication of this result on our central thesis is also obvious. The geologist was asked the question: "Is the hypothesis of the primordial polar Eden allowed?" Looking alone at the slowly cooling earth, he replied: ***"The Eden conditions were probably once found everywhere on the surface of the earth. Heaven might have been everywhere."*** Looking at the cosmic environment, however, he added, ***"But though Heaven may have been somewhere, the first parts of the Earth's surface that were cool enough to represent the conditions of Paradise life must have been at the Poles."*** [2]

2. Similar or identical are the thoughts of Professor Philip Spiller: *Die Weltschöpfung vom Standpunkte der heutigen Wissenschaft. Mil neuen Untersuchungen, 1868, 2d ed., 1873. Die Entstehung der Welt imd die Einheit der Näturkrdfte. Populäre Kosmogonie, 1872. Die Urkraft des Weltalls nach ihrem Wesen und Wirken auf alien Naturgebieten.* Berlin, 1879. In Professor Otto Kuntze's work, *Phytogeogenesis: Die vorweltliche Entwickehing der Erdkruste und der Pflanzen,* Leipsic, 1884, I also found traces of a recognition of the truth expounded by the above. See p. 51, 52, 53, 60, of his work.

• *Astronomical Geography*

"The nights are never so dark at the Pole as in other regions, for the moon and stars seem to possess twice as much light and brightness. In addition, in the north, there is a continuous light, whose varied shades and play are among the strangest phenomena of nature". - *Jean Pierre Rambosson, Astronomy, 1875*

We can think of an unbroken night of six months at the Pole. Eminent scientific authorities speak as if this conception were correct. Thus, Professor **Geikie**, in his admirable new manual of Geology, writing of the Arctic flora of the Miocene age, says: ***"When we remember that this vegetation grew luxuriantly at 8° 15' of the North Pole, in a region which is in darkness half the year…we can understand the difficulty of the problem in climate distribution that these facts present to the geologist"*** [1].

1. *Text-book of Geology.* By Archibald Geikie, LL. D., F. R. S London, 1882: p. 869.

In like manner **Sir Charles Lyell**, discussing the question of the possibility of whales reaching the supposed open sea at the Pole, says: ***"They could*** *pass under considerable barriers of ice, provided there were 'openings here or there;' and thus they might reach a more open sea near the Pole, and find their food during a day of more than five months' duration".* [2] From such representations as these, the reader is naturally led to the impression that daylight lasts at the Pole for little more than five months, while the rest of the year the region is shrouded in darkness. Were this true, it would certainly have been an unpromising region in which to seek a terrestrial paradise. Fortunately, our hypothesis, this conception of the duration of the polar night is very far from correct. The semi-annual reign of darkness exists only in the uninstructed imagination. Astronomical geography teaches that, in relation to daylight, polar regions are and always have been the most favored parts of the globe. Another popularizer of natural science such as the ***Rev. Thomas Dick*** stated the true facts as follows: ***"Under the Poles, where the darkness of the night would continue for six months without interruption if there were no refraction, total darkness does not prevail for one half of this period"***. When the sun sets at the North Pole, around September 23rd, the inhabitants (if there were any) enjoy the perpetual aurora until it descends 18° below the horizon. On its way through the ecliptic, the sun has two months before it reaches this point, during which time we have perpetual twilight. In two months, it again arrives at the same point, namely 18° below the horizon, when a new twilight begins, which increases steadily in brilliancy during the other two months, where at last the body of this beacon is seen to rise in all its glory.

2. *Principles of Geology,* New York ed., vol. i., p. 246.

So in this region, the light of day is enjoyed to a greater or less degree for ten months, without interruption from the effects of atmospheric refraction; and during the two months when the influence of the sunlight is entirely withdrawn, the moon shines above the horizon for two months and a half without interruption; and so it happens that they do not pass more than two separate double weeks or fortnights (14 days) in complete darkness, this darkness being relieved by the light of the stars and the frequent flashes of the Aurora Borealis. Hence it appears that there are no parts of our globe that enjoy during the year so large a proportion of sunlight as these northern regions. [3] Remarkable as this story of the polar day may be, it is worth noting the experience which repeatedly shows that the actual duration of light at high latitudes exceeds even the calculations of astronomers.

Thus, in the spring of 1873, the officers of the Austrian expedition, under Lieutenants *Weyprecht* and *Payer*, were surprised to see the sun three days before the date on which it was expected to rise. A late writer thus states the case; In the latitude (79° 15' N.) in which *Admiral Wilhelm von Tegetthoff* lay, the sun should have reappeared above the horizon on the 19th of February; but, owing to the effect of refraction, owing to the low temperature prevailing, -30°, the explorers were able to greet its rays three days earlier. [4]

3. Works of Thomas Dick, LL.D.; *The Practical Astronomer,* ch. ii. Hartford, vol. ii., second half, p. 30.

4. *Recent Expeditions in Eastern Polar Seas.* London, 1882: p. 83

Lieutenant Payer noted in his diary as follows:

"*Though the sun did not return to our latitude (78° 15' N., 71° 38' E. longitude) until the 19th of February, we were able to greet its rays three days before that date, owing to the strong refraction of 1° 40 ' which accompanied the temperature of – 30° R*" [5]. Even more remarkable was the experience of the *Barentz's* Arctic expedition, almost three hundred years before *Dr. Dick* to allude to it as follows:

"*The refracting power of the atmosphere has been found to be much greater, in certain cases, than that now stated. In 1595 (1596-1597) a company of Dutch sailors was wrecked on the coast of Novaia Zemlia, and obliged to remain in that desolate region during the night for more than three months (actually it was a little less than three months), they saw that the sun appearing on the horizon about sixteen days before the time at which he should have risen according to calculations, and when his body was actually more than four degrees below the horizon.*"

The only explanation of this astonishing phenomenon offered by the same writer is found in this appended clause -"*which circumstance has been attributed to the great power of refraction of the atmosphere in those intensely cold regions."* This is so unsatisfactory that not a few prefer to believe, which seems quite incredible, namely that *Barentz* and his men in a short space of less than three months made an error of sixteen days in their time record.

5. *New Lands within the Arctic Circle.* Lond. 1876: vol. i., p. 237.

Professor Nordenskjold referred to the case as follows: *"On the 14th [old 4th] November the sun disappeared and was visible again on 3rd February [old 24th January]*. These dates have confused many scientific men, because, in 76° north latitude, the upper edge of the sun should have ceased to be visible when the sun's southern declination in autumn became greater than 13° [6] and became visible again when the declination it again became less than that number; the sun was to be seen for the last time in the Ice Heaven of *Barentz* on the 27th [old 17th] of October and was to reappear there on the 14th [old 4th] February. It was assumed that the deviation resulted from a significant error in the counting of days, but this was unanimously denied by the wintering crew. [7] In a footnote, he provides evidence that seems conclusive that no such mistake was made. But while these experiences of *Barentz* and the Austrians indicate the duration of the darkness of the Pole to be less than sixty days out of the total of three hundred and sixty-five, some apparently good authorities extend the period to seventy-six or seventy-seven days. Thus *Captain Bedford Pim*, of the Royal Navy of Great Britain, makes the following statement: *"On the 16th of March the Sun rises, preceded by long dawn of forty-seven days, namely, from the 29th of January, when the first glimmer of light appears. On the 25th of September, the sun sets, and after a twilight of forty-eight days, namely, on the 13th of November, darkness reigns supreme, so far as the sun is concerned, for seventy-six days, followed by one long period of light, the sun remaining above the horizon one hundred and ninety-four days. The year, therefore, is thus divided at the Pole: 194 days sun; 76 darkness; 47 days dawn; 48 twilight".*" [8]

6. On the assumption of horizontal refraction of about 45'.

7. *The Voyage of the Vega.* London, 1882: p. 192.

8. Pim's *Marine Pocket Case:* quoted in *Kinn's Harmony of the Bible with Science.* London, 1882: 2d ed., p. 474.

Even according to this account we should have at the Pole only 76 days of darkness to 289 days of light in the year. In other words, instead of being in darkness a little short of half of the time, as at the equator, one would be in darkness but about one-fourth of the time. As far as light is concerned, therefore, even on this calculation the polar region is twice as favorable to life as any equatorial region that can be named. But whence this discrepancy among the astronomers? Why should some of them make the polar night sixteen days longer than others? The simple answer is that they proceed upon different assumptions as to atmospheric refraction in the region of the Pole. In our latitude twilight is usually reckoned to begin when the center of the rising sun is yet 18 below the horizon. Starting with this as the limit, and counting sunrise and sunset to be the moments when the sun s upper limb is on the horizon, we arrive at the division of the polar year given by **Captain Pim**. But astronomers say that in England twilight has been observed when the sun was 21° below the horizon. To be entirely safe some have therefore taken 20° as the limit of solar depression, and reckoning with this datum, instead of the 18° before mentioned, have found that at the Pole the morning twilight would begin January 20th, and the evening twilight would cease November 21st. This would make the period of darkness but 60 days, and the period of light 305. Thus a difference of only two degrees in the assumed limit of solar depression at the beginning and end of the twilights makes the difference of sixteen days in the supposed duration of darkness. Which of the two calculations, writes an eminent American mathematician, "*is the more correct is known, I imagine, by no one.* [9] To us, in the present discussion, the discrepancy is of very little moment. It is only a question as to whether at the Pole there is daylight three-fourths or five-sixths of the year. Both suppositions may be and probably are wrong. For if "in tropical climates 16° or 17° is said to be a sufficient allowance for the extreme solar depression, while, on the other hand, it is said in England to vary from 17° to 21°, it certainly looks as though in yet higher latitudes the light of the sun might be discernible when its body is as much as 21° or 22° below the horizon; and this would reduce the annual polar darkness to less than fifty days. This supposition is rendered the more probable by the fact that, while the expeditions already alluded to found much more of daylight than their astronomical calculations had led them to expect, we have no offsetting accounts where the sun was awaited in vain. The final and authoritative settlement of the question can be reached only by actual observation. Among the fascinating problems whose solution awaits the progress of Arctic exploration, we must therefore place the scientific determination of the unknown duration of the polar day. In view of the foregoing, we are certainly safe in conceiving of the polar night as lasting not over four fortnights. During two of these, as **Dick** reminds us, the moon would be walking in beauty through the heavens, and exhibiting all her changing phases of loveliness in unbroken successions. The other two would be passed beneath the starry arch of heaven, all whose sparkling constellations would be moving round and round the observer in exactly horizontal orbits.

9. Professor J. M. Van Vleck, LL. D., of Wesleyan University, in a letter to the author under date of October 11, 1883. Professor Van Vleck was for many years a collaborates upon the *American Ephemeris and Nautical Almanac.* He is the authority for the next quoted statement.

In such a perfect and regular stellar system kept in view so long and so continuously, the irregular movements of the "planets" or wandering stars, could not possibly escape observation. All their curious accelerations, retardations, conjunctions, and declinations, would be perfectly marked and measured on the revolving but changeless dial-plate of the remoter sky. Dwelling in such a natural observatory, any people would of necessity become astronomers. [10] And how magnificent and orderly would the on goings of the universe appear when viewed from underneath a firmament whose centre of revolution was fixed in the observer s zenith! After long months of unbroken daylight; how would one s soul yearn for a new vision of those stellar glories of the night ! Nor would the moon and silent stars be the only attractions of the brief period during which the light of the sun was withdrawn. The mystic play of the Northern Light would transform the familiar daylight world into a veritable fairy-land.

10. Even an equatorial position would probably have been less favor able. "The Peruvians had also their recurrent religious festivals; . . . but the geographic position of Peru, with Quito, its holy city, lying immediately under the equator, greatly simplified the

process by which they regulated their religious festivals by the solstices and equinoxes; and the facilities which their equatorial position afforded for deter mining the few indispensable periods in their calendar removed all stimulus to fiirther progress." Dr. Daniel Wilson on *"Pre-Aryan American Man"* in Proceedings and Transactions of the Royal Society of Canada. Montreal, 1883 : vol. i., sect. ii., p. 60.

In our latitude, the Aurora Borealis is a comparatively rare and tame phenomenon. In the highest Arctic regions, it almost nightly kindles its unearthly glories. [11] In itself it is lightning-diluted and sublimated to the point of harmlessness. [12] Sometimes these electric discharges not only fill the whole heaven with palpitating draperies, but also tip the hills with lambent flame, and cause the very soil on which one stands to prickle with a kind of life. [13] But after all the glories of the night begin the greater glories of the polar day. Who with any approach to adequacy has ever described dawn? What poet has not attempted it, and what poet has not failed? But if it is impossible to picture one of our brief and evanescent day-dawns, who shall attempt a description of that surpassing spectacle in which all the splendors and loveliness of sixty of our dawns are combined in one. No words can ever portray it. No poet s imagination, even, has ever given us such unearthly scenery. First of all, appears low in the horizon of the night sky a scarcely visible flush of light. At first, it only makes a few stars' light seem a trifle fainter, but after a little, it is seen to be increasing and to be moving laterally along the yet-dark horizon. Twenty-four hours later it has made a complete circuit around the observer and is causing a larger number of stars to pale. Soon the widening light glows with the luster of "Orient pearl". Onward it moves in its stately rounds, until the pearly whiteness burns into ruddy rose light, fringed with purple and gold. Day after day, as we measure days, this splendid panorama circles on, and, according to atmospheric conditions and clouds present more or less favorable conditions of reflection, kindles and fades, kindles and fades, fades only to kindle next time yet more brightly, as the still hidden sun comes nearer and nearer his point of emergence. At length, when for two long months such prophetic displays have been filling the whole heavens with these increscent and revolving splendors, the sun begins to emerge from his long retirement, and to display himself once more to human vision.

11. A lately published report, speaking of the last winter at one of these circumpolar stations of the far North, says: "Auroras have been seen here during the winter almost every night and during all weathers. The auroral forms or types which have appeared have been those generally known, from the grand corona to the modest, pulsating, little luminous cloud; but as a characteristic feature attending them all, I must mention the absence of stability in the types. Thus, only on a few occasions has there been an opportunity to watch the stationary arc, but in general, the aurorae have represented wafting draperies and shining streamers with ever-changing position and intensity". A. S. Steen" *The; Norwegian Circumpolar Station"* in Nature, October 11, 1883, p. 568.

12. "The electric discharges which take place in the polar regions between the positive electricity of the atmosphere and the negative electricity of the earth are the essential and unique cause of the formation of the polar light". M. de la Rive in *The Arctic Manual*, p. 742.

13. "Mr. Lemström concluded that an electric discharge which could only be seen by means of the spectroscope was taking place on the surface of the ground all round him, and that from a distance it would appear as a faint display of Aurora, a display like; the phenomena of pale and flaming light which is sometimes seen on the top of the Spitzbergen mountains*"; The Arctic Manual*, p. 739. Compare Elias Loomis, Aurora Borealis*, Smithsonian Report, 1865. H. Fritz, Das Polarlicht, Leipsic, 1881.*

After one or two circuits, during which his dazzling upper limb grows to a, full-orbed disk, he clears all hill-tops of the distant horizon, and for six full months circles around and around the world's great axis in full view, suffering no night to fall upon his favored home-land at the Pole. Even when at last he sinks again from view he covers his retreat with a repetition of the deepening and fading splendors which filled his long dawning, as if in these pulses of more and more distant light he were signaling back to the forsaken world the promises and prophecies of an early return. In these prosaic sentences, we aim at no description of the indescribable; we only remind ourselves of the bald facts and conditions which govern the unpicturable transformations of each year-long polar night and day. Enough, however, has been said for our purpose. Whoever seeks as a probable location for Paradise the heavenliest spot-on earth with respect to light and darkness, and with respect to celestial scenery, must be content to seek it at the Arctic Pole. Here is the true City of the Sun. Here is the one and only spot-on earth respecting which it would seem as if the Creator had said, as of His own heavenly residence, "***There shall be no night there***" – *Rev. of the Holy Apostle John the Theologian 22.5*

"The fact which gives the phenomenon of the polar aurora its greatest importance is that the earth becomes self-luminous; that, besides the light which as a planet it receives from the central body, it shows a capability of sustaining a luminous process proper to itself" – Alexander von Humboldt (1769 – 1859), German polymath, geographer, naturalist, explorer, and proponent of Romantic philosophy and science.

• *Physiographic Geology*

"A broad continent occupied this part of the globe when these strata were deposited" - Baron Adolf Erik Nordenskiöld

Baron Nordenskiöld was born in the Grand Duchy of Finland at the time when it was still part of the Russian Empire, where later, due to his political activity, he was forced to move to Sweden, where he became a member of the Swedish Parliament and Academy. He led the Vega Expedition along the northern coast of Eurasia in 1878-1879. This was the first complete Northeast Passage. The No*rdenskiöld's* are an old Finnish-Swedish family and members of the nobility. *Nordenskiöld's* father*, Nils Gustaf Nordenskiöld*, was a prominent Finnish mineralogist, civil servant and traveler. He was also a member of the Russian Academy of Sciences. As an explorer, *Nordenskiöld* was naturally interested in the history of Arctic exploration, especially as evidenced in old maps. This interest in turn led him to collect and systematically study early maps. He is remembered today for two important monographs, including many facsimiles, on early printed atlases and geographical maps, and medieval sea charts, respectively the Facsimile-Atlas of the Early History of Cartography (1889) and the Periplus (1897). He left his vast personal collection of early maps to the University of Helsinki, and it was inscribed on the UNESCO World Memory Register in 1997. Of the lithological line of evidence this eminent Arctic explorer, speaking of certain rock strata north of 69° N. latitude, says: *"A broad continent occupied this part of the globe when these strata were deposited*." [1] Everywhere he speaks of this ancient polar continent; as something already accepted and universally understood among scientific people.

1. Baron Nordenskiöld, *Expedition to Greenland. Arctic Manual,* London, 1875: p. 423.

He also alludes to the conspiratorial evidence of his former existence found in the various research departments. *"**These basalt beds; probably derived from a volcanic chain, active during the Tertiary period, which may have bounded the ancient polar continent, in the same way as is now the case with the eastern coast of Asia and the western part of America; thus, confirming the division of land and water in the Tertiary period, after which it is assumed that there were completely different lands**." - Arctic Manual, p. 420.2*

Our hypothesis calls for an antediluvian continent at the Arctic Pole. It is interesting to find that a writer upon the Deluge writing more than forty years ago advanced the same postulate. [2] Is the supposition that there existed such a continent scientifically admissible? Until very recently too little was known of the geology of the high latitudes to warrant or even to occasion the discussion of such a question. Even now, with all the contemporary interest in Arctic exploration, it is difficult to find any author who has distinctly propounded to himself and discussed the question of the geologic age of the Arctic Ocean. It will not be strange, therefore, if we have here to content ourselves with showing, first, that geologists and paleontologists do not think the present distribution of Arctic Sea and land to be the primeval one; and secondly, that in their opinion, incidentally expressed, a "continent" once existed within the Arctic Circle of which at present only vestiges remain.

2. "On peut supposer, et je tâcherai de developper cette ideé plus tard, qu'il a existé une periode géologique plus recoulée, . . . et qu'á cette époque l'Europe, l'Asie, et l'Amérique septentrionale se joignaient au pole nord de maniere á former un continent d'une étendue prodigieuse, se prolongueant vers le pole sud en trois presqu'iles, savoir: Amérique méridionale, l'Afrique, et l'Océanie. C'est des débris de cet ancien continent que des révolutions violentes ont forme les terres actuelles.; Fréderik Klée, *Le Déluge*, French ed. Paris, 1847: p. 83. (Danish original, 1842.)

We will begin with the distinguished *Alfred Russel Wallace*, who in speaking of the Miocene period presents us with a very different Northern hemisphere from ours of today. For instance, in his view, Scandinavia was at that time a vast island. He says:

"The distribution of the Eocene and Miocene formations shows that during a considerable portion of the Tertiary period an inland sea, more or less occupied by an archipelago of islands, extended across Central Europe between the Baltic and the Black and Caspian seas, and thence by narrower channels southeastward to the valley of the Euphrates and the Persian Gulf, thus opening a communication between the North Atlantic and the Indian Ocean. From the Caspian also, a wide arm of the sea extended, during some part of the Tertiary epoch, northwards to the Arctic Ocean, and there is nothing to show that this sea may not have been in existence during the whole Tertiary period. Another channel probably existed over Egypt into the eastern basin of the Mediterranean and the Black Sea; while it is probable that there was a communication between the Baltic and the White Sea, leaving Scandinavia as an extensive island. Turning to India, we find that an arm of the sea, of great width and depth, extended from the Bay of Bengal to the mouths of the Indus; while the enormous depression indicated by the presence of marine fossils of Eocene age at a height of 16,500 feet in Western Tibet renders it not improbable that a more direct channel across Afghanistan may have opened a communication between the West Asiatic and Polar seas". [3] Later, in the same book, **Mr. Wallace** incidentally shows that the facts of Arctic paleontology call for the supposition of a primitive Eocene continent in the highest latitudes, a continent that no longer exists. His language is *"The rich and varied fauna which inhabited Europe at the dawn of the Tertiary period as shown by the abundant remains of Mammalia wherever suitable deposits of Eocene age have been discovered proves that an extensive Palearctic continent then existed"*. [4]

Another most eminent authority in Arctic paleontology, the late **Professor Heer**, of Zurich, fully fifteen years ago arrived at and published the conclusion that the facts presented in the Arctic fossils plainly point to the existence in the Miocene time of a no longer existing polar continent. A **Fuller** reference to his views will be made in our next chapter. [5]

Another authority in this field, writing of the theory that continuous land once connected Europe and North America at the North, remarks *"In further support of this theory we have the fact that no trace of sea deposit of Eocene age has ever been found in the polar area, all the vestiges of strata remaining showing that these latitudes were then occupied by dry land"*. [6]

Finally, as our assumption of the early existence of a circumpolar Arctic continent is thus supported by the most competent geological authority, so is also our hypothesis that its disappearance was due to submergence beneath the waters of the Arctic Ocean. On this point what could be more explicit and satisfactory than the following, from one of the greatest of living geologists: *"We know very well that . . . within a comparatively recent geological period ... a wide stretch of Arctic land, of which Novaia Zemlia and Spitzbergen formed a part, has been submerged"*. [7]

3. Island Life. London, 1880: pp. 184, 185.

4. Ibid., p. 362.

5. Professor Heer, deceased Sept. 27, 1883. On the preeminence of his authority in this field, see *Nature,* Oct. 25, page 612.

6. J. Starkie Gardner in *Nature,* London, Dec. 12, 1878: p. 127.

7. James Geikie, LL. D., F. R. S., *Prehistoric Europe. A Geological Sketch.* London, 1881: p. 41. *Compare Louis Faliés, Études historiques et philosophiques sur les Civilisations Européenne, Romaine, Greque,* etc. Paris, 1874: vol. i., pp. 348-352.

As to the natural conditions and forces which may be conceived as having brought about this continental catastrophe, geologists are not so well agreed. The French savant, *Alfonse-Joseph Adhemar,* [8] has advanced a theory that this North-polar deluge was only one of an alternating series, which in age-long periods recur first at the North and then at the South Pole. Flammarion, writing of it, says: *"This theory depends on the fact of the unequal length of the seasons in the two hemispheres. Our autumn and winter lasted 179 days. In the southern hemisphere, they last 186 days. This seven days, or 168 hours of difference, increase each year the coldness of the pole. During 10,500 years the ice accumulates at one pole and melts at the other, thereby displacing the earth's center of gravity. Now a time will arrive when, after the maximum of elevation of temperature on one side, a catastrophe will happen which will bring back the center of gravity to the center of the figure, and cause an immense deluge. The deluge of the North Pole was 4,200 years ago; therefore, the next will be 6,300 hence."* [9]

Another recent theory teaches that the poles are periodically deluged, but simultaneously, not in alternation. The alternative movement is at the equator. The crust of the earth at the equator is all the time rising or sinking in a kind of eonian rhythm.

8. In his *Revolutions de la Mer.* 2 ed, 1860.

9. Flammarion naturally adds, "It is very obvious to ask on this, why should there be a catastrophe, and why should not the center of gravity return gradually, as it was gradually displaced? *Astronomical Myths, p. 426.* But a gradual displacement would produce a deluge, only a gradual one.

Whenever it sinks beyond the equilibrium figure, due to its actual rate of rotation, lands emerge at the poles; whenever it rises beyond the equilibrium figure, the polar lands sink and are submerged beneath the waters of the ocean. *Professor Alexander Winchell* thus expounds the view: *"It has been shown that one of the actions of tides upon a planetary body tends to diminish its rate of rotation. Correspondingly, its equatorial protuberance will tend to diminish. In the case of a planet still retaining its liquid condition, the equatorial subsidence will keep nearly even pace with the retardation. To whatever extent viscosity exists, the subsidence will follow the retardation. There will exist an excess of protuberance beyond the equilibrium figure due to the actual rotation, and this will act as an additional retardative cause. In the case of an incrusted and somewhat rigid planet, the excess of ellipticity would attain its greatest value. It would continue to augment until the strain upon the mass should become enough to lower the excessive protuberance to the equilibrium figure. The recovery of this figure might take place convulsively. The equatorial regions would then subside, and the polar would rise. In the case of an incrusted planet extensively covered, like the earth, by a film of water, retarded rotation would be attended by prompt subsidence of the equatorial waters and rise of the polar waters to about twice the same extent. In other words, the equatorial lands would emerge, and the polar lands would become submerged. The amount of emergence would diminish with an increase of distance from the equator, and the amount of submergence would diminish with an increase of distance from the pole. In about the latitude of 30, the two tendencies would meet and neutralize each other. Under these conditions, an incrusted and ocean-covered planet, since it must be undergoing a process of rotary retardation, must possess the deepest oceans about the poles and the shallowest about the equator. The first emergences of land, accordingly, will take place within the equatorial zone; and the highest elevations and greatest land areas will exist within that zone. The elevation of equatorial land masses would interpose new obstructions to the equatorial ocean current. This would divert it in new directions, and thus modify all climates within reach of oceanic influences. Changes of currents would necessitate the migration of marine faunas, and changes of climate would modify the faunas and floras of the land. "But the protrusion of the equatorial land mass could not increase indefinitely. The same central force which retains the ocean continually at the equilibrium figure strains the solid mass in the same direction. The strain must at length become greater than the rigidity of the mass can withstand. The equatorial land protuberance will subside toward the level of the ocean. Some parts of the ocean s bottom must correspondingly rise. Naturally, the parts about the poles will rise the most. Thus, some equatorial lands will become submerged, and some northern and southern areas may become newly emergent."*

But these vertical movements would not be arrested precisely at the point of recovery of the equilibrium figure. As suggested by **Prof. J. E. Todd**, and less explicitly by **Sir Wm. Thomson**, the movement would pass the equilibrium figure to an extent proportional to the cumulation of strain. The equatorial region would become too much depressed, and the polar regions too much elevated. The effect of this would be to accelerate the rotation sufficiently to neutralize the ceaseless tidal retardation. The day would be shortened. The ocean would rise still higher along the shores of equatorial lands, and subside along the shores of polar lands. An extension of polar lands would immediately modify the climates of the higher latitudes. They would become subject to greater extremes. A considerable elevation of polar lands would diminish the mean temperature, and the region of perpetual snow would be enlarged. These effects would visit the northern and southern hemispheres simultaneously. Such effects would follow from excessive subsidence of equatorial lands. But the constant retardative action of the tides would cause the equatorial lands again to emerge, and protrude beyond the limits of the equilibrium figure attained in a later age. Thus, the former condition would return, and the former events would be repeated. In the nature of force and matter, these oscillations should be repeated many times. *Professor Todd* suggests that the present terrestrial age is one of equatorial land subsidence and of high latitude emergence. Immediately preceding the present, the Champlain epoch was one of northern and probably of south polar subsidence; while further back, in the Glacial epoch, we have evidence of northern, and perhaps also south latitude elevation." [10]

10. *World-Life; or Comparative Geology*. Chicago, 1883: pp. 278- 280.

Leibnitz, *Deluc*, and others have presented a still different view of the etiology of all deluges, according to which they are the result of a steady shrinkage of the earth in a consequence of its secular cooling. According to this theory, after once a solid earth-crust had been formed, the cooling nucleus within it withdrew the support on which the crust had rested, in proportion as it shrank away from beneath it, until, as often as the subterranean voids thus created became too great for the strength of the crust, this of necessity fell in with the force of in computable tons, carrying the ruined surface to such a depth as to cause it immediately ta be overflowed and submerged by the adjacent water| of the ocean. The geologic history of the earth is divided into its strongly marked periods by these successive "collapsions" of the rocky strata which constituted the primitive crust. "Each succeeding cataclysm," says a recent advocate of the view, "considered as a universal catastrophe, must leave the globe a wreck, like the ruin of some immense cathedral whose dome and arches have fallen in. Cornice and frieze, pillar and entablature, broken and dislocated, lie at all angles of inclination and in the utmost confusion. So, it is with the ancient rocks and more modern strata. Only to this mighty wreck have been added the outgushings of molten matter into fissures, creating dikes, and the unsparing movements of oceans sweeping loose materials and perishing forms of all sorts from one place to another, partially covering up and disguising the desolation."

Again, the same writer says: "*The present sun face of the earth is comparatively recent. The last great cataclysm is, geologically speaking, not very ancient. Accumulating evidence compels us to believe that one of those destructive events has occurred since the human race was created. The facts I have presented plainly indicate that another is in the course of preparation. Each of these vast periodical voids between the nucleus and the crust is filled by collapsing of the surface. Thus, if we assume that the globe was one hundred or three hundred miles greater in all its diameters when its crust became hard and was bathed with the earliest seas, and when marine plants and trilobites and Mollusca began to appear, the lithological characteristics of the Paleozoic ages will be more acceptably deciphered. So successively with the carboniferous periods, whose vast areas have been folded up and overflowed, and whose fields for reproduction have been so numerous and extensive as to convince us that Arctic America, during those remote ages, presented tropical positions to the sun.*" [11]

11. C. F. Winslow, M. D., *The Cooling Globe, or the Mechanics of Geology*. Boston, 1865: pp. 50, 51. For the latest presentations and criticisms of this general theory, see Winchell's *World -Life*, 1883, pp. 302-308, and the literature there given. Among the older treatises constructed upon it, none is perhaps of so great interest to the general reader as the work on *The Déluge*, by Frédérik Klée (Danish 1842, German 1843, French 1847).

Although starting with no such purpose, the author, in expounding this *general **Leibnitzian*** theory of all deluges, incidentally explains the submersion of the primeval Arctic continent. In accordance with his theory, he asserts that "*the diameter of the earth at the poles must have been at some more ancient epoch very much greater than now. It must have been more than twenty-seven miles greater to permit such equatorial or tropical exposures to the sun as we know to be necessary for the production of those vegetable forms which abound in the coal measures of Arctic latitudes.* [12] *If it was fifty or a hundred miles greater during any portion of the carboniferous age, it might have been two hundred during the Taconic period, and perhaps three hundred or more when the life force began to fashion its primordial and rudimentary organisms upon its waiting surface.*" He furthermore distinctly asserts that ***Sir Isaac Newton***'s supposed demonstration that the oblateness of the earth's figure is due to the centrifugal force generated by its rotation *"is an error unworthy of further consideration among geologists."* The true explanation, as he regards it, is stated as follows: *"The shorter axes of the globe what at present are our poles are not the result of flattening by rotation, but by a sudden falling in of surface."* [13]

Here, of course, is just that down-sinking of wide polar regions, in "comparatively recent" geologic time, demanded by the facts of Arctic geology. It must have been greater than any of those which have occurred in other portions of the globe, for it has permanently modified the originally and naturally spherical figure of the earth. The author is "compelled to believe" that it, or one like it, "occurred since the human race was created." Moreover, this belief is in no wise built upon the Biblical record of the Deluge, for he speaks almost bitterly of "the retarding influence of Jewish legends upon the free expansion of the human intellect" and makes Moses one of the two men whose "declarations and authority, more than the statements of all others, have retarded the advancement of general knowledge. "Happily, for Moses, the second in this portentous duumvirate is no worse a man than *Sir Isaac Newton*!

12. Dr. Winslow seems here to forget that the primeval polar continent was of necessity the sunniest of all lands.

13. Ibid., p. 49

It is by no means necessary to commit ourselves to any one of these theories of deluges or to seek still other explanations of the recognized subsidence of the basin now occupied by the Arctic Ocean. Enough for the present that upon the authority of eminent physiographic geologists we have shown :

1. That the present distribution of land and water within the Arctic Circle is, geologically speaking, of very recent origin.

2. That the paleozoic data of the highest explored latitudes demand for their explanation of the hypothesis of an extensive circumpolar continent in Miocene time.

3. That lithological authorities affirm that such a continent existed.

4. That physical geography has reached the conclusion that the known islands of the Arctic Ocean, such as Novaia Zemlia and the Spitzbergen, are simply mountain tops still remaining above the surface of the sea which has come in and covered up the primeval continent to which they belonged.

5. And finally, that the problem of the process by which this grand catastrophe was brought about is now sporadically engaging the thoughts of terrestrial physicists and geologists. [14]

14. See the very interesting paper *"On Ice-Age Theories"* in *Transactions of the British Association*, 1884, by E. Hill, M. A., F. G. S. Also, in the same volume W. F. Stanley's criticism of the theory of Croll.

"Die arctische Geologie birgt die Schlüssel zu Lösung vieler Räthsel". - *Professor Heer*

"Arctic geology holds the key to the solution of many mysteries."

• Prehistoric Climatology

"*Ver illud erat, ver magnus agebat Orbis*" - *Vergil.*

"*It was a spring, a great spring in the world*".

Thus far, then, we have found theoretical geogony demanding a location at the Pole for the first country presenting conditions of Eden life; we have found the requisite astronomical conditions to give it an abundance of light; we have found the geologists attesting the former existence of such a country; we must now interrogate Prehistoric Climatology, and ascertain whether this lost land ever enjoyed a temperature which admits of the supposition that here was the primitive abode of man. The answer to our question comes, not from one, but from several sources. [1]

1. We have no use here for mere fancy sketches, like the following, which appeared on the loth of May 1884, in *The Norwood Review and Crystal Palace Reporter* (Eng.), and which looks very much like an unacknowledged loan from Captain Hall, of Arctic fame: "We do not admit that there is ice up to the Pole. No one has been nearer that point than 464 miles. Once inside the great ice barrier, a new world breaks upon the explorer; a climate first mild like that of England, and afterward balmy as that of the Greek Isles, awaits the hardy adventurer who first beholds those wonderful shores. Wonderful, indeed; for he will be greeted by a branch of the human race cut off from the rest of humanity by that change of climate which came over Northern Europe about 2,000 years ago, but surrounded by a profusion of life bewildering in the extreme." Speculations or fancies of this sort have ever clustered about this mysterious region of the Pole. As we shall hereafter see, they abounded in remote antiquity. Even the singular fancy known to the public as "Symmes Hole" antedates Symmes, and may be found in much more attractive form in Klopstock's Messiah. (*K. s'Sämmtliche Werke*. Leipsic, 1854: vol. i., pp. 24, 25.)

First, geogony gives us an almost irresistible tecedent probability. For if the earth from its earliest consolidation has been steadily cooling, it is hardly possible to conceive of a method by which any region once too hot for human residence can have become at length too cold except by passing through all the intermediate stages of temperature, some of which must have been precisely adapted to human comfort. Again, paleontological botany shows that in Europe in Tertiary times this hypothetical cooling of the earth was going on, and going on in the steady and regular way postulated by theoretic geogony. [2] But if a telluric process as essentially universal as this was going on in Europe, there is no reason why it should not have been going on in all countries, whether to the north, or to the south, or to the east, or to the west of Europe. But we are not left to inferences of this sort. It is now admitted by all scientific authorities that at one time the regions within the Arctic Circle enjoyed a tropical or nearly tropical climate.

2. "L'étude des flores nous démontre que le climat de 1'Europe, pendant les temps tertiaires, est toujours allé *en se refroidissant d'une mantire continue et reguilére*" *Le Préhistorique. Antiquité de l'Homme.* Par Gabriel de Mortillet, Professeur d'anthropologie préhistorique á l'École d'Anthropologie de Paris. Paris, 1883: p. 113 The study of the flora shows us that the climate of Europe, during the tertiary times, always went on cooling (A continuous and regular mantire) The Prehistoric Antiquity of the Man by Gabriel de Mortillet, Professor of préhistoric anthropology at the á l'École d'Anthropologie de Paris.

Professor Nicholson uses the following language: ***"In the early Tertiary period the climate of the northern hemisphere, as shown by the Eocene animals and plants, was very much hotter than it is at present; partaking, indeed, of a sub-tropical character. In the Middle Tertiary or Miocene period, the temperature, though not high, was still much warmer than that now enjoyed by the northern hemisphere; and we know that the plants of the temperate regions at that time flourished within the Arctic Circle."*** [3] *Mr. Grant Allen* says, ***"One thing at least is certain, that till a very recent period, geologically speaking, our earth enjoyed a warm and genial climate up to the actual poles themselves, and that all its vegetation was everywhere evergreen, of much the same type as that which now prevails in the modern tropics."*** [4] Alluding to those distant ages, *M. le Marquis de Nadaillac* remarks: ***"Under these conditions, life spread freely even to the Pole."*** [5] Similar is the language of *Dr. Croll*: ***"The Arctic regions, probably up to the North Pole, were not only free from ice but were covered with a rich and luxuriant vegetation."*** [6] *Keerl* holds that at the very Pole it was then warmer than now at the equator. [7]

Professor Oswald Heer s calculations would possibly modify *Keerl's* estimate to a slight degree, but only enough to make the circumpolar climate of that far-off age a little more Edenic than is that of the hottest portions of our present earth. [8]

3. *The Life-History of the Globe,* p. 335.

4. *Knowledge.* London, Nov. 30, 1883: p. 327.

5. *Les Premiers Hommes et les Temps Prehistoriqués.* Paris, 1881: tom, ii., p. 391.

6. *Climate and Time.* Am. ed., 1875: p.7

7. *Die Schöpfungsgeschichte und Lehre vom Paradies.* Basel, 1861: Abth. I., p. 634.

8. *Flora Fossilis Arctica.* Zurich, 1868: Bd. i., pp. 60-77. See also Alfred Russel Wallace, *Island Life.* London, 1880: ch. ix., pp. 163202. Well, therefore, sings a rollicking rhymester of the age, -

> *"When the sea rolled its fathomless billows*
> *Across the broad plains of Nebraska;*
> *When around the North Pole grew bananas and willows,*

And mastodons fought with the great armadillos
For the pine apples grown in Alaska."

Sir Charles Lyell, who in the discussion of this subject is characteristically cautious and "uniformitarian" does not hesitate to say, "*The result, then, of our examination, in this and in the preceding chapter, of the organic and inorganic evidence as to the state of the climate of former geological periods is in favor of the opinion that the heat was generally in excess of what it now is. In the greater part of the Miocene and preceding Eocene epochs the fauna and flora of Central Europe were sub-tropical, and vegetation resembling that now seen in Northern Europe extended into the Arctic regions as far as they have yet been explored, and probably reached the Pole itself. In the Mesozoic ages, the predominance of reptile life and the general character of the fossil types of that great class of vertebrata indicate a warm climate and an absence of frost between the 40th parallel of latitude and the Pole, a large ichthyosaurus having been found in lat. 77° 16 N."* [9] Averaging the above views and estimates of scientific authorities, we have at the Pole, in the age of the first appearance of the human race, a temperature the most equable and delightful possible; and with this, we may well be content.

9. *Principles of Geology,* eleventh ed., vol. i., p. 231.

"*One of the most startling and important of the scientific discoveries of the last twenty years has been that of the relics of a luxuriant Miocene flora in various parts of the Arctic regions. It is a discovery that was totally unexpected and is even now considered by many men of science to be completely unintelligible, but it is so thoroughly established, and it has such an important bearing on the subjects we are discussing in the present volume, that it is necessary to lay a tolerably complete outline of the facts before our readers*". A. R. Wallace (1880).

• *Paleontological Botany*

"It is now an established conclusion that the great aggressive faunas and floras of the continents have originated in the North, some of them within the Artic Circle". *Principal Dawson (1883).*

All traditions of the primeval Paradise require us to conceive of it as possessed of a tropical flora of the most beautiful and luxuriant sort, as adorned with "every tree that is pleasant to the sight, or good for food." Any theory, therefore, as to the site of Eden must of necessity present a locality where this condition could have been met. How is it with the hypothesis now under consideration? To reply that a polar Eden is scientifically admissible in this respect would be to state but a small part of the truth. Given in any country on the face of the globe a long-continued tropical climate, and tropical vegetation may well be expected. Anything else would be so abnormal as to require explanation. But the study of Paleontological Botany has just been conducted to a new and entirely unanticipated result.

The best authorities in this science, both in Europe and America, have lately reached the conclusion that *"all the floral types and forms revealed in the oldest fossils of the earth originated in the region of the North Pole, and thence spread first over the northern and then over the southern hemisphere, proceeding from North to South"*. This is a conception of the origin and development of the vegetable world which but a few years ago no scientific man had dreamed of, and which, to many intelligent readers of these pages, will be entirely new. Its profound interest, as related to the present discussion, will at once be seen. Without attempting a chronological history of this remarkable discovery, or in any wise assuming to assign to each pioneer student his share of the credit, we may say that *Professor Asa Gray*, of America, *Professor Oswald Heer*, of Switzerland, *Sir Joseph Hooker*, of England, *Otto Kuntze*, of Germany, and *Count G. de Saporta*, of France, have all been more or less prominently associated with the establishment of the new doctrine. *Sir Joseph Hooker* s studies of the floral types of Tasmania furnished data, before lacking, for a general trans-latitudinal survey of the whole field. He was struck by the fact that in that far-off Southern world "the

Scandinavian type asserts his prerogative of ubiquity." *Though at that time he seems not to have divined its significance, he clearly saw the paleontological and other vestiges of the great movement by which the far North has slowly clothed the north-temperate, the equatorial, and the southern regions with verdure. In one passage he describes the impression made upon him by the facts in the following graphic language: "When I take a comprehensive view of the vegetation of the Old World, I am struck with the appearance it presents of there, having been a continuous current of vegetation, if I may so fancifully express myself, from Scandinavia to Tasmania."* [1]

Light on this problem of the far South was soon to come from the far North. In 1868 **Professor Oswald Heer**, of Zurich, published his truly epoch-making work on the fossil flora of the Arctic regions, in which he modestly yet with much confidence advanced the idea that the *Bildungsherd*, or mother-region, of all the floral types of the more southern latitudes, was originally in "**a great continuous Miocene continent within the Arctic Circle**" and that from this center the southward spread or dispersion of these types had been in a radial or out-raying manner. [2] His demonstration of the existence in Miocene times of a warm climate and of a rich tropical vegetation in the highest attainable Arctic latitudes was complete and overwhelming. Our latest geologists are still accustomed to speaking of his result as "**one of the most remarkable geological discoveries of modern times**." [3] His theory of a primeval circumpolar mother region whence all floral types proceeded is also at present so little questioned that today among representative scholars in this field the absorbing and only question seems to be, who first proposed and to whom belongs the chief honor of the verification of so broad and beautiful a generalization? [4]

1. The Flora of Australia. London, 1859: p. 103. On the remarkable qualifications of Dr. Hooker to speak on this subject, see Sir Charles Lyell, *The Antiqtiity of Man,* pp. 417, 418.

2. Flora Arctica Fossilis: Diefossile Flora der Polarldnder. Zurich, 1868: I. Vorwort, pp. iii., iv., and elsewhere.

3. Archibald Geikie, LL. D., F. R. S., *Textbook of Geology.* London, 1882: p. 868.

4. Some twenty-five years ago, in a paper on *"The Botany of Japan"* (Memoirs of the American Academy of Science, 1857, vol. vi., pp. 377458), Professor Asa Gray suggested the possibility of the common origination in high northern latitudes of various related species now widely separated in different portions of the north-temperate zone. In 1872, four years after the publication of Heer's work, in treating of *"The Sequoia and its History"* in an address (see *Joiurnal of the Am. Ass. for the Advancement of Science,* 1872), he renewed in a clearer and stronger manner his advocacy of the idea. In the same year, and in 1876, Count Saporta, with due acknowledgment of the work of Professor Heer, gave currency to the theory in the scientific circles of France. Alluding to this, the Count has recently written "Asa Gray was not the only botanist who had the idea of explaining the presence of disjoined species and genera dispersed across the boreal temperate zone and the two continents, by means of emigrations from the pole as the mother-region whence these vegetable races had radiated in one or several directions. This had been parallelement conceived and developed in France upon the occasion of the remarkable works of Professor O. Heer." *Am. Journal of Science,* May, 1883, p. 394. The annotation appended to this by Professor Gray may be seen on the same page. For a German acknowledgment see Engler, *Entwickelungsgeschichte der Pflanzenwelt,* Th. i., S. 23; for an English, see *Nature, London,* 1881, p. 446; for an American, J. W. Dawson, *"The Genesis and Migration of Plants"* in *The Princeton Review,* 1879, p. 277. But Dr. Dawson, referring to Saporta *s'Ancienne Vegetation Polaire,* Hooker's *Presidential Address* of 1878, Thistleton Dyer's *Lecture on Plant Distribution,* and J. Starkie Gardner's *Letters in Nature,* 1878, well remarks that "the basis of most of these brochures is to be found in Heer's *Flora Fossilis Arctica.*"

Arctic plants and animals which in the beginning of the Quaternary ages came southward into Europe. [5] But it may be that the testimony of Paleontological Botany is not yet exhausted. What if it should at length appear that along with the plant's prehistoric men and civilized men at that must have descended from the mother region of plants to the place where history finds them? Without any reference to or apparent recognition of the great anthropological interest of such a question, at least one botanist of Germany, reasoning from botanical facts and postulates alone, has reached precisely this conclusion. This savant is **Professor Otto Kuntze,** who has made special studies of cultivated tropical plants. What other botanists had found true of the wild flora in continents separated by wide oceans he finds true of domesticated plants. But the problem of the spread of these plants from continent to continent raises peculiar and most interesting questions. Taking the banana-plantain, which was cultivated in America before the arrival of Europeans in 1492, **Professor Kuntze** asks, **"In what way was this plant, which cannot stand a voyage through the** *temperate zone, carried to America*? "The difficulty is that the banana is seedless, and can be propagated in a new country only by carrying thither a living root and planting it in a suitable soil. Its very seed lessness is evidence of the enormous length of time that it has been cared for by man. As the Professor says, *"A cultivated plant which does not possess seeds must have been under culture for a very long period, we have not in Europe a single exclusively seedless, berry-bearing cultivated plant, and hence it is perhaps fair to infer that these plants were cultivated as early as the middle of the diluvial period*." But now as to its transportation from the Old World to the New, or vice versa. *"It must be remembered,"* he says, *"that the plantain is a tree-like, herbaceous plant, possessing no easily transportable bulbs, like the potato or the dahlia, nor propagable by cuttings, like the willow or the poplar. It has only a perennial root, which, once planted, needs hardly any care."* After discussing the subject in all aspects, he reaches the twofold conclusion, first, that civilized man must have brought the roots of the plant into any new regions into which it has ever come; and secondly, that its appearance in America can only be accounted for on the supposition that it was carried thither by way of the north polar countries at a time when a tropical climate prevailed at the North Pole. [6]

5. Geikie, *Textbook of Geology, p. 874.* Compare Wallace: "We have now only to notice the singular want of reciprocity in the migrations of northern and southern types of vegetation. In return for the vast number of European plants which have reached Australia, not one single Australian plant has entered any part of the north temperate zone, and the same may be said of the typical southern vegetation in general, whether developed in the Antarctic lands, New Zealand, South America, or South Africa." *Island-Life.* London, 1880: p. 486. *In like manner Sir Joseph Hooker affirms: "Geographically speaking, there is no Antarctic flora except a few lichens and seaweeds." Nature,* 1881: p. 447. Possibly, however, the progress of research may bring to light evidence of a second and less powerful polar Bildiingsherd of primitive flora forms in the Antarctic region. Some of the discoveries of F. P. Moreno look in that direction. See Patagonia, resto de un antiguo continente hoy sumerjido." Also, *"La faune éocéne de la Patagonie australe et le grande continent antarctique." Par M. E. L. Trouessart. Revue Scientifique,* Paris, xxxii., стр. 588 ss. (Nov. 10. 1883). Also, Samuel Haughton in his last lecture for *Physical Geography.* Dublin, 1880.

6. *Pflanzen als Beweis der Einwanderung der Amerikaner aus Asien in praglazialer Zeit.* Published in Ausland, 1878, p. 197, 198.

"Damals von dort aus - d. h. aus diesem Bildungsherdfur die Pflanzen sudlicher Breiten im hohen Norden hat eine strahlenfdrmige Verbreitung von Typen stattgehabt". – Professor Oswald von Heer (1809-1883)

"At that time from there - from this center of formation for the plants of southern latitudes in the far north there has been a radiating distribution of types."

• *Paleontological Zoology*

"All the evidence at our command points to the Northern hemisphere as the birthplace of the class, Mammalia, and probably of all the orders". - Alfred Russel Wallace (1823 –1913, famous British naturalist, explorer, geographer, anthropologist, and biologist).

But in settling the site of Eden the animal kingdom must also have a voice. According to the Hebrew story, the representatives of this kingdom were an earlier creation than Adam, and in Eden was the world-fest of their christening. Evidently, the lost cradle of humanity must be fixed in time posterior to the beginnings of animal life, and in space so located that from that spot as a center all the multitudinous species, genera, orders, and families of the whole animal creation might have radiated forth to the various habitats in which they are respectively found. Now it is one of the striking facts connected with Zoology that if we pass around the globe on any iso thermal line, at the equator, or in any latitude south of it, or in any latitude north of it, until we come to the confines of the Arctic zone, we find, as we pass from land to land, that the animals we encounter are specifically unlike. Everywhere we find, along with like climatic and telluric conditions, different animals. The moment, however, we reach the Arctic zone, and there make the circuit of the globe, we are everywhere surrounded by the same species. On the other hand, if we take great circles of the earth s longitude, and pass from the Arctic region down along the continental masses of the New World to the South Pole, thence returning up a meridian that crosses Africa and Europe, or Australia and Asia, we shall find in the descent abundant fossil evidence that we are moving forward on the pathway along which the prehistoric migrations of the animal world proceeded; while on our return on the other side of the planet we shall find that we are no longer following in the track of ancient migrations, but are advancing counter to their obvious movement. All this is as true of the flora of the world as it is of the fauna. Hence the language of the late *Professor Orton*: "*Only around the shores of the Arctic Sea is the same animals and plants found through every meridian, and in passing southward along the three principal lines of land specific identities give way to the mere identity of genera; these are replaced by family resemblances, and at last, even the families become in a measure distinct, not only on the great continents but also on the islands, till every little rock in the ocean has its peculiar inhabitants.*" [1]

Another well-known naturalist says: "*It should also be observed that in the beginning of things the continents were built up from North to South, such has been, at least, the history of the North and South American and the Euro-Asiatic and the African continents; and thus it would appear that north of the equator, at least, animals slowly migrated southward, keeping pace as it were with the growth and southward extension of the grand land-masses which appeared above the sea in the Paleozoic ages. Hence, scanty as is the Arctic and Temperate region of the earth at the present time, in former ages these regions were as prolific in life as the tropics now are, the latter regions, now so vast, having through all the Tertiary and Quaternary ages been undisturbed by great geological revolutions, and meanwhile been colonized by emigrants driven down by the incoming cold of the glacial period.*" [2] As long ago as 1876 *Mr. Alfred Russel Wallace* wrote "*All the chief types of animal life appear to have originated in the great north temperate or northern continents, while the southern continents have been more or less completely isolated during long periods, both from the northern continent and from each other.*" [3] And again, speaking of Mammalia, he said "*All the evidence at our command points to the Northern Hemisphere as the birthplace of the class, and probably of all the orders.*" [4]

1. *Comparative Zoology.* New York, 1876: p. 384.

2. A. S. Packard, *Zoology*. New York, 2d ed., 1880: p. 665. In his *Elements of Geology,* New York, 1877, p. 159, Le Conte gives a graphical representation of the polo-centric zones of the earth s flora and fauna (Fig. 131), which ought to have suggested the true genetic connection of the whole.

3. The Geographical Distribution of Animals. New York ed., vol. i. p. 173.

4. Ibid., vol. ii., p. 544.

From all the facts but one conclusion is possible, and that is that like as the Arctic Pole is the mother region of all plants, so it is the mother region of all animals, the region where, in the beginning, God created every beast of the earth after his kind, and cattle after their kind, and everything that creped on the earth after his kind. And this is the conclusion now being reached and announced by all comparative zoologists who busy themselves with the problem of the origin and prehistoric distribution of the animal world. But to believe that **Professor Heer's** "Miocene Arctic Continent" was the cradle of all floral types and the cradle of all faunal forms, and yet deny that it was also the cradle of the human race, is what few philosophical minds are likely long to do.

C'est a des emigrations venues, sinon du pole, du mains des contrees attenantes au cercle polaire, qu il faut attribuer la presence constatee dans les deux mondes de beaucoup danimaux propres a Phemisphere boreal. - *Count Saporta (1823 –1895, French aristocrat, paleobotanist).*

"It is to emigrations coming, if not from the pole, from the lands adjoining the polar circle, that we must attribute the presence observed in the two worlds of many animals specific to the boreal hemisphere."

• *Paleontological Anthropology and Ethnology*

Quittons done pour un instant les jardins d'Armide, et, nouveaux Argonautes parcourons les régions hyperborées; cherchons-y, armes de patéence et surtout de scepticism, Vorigine de'la plupart des nations et des langues tnodernes, celle meme des habitans de l'Attique, et des autres peuples de la Gréce, objets de noire savante idolatrie. (Let us therefore leave the gardens of Armide for a moment, and, new Argonauts, let us traverse the hyperborean regions; let us seek there, armed with patience and above all with skepticism, the origin of the majority of modern nations and languages, that of the inhabitants of Attica, and of the other peoples of Greece, objects of our learned idolatry). – Charles de Pougens (A. D. 1799).

Man is the one traveler who has certainly been in the cradle of the human race. He has come from the land we are seeking. Could we but follow back the trail of his journeyings it would assuredly take us to the garden of pleasantness from which we are exiled. Unfortunately, the traveler has lost whole volumes of his itinerary, and what remains is in many of its passages not easy of decipher. What says anthropologic and ethnic Paleontology or what some French writers are beginning to call *Paleoethnique Science* respecting the hypothesis of a Polar Eden? One of the strongest proofs he could then find that a new light was about to dawn on this field was in their cited work of **Quatrefages**, entitled "***The Human Species***". [1] Accordingly, in discussing the probable verdict of this science upon the admissibility of the new theory of human distribution, the lecturer presented the following paragraph, and there rested the case: "***Anthropology, as represented by Quatrefages, seems to be actually feeling its way to the same hypothesis. This writer first argues that in the present state of knowledge we should be led to place the cradle of the race in the great region bounded on the south and southwest by the Himalayas, on the west by the Bolor mountains, on the northwest by the Ala-Tau, on the north by the Altai range and its offshoots, and on the east by the Kingkhan, on the south and southeast by the Felina and Kwen-lun.*** Later, however, he says that *paleontological studies have very recently led to results that are capable of modifying these primary conclusions. And after briefly stating these results, he starts the question of whether or not the first center of human appearance may not have been considerable to the north of the region just mentioned, even in polar Asia! Without deciding, he adds, perhaps prehistoric archeology or paleontology will someday confirm or confute this conjecture*".

The cautious anticipation here expressed was quickly fulfilled. At the concluding lecture of the same first course it was possible to present the following as the ripe conclusion of a fellow countryman of **Quatrefages**, one of the foremost savants of Europe, ***Count Saporta***: [2] "***We are inclined to remove to the circumpolar regions of the North the probable cradle of primitive humanity. From there only could it have radiated as from a center to spread into several continents at once, and to give rise to successive emigrations toward the South. This theory best agrees with the presumed march of the human races.*** " [3]

1. New York edition, pp. 175, 177, 178. *See M. Zaborowski's support of Quatrefages conjecture in the Revue Scientifigue,* Paris, 1883, p. 496.

2. The following note appeared in the Boston Daily Advertiser of May 25, 1883:

The Cradle of the Race.

A few years ago, about the time of the appearance of the first edition of Dr. Winchel's Preadamites, in a letter addressed to its learned author, I expressed my belief that the Garden of Eden, the first abode of man, was to be sought in a now submerged country, situated at the North Pole. More than a year ago, in a printed essay on Ancient Cosmology, I made the statement that "*all ethnic traditions point us thither for the cradle of the race.*" Early last January I began a course of lectures in the post-graduate department of the university, setting forth my view and the astonishing mass of cosmological, historic, mythologic, paleontologic, paleolithic, and other evidence which conspire to its support. Last Monday afternoon, about twenty minutes before I was to give the concluding lecture of the course, I opened the fresh-cut leaves of the Revtte des Deux Mondes, the number for the first of this month. In it my eye quickly fell upon *Un Essai de Synthése Paléoethnique*, in which M. le Marquis G. de Saporta sums up and sets forth the latest results of paleontological research, so far as they bear upon ethnology. Judge of my gratification to find some twenty pages devoted to the question of the cradle of the human race in the light of the latest science, and to read as the conclusion of this learned savant that this cradle must have been "*within the Arctic Circle* "As Count Saporta has lately shown a little anxiety that American scholarship should not receive too exclusive credit for first proposing a closely related doctrine which he holds in common with our Professor Gray, and with Switzerland's Professor Heer (see *American Journal of Science*, May 1883, p. 396, footnote), he will doubtless pardon the public statement of this, tome, a most interesting coincidence.

Boston, May 24, 1883.
William F. Warren.

In the foregoing, we have more than a demonstration of the bare admissibility of our hypothesis. We have in it the latest word of anthropological science respecting the birthplace of the human race. To make it a complete confirmation of our theory so far as this field of knowledge is concerned, but one thing is lacking, and that is a clearer recognition of the great natural revolution or catastrophe which destroyed man s primitive home and occasioned the worldwide post-diluvian dispersion. This lack, however, is abundantly supplied by the foremost German ethnographers, and even by such who represent the most radical Darwinian views. Thus **Professor Friedrich Muiller**, of Vienna, and **Dr. Moritz Wagner**, both of whom place the probable cradle of the race in some high latitude in Europe or Asia, lay the utmost stress upon the mighty climatic revolution which came in with the glacial age, ascribing to it the most stupendous and transforming influences that have ever affected mankind. [4] In our view the deterioration of the natural environment reduced the vigor and longevity of the race; in theirs, it changed one of the tribes of the animal world into men! Which of these views is the more rational may safely be left to the reader's judgment. Few will be disposed to accept the doctrine that man is simply judiciously-iced pithecoid

3. Es muss dort, wo der Mensch aus dem Zustand, den er mit den Thieren gemeinsam hat, sich entwickelte, ein gewaltiger Wechsel der Naturkräfte und seiner Umgebung stattgefunden haben. Nichts ist natiirlicher als an die Eiszeit des Endes der Pleiocänen und der Diluvial-Periode, welche durch eine Reihe schlagender geologischer Thatsachen für das nördliche Europa, Asien und America bestatigt wird, zu denken. Damals, wo das Paradies des in der Befriedigung leiblicher Bediirfnisse einzig und allein dahinlebenden, unschuldigen, Gutes und Boses noch nicht unterscheidenden- Menschen mit eisiger Hand zertrlimmert wurde, damals fing der Mensch *den eigentlichen Kampf urns Dasein an, und stieg durch Anspannung aller seiner Krafte zum Herrn der Natur empor.* (There must have been a tremendous change in the forces of nature and in his environment where man developed from the condition he has in common with the animals. Nothing is more natural than to think of the Ice Age of the end of the Pliocene and of the Diluvial Period, which is corroborated by a number of striking geological facts for northern Europe, Asia and America. At that time, when the paradise of the innocent human being, who lived solely and solely in the satisfaction of bodily needs, and who did not yet distinguish between good and evil, was shattered with an icy hand, then man began the actual struggle for existence and rose by exerting all his strength up to the lord of nature." As the tree no more bore fruit the "climber" was forced to "become a runner" this differentiated the foot from the hand, modified the leg, and in time changed the pithecoid ancestors of humanity into men) There must have been a tremendous change in the forces of nature and in his environment where man developed from the condition he has in common with the animals. Nothing is more natural than to think of the Ice Age of the end of the Pliocene's and of the Diluvial Period, which is corroborated by a number of striking geological facts for northern Europe, Asia and America. At that time, when the

paradise of the innocent human being, who lived solely and solely in the satisfaction of bodily needs, and who did not yet distinguish between good and evil, was shattered with an icy hand, then man began the actual struggle for existence and rose by exerting all his strength up to the lord of nature. "As the tree no more bore fruit the "climber" was forced to "become a runner" this differentiated the foot from the hand, modified the leg, and in time changed the pithecoid ancestors of humanity into men. Friedrich Müller, *Allgemeine Ethnographic*. Wien, 1873: p. 36

Telle est la théorie qui s'accord le mieux avec la marche présumlé des races humaines. - *Count Saporta, 1883, "Such is the theory which agrees best with the presumed progress of the human races."*

• *Arctic migration of the birds*

*"**This ability to navigate by Earth's magnetic fields has confounded us for decades**" - Kyle Horton, University of Oklahoma*

Another unsolved equation that may shed some light on our subject is the mysterious migration of birds to the Arctic region. The Arctic tern (Latin: *Sterna paradisaea*), a black-crowned seabird weighing no more than a bar of soap, flies from the top of the world to the bottom and back again every year. That's 40,000 kilometers as the crow flies. But when researchers equipped terns with satellite tracking devices, they discovered that these birds don't take the shortest path. One individual, tracked in 2015, ended up covering close to 100,000 kilometers – equivalent to more than twice around the planet.

"Bird enthusiasts have been ringing (marked with a numerical metal or plastic tag on the leg or wing) birds since the 1890s," says **Anders Hedenström** at Lund University in Sweden. "But ringing (marking) data only tell you where birds have been recaptured. They don't tell you what they're up to once they've disappeared over the horizon." Thanks to lightweight trackers, we can now follow even the smallest birds on their spectacular journeys. What we're finding along the way is amazing, says *Hedenström*. **"In just a few years, we've learned more about migration strategies than from a century of ringing." Meanwhile, mathematical modeling and molecular biology are also bringing fresh insight into why**

and how they do it. There is still a lot to learn, but from where these birds really go and how they navigate to the tricks they use to prepare for such epic journeys, the story of avian migration is not standing still. It's not hard to see why migratory birds leave places such as northern Europe for warmer climes like central Africa as winter draws in: why to struggle through colder temperatures, shorter days, and scarcer food supplies when you can be somewhere with pleasant temperatures and plentiful food. But that raises another question: why do these birds risk their lives by flying thousands of kilometers back each spring? Why not stay where it's warm? One theory is that it comes down to real estate. "In the tropics, competition for nesting space is fierce," says Hedenström. " So it may well pay to opt-out of that fight and fly north, where the food supply peaks in summer and there is more room for nesting – at least if you get there in time, because the best spots may get filled fairly rapidly."

That might explain why many migratory birds are in such a hurry during their spring migration. Last year, when **Hedenström** and his colleagues tracked common swifts flying across the Mediterranean and the Sahara desert, they found that some birds took more than two months to complete the southern journey in autumn, while all the birds they tracked heading north in spring crossed in under two weeks.

Then again, in terms of the evolution of intercontinental migration, it's far from clear that all birds making these journeys today started out traveling north from the tropics during the summer. In 2014, **Ben Winger**, now at the University of Michigan in Ann Arbor, and his colleagues built a mathematical model to reconstruct the geographical ranges of the ancestors of hundreds of living species of American songbirds. They found that most long-distance migrants began in the north and started flying south for winter, as opposed to being tropical birds flying north for summer. All of which still leaves open the question of why some species fly tens of thousands of kilometers every year. Why not find somewhere closer for a winter escape? We're still a world away from a conclusive answer. One idea is that favorable winter-summer habitats slowly drifted further apart as a result of plate tectonics, forcing birds to cover just a few extra millimeters each year – but vast distances millions of years later.

Even that can't explain the curious long-haul journey of the ancient murrelet, a member of the auk family that includes puffins and guillemots. Tracking studies from 2014 showed that these birds fly almost 8000 kilometers across the north Pacific, from Canada to Japan and China, even though there is little difference in the conditions at the two destinations.

Migratory birds are extraordinary endurance athletes – and their feats require some serious preparation. In the weeks before take-off, many undergo extreme physiological changes. Most obviously, they load up on fats. In many cases, that means temporarily supersizing their digestive organs to ingest as much food as possible. Then, immediately before departure, they shrink their digestive organs to reduce their flying weight. But that's not all. At least one species indulges in what ***Jean-Michel Weber*** at the University of Ottawa, Canada, describes as "natural doping". Weber noticed that the semipalmated sandpiper, which flies non-stop from the Bay of Fundy on the east coast of Canada to South America at the end of every summer, mainlines on mud shrimp before departing. Mud shrimp are loaded with omega-3 fatty acids, and Weber suspected that these compounds boosted the efficiency of the sandpipers' muscles. To isolate their effects from other factors, he turned to a more sedentary bird. Sure enough, when he fed bobwhite quails a cocktail of fatty acids equivalent to the diet of the sandpipers, the amount of oxygen that their muscles could use shot up by 58 percent. Migrants' preparations don't stop there. Several species, including the red knot, are known to bulk up their heart muscles so they can pump more oxygen-rich blood around the body. The bar-tailed godwit, however, might have the most effective way to supercharge aerobic capacity. Its levels of hemoglobin, the molecule that carries oxygen around the blood, increase considerably in the weeks before migration.

That helps explain how the godwit can fly for more than 11,000 kilometers without rest. This epic journey, revealed back in 2007 by one of the first big satellite-tracking studies, makes it the longest-known non-stop journey by any bird (see diagram). Another factor is that the godwit doesn't rely on fat alone. ***"Many birds will also break down muscle tissue along the way,"*** says ***Hedenström***. ***"Muscle proteins contain plenty of water, which helps to avoid dehydration."***

But what triggers migration? Migratory birds are punctual when it comes to departure times: all individuals in a species tend to leave at roughly the same time. But they do appear to be able to respond to shifts in conditions from year to year, so they arrive at their destination when the going is good. This suggests they respond to an external stimulus, something triggering that irresistible migratory urge known as Zugunruhe – from the German Zug, meaning movement, and unruhe, or restlessness. But what tells them to depart? The most important indicator that the seasons are changing is probably sunlight. It's clear that shifts in the length of days are a major factor in triggering Zugunruhe. It is far from the only thing they pay attention to, however: in studies where day length was artificially kept constant, several species of migratory birds still knew when to leave. What's more, for birds leaving from the tropics, where day length barely changes all year round, there has to be something else.

Changes in air pressure, predictive of incoming weather, seem to have an influence, as does food availability. In 2011, **Peter Marra** at the Smithsonian Migratory Bird Center in Washington DC demonstrated that American redstarts delay their spring departures if dry conditions in their overwintering areas mean they struggle to find enough food to prepare for the journey.

How do birds pick their route?

"Tracking is teaching us that different birds may follow very different routes, and they are often far from straight," says **Hedenström**. Take the Arctic tern, whose monster detour means it may travel 60,000 kilometers a year farther than the most direct trip. Such diversions are typically down to finding suitable rest stops, but the wind has a big say too. Because birds fly at speeds comparable to typical wind speeds, head and side winds can pose a considerable challenge. Several tracking studies have revealed that birds take hefty diversions to find favorable winds, allowing themselves to drift when it is more energy efficient than keeping to a straight line, says **Hedenström**. Last year, for instance, a team led by **Kyle Horton** at the University of Oklahoma used weather radar to track flocks of songbirds that migrated by night across North America. They found that the birds

drifted sideways on crosswinds but then adjusted their course near the Atlantic coast to get back on track.

"This ability to navigate by Earth's magnetic fields has confounded us for decades"

Another recent tracking study, this time following frigate birds migrating across the Indian Ocean, revealed not only that they seek out cumulus clouds so they can ride on the strong updraughts beneath them, but also that they appear to sleep as they ascend. Bar-headed geese, which migrate over the Himalayas, have a similar appreciation for optimal elevation. They constantly change the height, descending into valleys where the air is denser and more oxygen-rich whenever they can, then climbing when necessary, using updraughts where possible. This significantly reduces the energetic cost and physiological strains of the trip.

"2.4 million kilometers Average distance traveled by an Arctic tern over its life – equivalent to three trips to the moon and back".

In any case, the choice of route is critical: a 2016 study tracking cuckoos, for example, found that at least two-thirds of the birds following an eastern route through Italy or the Balkans were likely to survive, whereas animals choosing a shorter route across Spain or Portugal faced a much higher risk of dying on the trip. The researchers suspect that drought conditions in Spain, increasingly common over the years they studied, are to blame. How do birds navigate? The senses that birds rely on to find their way largely remain mysterious. This is especially true for species that travel individually, which means young birds have to figure out where to go without a flock to follow. It is safe to say that birds probably use all their senses: visual landmarks as well as the sun and the stars provide them with information on their position, as do smells for some species, especially seabirds. But there must be something else because birds still show a clear tendency to take off in the right direction even in total darkness. That something is an ability to detect and navigate by Earth's magnetic field lines that have confounded scientists for decades. At this point, there are two main contenders for the molecular mechanism underlying "magnetoreception" in birds. The first relies on crystals of magnetite, a form of iron oxide, found in the upper beaks of several species, including European robins and garden warblers. But it has proven maddeningly difficult to demonstrate that magnetite plays a part in magnetoreception. Perhaps the most promising work comes from fish. In 2012, **Michael Winklhofer** at the Ludwig Maximilian University of Munich, Germany, took cells containing magnetite clusters from the snouts of rainbow trout and placed them under a microscope around which an artificial magnetic field was rotated. Sure enough, the cells also rotated – and their sensitivity was much greater than expected. However, it's not yet clear how those cells might send signals to the brain. The alternative explanation involves light-sensitive proteins called cryptochromes, found in the eyes of all kinds of migratory animals. The idea is that magnetic fields alter a quantum property called spin in the electrons within these molecules, flipping them back and forth between two different states. That in turn changes the chemical behavior of those molecules, which results in Earth's magnetic fields being superimposed on the birds' vision. Studies have shown that these proteins are sensitive to magnetic fields. Again, though, the task is to see the process in action in a living being and show it is connected to its brain.

The question remains open: *Do these birds still have some ancient code from the era when a mild and pleasant climate reigned in the north? Is there still a record in their collective unconscious that indicates that this is the path of their ancestors? Why would they travel so long and extreme even to the North Pole, where they also risk their own lives? Is there a code engraved in their memory that still motivates them to sow the last land? Our Arctic Eden hypothesis appears to have the potential for solving this biological mystery.*

• *The Arctic Home of the Vedas*

"If we trace the history of any people back into the past, we come at last to a period of myths and traditions which eventually fade into impenetrable darkness." - *Bal Ghandahar Tilak, The Arctic Home of the Vedas 1903*

Bal Ghandahar Tilak (23 July 1856 – 1 August 1920), known by the nickname *Swarajya* (Self-Governor) was a mathematician, astronomer, historian, journalist, philosopher, and political leader of India in the 1880s and 1920s. He was a contemporary of Gandhi and a campaigner for the independence of India. He was also given the honorary title "*Lokmānya*", which literally means "accepted by the people as their leader". He advocated and propagated the theory that the original home of the Aryans was not Asia, as long thought, but the North Pole in the pre-glacial or inter-glacial period. *Bal Ghandahar Tilak* in his epochal work "*Arctic Homeland of the Vedas*" from 1903, builds a theory according to which Indo-Europeans lived in the Arctic or Artic Circle long before the last great climatic changes in Eurasia. *The Arctic Home of the Vedas* was written sometime in late 1898 but was first published in March 1903, in the city of Pune.

Apart from the fact that he researched the Vedas and other ancient writings in detail, he still receives strong support in his theory from the holy book Avesta of their first Aryan cousins - the ancient Persians. Due to the great affinity of the oldest written languages, namely the Sanskrit from India and the Avestan language from Persia, the theory that migrant Aryan people are actually Proto-Indo-European is built on its own. The simplest comparative ethnological analysis of the Indo-European peoples shows the great role of epic poetry, which served as a transmitter of all kinds of knowledge, and the great role of the cult of the sun and light. Epic poetry, embedded in such deep and extensive knowledge and philosophical principles, cannot be the result of the imaginations of individuals over a period of several centuries. It is quite logical that such a grandiose result of spirituality can be formed only after thousands of years of living in stable conditions, with a great role of the sun and its cycle. In his conclusion, *Tilak* uses the results of astronomical studies of the Earth's motion around the sun and the theory of insolation as an explanation for the Ice Age cycles. He believes that we have sufficient reason to believe that the Arctic region had a mild climate during the interglacial period. *Tilak* also emphasizes that the new scientific discoveries do not refute the claims made in the Vedas, which indicate that their creators once lived in the Arctic, but rather complement them. Using the astronomical method and deep analysis of the content of the most ancient written literature known to mankind today, he came to the conclusion that it also originated from these northern regions. By analyzing the relief of the northern part of Siberia and the depth of the Arctic Ocean, *Tilak* concludes that there is a strong possibility that in the period before the end of the Last Ice Age there was a vast land near the North Pole with a mild climate. It also follows the movement of the North Star during the precession of the Earth's axis with a cycle of about 21,000 years and its movement through the constellations; the orbit of the stars in the sky and the horizon, as well as the orbit of the sun in the horizon; then he analyzes the polar day, long dawns and polar nights, etc. Observing all these phenomena as reality and placing himself in the position of an observer, *Tilak* finds in his analysis of the Vedas passages which he easily recognizes as appropriate descriptions of such phenomena as are extremely typical of the northern geography namely the Artic and the plain it occupies. By studying in depth some of the described phenomena and relative positions of the stars and constellations in recent millennia, the descriptions in the Vedas, in addition to finally concluding that they originated in the Arctic region, also reasoned that they describe situations that are older than 4,500 BC. According to him, the ancient Indo-Europeans lived in the interglacial period on the vast land of the Arctic near the North Pole, Greenland, and probably Siberia. In the period from 10,000 - 8,000 years BC. concludes that this land was destroyed by ice and sinking. Of course, these descriptions, as we can hear, have their own echo in *Plato's* myth about the sunken and destroyed Atlantis. In the second volume of this book we will pay more attention to various hypotheses related to the causes of climate change and the beginning of the Ice Age.

We can say that Paleolithic man during the inter-ice age inhabited that area, where his conditions were very pleasant, because the sun was on the horizon for a longer period of days of the year, depending on the place of latitude were *Sir Frederick William Herchel* [1] described that climate as – *eternal spring*. The harsh climate now raging in the Arctic regions dates back to the post-glacial age.

1. Sir Frederick William Herschel - (November 15, 1738 – August 25, 1822) was a German-born British astronomer and composer. He often collaborated with his younger sister and fellow astronomer Caroline Lucretia Herschel (1750–1848). Born in the Electorate of Hanover, William Herschel followed his father into the Hanoverian military before emigrating to Great Britain in 1757 at the age of nineteen.

Tilak gives his reasoning, that it would be logical to assume that not all inhabitants lived exactly in the area of the North Pole, but also in the vicinity of the Arctic Circle, that is, at a slightly different latitude. What is really impressive here is the fact that we can have a long and uninterrupted sunny day lasting from 6 to 11 months. The picture of the characteristics of the North Pole in terms of the division of the day into 6 months and night along with twilight and dawn also into 6 months is not only acceptable but scientifically tenable. However, as we have seen depending on the latitude can be areas where the sun can be visible even longer than 6 months. According to the author, it turns out that there were places, that is, geographical latitudes, where the ratio between day and night in terms of months could be 6:6 exactly at the North Pole itself, but in the Arctic Circle it seems that we could have the following parameters: 7:5 in favor of the day, 8:4, 9:3, 10:2 and finally 11:1, that is, the maximum day should last 11 months and only 1 month should be night. Namely, in his book he gives us an account from the hymns where symbolically the chariot of Surya or the personification of the sun was once pulled by 7 horses and sometimes by 10 horses, as well as many other examples from the myths related to the deities that, according to the etymologists' interpretations, symbolize the months. About the Vedas, there is a tradition that in the beginning there was only one Veda, which was later divided into four parts (*Rig-Veda, Yajur-Veda, Sama-Veda, Atharva-Veda*) due to the decline of consciousness that depended on the change of ages, a phenomenon that later in the following chapters it will be presented. According to tradition, it is said that they were originally transmitted orally and that then people had even greater mental capacities. So later each priest would choose one or two of the four Vedas to memorize and recite correctly and symmetrically. These sages known as *rishis* [2] knew the hymns exactly by heart, but as follows from tradition it is said that at some point they decided to write them down, as the memory capacities of people became more and more limiting. The sages remained consistent and persistent in their mission and the Vedas managed to survive to this day.

2. Rishi (Sanskrit: हिषि,: Ṛṣi), in Cambodia, Thailand, and Laos also known as Ruesi / Rusi (Khmer: তানিনি, Thai: তহনি, Lao: লাসি) or राम् Rase is a term for a realized and enlightened person. They are mentioned in various Hindu Vedic texts. The Rishis are believed to have composed the hymns of the Vedas. The post-Vedic tradition of Hinduism regards rishis as "great yogins" or "sages" who after intense meditation have realized the ultimate truth and eternal knowledge. They are monks of the highest rank.

Through the very hymns in the Vedas as the oldest literature and world treasure, the ingenious Indian fell asleep to investigate and determine their age, guided by the data left in the ancient writings in which the lunar houses or asterisms (Nakshatras) began the Vedic year during the Vernal Equinox. That Vedic calendar, as he himself concluded, is not tropical, but sidereal. According to his calculations, *Tilak* in his equally monumental work "*Orion or the Antiquity of the Vedas*" of 1893, managed to arrive at some results when the scriptures were compiled according to the passages he found in them:

• 10,000 - 8,000 years ago – the destruction of the arctic paradise occurs with the last glaciation and the beginning of the post-glacial age.

• 8000 - 5000 years ago – the time of migrations. The surviving representatives of the Indo-Europeans wandered across Europe and North Asia in search of new territories. The Vernal Equinox was located in *Purnavasu*, where he named the period after the deity who ruled that constellation, that is, the period of *Aditi*. *Punarvasu* is a nakshatra in Vedic astrology that refers to the two brightest stars in the constellation or constellation Gemini, the stars Castor and Pollux.

• 5000 – 3000 years ago – the period of the *Mrigashīrsha* or Orion nakshatra. When the Vernal Equinox was in Orion, where numerous Vedic hymns correspond to that period, where it seemed to him that the Vedic bards had not yet forgotten the importance or significance of the Artic land that had been handed down to them from generation to generation. This period is called the period of the Vedas, which according to him they were written 4500 years ago.

• 3000 – 1400 years ago – the period of the *Krittikas*, where the Vernal Equinox was in the constellation of Pleiades. Into this period come writings like the *Taittirîya Samhita* and the *Brāhmaṇas*, which obviously had to be placed in this period of the Pleiades. The legends about the Arctic origin are fading more and more and the Vedic hymns are becoming less and less understandable. At the end of that period, **Vedanga-Joytisha** was also composed.

• 1400-500 years BC. - the pre-Buddhist period, when the **Sutri** and philosophical systems arise.

Tilak for the "**Arctic theory of the Vedas**", paid special attention to the long days and nights, and of course, the long dawns that are sung in the hymns and writings, where it is especially emphasized that the day of the Gods or Devas lasted for six months. In the **Taittirîya Brâhmana** (*III, 9, 22, 1*) there is a passage that clearly says: "*That which is a year is but a single day of the Gods.*" [3]

This statement is so clear that there can be no doubt as to its meaning. A year for mortals will be but one day for the Gods.

3. *Taittirîya Brâhmana* III, 9, 22, I, (ekam va etaddevānāmahah yatsanvatsarah). See: *Orion*, p. 30, note (1955 edition).

Deeper research, however, forced me to conclude that the tradition represented by this passage indicated the existence of a polar homeland in ancient times, so I later found evidence that allowed me to reach the previous conclusion. There are several theories from which the above statements from the **Taittirîya Brâhmana** can be explained. We can consider them as a pure figment of the imagination or a metaphor that expresses a fact completely different from the one described, but they can also be the result of the actual observation of the writer himself or of the third person from whom he received the information. It can also be considered to be based on later astronomical calculations because what was initially an astronomical derivation could later turn into an actual fact of observation. **Tilak** gives his final conclusion, according to which ancient Indo-Europeans lived in the interglacial period on a vast Arctic land near the North Pole. In the period from 10,000-8,000 BC. this land has been destroyed by sedimentation and sinking.

• *Conclusion*

"We must now be prepared to admit that God can plant an Eden even in Spitzbergen; that the present state of the world is by no means the best possible in relation to climate and vegetation; that there have been and might be again conditions -which could convert the ice-clad Arctic regions into blooming Paradises". – Principal J.W. Dawson

We are at the end of the first series of tests, and with what results?

1. Scientific Cosmology, searching for the place where the physical conditions of Eden-life first appeared on our globe, is brought to the very spot where we have located the cradle of our race.

2. Contrary to all ordinary impressions, we have found this same spot the most favored on the globe, not only with respect to the glories of the night but also with respect to the prevalence of daylight.

3. In its geology we have found scientific evidence of the vast cataclysm which destroyed the antediluvian world and permanently transferred to lower latitudes the habitat of humanity.

4. We have found scientifically accepted evidence that at the time of the advent of man the climate at the Arctic Pole was all that the most poetic legends of Eden could demand.

5. From Paleontological Botany we have learned that this locality was the cradle of the floral lifeforms of the whole known earth.

6. By Paleontological Zoology we have been assured that here too originated, and from this center eradiated, the fauna of the prehistoric world.

7. And lastly, we have found the latest ethnographers and anthropologists slowly but surely gravitating toward the same Arctic Eden as the only center from which the migrations of the human race can be intelligibly interpreted.

8. Finally, even the most ancient writings known to mankind today, such as the Vedas of India, according to some scholars, and even the sacred Avesta of the ancient Iranians or Persians, provide enormous support and numerous pieces of evidence, which as will see in the following pages, indicate that at the time they were composed, the ancient poets were in the immediate vicinity of the Arctic region, while later, during the glaciation period, they were transferred to new countries that offered stable climatic and living conditions.

We asked of these sciences simply, Is our hypothesis admissible? "Their answer is more than an affirmative; it is an unanticipated and pronounced confirmation. Some months after the foregoing chapters had been written and delivered in lectures before classes of students in the University, a very interesting reinforcement of the views therein advanced appeared in a little work by *Mr. G. Hilton Scribner*, of New York, entitled *Where did Life Begin?*" [1]

As *Mr. Scribner* was conducted to a belief in the north polar origin of all races of living creatures by considerations quite independent of those mythological and historical ones which first led the present writer to the same opinion, the reader of these pages will find in the following extracts a special incentive to procure and read the entire treatise from which they are taken. That two minds starting with such entirely different data should have reached so nearly simultaneously one and the same conclusion touching so difficult and many-sided a problem is surely not without significance.

1. Published by Charles Scribner s Sons, New York. I2mo, pp.64. Ex-Chancellor Winchell (anonymously) reviews the work with much respect in Science, March 7, 1884, p. 292. For courteous permission to quote from the treatise without restriction, I publicly return the author my thanks.

Our first extract is from pp. 21-23, where the following summary of previous reasonings and conclusions is given: "We may therefore safely conclude if the code of natural laws has been uniformly in force,

First - That life commenced on those parts of the earth which were first prepared to maintain it; at any rate, that it never could have commenced elsewhere.

Second - As the whole earth was at one time too hot to maintain life, so those parts were probably first prepared to maintain it which cooled first.

Third - That those parts which received the least heat from the sun, and which radiated heat most rapidly into space, in proportion to mass, and had the thinnest mass to cool, cooled first.

Fourth - That those parts of the earth s surface, and those only, answering to these conditions are the Arctic and Antarctic zones.

Fifth - That as these zones were at one time too hot, and certain parts thereof are now too cold, for such life as inhabits the warmer parts of the earth, these now colder parts, in passing from the extreme of heat to the extreme of cold, must have passed slowly through temperatures exactly suited to all plants and all animals in severalty which now live or ever lived on the earth.

Sixth - If the concurrent conditions which have usually followed lowering temperature followed the climatic changes, in this case, life did commence on the earth within one or both of certain zones surrounding the poles, and sufficiently removed therefrom to receive the least amount of sunlight necessary for vegetal and animal life.

It seems almost superfluous to say that those parts of the earth which first became cool enough to maintain life had a climate warmer at that time than that which we now call torrid. It was for an epoch, and probably a very long one, as hot as it could be and maintain life. It is also quite obvious, in the light of the foregoing considerations, that as the temperate zones have always received more heat from the sun, and have had more mass per square foot to cool, in proportion to radiating surface, than the polar zones, so, on the other hand, they have always received less heat from the sun and have had less mass to cool, in proportion to the radiating surface, than the torrid zone; and so when the arctic zones cooled from a tropical to what we now call a temperate climate, the temperate zones had cooled down to that temperature which we now call a torrid climate, while the equatorial belt was still too hot for any form of life. Thus, the lowering of temperature, climatic change, and that life which made its advent in these zones surrounding the poles have crept thence slowly along, *pari passu*, from these polar regions to the equator. Farther on (pp. 26, 27) he claims that the progressive cooling of the region at the Pole is all-sufficient, as a natural cause, to account for that dispersion of life, vegetable, and animal, which proceeded from the Arctic center southward: "As might be readily supposed, these Arctic regions which first became cool enough to maintain life would from the same causes be the first to become too cold for the same purpose. And this cold would occur first as a temperate climate near and around the pole; at any rate, in the center of a zone just sufficiently removed from the pole to combine the influence of the sun with its own cooling temperature, to become the first fit habitation of life. This central cold creating a temperate climate would thus have become the first and all-sufficient cause of dispersion and distribution of both the tropical plants and animals over another zone next south, next further removed from the pole, and next sufficiently cool to maintain such life. Moreover, this cooler climate occurring in the center would have driven out and dispersed such life equally, in all possible directions. So, if the first habitable zone included the northernmost land of all the great continents which converge around the North Pole, this dispersion from an increasing cold to the north of each of them would have sent southward plants and animals from a common origin and ancestry to people and to plant all the continents of the earth, with the possible exception of Australia, whose flora and fauna are certainly anomalous and possibly indigenous. In section fourth *(pp. 28-34)* the author briefly touches upon some of the surface features of the globe peculiarly favorable to the southward migration of plants and animals: "Let us now see how admirably the earth is adapted, by its surface formation and topography, for a southern migration from a zone surrounding the North Pole. In the first place, nearly the whole of the earth s surface (and all the northern hemisphere) is corrugated north and south with alternate continents and deep-sea channels almost from pole to pole. Both the eastern and western continents extend with unbroken land connections from the Arctic zone through the northern temperate, the torrid, and through the southern temperate, almost to the Antarctic zone. Between these great continents lie the deep oceans, whose channels run north and south through as many degrees of latitude. The great air and ocean currents run north or south; all the mountain ranges of the western continent and many of the eastern continents run mainly north and south. Nearly all the great rivers of the northern hemisphere run north or south. To a southern migration, in other words, a migration from the Arctic region toward the equator these peculiarities of topography, these great corrugations and mountain ranges, these channels, and currents, are roads and vehicles, guides and helps; while to an east and west migration the same features are not only obstacles and hindrances, but in the main barriers insuperable. The impassability of mountain ranges for most plants is shown by the fact that strongly marked varieties in great numbers and many distinct species occur upon the eastern slopes of the Rocky Mountains, the Sierra Nevada, the Alleghanies, and even lower ranges, which are not found at all upon their western sides, and vice versa. Such a condition of things, incompatible as it is with an eastern and western migration, is quite consistent, however, with a north and south movement. For all the climatic conditions, especially that of rainfall, are so different on the opposite sides of all long mountain ranges that the same variety, split and separated by the northern extremities of these ranges, would, in moving southward along their eastern and western sides, and encountering such diverse conditions, have become in the course of time, under the laws of adaptation, distinct varieties, and probably different species. It may be well now to examine some of the conditions assisting this movement. Hot air being lighter than cold, the heated air of the northern equatorial belt has always risen and passed mainly toward the North Pole in an upper current, while the cooler and heavier currents from the north have swept southward, hugging the surface of the continents, laded with pollen, minute germs and spores, and all the winged seeds of plants, bending grass and shrubs and trees constantly to the southward, and so, by small yearly increments, moving the whole vegetal kingdom through valleys and along the sides of mountain ranges, down the great continents, always moving with, and never across, these great surface corrugations. It is unnecessary to add that all insects and herbivorous animals would follow the plants, or that the birds and carnivorous animals would follow the herbivorous animals and the insects. So, too, the currents of the ocean have been established in obedience to similar laws: as hot water is lighter than cold, great surface currents have been formed in both the Atlantic and Pacific oceans, flowing from the equator to the Arctic regions; while the cooler and heavier currents from the Arctic have swept the floor of both oceans from shore to shore to the southward, carrying all kinds of marine life from the pole toward the equator with them. It may be well in this connection to allude to another fact seriously affecting the bottom currents from the pole toward the equator of both air and ocean. By reason of the revolution of the earth upon its axis, a given point upon its surface 1,000 miles south of the North Pole moves eastward at the rate of about 260 miles an hour, while another point in the same meridian at the equator would be moving to the eastward a little more than 1,000 miles an hour; so every cubic yard of air and water which starts in a bottom current from the polar regions for the equator must, before reaching the equator, acquire an eastward motion of about 750 miles an hour. The tendency, therefore, of all bottom currents of air and ocean moving to the south is to press to the westward every obstacle met within its course, and the result, both as to the currents and all movable things they come in contact with, would be to give them a southwestern course and movement. Now it is a strange coincidence, if nothing more, that the eastern coasts of all the continents have a southwestern trend, is full of bays, inlets, and shoal water, as though the floor of the ocean was being constantly swept up against them; while the western coasts are more abrupt, straight, and touch deeper water, as though the sweepings from the land were being constantly rolled into the sea along their entire lines. Notwithstanding all these indications of a southern or southwestern movement, ever since the migration of plants and animals first attracted attention, students of natural science, careful and conscientious observers, able and discriminating investigators, have, almost with one accord, been looking east and west across these great north and south corrugations and natural barriers for the paths of their journeyings; searching along every parallel of latitude, across lofty mountain ranges, broad continents, deep and wide oceans, and ocean currents, to and from and if perchance they looked north or south it was only in search of some ferry or ford south of the ice-fields by which to pass the flora and fauna from one continent to another, and thus account for what is very evident, namely, that many widely distributed species and varieties have come from the same locality and had a common ancestry and origin. Is it not evident that the very plants and animals (in a tribal sense) whose migrations they have been engaged in unraveling were as much older than ice and snow on the earth as it would require in time to lower the average temperature over a vast area from a tropical to a frigid climate? The portion of the little treatise least satisfactory, even to its author, is the part that relates to man (pp. 52-54). By making the human race descendants (or, as on Darwinist principles we ought rather to say, the ascendants) of one or more pairs of lower animals, and assuming that our animal ancestry had already been driven from the polar region before they were blessed with this unanticipated progeny, the author suggests a possible manner in which the absence on the earth of our immediate predecessor, the missing link, might be accounted for. He says, "if it is true that, in common with many existing plants and animals, the ancestry of man some animal with a thumb, and so having the possibility of all things shared this northern home, this common and immensely remote origin, earlier by long epochs than the glacial period, it would afford a possible ground for the claim of the unity of the origin of man, and also a reason for the absence on earth of his immediate predecessor. His arboreal progenitor in the pioneer ranks of this great southern movement, ages before the Quaternary (during all of which period man has probably inhabited the earth), was possibly driven naked by the ever-following, merciless cold, thus keeping him within the southward-moving tropical climate, down the eastern and western continents alike, until it and he, arriving in the lapse of ages at the equatorial belt, and being always at the head and still rising in the scale of being by this movement, discipline, and process, became sufficiently advanced by slow degrees to build fires, clothe himself, make implements, and, possibly, domesticate animals, at least the first and most useful to primitive man, the dog, and so prepared for conflict and for all climates, turned backward to the verge of everlasting ice, subduing, slaying, and exterminating, first his own ancestry, his nearest but now weak rival, which by lingering behind and struggling for life in a climate of increasing cold, would have become extremely degenerated and so easily disposed of, if not actually exterminated by the climate itself ; thus leaving as the nearest in resemblance to man, and yet the remotest in actual relationship both to him and to his ancestry, the later tribes of anthropoid apes since developed, nearer to the equator, from the next lower animals which accompanied him in his south ward march." In this speculation, it will be observed, the place of the origin of the human race is entirely indeterminate. When its far-off arboreal ancestor left the Pole his only prophetic endowment was "thumb". But possessing this, he "had the possibility of all things. In his successors, ages afterward, the real transition from the plane of animal to that of human life seems to be represented as having taken place "at the equatorial belt." Unfortunately, however, for the theory, the claim of the new men to the virtue and name of humanity was now poorer than before the change, for their first act was to turn fiercely upon those who brought them into being, "subduing, slaying, and exterminating their own ancestry" in a frenzy worse than brutal. The shock the feelings of the near but younger relatives of the massacred victims the mild-mannered apes must have been violent in the extreme. In fact, among all the tens of thousands of their descendants, not one, from that day to this, has ever been seen to smile. But in justice to our author, it should be stated that he attaches little, if any, weight to this Darwinistic episode. He frankly says, "*This last proposition, however, is but a vague and very deductive supposition, for which nothing is claimed beyond a possibility or bare probability*." It is possible that he is only slyly indulging in a bit of quiet pleasantry at the expense of the new-school anthropologists. Whether so or not, he hastens without further words to return from it to the impregnable positions of his main argument and to reinforce them by a fresh study of the power and function of heat in the cosmic unfoldment and distribution of life. The next two divisions of the present work will show us that the birth memories of mankind conduct us, not to the equatorial belt, but to the polar world, and that in *Mr. Scribner's* answer to the question, "*Where did Life begin?* - human, as well as floral and faunal life, should be included. After examining these fresh lines of evidence, it is believed that the reader will find more impressive than ever the words with which our author concludes his charming tractate: "*Thus the Arctic zone, which was earliest in cooling down to the first and highest heat degree in the great life-gamut, was also first to become fertile, first to bear life, and first to send forth her progeny over the earth. So, too, in obedience to the universal order of things, she was first to reach maturity, first to pass all the subdivisions of life-bearing climate and finally the lowest heat degree in the great life range, and so the first to reach sterility, old age, degeneration, and death. And now, cold and lifeless, wrapped in her snowy winding sheet, the once fair mother of us all rests in the frozen embrace of an icebound and everlasting sepulcher. All these things happened in the North; and afterward, when men were created, they were created in the North; but as the people multiplied they moved toward the South, the Earth growing larger also, and extending itself in the same direction -* H. H. Bancroft, Native Races, vol. iii., p. 162. (1832 – 1918).

Chapter II
Cosmologia

Not enough credit has been given to ancient astronomers. For instance, there is no time within the scope of history when it was not known that the earth is a sphere and that the direction down at different points is toward the same point at the earth's center. Current teaching in the textbooks as to the knowledge of Astronomy by the ancients is at fault. [1] - *Simon Newcomb, LL. D.*

1. Lowell Lecture. *Boston Daily Advertiser, Nov. 29, 1881.*

Back of every mythological account of Paradise lies some conception of the world at large, and especially of the world of men. Rightly to understand and interpret the myths, we must first understand the world conception to which they were adjusted. Unfortunately, the cosmology of the ancients has been totally misconceived by modern scholars. All our maps of "*The World according to Homer*" represent the earth as flat, and as surrounded by a level, flowing ocean stream. *"There can be no doubt,"* says **Bunbury** "that **Homer** (Ὅμηρος *c. 8th century BC*), in common with all his successors down to the time of **Hecataeus** (Ἑκαταῖος ὁ Μιλήσιος; *c. 550 BC – c. 476 BC*), believed the earth to be a plane of circular form." [2] As to the sky, we are generally taught that the early Greeks believed it to be a solid metallic vault. [3]

2. E. H. Bunbury, *History of Ancient Geography among the Greeks and Romans,* London, 1879: vol. i., p. 79. Professor Bunbury was a leading contributor to Smith's *Dictionary of Ancient Greek and Roman Geography*. Compare Friedreich, *Die Realien in der Ilias und Odysee.* 1856, 19. Buchholz, *Die Homerische Realien.* Leipsic, 1871: Bd. i., 48.

3. See Voss, Ukert, Bunbury, Buchholz, and the others.

Professor F. A. Paley aids the imagination of his readers as follows: "*We might familiarly illustrate the Hesiodic notion of the flat circular earth and the convex overarching sky by a circular plate with a hemispherical*

dish-cover of metal placed over it and concealing it. Above the cover (which is supposed to rotate on an axis, πόλος) live the gods. Round the inner concavity is the path of the sun, giving light to the earth below. "[4] That all writers of Greek mythology, including even the latest, [5] should proceed upon the same assumptions as the professed Homeric interpreters and geographers building upon their foundations is only natural. And that the current conceptions of the cosmology of the ancient Greeks should profoundly affect current interpretations of the cosmological and geographical data of other ancient peoples is also precisely what the history and inner relationships of modern archaeological studies would lead one to expect. It is not surprising, therefore, that the earth of the Ancient Hebrews, Egyptians, Indo-Aryans, and other ancient peoples has been assumed to correspond to the supposed flat earth of the Greeks. [6]

4. *The Epics of Hesiod, with an English Commentary*. London, 1861: p. 172.

5. See, for example, Sir George W. Cox: *An Introduction to the Science of Comparative Mythology and Folk-Lore,* London and New York, 1881: p. 244. *Decharme, Mythologie de la Gréce Antique.* Paris, 1879: p. n. 11

6. It is true that Heinrich Zimmer remarks, "Die Anschauung die sich bei Griechen und Nordgermanen findet, dass die Erde eine Scheibe sei, um die sich das Meer schlingt, begegnet in den vedischen Samhita nirgends." *Altindisches Leben.* Berlin, 1879: p. 359. But even he does not advance from this negative assertion to an exposition of the true Vedic cosmology. Compare M. Fontane:" Leur est embryonaire. La cosmographie terre est pour l'Arya ronde et plate comme un disque. Le firmament védique, concave, vien se souder á la terre, circulairement, á'horizon.*" Inde Védique,* Paris, 1881: p. 94. With this agrees Bergaine, *La Religion Védique.* Paris, 1878: p. I.

A protracted study of the subject has convinced the present writer that this modern assumption, as to the form of the Homeric earth is entirely baseless and misleading. He has, furthermore, satisfied himself that the Egyptians, Akkadians, Assyrians, Babylonians, Phoenicians, Hebrews, Greeks, Iranians, Indo-Aryans, Chinese, and Japanese, in fine, all the most ancient historic peoples, possessed in their earliest traceable periods a cosmology essentially identical, and one of a far more advanced type than has been attributed to them. The purpose of this chapter is to set forth and illustrate this oldest known conception of the universe and of its parts. In ancient thought, the grand divisions of the world are four, to wit: the abode of the gods, the abode of living men, the abode of the dead, and, finally, the abode of demons. To locate these in right mutual relations, one must begin by representing to himself the earth as a sphere or spheroid, and as situated within, and concentric with, the starry sphere, each having its *axis perpendicular*, and its north pole at the top. The pole star is thus in the true zenith, and the heavenly heights centering about it are the abode of the supreme god or gods. According to the same conception, the upper or northern hemisphere of the earth is the proper home of living men; the under or southern hemisphere of the earth, is the abode of disembodied spirits and rulers of the dead; and, finally, the undermost region of all, that centering around the southern pole of the heavens, the lowest hell. [7] The two hemispheres of the earth were furthermore conceived of as separated from each other by an equatorial ocean or oceanic current.

To illustrate this conception of the world, let the two circles of the diagram which constitute the frontispiece of this work represent respectively the earth-sphere and the outermost of the revolving starry spheres. *A* is the north pole of the heavens, so placed as to be in the zenith. *B* is the south pole of the heavens in the nadir. Line *A B* is the axis of the apparent revolution of the starry heavens in a perpendicular position. *C* is the north pole of the earth; *D* is its south pole; the line *C D* is the axis of the earth in a perpendicular position, and coincident with the corresponding portion of the axis of the starry heavens. The space *I I I I* is the abode of the supreme god or gods; *2*, Europe; *3*, Asia; *4*, Libya, or the known portion of Africa; *5 5 5*, the ocean, or "ocean stream" *666*, the abode of disembodied spirits and rulers of the dead; *7777*, the lowest hell.

7. It is worthy of notice that the sight of portions of the south polar heavens, especially the starless region known as "the black Coal Sack "is to this day capable of suggesting the associations of the bottomless pit. Thus, in a recent traveler s letter of the ordinary kind we read, "Every clear evening we could see the Magellan Clouds, soft and fleece-like, floating airily among the far-off constellations. These mysterious bodies look like star spray, or borrowed bits of the Milky Way. Then, too, our eyes would seek out, as by some strange fascination, those still more mysterious chambers of the South, the black Coal Sack, with its retreating depths of darkness, wherein no star shines. These irregular spaces, emptinesses, as it were, in the heavens, impress one with a sense of something uncanny, as though these were, indeed, the blackness of darkness forever. "*The Sunday School Times*. Philadelphia, 1883: p. 581.

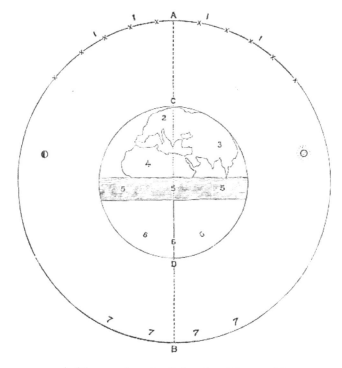

A. The north celestial pole at the zenith.

A B. The axis of the heavens in a normal position.

C D. Earth's axis in normal position.

1111. Abode of the supreme God, or gods.

2, 3, 4. Europe, Asia and the known part of Africa.

555. The Equatorial Ocean-river that surrounds the Earth.

666. Abode of disembodied human souls.

7777. Abode of demons.

C. Location of submerged Eden.

C A. The strength of Zion's Hill

Now, to make this key a graphic illustration of Homeric cosmology, it is only necessary to write in place of *I I I I* "*Lofty Olympus*" (Ὀλυμπος); in place of **555**, "*The Ocean Stream*" (Ὠκεανός) in place of **666**, "*House of*

Aides" (Hades, Ἄιδης, *Háidēs*); and in place of *7 7 7 7*, "*Gloomy Tartaros*" (Τάρταρος, *Tártaros*). Imagine, then, the light as falling from the upper heavens, the lower terrestrial hemisphere, therefore, as forever in the shade; imagine the Tartarean abyss as filled with Stygian gloom and blackness, fit dungeon-house for dethroned gods and powers of evil; imagine the "men illuminating" sun, the "well-dressed" moon, the "splendid" stars, silently wheeling round the central upright axis of the lighted hemispheres, and suddenly the confusions and supposed contradictions of classic cosmology disappear. We are in the very world in which the immortal **Homer** (Ὅμηρος *Hómēros*) lived and sang.1 It is no longer an obscure crag in Thessaly, from which heaven-shaking Zeus proposes to suspend the whole earth and ocean. The eye measures for itself the nine days fall of **Hesiod** (Ἡσίοδος) s brazen anvil from heaven to earth, from earth to Tartarus. Hyperboreans are now a possibility. Now a *descmsus ad inferos* can be made by voyagers in the black ship. Unnumbered commentators upon **Homer** have professed their despair of ever being able to harmonize the passages in which Hades is represented as "beyond the ocean" with those in which it is represented as "subterranean". Conceive of man s dwelling place, of Hades, and the ocean, as in this key, and the notable difficulty instantaneously vanishes. Interpreters of the **Odyssey** have found it impossible to understand how the westward and northward sailing voyager could suddenly be found in waters and amid islands unequivocally associated with the East. The present key explains it perfectly, showing what no one seems heretofore to have suspected, that the voyage of **Odysseus** (Ὀδυσσεία) is a poetical account of an imaginary circumnavigation of the mythical earth in the upper or northern hemisphere, in chiding a trip to the southern or under hemisphere and a visit to the Ὀμφαλός θάλασσής or the North Pole. In this cosmological conception, the upright axis of the world is often poetically conceived of as a majestic pillar, supporting the heavens, and furnishing the pivot on which they revolve. **Euripides** (Εὐριπίδης, *c. 480 – c. 406 BC*) [8] and **Aristotle** (Ἀριστοτέλης, *384–322 BC*) [9] unmistakably identify the *Pillar of Atlas* with this world-axis. How interesting a feature this pillar became in ancient mythologies will be seen below in chapter third of this part, in chapter second of part six, and elsewhere in this volume. Again, according to this view the highest part of the earth, its true summit, would of course be at the North Pole. And since the whole of the upper or northern hemisphere would in this case be conceived of as rising on all sides from the equatorial ocean toward that summit, nothing would be more natural than to view the entire upper half of the earth as itself a vast mountain, the mother and support of all lesser mountains. [10]

9. *Peirithous,* 597, 3-5, ed. Nauck.

10. *De Anim.* Motione, c. 3.

11. See *Bundahish* chaps, viii., xii., etc.

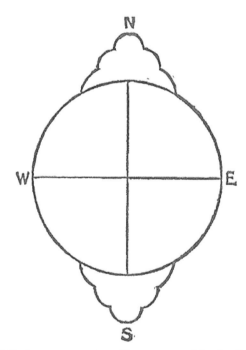

The Antipodal Polar mountains. Compare with the flag of Antartica.

Moreover, as the abode of the supreme God or gods was thought to be directly over this summit of the earth, it would be extremely easy for the imagination to carry the summit of so stupendous a mountain into and far above the clouds, and even to extend it to such a height that the gods of heaven might be conceived of as having their abode upon its top. This is precisely what came to pass, and hence in the cosmology of the ancient Egyptians, Akkadians, Assyrians, Babylonians, Persians, Indians, Chinese, and others we find, under various names, but always easily recognizable, this *Weltberg*, or *"Mountain of the World"* situated at the North Pole of the earth, supporting, or otherwise connecting with the city of the gods, and serving as the axis around which sun, moon, and stars revolve.

Flag of Antarctica

The True South proposal was designed by Evan Townsend in 2018. The flag has the following meaning: Horizontal stripes of navy and white represent the long days and nights at Antarctica's extreme latitude. In the center, a lone white peak erupts from a field of snow and ice, echoing those of the bergs, mountains, and pressure ridges that define the Antarctic horizon. The long shadow it casts forms the unmistakable shape of a compass arrow pointed south, an homage to the continent's legacy of exploration. Together, the two center shapes create a diamond, symbolizing the hope that Antarctica will continue to be a center of peace, discovery, and cooperation for generations to come.

Often, we also find evidence that the under hemisphere was in like manner conceived of as an inverted mountain, antipodal to the mountain of the gods, and connecting at its apex with the abode of demons. [11] The adjoining figure may illustrate this conception of the earth, the upper protuberance being the *"Mount of the Gods"* and the lower the inverted *"Mount of Demons."* A clear view of the first of these remarkable World-Mountains are so essential to any right understanding of mythical geography and of the mythical terrestrial Paradise that a more extended examination of the subject seems a necessity. Beginning with the Egyptians we may note this remarkable fact; notwithstanding his sharing the common and mistaken modern assumption that the Egyptians conceived of the earth as flat, **Brugsch**, confessedly the foremost authority in ancient Egyptian geography, places the highest and most sacred part of the Egyptians earth at the North, making the land there to rise until in actual contact with heaven.

11. "Dans les conceptions de la cosmogonie mythique des Indians on oppose au Sou-Merou le bon Merou, du Nord, tin Kou-Merou mauvais et funeste, qui y fait exactement pendant et en est l'antithése. De meme les Chaldéens opposaient a la divine et bienheureuse montagne de'1 Orient accadien '*garsag-babbarra* = assyrien *śad çit śamśi*, une montagne funeste et ténébreuse . . . accadien, *garsag-gigga* = assyrien *śad erib śamśi*, situeé dans les parties basses de la terre." Lenormant, *Origines de'l' Histoire*, tom. ii. I, p. 134.

He also places at the farthest southern extremity of the earth another lofty mountain, *Apen-to* or *Tap-en-to*, literally "*The horn of the world.*" [12] Now, while several professed Egyptologists have recently come to the conviction that the earth of the Egyptians was a sphere, no one has brought out the fact that these two heights are two antipodal polar projections of the spherical earth, the upper or celestial one being the mount of the gods, and the lower or infernal one the mount of demons. Of the former the following passage in the "*Book of Hades*" may naturally be understood to speak:

"Draw me [the nocturnal sun], infernal ones! . . .

"Retreat towards the eastern heavens, toward the dwellings which support Sar, that mysterious mountain that spreads light among the gods [or, that I may spread light among the gods?], who receive me when I go forth from amongst you, from the retreat." [13]

12. Geographische Inschriften altagyptischer Denkmäler. Leipsic, 1858: vol. ii., p. 37.

13. Records of the Past, vol. x., p. 103. I understand this to refer to the (northward and southward) *annual,* and not to the diurnal, movement of the sun.

To the inverted infernal mountain seem to apply the expressions in chapter one hundred and fifty of the "***Book of the Dead***":

"Oh, the very tall Hill in Hades! The heaven rests upon it. There is a snake or dragon upon it: Sati is his name" etc. [14] In another chapter of the same book a place is spoken of as "the inverted precinct" which place is Hades. [15] Moreover, the translator of another text, called the **"Book of Hades"** describes a "pendant mountain" as a curious feature in the vignette illustrations of the original. This can hardly be anything other than *Ap-en-to*, the inverted mountain of Hades. [16]

14. The mention of the starry serpent or dragon completes the parallelism between the North Polar and South Polar mountains. "Mr. Procter has remarked that when the North Pole Star was *Alpha Draconis*, the Southern was most probably the star *Eta Hydri*, and certain to have been in the constellation Hydra. The encircling Serpent, the symbol of eternal going around, was figured at both Poles, the two centers of the total starry revolution. "Massey, *The Natural Genesis,* vol. i., p. 345. In our discussion of the Pillar of Atlas, we have spoken of the identity of Draco with the dragon that assisted the nymphs in watching the golden apples in the North Polar Gardens of the Hesperides. See Depuis, *Origines des Constellations, p. 147.* The same parallelism is alluded to in the following: "The hydrocephalus in question is divided into four compartments, two of which are opposed to the two others as if to indicate the two celestial hemispheres; the upper one above the terrestrial world and the lower one below it. *"Proceedings of the Society of Biblical Archeology,* March 4, 1884. London, 1884: p. 126. See also Revue *Archeologiqué.* Paris, 1862: vi., p. 129.

15. Bunsen, *Egypt's Place in Universal History*, vol. v., p. 208.

16. *Records of the Past*, vol. x., p. 88. Two years after the above was written I met with the following: "The god advancing in a reversed position" (in a certain New Zealand legend) "is the sun in the Underworld. The image exactly accords with an Egyptian scene of the sun passing through Hades, where we see the twelve gods of the earth, or the lower domain of night, marching towards a mountain *turned upside down,* and two typical personages are also turned upside down. This is an illustration of the passage of the sun through the Underworld. The *reversed* on the same monument are the dead. Thus, the Osirified deceased, who has attained the second life, in the Ritual says exultingly, I do not walk upon my head! The dead, as the Akhu, are the spirits, and the Atua [of the New Zealand legend] is a spirit who comes walking upside down." Massey, *The Natural Genesis.* London, 1883: vol. i., p. 529. (The italics are Massey s.) The passage is the more remarkable from the fact that Massey elsewhere states that the earth" was considered flat by the first myth-makers" who in his scheme appear to have been the Egyptians. Ibid., vol. i., p. 465.

The Akkadians, who antedated even the most ancient empires of the Tigro-Euphrates valley, had in like manner a *"Mountain of the World"* which was unlike all other mountains in that it was support on which the heavens rested and around which they revolved. It was called *Kharsak Kurra*. It was so rich with gold and silver and precious stones as to be dazzling to the sight. An ancient Akkadian hymn respecting it uses this language: "O mighty mountain of *Bel, Im-Kharsak*, whose head rival's heaven, whose root is in the holy deep! "Among the mountains like a strong wild bull, it lieth down." Its horn like the brilliance of the sun is bright." Like the star of heaven, it is filled with sheen." [17] In another hymn, apparently of great antiquity, we find the goddess Ishtar addressed as "*Queen of this Mountain of the World*", which is further located and identified by its connection with "*the axis of heaven*" and with "*the four rivers*" of the Akkadian Paradise. [18]

17. *Records of the Past.* London, vol. xi., pp. 131, 132. Lenormant, *Chaldaean Magic*, p. 168. Lenormant's latest revised translation may be seen in *Les Origines de l'Histoire*, tom. ii. i, pp. 127, 128.

18. George Smith, *Assyrian Discoveries*, pp. 392, 393. Mr. G. Massey remarks, "In an Akkadian hymn to Ishtar, the goddess is addressed as the Queen of the Mountain of the World and Queen of the land of the four rivers of Erech; that is, as the goddess of the mythical Mount of the Pole and the four rivers of the four quarters, which arose in Paradise. The Mountain of the World was the Mount of the North." *The Natural Genesis*, vol. ii., p. 21.

Lenormant places this mountain in the North (but sometimes incorrectly in the East or Northeast), and makes it the "*lieu de rassembled des dieux*" but when he locates the corresponding antipodal mountain of Hades in the West, instead of in the South, he seems to have gone entirely beyond the evidence. At least, **Dr. Friedrich Delitzsch** affirms that in the cuneiform literature thus far known he has discovered no trace of such a location. [19] But on this question of the site of these mountains more will be said in chapter sixth of the present division. The Assyrians and Babylonians inherited the Akkadian conception. One of the titles of the supreme divinity of the Assyrians related to the sacred mount. An invocation to him opens thus:

"**Assur, the mighty god, who dwells in the temple of Kharsak Kurra.**" [2]
An Assyrian hymn speaks of the "feasts of the silver mountain, The

heavenly courts" and the translator makes the expression refer to this "*Assyrian Olympos*". [21]

19. Wo lag das Paradies? Leipsic, 1881: p. 1 2 1.

20. Cuneiform Inscriptions of Western Asia. London: vol. i., pp. 44, 45. Translated by Mr. Sayce in *Records of the Past,* vol. xi.,

21. Records of the Past, vol. iii., p. 133.

Sayce finds in the following a plain reference to the same: "***I am lord of the steep mountains, which tremble whilst their summits reach to the firmament.***

Ancient Israelite Cosmology from the Bible

"The mountain of alabaster, lapis, and onyx, in my hand I possess it." [22] How current the idea must have been among the Babylonians is shown by the rhetorical use made of it by the prophet Isaiah. Rebuking the arrogance of the king of Babylon and pre-announcing to him his doom, the prophet beholds his fall as already accomplished, and in a passage of wonderful pictorial power and beauty exclaims, *"How art thou fallen from heaven, O Lucifer, son of the morning! How art thou cut down to the ground, which didst weaken the nations! For thou hast said in thine heart, I will ascend into heaven, I will exalt my throne above the stars of God: I will sit also upon the mount of the congregation in the sides of the North (or more correctly in the uttermost parts of the North, in the extreme northern regions), I will ascend above the heights of the clouds; I will be like (or equal to) the Most High. Yet thou shalt be brought down to Sheol, to the sides (or regions) of the pit."* [23] Since the publication of *Gesenius's* commentary on this passage and his excursus upon the "*Gotterberg im Norden*" appended to it, no question has remained in the minds of scholars as to the character of the *Har Moed* the "*Mount of the Congregation*" in the far-off North. Among the Chinese we find a similar celestial mount, the mythical *Kwen-lun*. It is often called simply "*The Pearl Mountain*." On its top is Paradise, with a living fountain from which flow in opposite directions the four great rivers of the world. [24]

22. *Records of the Past,* vol. iii., p. 126.

23. *Isaiah xiv.* 12-15.

24. Stollberg, *Mémoires concernant les Chinois*, t. i., p. 101, cited in Keerl, *Lehre vom Paradies*. Basle, 1861: p. 796.

Around it revolves the visible heavens; and the stars nearest to it, that is nearest to the Pole, are supposed to be the abodes of the inferior gods and genii. To this day, the Taoists speak of the first person of their trinity as residing in *"The Metropolis of Pearl Mountain"* and in addressing him turn their faces to the northern sky. [25] A striking parallel to the Egyptian and Akkadian idea of two opposed polar mountains, an Arctic and the Antarctic, the one celestial and the other infernal, is found among the ancient inhabitants of India. The celestial mountain they called *Su-Meru*, the infernal one *Ku-Meru*. [26] In the Hindu Puranas, the size and splendors of the former are presented in the wildest exaggerations of Oriental fancy. Its height, according to some accounts, is not less than eight hundred and forty thousand miles, its diameter at the summit three hundred and twenty thousand. Four enormous buttress mountains, situated at mutually opposite points of the horizon, surround it. One account makes the eastern side of Meru of the color of the ruby, it's southern that of the lotus, it's western that of gold, it's northern that of coral. On its summit is the vast city of Brahma, fourteen thousand leagues in extent. [27] Around it, in the cardinal points and the intermediate quarters, are situated the magnificent cities of Indra and the other regents of the spheres. The city of Brahma in the center of the eight is surrounded by a moat of sweet flowing celestial waters, a kind of river of the water of life *(Gangâ),* which after encircling the city divides into four mighty rivers flowing towards four opposite points of the horizon, and descending into the equatorial ocean which engirdles the earth. [28]

25. Joseph Edkins, *Religion in China.* 2d ed., 1878: p. 151. The Ainos of Japan, although declared to be "ausserordentlich arm an Sagen" have nevertheless their corresponding mythical Gold-mountain, Kogane-yama. Dr. B. Scheube, *Die Ainos.* Yokohama, 1882: p. 24.

26. "Meru, in Sanskrit, signifies an *axis or pivot.* "Wilford in A*siatic Researches.* London, 1808: vol. viii., p. 285. The prefix "Su"signifies "beautiful".

27. In Brugsch's *Astronomische Inschriften,* p. 177, we read, "Es gab ein himmliches *Anu or Ón*, Heliopolis, dessen *östliche Lichtseite* und *westliche Lichtseite* öfters erwähnt werden." Was this perhaps the Vorbild and Egyptian counterpart of the city of Brahma, the city of Sakra, and all the other Asiatic *Götterstädte* in the celestial pole? It would be very interesting to know.

Sometimes Mount Meru is represented as planted so firmly and deeply in the globe that the Antarctic or infernal mountain is only a projection of its lower end. Thus, the **Sûrya Siddhânta** says:" *A collection of manifold jewels, a mountain of gold, is Meru, passing through the middle of the earth-globe (bhu-gola) and protruding on either side. At its upper end are stationed along with Indra the gods and the Great Sages (maharishis); at its lower end, in like manner, the demons have their abode, each (class) the enemy of the other. Surrounding it on every side is fixed, next, this great ocean, like a girdle about the earth, separating the two hemispheres of the gods and of the demons*". Conceiving Meru in this way, as a kind of core extending through the earth and projecting at each pole, one can easily understand the following passage, in which two pole stars are spoken of instead of one: *"In both (i. e., the two opposite) directions from Meru are two pole-stars fixed in the midst of the* *heavens, it is correctly added that "to those who are situated in places of no latitude (i. e., on the equator) both these pole-stars have their place in the horizon."* Farther on in the same treatise the common designation used for the northern hemisphere is the hemisphere of the gods and for the southern the hemisphere of the asuras, or demons. [29] A picture of *"The Earth of the Hindus"* showing the exact position of Meru and its buttress mounts, will be given below. That the cosmology of ancient India should have been retained and propagated in its main features by all the followers of Buddha was only natural. Accordingly, in their teachings our earth, and every other, has its *Sumeru*, around which everything centers. [30]

28. Chapter xii., sections 45-74. On the origin and age of this treatise see the notes of the translator, Rev. Ebenezer Burgess, in the *Journal of the American Oriental Society*, vol. vi. New Haven, 186: pp. 140-480.

29. Its name, in Japanese, is written *Sxi-meru*; in Chinese, *Si-miliu*, or *Siu-mi;* in Tibetan, *Rirap*, or *Ri-rap-hlumpo*; in Mongolian (Kalmuck), *Sümmer Sola*, or *Sjumer Sula*; in Burmese, Miem-mo. C. F. Koeppen, *Die Religion des Buddhas*. Berlin, 1857: vol. i., p. 232. See, also, A. Bastian, *Die Völker des ostlichen Asiens*, Bd. iii., 8- 352, 353 5 vi., 567, 568, 576, 578, 580, 587, 589, 590. Spence Hardy, *Manual of Buddhism*, pp. 1-35. The same, *Legends of the Buddhists*. London, 1866: pp. xxix., 42, 81, 101, 176, etc.

Its top, according to the **Nyâyânousâra Shaster**, is four-square, and on it are situated the three and thirty (Trayastriñshas) heavens. Each face of the summit measures 80,000 yojanas. Each of the four corners of the mountain-top has a peak seven hundred yojanas high. These, of course, are simply the four buttresses -mountains of the Hindu Meru lifted to the summit and made the culminating peaks. They are ornamented, we are told, with the seven precious substances, gold, silver, lapis-lazuli, crystal, cornelian, coral, and ruby. One of the cities on the summit is called *Sudarsana*, or *Belle-vue*. It is 10,000 yojanas in the circuit. The stoned gates are 1½ yojanas high, and there are 1,000 of these gates, fully adorned. Each gate has 500 blue-clad celestial guards, fully armed. In its center is a kind of inner city called the Golden City of King Śakra, whose pavilion is 1,000 yojanas in the circuit, and its floor is of pure gold, inlaid with every kind of gem. This royal residence has 500 gates, and on each of the four sides are 100 towers, within each of which there are 1,700 chambers, each of which chambers have within it seven Devas, and each

Devî, is attended by seven handmaidens. All these Devas are consorts of King Sakra, with whom he has intercourse in different forms and personations, according to his pleasure. The length and breadth of the thirty-three heavens are 60,000 yojanas. They are surrounded by a sevenfold city wall, a sevenfold ornamental railing, a sevenfold row of tinkling curtains, and beyond these a sevenfold row of Talas trees. All these encircle one another and are of every color of the rainbow, intermingled and composed of every precious sub-stance. Within, every sort of enjoyment and every enchanting pleasure is provided for the occupants. Outside this wonderful city of the gods, there is on each of its four sides a park of ravishing beauty. In each park, there is a sacred tower erected over personal relics of Buddha. Each park has also a magic lake, filled with water possessing eight peculiar excellences. Thus, beauties are heaped upon beauties, splendors upon splendors, marvels upon marvels, until in sheer despair the wearied and exhausted imagination abandons all further effort at definite mental representation. [31] It is worthy of note that, while most scholars have supposed the *Sumeru* of Buddhism to be simply a development of the Indian idea, **Mr. Beal**, a high authority, has, in one of his latest publications, claimed for it an independent and coordinated, if not primitive, character. [32] Other peculiarities in Buddhist cosmography, especially the detachment of *Uttarakuru* and of *Jambu-dwîpa* from Mount Meru, in both of which particulars the Buddhist cosmos differs from the Puranic, lend some apparent confirmation to this claim. In ancient Iranian thought, this same celestial mountain presents itself to the student. Its name is *Harâ-Berezaiti*, the mythical *Albordj*, [33] *"the seat of the genii: around it revolves sun, moon, and stars; over it leads the path of the blessed to heaven."* [34] Serbian historian and archeologist, **Miloš S. Milojević** in his book from 1872 comparing the Vedic concept of *Svarga* with the Slavic god *Svarog* he wrote the following: *"The highest surface of that Mera or Su-Mera, which means: the beautiful and brightest Mera, is round and surrounded by the wreath of Ilavrad, which is worshiped under the name Svargabumi - our Svarog - of the heavenly abode on earth, even today in various nations "Meru is important in Indian and other surrounding peoples mythology as the abode and abode of the gods and righteous souls. On all four sides of* *that legendary mountain, it rests on various precious rocks made of the most precious metals and stones*." [35]

30. See Beal, *Catena of Buddhist Scriptures,* pp. 75-81. Comp. Beal, *Lechtres on Buddhist Literature in China,* pp. 146-159.

31. "I cannot doubt that the Buddhist myth about Sume or Sumeru is distinct from the later Brahmanical account of it, and allied with the universal belief in and adoration of the highest." *Buddhist Literature in China.* London, 1882: p. xv. 3"

32. Das erste Vorkommen des Namens im Zend ist im Gebet an Mithra (invoco, celebro supremum umbilicum aquarum, nach Duperrons Uebersetzung) welches E. Burnouf wortgetreuer übersetzt: Ich preise den hohen göttlichen Berggipfel, die Quelle der Wasser, und das Wasser des Ormuzd, wo die Bezeichnung eine ganz allgemeine ist. Vom Adjectiv *berezat*, d. i. erhaben in der Parsen Uebersetz ung, stammt erst der *Bordj* d. i. der *Erhabene*. Als Berg aus dem die Wasser hervortreten, wird er im Zend 'Nafedrô' (*Nabhi* im Sanskrit.) d. i. *der Nabel* genannt, als Erhohung welche Wasser giebt; und als Berg der das befruchtende Princip enthält zum Genius der Frauen erhoben." Ritter, *Erdkunde*, viii. 47.

33. Spiegel, *Erânische Alterthumskunde*. Leipsic, 1871: Ed. i., S. 463. *The Venîdâd.* Fargard xxi., *et passim*. See references in Index to *Pahlevi Texts*, translated by E. W. West. Vol. v. of *Sacred Books of the East.* Also, Haug, *Religion of the Parsees.* 2d ed., Boston, 1878: pp. 5, 190, 197, 203-205, 216, 255, 286, 316, 337, 361, 381, 387, 390.

34. Milos S. Milojevic, (1840 – 1897, Милош С. Милојевић, *Историје Срба и Српских - Југословенских Земаља у Турској и Аустрији*), in *Histories of Serbs and Serbian-Yugoslav Countries in Turkey and Austria*, 1872, стр, 32; "Најузвишенија површност те Мере или Су-Мере, што значи: прекрасне и најсветлије Мере, округла је и окружена венцем Илаврада, који се под именом Сваргабуми - наш Сварог - небесног пребивања на земљи, и дан данашњи у разних народа обожава. С тога Су-Меру има значај у инђијској и осталих околних народа митолођији као жилиште и становање богова, и умрлих праведника. Са све четири стране те баснословне планине, она се одупире на разне драгоцене стене од најдрагоценијих ковова и камења". This theonym Svarog is preserved in several forms, in the Russian Primary Chronicle as Соварога, Sovaroga, Сварогъ, Svarogŭ, Сварогом, Svarogom, Сварога, Svaroga, and in the Sofia Chronograph as: Сварог, Svarog, Сварож, Svarož. The fire etymology was one of the first to be proposed by the Slovene linguist Franc Miklošič (1875), who explained the theonym Svarog as consisting of the stem svar 'heat', 'light', and the suffix -og. The stem svar itself was to be derived from an earlier *sur "shining". I guess Svarog is another name for Perun (Indra).

The following description of it in one of the invocations of *Rashnu* in the *Rashn Yasht* forcibly re-minds one of the *Odyssean* descriptions of the heavenly *Olympos*: "*Whether thou, O holy Rashnu, art on the Harâ-Berezaiti, the bright mountain around which the many stars revolve, where come neither night nor darkness, no cold wind and no hot wind, no deathful sickness, no uncleanness made by the Daevas, and the clouds cannot reach up to the Haraiti Bareza; we invoke, we bless Rashnu.*" [36] The following description is from *Lenormant*: "*Like the Meru of the Indians, Harâ-Berezaiti is the Pole, the center of the world, the fixed point around which the sun and the planets perform their revolutions. Analogously to the Ganga of the Brahmans, it possesses the celestial fountain Ardvî Sûra the mother of all terrestrial waters and the source of all good things. In the midst of the lake formed by the waters of the sacred source grows a single miraculous tree, similar to the Jambu of the Indian myth, or else two trees, corresponding exactly to those of the Biblical Gan-Eden. There is the garden of Ahuramazda, like that of Brahma on Meru. Thence the waters descend toward the four cardinal points in four large streams, which symbolize the four horses attached to the car of the goddess of the sacred source, Ardvî Sûra - Anahita. These four horses recall the four animals placed at the source of the paradisiac rivers in the Indian conception.*" [37]

35. Darmesteter, *The Zend-Avesta,* ii. 174.

36. "Ararat and Eden" *The Contemporary Review*, September, 1881, Am. ed., p. 41. Compare the following: "L'Albordj des Perses cor respond parfaitement au Merou des Hindous; de même que la tra dition de ceux-ce divise la terre en sept Dvipas ou isles, de même les livres zends et pehlvis reconnaissent sept *Keschvars* ou contrées groupées egalement autour de la montagne sainte" etc. *Religions de l'Antiquité*. Trans. The Albordj of the Persians corresponds perfectly to the Merou of the Hindus; just as the tradition of these divides the earth into seven Dvipas or islands, so the Zend and Pehlvis books recognize seven Keshvars or lands also grouped around the holy mountain" etc). *Religions of Antiquity*. Creuzer, trans. Guigniaut. Tom. I., pt. ii., p. 702, footnote.

The Hellenic and Roman myths concerning the "*World Mountain*" were numerous, but in later times not a little confused, as *Ideler* has learnedly shown. [37] By some, as for example *Aristotle (Ἀριστοτέλης, 384–322 BC),* it was identified with the Caucasus, and it was asserted that its height was so prodigious that after sunset its head was illuminated a third part of the night, and again a third part before the rising of the sun in the morning. This identification explains the later legend, according to which, in order to prove his rightful lordship of the world, ***Alexander the Great*** plucked ***"the shadowless lance"*** (the earth s axis) out of the topmost peak of the Taurus Mountains. [38] More commonly the mount is called Atlas, or the Atlantic mountain. ***Proclus*** *(Πρόκλος, 8 February 412 – 17 April 485)*, quoting ***Heraclitus*** *(Ηρακλειτος, c. 500 BCE)*, says of it, ***"Its magnitude is such that it touches the ether and casts a shadow of five thousand stadia in length. From the ninth hour of the day, the sun is concealed by it, even to his perfect demersion under the earth."*** [39] ***Strabo***'s *(Στράβων, 64 or 63 BC – c. 24 AD)* account of it is full of the legendary features characteristic of a *"Terrestrial Paradise"*. The olive - trees were of extraordinary excellence, and there were there seven varieties of refreshing wine. He informs us that the grape clusters were a cubit in length, and the vine trunks sometimes so thick that two men could scarcely clasp around one of them. ***Herodotus*** *(Ἡρόδοτος, c. 484 – c. 425 BC)* describes the mountain as "very tapering and round; so lofty, moreover, that the top (they say) cannot be seen, the clouds never quitting it either summer or winter. The natives call this mountain [40] *"The Pillar of Heaven"*, and they themselves take their name from it, being called *Atlantes (Ἀτλαντὶς νῆσος, Atlantis nesos, "island of Atlas")*. They are reported not to eat any living thing and never to have any dreams." [41] Equally strange is the story told by ***Maximus Tyrius***, according to which the waves of the ocean at high water stopped short before the sacred mount, ***"up like a wall around its base, though unrestrained by any earthly barrier*** *."* ***"Nothing but the air and the sacred thicket prevent the water from reaching the mountain*** *."* According to other ancient legends, a river of milk descended from this marvelous height. Noticing such curious stories, ***Pliny*** *(Gaius Plinius Secundus AD 23/24 – 79)* well describes the mountain *fabulosissimum. (The most beautiful).* [42]

37. On the Homeric and Hesiodic Olympos, see below, part sixth, chapter second.

38. "Auch in den Alexandersagen des Mittelalters ist die Erinnerung an das Naturcentrum im Nordpol erhalten, und zwar in merkwürdiger Uebereinstimmung der morgen- und abendländischer Dichter. In dem altenglischen Gedicht von Alisaunder (bei Jacobs und Uckert, 8.461) findet Alexander der Grosse auf dem hochsten Gipfel des

Taurus eine schattenlose Lanze, von welcher geweissagt war, wer sie aus dem Boden reissen könne, werde Herr der Welt werden. Alexander aber riss sie heraus. Die Lanze ist ein Sinnbild der Weltachse. Sie weist vom höchsten Berge auf den Nordpol hin, und ist schattenlos weil von dort urspriinglich alles Licht ausging. Trans. The memory of the nature center in the North Pole is also preserved in the Alexander sagas of the Middle Ages, and indeed in a remarkable agreement between the poets of the East and West. In the Old English poem by Alisaunder (in Jacobs and Uckert, 8.461), Alexander the Great finds a shadowless spear on the highest peak of the Taurus, from which it was prophesied that whoever could tear it out of the ground would become master of the world. But Alexander tore them out. The lance is a symbol of the axis of the world. It points from the highest mountain to the North Pole and has no shadow because all light originally came from there". "Menzel, *Die vorchristliche Unsterblichkeitslehre, Bd.* i., S. 86.

39. See Taylor's *Notes on Pausamas,* vol. iii., p. 264.
40. Herodotus, Bk. iv. 184.
41. "When Cleanthes asserted that the earth was in the shape of a cone, this, in my opinion, is to be understood only of this mountain, called Meru in India. Anaximenes said that this column was plain and of stone: exactly like the Meru-pargwette of the inhabitants of Ceylon, according to Mr. Joinville in the seventh volume of the Asiatic Researches. This mountain, says he, is entirely of stone, 68,000 yojanas high, and 10,000 in circumference from top to bottom. The divines of Tibet say it is square, and like an inverted pyramid. Some of the followers of Buddha in India insist that it is like a drum, with a swell in the middle, like drums in India; and formerly in the West, Leucippus said the same thing." F. Wilford, in *Asiatic Researches*, vol. viii., p. 273.

Everywhere, therefore, in the most ancient ethnic thought, in the Egyptian, Akkadian, Assyrian, Babylonian, Indian, Persian, Chinese, and Greek, everywhere is encountered this conception of what, looked at with respect to its base and magnitude, is called the "*Mountain of the World*" but looked at with respect to its glorious summit and its celestial inhabitants is styled the "*Mountain of the Gods*". It is also interesting to note that the Etruscans who called themselves *ꝒꝆꝎꝆ (Rasenna)* i.e., *Raseni* or *Rashani* (literally Russians) and who were the basis and forerunner of the later Roman civilization and culture also have an interesting cosmological worldview. Among the Etruscans, one can clearly see the hermetic foresight that the sky mirrored the earth, and the macrocosm was reflected in the microcosm. The sky was divided into 16 parts, which were inhabited by different deities: the main ones were in the East, dead souls and earthly deities in the South, underground and evil creatures in the West, and the most powerful and mysterious gods of fate in the North. We need not pursue the investigation further. Enough has been said to warrant the assertion of **Dr. Samuel Beal**: "*It is plain that this idea of a lofty central primeval mountain belonged to the undivided human race!*" [42] Elsewhere the same learned Sinologue has said, "*I have no doubt I can have none that the idea of a central mountain, and of the rivers flowing from it, and the abode of the gods upon its summit, is a primitive myth derived from the earliest traditions of our race.*" [43] The ideas of the ancients respecting the Underworld, that is the southern hemisphere of the earth beyond the equatorial ocean, are sufficiently In all these studies one important caution has too often been overlooked. In interpreting the cosmological and geographical references of ancient religious writings it should never be forgotten that the ideas expressed are often poetical and symbolical, religious ideas, hallowed in sacred song and story. If, some thousands of years hence, one of **Macaulay's** archaeologists of New Zealand were to try to ascertain and set forth the geographical knowledge of the Christian England of to-day by a study of a few fragments of English hymns of our period, critically examining every expression about a certain wonderful mountain, located sometimes on earth and sometimes in heaven, and bearing the varying name of "Sion" or "Zion" then making a microscopical study of all the references to the strange river, which according to the same texts would seem to be variously represented as u dark "*and as possessed of stormy banks*" and as "*rolling between*" the singer living in England and the abode of the dead located in Western Asia, and called "Canaan" a river sometimes addressed and represented as so miraculously discriminating as to know for whom to divide itself, letting them cross over "dry shod" surely, under such a process of interpretation, even the England of the nineteenth century would make in geographical science a very sorry showing. Or again, if some **Schliemann** of a far-off future were to excavate the site of one of the dozen American villages known by the name of "Eden" and, finding unequivocal monumental evidence that it was thus called, were thereupon to conclude and teach that the Americans of the date of that village believed its site to be the true site of the Eden of sacred history, and that here the race of man originated, this would be a grave mistake, but it would be a mistake precisely similar to many an one which has been committed by our archaeologists in interpreting and reconstructing the geography of the ancients.

42. Buddhist Literature in China, p. 147.
43. Ibid., p. xiv.

In concluding this sketch of ancient cosmology one further question naturally and inevitably thrusts itself upon us. It is this: How are the rise and the so wide diffusion of this singular worldview to be explained? In other words, how came it to pass that the ancestors of the oldest historic races and peoples agreed to regard the North Pole as the true summit of the earth and the circumpolar sky as the true heaven? Why were Hades and the lowest hell adjusted to a south-polar nadir? The one and sole satisfactory explanation is found in the hypothesis of a primitive north-polar Eden. Studied from that standpoint, the appearances of the universe would be exactly adapted to produce this curious cosmological conception. Thus, the very system of ancient thought respecting the world betrays the point of view from which the world was first contemplated. This, though indirect evidence of the truth of our hypothesis, is for this very reason even more convincing.

Chapter III
Tao

"When the cold goes, the heat comes, and when the heat comes, the cold goes." "When the sun reaches its peak, it sets, and when the moon becomes full, it begins to set" - The Book of Changes, Lao Tzu (老子)

Tao or Dao is a metaphysical concept found in Taoism, Confucianism, and ancient Chinese philosophy in general. Although the term itself is translated as "the way" or "principle", it is most often used to denote the basis or true nature of the world, that is, the lawfulness of the universe. The common theory of various schools of Chinese philosophy is that when the development of one thing reaches one extreme, there is a turn to the other extreme. This is one of the main theses of the philosophy of Lao Tzu (老子) as well as the Book of Changes. The term Tao is related to the Vedic concept *Ṛta*, the Indian term *Dharma* (धर्म, law), and the Greek λόγος (logos) [1]. The term can mean a path or principle. The term *Tao* was not originally associated with the meaning given to it by the Taoists.

The two aspects of Taiji (太極兩儀) are known as the Yin-Yang symbol; Yin-dark while Yang represents light.

In the beginning, *Tao* meant the lawfulness of the movement of heavenly bodies around the Earth, and this regularity is understood as the cause and symbol of all earthly events. The theory of movement through change was inspired by the movement of the Sun and Moon and the change of the four seasons.

It is the eternal dynamic interaction (*Taiji*) between heaven or sun - (light, heat, dryness) - *Yang* and earth (darkness, cold, wetness) - *Yin*, and the relationship between the heavenly father and mother earth. And this interaction is perfectly depicted by the *Taijitu* diagram or the *Yin–Yang* dualism.

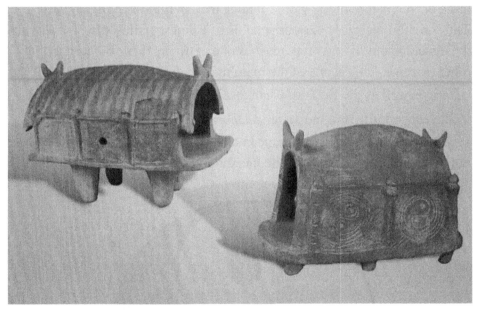

Well, here's something even more interesting for us. This is the oldest representation of this sacred symbol that originates from our Danubian culture. These are the two "sanctuaries" of the Old European Neolithic-Eolithic Cucuteni-Trypillia culture, also known as the Tripolye culture which flourished between 5200 BC. and 3500 BC. in Eastern Europe, which we can freely consider as a kind of cultural expansion of Vinča culture, covering the region from the Carpathians to the Dniester and Dnieper regions, centered in modern Moldavia and covering significant parts of western Ukraine and northeastern Romania. Roughly speaking, this is the historical area, which, as we know, is one of the primordial epicenters of the Slavic nations. But is this all just a coincidence? The symbol *Yin-Yang* (darkness-light) perfectly depicts the process of the endless cyclical change of the duration of day and night that causes the endless cyclical change of heating (*Yang*) and cooling (*Yin*) of the Earth in a physical sense. However, this concept also has its metaphysical analogy, which we will now pay more attention to because it also represents a kind of torch that further illuminates our polar hypothesis.

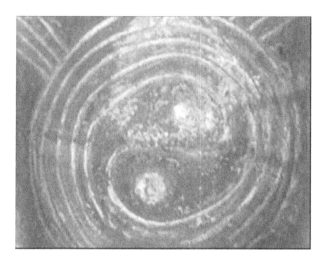

The Serbian folk calendar *(Godishnjak vremenski)* [1] is a set of more or less unwritten rules that the Serbian people have adhered to for centuries, parallel to church rules. The national calendar was based on the church calendar of the Serbian Orthodox Church, but it is completely different from it: according to the names of the holidays, which gave their specific characteristics, the months were called with Old Slavic names or the names of the holidays from the Old Slavic mythology, which gave its own interpretations and calculation methods. The Serbian national calendar was the official calendar of the medieval Serbian states, when it was included in the church codex by Saint Sava himself, and lasted until the 19th century when it was excluded from use after the Berlin Congress.

According to him, charters, laws, decisions, and obligations were written. The oldest record of the Serbian calendar is a tombstone from the 6th century. In the monument of **Tsar Lazar**, it is stated that the battle of Kosovo took place in the year 6897.

According to the Serbian national calendar, today is the year 7530 (or 2022 AD) from the time when, according to tradition, the great flood took place, that is, the "new creation of the world". Here is a pictorial example:

Tombstone of the enochiar (cup maker, middle-age title) Dabizhiv (Дабижив) in the Treskavac monastery today Prilep, North Macedonia.

An inscription on the plaque reads: „*Месца генара оуспе рабь беи Дабиживь енохіарь цра Оуроша вьсе срьбьскье земьле грьчьскіе и поморьскіе в лте sⱳо еньдкта еі*".

Translation: "*In the month of January, God's servant Dabiziv enochiar of the king Uros succeeded in all the Serbian lands, Greek and Maritime lands, in the summer of 6870, indict 15*".

The one who is further interested can investigate in more detail what exactly the term *indict* means. Otherwise, according to the old calendar, the year 6870 is analogous to what we know today as the year 1362 of the new calendar. In Russia, this calendar was changed much earlier, even in the age of reforms by **Peter the Great.** In this case, the term summer (лето) meant year, because the year always started in the summer phase. The year in the old calendar was divided into two phases - the summer and winter phases.

This analogy for the division of the year has its own metaphysical, that is, macrocosmic and microcosmic aspects. We have morning, day, evening, and night, while transitional phases and transitions can be considered as dawn and dusk, which in turn are analogous to the Spring and Autumn Equinoxes, and the warm noon with its maximum corresponds to the Summer Solstice, while the dark and cold night with Winter Solstice. The division of the year also corresponds to six months of summer and six months of winter, where summer began with St. George's Day (April 23rd according to the new calendar, i.e. May 6th according to the old calendar) and ends with St. Dimitri's Day or Mitrovden (26th October according to the old calendar and November 8 according to the new calendar), where the winter phase of the year began. We also have this calendrical division of the year into summer and winter among the insular Celts, where the year was divided into a light half and a dark half. As the day was considered to begin with the rising sun, so the year began with the bright half of the year beginning with *Calan Haf or Bealtaine* (around May 1, modern calendar). The dark phase began with the feast of *Oíche Shamhna*. This observance of festivals beginning the evening before the day of the festival is still seen in celebrations and folkloric practices among the Gaels, such as the traditions of *Oíche Shamhna* (Samhain Eve) among the Irish and *Oidhche Shamhna* among the Scots. [2]

1. See in detail: *"Serbian View of the World", From Lepenski Vir, via Tribals to Saint Sava, 7528 (2020)* - Aleksandar Šargiđ, Chapter: Serbian Dialectic: Perun and Veles (Belbog and Crnbog), p. 227.

2. Lyle, Emily B. (1994). *"The starting-points in the Coligny Calendar"*. Études celtiques. 30: 285–289.

• *The Path of the Gods and the Path of Mortals*

In the same way, the ancient Vedic scriptures as we said make two main divisions (*ayanas*) of the year - *Devayana,* or the path of the gods, life and light, and *Pitrayana* - the path of the dead, ancestors, darkness to the very underworld of demons, i.e. the path of the so-called "*Black Sun*", which is known today as one of the symbols of Nazi Germany. If we look at this phenomenon through the prism of astrology, we have the impression that the first six signs or constellations through which the sun transits: ***Aries, Taurus, Gemini, Cancer, Leo,*** and ***Virgo*** represent the summer solar half-year - *Devayana,* and when the sun travels through the constellations of ***Libra, Scorpio, Sagittarius, Capricorn, Aquarius,*** and ***Pisces*** – the sun travels through the winter or lunar half-year - *Pitrayana*. But what is so fascinating is that the beginning of the year at the North Pole begins after long dawn with the sunrise itself, a phenomenon that occurs in that region exactly at the time of the Vernal Equinox on 21.03, where then the culmination or solar maximum occurs exactly at during the Summer Solstice on 21.06 and then the sun will begin to slowly descend and sink, where after the Autumnal Equinox 22.10 it will be lowered below the horizon where the twilight phase will occur (the Celtic holiday Samhain) which is known in Slavic folklore and as the evening dawn and at the latest it will reach the point of the solar minimum - the Winter Solstice on 21.12.

The Old Germanic calendar year was divided into a summer half and a winter half, as attested in Old English and medieval Scandinavian sources. In Scandinavia this continued after Christianization; in Norway and Sweden, the first day of summer is marked by *Tiburtius Day* (14 April) and the first day of winter by *Calixtus Day* (14 October). [1]

1. Jansson, Svante (2011). *"The Icelandic calendar"* In Óskarsson, *Veturliði (ed.). Scripta islandica. Scripta Islandica: Isländska Sällskapets Årsbok.* Vol. 62. pp. 65–66.

This division of the solar and lunar phase of the year can be most vividly experienced in this fresco located in the Lensonvo Monastery [2] in today's Republic of North Macedonia. Here we clearly see that even the signs of the zodiac are written down in words. Jesus Christ is in the center surrounded by thirty-three saints, which is analogous to the thirty-three Devi, the thirty-three gods or *Tridasha* [2] (Sanskrit: त्रिदश *tridaśa* "three times ten") the pantheon of Hindu deities – the guardians of Mount Meru or Mountain of the Gods. The *Trāyastriṃśa* [3] heaven is the world of the Devas in the Buddhist cosmology as well.

The Fresco depicts the Zodiac from Lesnovo Monastery in today's R. North Macedonia. In the bright solar phase on the left, the signs from Aries to Virgo, which make up the first six months, are shown and visible, while the signs from the lunar phase, which make up the remaining six months of the year, are almost completely erased and pale, but the moon is clearly visible as a body that is visible during the arctic night.

The word *trāyastriṃśa* is an adjective formed from the numeral *trayastriṃśat* meaning thirty-three, "33" and can be translated as "belonging to the thirty-three Devas".

2. The Lesnovo monastery (dedicated to the Holy Archangel Michael and the hermit Gavril Lesnovski) is located near the village of the same name, between Kratovo and Zletovo in today's North Macedonia. It was built in 1341 by the great Serbian Duke

Jovan Oliver Grčinič, on the foundations of a basilica from the time of the local hermit Gavril Lesnovski, whose hermitage cave is located nearby.

3. The Thirty-Three Gods or Tridasha (Sanskrit िदश्रिदश tridaśa "three times ten") is a pantheon of Hindu deities, of Vedic origin, with some developing later. Tridasha generally includes a set of 31 deities consisting of 12 Ādityas, 11 Rudras and 8 Vasus, while the identity of the other two deities that complete the 33 varies. 33 are:

· 8 Vasus (deities of material elements) are: Dyauṣ - "Heaven", Pṛthivī - "Earth", Vāyu - "Wind", Agni - "Fire", Nakṣatra "Stars", Varuṇa - "Water", Sūrya - "Sun". ", Chandra - "The Moon."

· 12 Ādityas (personified deities) - Vishnu, Aryaman, Indra (Śakra), Tvāṣṭṛ, Varuṇa, Bhaga, Savitṛ, Vivasvat, Aṃśa, Mitra, Pūṣan, Dakṣa. This list sometimes differs in details.

· 11 Rudras, composed of The Five Abstractions - Andananda "bliss", Vijñāna "knowledge", Manas "thought", Prāṇa "breath" or "life" Vāc "speech", then the Five Names of Shiva - Īśāna "revealing aspect", Tatpuruṣa 'hidden aspect', Aghora 'destructive aspect Bhairava, Vāmadeva 'preservation aspect', Sadyojāta 'creation aspect' and Ātmā 'the self'

· Other sources include the 2 Aśvins (or Nāsatyas), the solar divine twins corresponding to Saint George and Saint Demetrius.

· The Trāyastriṃśa heaven is the second of the Kāmadhātu heavens, just above the Catumaharajika or realm of the four heavenly kings, and is the highest of the heavens that maintains a physical connection with the rest of the world. Trāyastriṃśa is located on top of Sumeru - the central mountain of S The Trāyastriṃśa heaven is the second of the Kāmadhātu heavens, just above the Catumaharajika or realm of the four heavenly kings, and is the highest of the heavens that maintains a physical connection with the rest of the world. Trāyastriṃśa is located on top of Sumeru, the Central Mountain of the World World. In the New Testament, the Transfiguration of Jesus is the event where Jesus is transformed and becomes resplendent in glory on a mountain. The Synoptic Gospels (Matthew 17:1–8, Mark 9:2–8, Luke 9:28–36) describe him, and the Second Epistle of Peter also refers to him (2 Peter 1:16–18). It is also assumed that the first chapter of the Gospel of John alludes to it (John 1:14). At the top of the mountain, Jesus begins to shine with rays of light.

Even astrologers today do not know why the signs from Libra to Pisces are traditionally considered lunar. However, with the help of the Arctic hypothesis, we now clearly know that after the Autumnal Equinox, the sun begins to sink below the horizon, and with that begins the long polar night where the moon becomes visible in the night sky. If indeed our ancestors were living witnesses in these northern regions, they must have had the most direct insight into when the most important four points or holidays occur during the year. Many would legitimately wonder how the ancient peoples knew exactly when during the year these holy processes in nature took place because without having the appropriate technology, it would be really difficult to determine Vernal or Autumn Equinox, Winter or Summer Solstice correctly. However, this cult definitely originated from where these points were practically directly visible with our eyes. They would be able to spot exactly when these events occur in nature, without a single error in the calculation. It, therefore, remains for us to check the sacred literature of the ancestors and try to extract key information for our hypothesis in the search for the lost paradise on earth.

In the ancient scripture **Sûrya Siddhânta** *XII, 45-50* we find the following stanzas:

45. In the semi-revolution beginning with Aries, the Sun, in the hemisphere of the gods, is visible to the gods: but when it is in Libra, it is visible to the demons, then it moves in their hemisphere.

46. Hence, on account of his great proximity, the rays of the Sun are hot in the hemisphere of the gods in summer, but when he is in that hemisphere of the demons in winter: in the opposite season, they are weak.

47. On the Equinox, both gods and demons see the Sun on the horizon; their day and night are mutually opposed.

48. The sun, rising at the beginning of Aries, while moving further north for three signs, completes the half of the day for the inhabitants of Meru;

49. In like manner, as he moves through the three signs beginning with Cancer, he completes the second half of their day: he accomplishes the same for the enemies of the gods as he moves through the three signs beginning with Libra, and the other half of the three signs beginning with Capricorn, respectively.

50. Hence night and day are mutually opposed to each other, and the measure of day and night is until the completion of the solar revolution.

For the first people, especially the Indo-Europeans, it turns out that the "*Garden of Paradise*" was located at the Pole, where according to the scriptures there could be only one day and one night in the whole year. Moreover, at the break of that strange day the sun had to rise, not in the east, as in post-flood times and now on our latitude, but in the south. Do the traditions or sacred books of the ancient world give any hint of such a sunrise and such a heavenly day or polar night? A partial answer to this question is found in the beliefs of the ancient Scandinavians. A learned Danish writer extraordinarily informs us; that the Scandian seafaring mythology informs us that before the present order of the world was established, the sun, which now rises in the east, "rose in the south."[3]

3. Ce qu'il y a de plus remarquable dans la mythologie du Nord, c'est qu'elle nous reconte qu'avant l'ordre actuel des choses (avant que les fils de Bor, c'est-à-dire les dieux, eussent créé Midgard), le soleil se levait au Sud, tandis qu'à présent il se lève à l'Est."— What is most striking in the mythology of the North is that it tells us that before the true order of things (before the sons of Bor, i.e. the gods, created Midgard), the sun rose in the South, while now it rises in the East – Frédérik Klee, *Le Déluge*, Fr. ed. Paris, 1847: p. 224.

Pitryāna पितृःयान - the path of the ancestors through the gate of death; from the epic period onwards, it is increasingly seen as contrasted with *Devayana*, which involves liberation from existence through wisdom (Sanskrit: *jñāna*; Slavic: *znanje*, knowledge). This depiction of ancestors or elder demons is the lunar and dark path, while the divine is solar.

"Devayana is the path of Vishnu, while the Pitrayana path is dark; these are the two paths after death – one path leads upwards, the other downwards" - *Mahabharata XII, 315.30.*

The very Sanskrit word *Pitris* (पित्र), is also translated as old men, ancestors (*pater, piter, frater*) until its negative connotation and identification with the dead, vampires, and demons. Although they are symbols of the dead and death, in the Puranas a distinction is made when it is said: *devāḥ pitaraḥ* (godlike ancestors), whence seems to arise the cult of the dead in the year, where one is celebrated in the summer, while the other in the winter half of the year. the year.

Therefore, it is not by chance that the great **Dr. Veselin Chaikanov** *(Веселин Чајкановић, 1881 – 1946)* [4] noted:

  "It would take us far to count all the chthonic demons. This much can be said that the number of these demons is infinitely large. And the ordinary dead, our relatives, our ancestors, the known and the unknown dead are also demons. The souls of the dead can be, as when, both good and bad demons, but even the best are nervous and sensitive, and an irresistible longing for life makes them malicious and envious; this is especially true of the souls of those who died without fulfilling their duties or experiencing life - that is, the souls of young boys and girls, women who died in childbirth, people who are tired of violent death."

4. Veselin Čajkanović (Веселин Чајкановић) *Myth and Relgion in Serbs (org. title "Мит и Религија у Срба - изабране студије") (1973)*, стр. 46. Čajkanović (1881–1946) was a Serbian classical scholar, philologist, philosopher, ethnologist, orientalist, religious history scholar, and Greek and Latin translator.

From this remark of his, we can draw a logical conclusion that some of our ancestors after death, if they did not die righteously or in a natural way, if they did not get rid of their sinful earthly activities or did not realize themselves during their life, can become dangerous in some way and disturbing for the descendants, and only the righteous and virtuous deeds of the descendants such as fasting, austerities, prayers, and virtuous services and memorial remembrance of the dead, can help in their liberation and advancement to higher spiritual instances.

These two paths of the sun's motion, namely *Devayana* and *Pitrayana*, and also the appearance of the moon, which, as we have seen, is constantly visible in the far north during the dark period or winter phase of the year, at the moment when the sun is "submerged under water" ", during his transition through the *Pitrayana*, we can trace these dualities in the very posthumous rituals by which the dead ancestors were sent off once and today. We will now briefly deviate from the main course and try to penetrate some archetypal views, customs, or superstitions, which, as it seems, may have arisen from these primordial aspects of creation.

As *Čajkanovic* himself spoke extensively in his book, he stated that our people were cautious when it came to the dead ancestors, who otherwise we could anger, and that the cult of the dead was so widespread that some even think it is so old and primitive that all religion developed from him. There is also a belief that the other world is on an island, which is sometimes visited only by selected, great people, sometimes all the deceased. [5]

5. Veselin Čajkanović, (Веселин Чајкановић) *Myth and Religion in the Serbs,* 1892, Kolo LXVI Book 443 (published since 1973).

In his detailed and extensive study in the book "*The Ancient Faith of Serbs and Croats*" from 1885, the Dalmatian Serb *Natko Nodilo* notes the following:

"*The old phrase "bčajnik" means, for us, an undissolved body in the grave, and an old saying in Montenegro says: "It has not been despaired of for a thousand years!" So, it is a great misfortune to "despair" (očajavao) for a long time in the rough with the whole body. The Romanians also stick to this. But that goes hand in hand with Christian thought, according to which the incorruptible body is above all a sign of holiness and befitting of saints. For the pagan Slavs, the faster the body disintegrated, the faster the soul was ushered into the other world*."

As it seems to me, there is a common Serbian and Croatian belief in the relationship with it. The unfortunate body, if it is not dissolved, is again taken over by the unfortunate soul, and the poor dead person comes to life, wandering, not even knowing where he is. At least that's what is meant for *tenac* (living dead), in the region of Boka Kotorska. "*Tenac*" or "*Tenjac*" is not a real werewolf, in the current meaning of these words, they are beating in front of themselves, as they now call a man from whom a spirit springs in a dream in the place called Risna.

"Dead people can become *tenci*, just as they can, on the other hand, "vampirize". *Vrčević* thus describes a case of accentuation [6]:

"We say that the late Jokan Markišin has become tenac, and that at night he is lying on the grave. Everyone alive died of fear. They made a thorn stake, and tied a black ugič (ram leader) to it. We went to the cemeteries. He put the petrahil (priestly robe), I read the Easter prayer, he burned the grave, and they began to dig up the grave to the corpse. He lifted the flap as well. The deceased had not yet begun to decompose, but he was bloated, and his two eyes were gouged out. He took a stake and pierced it, and a black ram slaughtered it over it, poured its blood over it, then turned the plate again and covered it with earth. The sons of the deceased Jovan paid and ordered today to mention him at the liturgy, and thus to free him from sin".

In the saying, despite the agreement between the new and the old faith, the pagan sacrifice of the black ram and its blood, to satisfy the deceased, is evident. From this undoubtedly ancient practice, we only note here that the unwilling *tenac* lay completely in the grave: "*it did not even begin to decay.*"

6. Nadko Nodilo, *The Ancient Faith of Serbs and Croats, org. title: Stara vjera Srba i Hrvata, 1885, пог.* Религија гроба, стр.369-370, Niz prip., na str. 331—2. Кажу ми, да се покојни Јокан Маркишин потенчио, и да ноћу излази из гроба. Свак жив од страха умро. Приправили трнов колац, и при њему црног везали угича привезли. Погојсмо у гробље. Ставих петрахиљ, очитах васкрену молитву, пра прекадих гроб, а они навалише откопавати све до прељеша. Дигоше и преклопнице, кад ли сбиља! Не бијаше се ни још покојник почео распадати, но се надуо као кабао, а оба ока издубљио. Узеше колац и прободоше га, а над њим заклаша угића, прелиша га крвљу угића (ован, предводник), па опет плочама преклошие и земљом затрпаше. Синови покојног Јокана платише и наредише, да га данас на летургију споменем, и тако да го од грехова ослободим.”

Therefore, it is important for us that *Nodilo* himself in the essence of this book explains that now it is easy for us to understand the main reason why *"the Slavs and other Aryans, from time immemorial, even from Vedic times, burned the bodies of the deceased"*. At that time, *Nodilo* seems to have been absolutely aware of the connection between Slavs and Aryans from Central Asia. In his precious book, which also leaves a rich testimony to our mythology, folklore, and customs, he also poses the question - "***Did the Serbs and Croats burn the dead***?" His answer is:

"*I would say yes, at least for the Serbs. Already in the late period, and that in the time when the faith of Christ was already accepted, when in 1335 Tsar Dusan the Strong passed over, "The body of that knight," says Lukarić, the historian from Dubrovnik, was brought to Macedonia and buried with holy fire, in St. Arangel, outside the fortress of the city of Prizren. That holy fire is not Christian.* [7]

7. Nadko Nodilo, *Ancient Faith of Serbs and Croats*, 1885, ch. Religion of the grave, p. 371, Luccari, *Annali di Rausa*, 1. II, p. 6: "Il corpo di questo heroe (Dussan) fu portato in Macedonia, et con fuochi sacri fu sepellito in S. Angelo fuori delle mura di Prizrien".

Now we clearly understand the main reason why the Slavs and other Indo-Europeans, before being baptized, began to burn the dead bodies of their loved ones. Slavs, as well as the Aryans, from time immemorial, even since Vedic times, have either buried their bodies directly in the ground, or previously in the palace, but for most Slavs, the most difficult of these two methods of burial is cremation or burning. I say more than them because all Slavic tribes did not burn corpses in a certain period, as can be seen from the old Slavic graves excavated. And among the Slavs, where cremation was common, it was not always done. Many people could not arrange it because it would be much more expensive to burn a corpse than to simply bury it. The especially solemn Slavic custom of taking the dead to a ship or boat, which will then be released along with the burnt body down the water, was very expensive and suitable only for nobles, gentlemen, and important people. According to historical evidence, most of their dead were burned by the huge eastern branch of the Slavs known as the Antes.

The Aryan peoples most often practiced burying the dead through purifying and holy fire, where the last ritual or the Vedic *Antima Sanskar* (अंत्येष्टी) represented the essence of a fiery funeral ceremony that is still practiced in India today.

On the other hand, the burying of the dead on the earth, according to Maori beliefs, seems to represent the *Pitrayana* feature and the cult that derives from that path. We see that there is one view of the world and a natural dualism between these opposing forces. *Whiro* or *Whiro-te-tipua* is the lord of darkness and the embodiment of all evil in New Zealand Maori mythology. Just as the Vedic asura (demon) *Vritra* (वृत्र), also known as *Vala* and sometimes as his brother, represents in the Vedas the personification of evil and darkness, where we see the same archetype carried by this dark Maori deity. He lives in the underworld and is responsible for the diseases of all people, which is in contrast to his enemy *Tāne* or *Tāne-mahuta*. [8]

8. Best, Elsdon (1924). *The Maori – Volume 1.* Harry H. Tombs, Wellington. p. 66

Elsdon Best suggests that evil seems to have entered the world when the primordial parents divided, a fact that recalls the symbolic representation of the separation of two principles and polarities - male and female (light and dark) from the third one that keeps them in balance and harmony. According to some tribes, when people die, their bodies go down to the underworld, where they are eaten by Whiro. Every time when Whiro eats a body, he becomes stronger. This process, according to the devotees, will eventually make him powerful enough to free himself one day from the underworld, and at that moment he will "come to the surface and devour everything and anything that lives on earth". That's why some followers of ancient wisdom recommend cremation or a fiery farewell to the deceased to prevent this process, because according to beliefs, Whiro cannot get power from ashes, but the fire itself had transcendental lighting and purifying properties. [9]

9. Black hole "resembles Whiro, atua of darkness" – *Māori astronomer".* Cremation is therefore recommended to prevent this, because Whiro cannot gain strength from ashes.

Taiwhetuki was the "*House of Death*" where Whiro was the lord. It was a deep and dark cave where all evil things are kept, including black magic. According to legends, it is a place where countless personifications of diseases and infections live, corresponding to demons and hell itself. Geckos, snakes, and other reptilian creatures, especially poisonous ones, correspond to his archetype. As for this meaning and culture of the Maori people, I must emphasize that they exist, especially in the past so-called white Maori, because a huge number of mummies with light and red hair were found, although even today one can meet a certain percentage of characteristic European features and light hair and eyes among the natives. Their higher tribal caste is called *Ariki*, which phonetically and essentially seems to correspond to the Aryans from the east, who were the upper castes in the varna system in India. In the same way, the *ariki* (New Zealand, Cook Islands), 'ariki (Easter Islands), *aliki* (Tokelau, Tuvalu), *ali'i* (Samoa, Hawaii), *ari'i* (Society Islands, Tahiti), *aiki* (Marquesas Islands), the *akariki* (Gambier Islands) are members of the hereditary chieftainship tradition or noble caste in Polynesia. As we can see, the *arikis* had a noble and divine status throughout the tribal communities in Polynesia. Political leadership or governance in the Maori community traditionally comes from two different groups of people - the ariki and the *rangatira*.

The *Ariki* are "persons of the highest rank and seniority". As "high-ranking first-born children to first-born children" - the chosen people, the Ariki inherit their positions from their predecessors. In particular, their "top rank derives from the connection with a large number of descendant lines originating from the founder's ancestors, and finally from the divine summit". [10]

10. Halle, Horatio (1846). The United States Exploring Expedition During the Years 1838, 1839, 1840, 1841, 1842: *Ethnography and Philology*. 6. Philadelphia: Printed C. Sherman. p. 294. See also Fornander, Abraham; Stokes, John F. G. (1885). *An Account of the Polynesian Race*. 3. London: Trübner & Company. p. 55–56. Ibid Ballara, A. (1998). Iwi: *The dynamics of Māori tribal organization* from c.1769 to c.1945. Wellington, New Zealand: Victoria University Press. (p. 205).

*Atama Takahipaetu Paparangi, born - May 1821 - died 31? 1915 (age 93–94)
Mitimiti, Far North District, Northland, New Zealand. The elongated
(Dolichocephalic) skull and light hair can easily be noticed.*

*Mummified Maori skull, Cologne's Rautenstrauch-Joest Museum of World
Cultures*

In Maori culture, the arikis were both male and female, which is an interesting feature of the old order, especially a feature that was expressed among the Indo-European peoples, the Celts, the Illyrians, etc. A contemporary example of a woman in this leadership role is *Te Atairangikaahu*, the Maori paramount chief or queen of the Waikato Federation of Tribes. In this case, it seems that this Maori culture was brought to the southernmost islands of the country, precisely by the post-flood travelers who were looking for a new and stable life.

As we said Avesta is the collection of holy books from the religion of the ancient Iranians (Parsis, Persians), who kept the teachings of Zarathustra known as Zoroastrianism or Mazdaism. The collection is believed to have been created during the lifetime of Zarathustra himself. The Avesta was written in the original language of the ancient Iranians, namely Parsi. in the Avestan language, which today is considered the first cousin of Sanskrit. In this stanza it is clearly emphasized that burying the dead in the ground is a great sin.

13. "*The tenth of the good lands and regions, which Ahura Mazda created, was the beautiful Harauvati - Then came Angra Mainu, who is all death, and with his magical powers created the sin that cannot be forgiven, which is burying the dead in the ground*." - *Avesta, Vendidad 13 (45),*

Aḥmad ibn Faḍlān – the Arab travel writer who personally visited Eastern Europe in the year 922, described the funeral of a Russian (*Rūsiyyah*) nobleman who died while swimming in the Volga:

"*Then the nearest relative of the deceased came, took a torch and lit it, then went to the ship, so that he would not see it, and set fire to the wood piled under the ship. And the fire went first to the wood, and then to the funeral ship, and the tent, and the dead man, and all that belonged to him. The great, terrifying wind fueled the flames which flared up and were unstoppable. And there was a man standing next to me, a Russian, who said: "Truly you Arabs are a crazy people. You put your dead in the ground, where worms eat the bodies, and we burn them in the blink of an eye, so they immediately enter heaven." Indeed, in less than an hour, the ship and the timbers, and the man, were reduced to ashes. Then the Russians made something similar to a holma (round mound) at the place of that ship, and in its middle, they put six white poplars, and on them, they wrote the name of the man and the king of the Russians and left.*" [11]

11. Fadlan, Ahmad Ibn; Frye, Richard N. (trans.) (2005). Ibn Fadlan's Journey to Russia: A Tenth-Century Traveler from Baghdad to the Volga River. Princeton, New Jersey: Markus Wiener. p. 63–71. See also Ibn Fadlān (2012). *Ibn Fadlān and the Land of Darkness: Arab Travelers in the Far North*, p. 49

This testimony of *ibn Faḍlān* in 922, apart from giving us clear evidence that the Slavs (specifically the Russians) had a letter and knew how to write before the Roman missionaries and brothers *Constantine the Philosopher* and *Methodius* appeared on the scene, also leaves us with a very clear picture of the funeral ritual which corresponds to the rituals of the Vedic epoch which are still typical of India today.

Among the old Slavs or Germans there was a custom to lay the dead in a boat and send them by sea; or to be buried or burned in a boat; or, finally, to make their grave look like a boat. According to the German Protestant theologian and historian of religion *Carl Clemen*, the reason for this burial is that our ancestors wanted to send the dead to that imaginary island where the dead go. Classical peoples believed that an idyllic and eternally happy life was lived on that island and tried to localize it in different parts of the world. But it seems that this supposedly imaginary island is actually the *"Terrestrial Paradise"*, the Garden of Eden of the Bible or Atlantis which once really existed in the far north and which probably became the inspiration for this idea of our forefathers.

The Serboi (*Σέρβοι, Sérboi, Serbs*) were an ancient Sarmatian tribe mentioned by the Greco-Roman geographer *Ptolemy* (Lat. *Claudius Ptolemaeus*, Greek: *Κλαύδιος Πτολεμαῖος*), who lived in the Caucasus (Sarmatia Asiatica) somewhere near present-day Chechnya and Dagestan from ancient Iberia and Albania. *Pliny the Younger* (Lat. *Gaius Plinius Caecilius Secundus, 63 ~113*), in his *work "Plinii Caecilii Secundi Historia naturalis"* from the 1st century AD. mentions the *Serboi* who lived near the Cimmerians, probably near the Black and Azov Seas.

Herodotus (Ἡρόδοτος) mentions the Sarmatians as having descended from the Amazons, who married young Scythian men, who migrated together with the women "when they crossed the Tanais (the Don River), they traveled eastward from the Tanais for three days, and from Lake Meotida three days in the north". The same tribe, but under the name *Sarbini* [12] was recorded in the Caucasus region by the Arab geographer *Al-Masudi* (*Abu al-Hasan Ali ibn al-Husayn al-Mas'udi*) in the 10th century.

Dr. Đorđe Janković (Ђорђе Јанковић 1947 - 2016) is one of the most famous archaeologists in the Balkans, doctor of sciences and university professor, in his work **"Srpske Gromile"** from 1998, he says that much more information about the Slavic burial was left by Arab writers. Important information about the Serbs is preserved in the work of *Al-Masudi (died 956 / 7)*. *Janković* says that his data dates back to the 8th century, as can be deduced from the names of peoples and tribes that later disappeared - Lombards (Nukabardi), Avars (Avandza), Dulyebs (Dulaba), etc. It is possible that the Serbs are also mentioned in other Arabic sources, but they are not recognized due to the Arabic way of writing. I am quoting *Al-Masudi's* data on the Russian and Polish translations that were available to me (in brackets there are different possible readings according to the authors of the translation):

"...the tribe called the Sarbini; that tribe is exceedingly terrible to their adversaries for reasons which would be too long to mention, for the characteristics of which it would be at great length to exhibit, and for the absence of law among them, to whom they would obey, or because of their disobedience to any nation. The tribe we have mentioned under the name of Sarbini burn their dead on a pyre; when their ruler or headman dies, they burn his riding horse also. They have a custom similar to that of the Hindus; we have mentioned this in part earlier in this part, in describing the Kaba mountains and the Khazar lands, when we said that there are Slavs and Russians in the Khazar lands and that they also bury the dead on a pyre." [12]

This fact is also repeated by **Ibrahim ibn Yaqub** (إبراهيم بن يقوب *Ibrâhîm ibn Ya'qûb al-Ṭarṭûshi or al-Ṭurṭûshî*): "*The tribe we mentioned, which is called Sernin / Sarbin, burns the dead in the fire, when their leader dies they also burn his riding horses. Their action is (in this respect) similar to that of the Hindus.*" [13]

12. T. Lennitsky, 1955, p. 130. and elsewhere, L. A. Dinces, 1947, pp. 76-79.
13. PVL, I, 15, 211.

Al-Masudi here compares the burial of the Serbs with the burial of the Slavs and Russians living in Khazaria, which resembles the burial in India; they burn them with a riding horse, but for the Serbs, it is noted that they burn rulers and leaders (*zupani*), and for the Russians, it is said that they burn them with weapons and jewelry [14]. In India, both Brahmanists and Buddhists burned the dead, and they still do so today, and neither of them erect gravestones. About the same time as the burials of the burnt dead appeared in Europe - somewhere in the third millennium of our era, but the burial data from later times is not known to me [15]. The record of the Russian tradition "**Повѣсть времянныхъ лѣтъ**" also known as "***Nestor's Chronicle***" or "***Primary Chronicle***", finally formed at the beginning of the 12th century, is especially important for the cremation: [16] "***And the Radimichi, Vyatichi and the Severyani tribe had a general custom ... they made a large wooden chamber, laid the dead and burned them, and then, collecting the bones, put them in a bowl and left them on the pillars by the roads, as the Vyatići do even now. Kriviqi and other heathens also adhered to this custom, not knowing God's law, but doing it according to God's law***".

14. Masudi, *Golden Liquor,* Chapter XXXIV, after A. Þ. Garkavi, 1870, 129, 136-137
15. About burial in India R. B. Pandey, 1990, 189-217.
216. PVL, I, 15: Vyatichi finally abandoned burning the deceased, according to archaeological evidence, during the XII century - V. C. Sedov, 1982, 146-147.

In addition to the information that the Serbs, including the leaders, are ritually cremated, in *Al-Masudi's* note, there is also important information that the Serbian funeral is similar to the Hindu one. Arab scribes also note this about some other Slavs. The comparison of Serbs with Hindus cannot only refer to the cremation of the dead but also other rituals. In India, Buddhists and Brahmins have been using cremation of the dead without interruption since ancient times. The burnt remains of the deceased are usually not buried, so there are no graves. But in the past, and even today, there is a burial in urns and burial in mounds. In India, funeral rites are elaborate, there are different schools and extensive descriptions [16]. Only those data that are interesting due to the comparison with the burial of the Slavs in the past will be presented here. *Agni* (अग्नि , Slavic: Oganj, the deity of Fire) is the messenger of the gods on earth, who conveys sacrifices to the gods because materially it cannot be conveyed. Therefore, the soul of the deceased can be released only by burning and uniting with the souls of the ancestors, and the souls of the *Niritti* villains go to hell. The souls of those buried in the ground become evil spirits. Pregnant women, children, and goddesses do not have to be burned, because they are "clean". Before dying, the mortal chooses the place of burial: on good ground, from where the waters flow to the south and west and flow to the north and east. After the death of the deceased, the fire that was burning on the hearth at that moment was removed from the house. It was used to light a funeral pyre. Various household items and sacrificial food may be placed on the deceased before cremation. Widow burning was abandoned in Vedic times, but was preserved symbolically as part of the ritual. That's why it was renewed periodically until recently. When the burning was over, a feast followed and a new fire was lit in the house. In Vedic times, play and revelry began with the feast. The next day, the remains of the deceased could be placed in an urn or in a bundle of black antelope skin that was hung on a certain type of tree. The urn is buried, or the bones are poured into the river, or the sea. A boat, a ship, sometimes appears in funeral rites, although often symbolically. A mound can be erected and various rituals performed. [17] Food is placed in the mound, and the containers that have been used are then broken. Broken vessels used for bathing the deceased and other rituals may be kept in separate pits. The base of the mound is previously cleaned, sprinkled with small pebbles, plowed, and sown. This kind of burial and similar rites were practiced by all Indo-Europeans and were probably introduced by the Aryans. Unlike other Indo-Europeans in Europe, the Slavs kept this burial and rituals much longer. In addition to the Slavs, such a funeral rite was also preserved by the Baltic people until the 12th century. [18]

Arab writers describe the burial of Russians in more detail, and in those descriptions, there is interesting information about all Slavs. Thus, **Ahmad ibn Rustah** (حمد ابن رسته اسفاهانی *Aḥmad ibn Rusta Iṣfahānī*) notes that a temporary house-like tomb, with a roof, was made for the dead noble Russians. [19]

"One of the different pagan peoples living in his country (it means Khazaria) are Sakalibah (Slavs in translation from Arabic), and the other is Rus (Russians). They live in one of the two sides of this city: they burn the dead with their livestock, utensils, weapons, and ornaments".

16. V. C. Sedov, 1982, 144. and elsewhere.

17. L. A. Dinces 1947, B. A. Rubakov, 1987, p. 89-92.

18. The same; compare C. C. Milúkov, 1981, p. 31.

19. Sh. Beshlagi, 1982. p. 372-379.

The mythic dualism in Slavic mythology between *Perun (Перунъ)* and *Veles (Велесъ)* perfectly corresponds to the Vedic dualism between *Indra* (also known as *Purandar*) and *Vrithra* (also known as *Vala*). The idea that night and day last for six months is very widespread not only among the Aryans of the Vedic or post-Vedic epoch but also among other Indo-European peoples. In the writing of the ancient Persians, *Vendidad (II,40)* [20] we find the verse: "*Tae cha araya mainyaente yat yare*"; which means: "*they have a day what is a year*". Even in the most ancient times, the Vedic year, as we said, was also divided into two parts: *Devayana* and *Pitriyana*, which originally corresponded to another Vedic term *Uttarayana* and *Dakshinayana*, i.e. summer and winter, which are symbolically expressed in the sacred dualistic symbol known in Taoism as Yin- Yang, and whose oldest traces, as we have seen, comes from the Neolithic age. Devayana in the ***Rig-Veda Samhita*** [21] literally means "*The Path of the Gods*".

In ***Rig-Veda*** 7,76,2 the poet says:

पर मे पंथा देवयाना अद्रश्रन्नमर्धन्तो वसुभिरिष्कृताः |
अभुदु केतुरुषसः पुरस्तात पर्तिषेगादधि हरम्येभ्यः ||

pra me panthā devayānā adṛśrannamardhanto vasubhiriṣkṛtāsaḥ |
abhūdu keturuṣasaḥ purastāt pratīcyāghādadhi harmyebhyaḥ ||

"*The path of the Gods became visible to me*
The banner of the dawn has appeared in the East.*"

21. Vendidad or Videvdat is a collection of texts within the larger Avesta list. However, unlike other Avesta texts, the Venidad is a code, not a liturgical manual.

22. Samhita (सम्) Samhita literally means "assembly, joining, union", "collection", and "methodical, rule-combined text or verses". Samhita also refers to the oldest layer of text of the Vedas, which consists of mantras, hymns, prayers, liturgies, and benedictions.

Here it is clearly explained that *Devayana* is the stage that began with the dawn and the end of the long night and that this is the path on which the morning deities like Agni, Surya, Ashvins, Ushas, etc. traveled during their celestial movement. The path of *Pitris* is described as the path of death, the opposite of *Devayana*.

In ***Rig-Veda*** *10,88,15* the poet says:

परं मरत्यो आनु परेहि पंथां यस्ते सव आत्रो देवयानात |

param mṛtyo anu parehi panthām yaste sva itaro devayānāt |

"Go, thence, O Mortal, follow your own special path, separate from that which the Gods are not wont to travel".

While **Rig-Veda** *10,88,15* says:

दवे सरुती अश्नवम पितृणमहं देवानामुतमत्र्यानाम

dve srutī aśṛṇavaṃ pitṝṇāmahaṃ devānāmutamartyānām |

"I have heard that there are only two paths, the path of the Demons and the path of the Gods".

If the path of *Devayana* began with the dawn from which the day followed, we must assume that the path of the *Pitrayana* began with the dusk after the Autumnal Equinox from which followed the night. As we see, we can now clearly conclude that the year was definitely divided into two parts, one with uninterrupted light and the other with uninterrupted darkness, and this culture and proto-religion definitely derives from the Arctic regions, where the ancestors with their physical eyes could see them and observe the four holiest ancient holidays of the year: the Spring Equinox, the *Midsommer* or Summer Solstice, the Autumn Equinox, and the Winter Solstice, where then this cult from this center was transferred to other regions where the Indo-Europeans had to migrate. Let's follow the example of one of the most significant Mesolithic and Neolithic archaeological sites - Lepenski Vir, which is located today in Serbia on the very border with Romania. Using computer simulations of the sunrise, as well as determining the night starry sky, the experts concluded that the Sun was rising directly over the peak of Treskavac, which represented a natural marker. The first archeo-astronomical research were conducted during the Winter Solstice in 2014. They pointed to the possibility of the "double sunrise" occurring during the Summer Solstice. The volcanic hill of Treskavac, located across the Danube from Lepenski Vir, has a rocky outcrop near the top and a slope greater than the slope of the Sun's apparent orbit. The sun appears over Treskavac, then goes behind the spout and reappears. The phenomenon was observed and confirmed during the Summer Solstice in 2015. The entire passage, which was recorded, lasts a little more than 4 minutes. The scientific literature mentions two archaeological sites in Great Britain where a "double sunset" was observed during the Summer Solstice, but a "double sunrise" was not observed. As the axial tilt has since changed, a geospatial analysis using GPS was carried out, which proved that the "double sunrise" also occurred at that time and was visible from the original location of Lepenski Vir. The phenomenon was investigated by *Pavlović* and *Aleksandra Bajić*, who published their findings in the 2016 book "*The Sun of Lepenski Vir*". As only the specific position of the Sun during the winter and summer solstices was necessary to calculate the time using a reference point that repeats after one year, they believe that Lepenians used the "double sunrise" as a basis for some kind of solar calendar which dated to 6300–6200 BC. As Lepenski Vir was a sedentary community for several millennia, *Pavlović* and *Bajić* hold that the inhabitants must have observed the phenomenon, especially since people were then much more observant of natural phenomena than they are today. Even *Srejović*, who died in 1996 and was unaware of the phenomenon, said that, based on the geographical configuration of the gorge, *the "dance of light and shadows occasionally reach the levels of hierophany"*. The terrain was further surveyed by theodolite, and an astrogeodetic analysis was conducted in 2017. The results show that the "double sunrise" was visible from the northernmost part of the settlement. Viewed from the southernmost part, the summer solstice Sun rose on the southern part of the flattened top of Treskavac. So, the whole settlement was accurately measured with respect to the astronomical event. [22]

22. Hristivoje Pavlović (21 September 2017), *"Tajne Lepenskog Vira XXXIII*- Mesto gde se sunce razada dva puta", Politika (on Serbian),

Such a masterly arrangement of the site and the sanctuaries in it could not be the product of some chance by the "primitive man" of the Mesolithic, but only the product of deep astronomical knowledge and experience where the ancient solar tradition seems to have been transferred to the new geography in the post-flood period. It could probably be experimentally proven that the sun's rays fall between the two sculptures from the site on the day of the equinox, at sunrise. Since then, the sun separates its path at sunrise, north or south, returning to this point twice a year. Judging from the size, position, orientation, and contents of this shrine, there is no doubt that the shrine known as No. 54 records the solar Spring and Autumn Equinoxes and that the key to organizing the position of the shrine is the celestial sphere of the day, as a place to follow the annual path of the sun. It may indicate that there is something else in the organization of the spheres (seasons), which is invisible for now. It is obvious that the builders of *Lepenski Vir I,* had knowledge of the path of the sun and the consequences of its movement, which are expressed by the position of the sanctuary, and consistently explained in the sculpture with visual symbols. They probably also had knowledge of the course of day and night, years and hours, as well as the seasons. Knowledge of spatial orientation, also grounded in sunrise and sunset, is visible in every detail of the organization of each individual sanctuary and the settlement as a whole. Unlike the shrines of the day celestial sphere, the shrines of the night celestial sphere are almost illegible. Their circular arrangement reveals nothing, and the usual orientation, as in the sphere of the day (except for exceptions), only confirms the rule that all sanctuaries record sunrise and sunset by orientation. There was no deviation from this rule in the celestial sphere of the day; while in the sphere of the night there are four exceptions. [23]

23. Ljubinka Babović, *Svetilišta Lepenskog Vira,* 1997.

To repeat, in **Taittirīya Brāhmaṇa** (*III,9,22,1*) [24] it is explicitly and clearly stated that: "*what constitutes a year is only one day (day-night) of the Gods*". The Aryans apparently had the same idea in the "*Laws of*

Manu": "*The Year of Mortals is one day and one night of the Gods* **or regents of the universe seated around the North Pole;** and again, their division is: *"the day is the northern and the night the southern course of the Sun.*" [25]

24. *Taittirīya Brāhmaṇa* - (Sanskrit तैत्तिरीयब्राह्मण, meaning "Brāhmaṇa of the school of Titri") is a commentary on the Krishna Yajurveda. Brahmāna (ब्राह्मण) means "explanations of sacred knowledge or doctrine". Taittirīya (तित्तिरीय) derives from the name of the sage Taitiri (or Tittiri, तित्तिरि). The Yajurveda (Sanskrit: यजुर्वेद, Jajurveda, from yajus meaning "worship" and veda meaning "knowledge") is a Veda primarily of prose mantras for ritual rites of worship. The Yajurveda is broadly grouped into two parts - the "black" or "dark" Krishna Yajurveda and the "white" or "light" Shukla Yajurveda. This probably corresponds with the later deities of the brothers Krisha and Belarama (Baladeva) who correspond with the cult of Dionysus/Apollo, i.e. the Slavic Koledo/Kupala. Accordingly, the Krishna Yajurveda is probably associated with the winter half-year and rites prescribed for that phase, and Krsna itself literally means black. Kṛṣṇa, which is primarily an adjective meaning "black", "dark", "dark blue" or "the all attractive". The waning moon is called Krishna Paksha, relating to the adjective meaning "darkening".

25. *Code of Manu. I, 67.*

Similarly, in ***Sûrya Siddhânta***, **chapter *XII, 74*.** we read: "***The gods see the Sun after it has risen once, in half a year.***" According to ***Surya Siddanta***, demons and gods see the Sun for six months at a time. Mount Meru, the holy mountain that we will talk about in the next chapter is the North Pole for our astronomers, and the ***Sûrya Siddhânta***, *XII, 67*, says: "***On Meru, the gods observe the Sun during half its rotation***". Thus, it easily and naturally explains their night and day, which last half a year; and all astronomers and magicians have allowed the correctness of that explanation. The "*Day of the Gods*" corresponds to the passage of the Sun from the Vernal to the Autumnal Equinox, when the sun is visible at the North Pole or Meru; and night corresponds to the passage of the sun through the southern hemisphere, from Autumn to the Vernal equinox. But

Bhāskarāchārya (born c. 1114–1185), [26] who misunderstood the place where it is said that "*Uttarâyana is the day of the gods*", wondered how *Uttarâyana* was a term that once referred to the passage of the Sun from the Winter Solstice to the Summer Solstice, could be the day of the gods located at the North Pole, but an observer located at the pole can only see the Sun at the time of its passage from the Vernal to the Autumnal Equinox.

26. Bhāskara II (c. 1114–1185), also known as Bhāskarāchārya ("Bhāskara, teacher") and as Bhāskara II to avoid confusion with Bhāskara I, was an Indian mathematician and astronomer. From the verses, in his major work, *Siddhanta Shiromani* (सिद्धान्तशिरोमणी), it can be deduced that he was born in 1114 in Vijayalavida (Vijadavida near Mount Patasha, in the present-day area of Mount Khadhari) region of Maharashtra. He is the only ancient mathematician who is immortalized on a monument. In a temple in Maharashtra, an inscription said to have been created by his grandson Changadeva lists Bhāskarāchārya's ancestral lineage several generations before him, as well as two generations after him. Colebrook, was the first European to translate (1817) the mathematical classics of Bhāskarāchārya II.

Equally unmistakable is the language of probably more ancient work, translated into English more than a century ago under the title "*The Institutes of Vishnu*" 1880, which reads as follows:
"*The Northern Progress of the Sun is the day of the Gods; the Southern Progress of the Sun (at them) is the night. "A year is one day and one night"*.

The Arab medieval historian and travel writer *Al-Mas'udi* in his book entitled "*Meadows of Gold and Mines of Precious Stones*" around the year 956 notes the following: *"The Targiz (translated as Bulgarians) are a great and powerful nation: they are brave and have subdued their neighbors; and one horseman of theirs, who has converted a Muslim, to whose number the king also belongs, can oppose three other horsemen and two hundred infidels. The inhabitants of Constantinople cannot defend themselves against them except by their walls; the same is the case with other areas in that settlement; their only protection is fortresses and walls. The night is extremely short in the land of the Bulgarians throughout the year; some believe that the Bulgarians cannot cook the meat in the cauldron before the morning comes. We have explained the cause of this phenomenon in our former books, depending on the spherical shape (of the earth); we also said that the night in some parts of the world lasts for six months without interruption; and then again, that there are six months of day and no night. It is about (the time when the sun is in) capricornus* جدْيٌ *. The authors of the astronomical tables also state the reasons related to the spherical shape (of the earth)".* [27]

27. Mas'ûdi Ali-Abu'l-Hassan, ca. 956. "*Meadows of gold and mines of gems*" Publication date 1841 Publisher London : Printed for the Oriental Translation Fund of Great Britain and Ireland, Contributor University of California Libraries, Language English, Les Prairies d'or (Arabic text with French translationof *Kitāb Murūj al-Dhahab wa-Maʿādin al-Jawhar*). Translated by Barbier de Meynard and Pavet de Courteille. 9 vols. Paris, Societe Asiatique, Imprimerie impériale, 1861–69; Imprimerie nationale, 1871–77. Revised Arabic edition by Charles Pellat 5 vols. Universite Libanaise, Beirut, 1966–74. Incomplete revised French edition by Pellat. Lunde and Stone's English edition of Abbasid material, 1989.

See also Mavro Orbini's book *"The Kingdom of the Slavs"* org. us. *Il Regno Degli Sclavi,* from 1601 published in Pesara, which was immediately on the list of banned books of the Vatican, the author wrote the following on p. 382 (in the original Italian): *"The Slavic people Bulgars, came from Scandinavia (as it reports by Methodius Martyr, Jordanes Alanski and Francesco Irenik in VI book, ch. 32) and stopped for a short time at that end of Germany where the waters of the Pomeranian Sea (Pomorje), otherwise called the White Sea (Baltic Sea) splash. Later, going there, ravaging and burning, they occupied the fields around the Volga river, after which they began to be called Volgari, and later they were also called Bulgaros by Byzantium. Leaving later, over time, a part of them moved from the Volga to the Danube, and from there they finally penetrated into Thrace."*

I bulgari natione Slaua vennerò di Scandináuia (secondo che riferiscono Methodio Martire, Giornando Alano, & Francesco Irenico al 6. lib.cap.32.) & fermatisi in quell'estremo dell'Alamagna, ch'è bagnato dal mar Pomerico, altrimente chiamato Baltico, vi si posarono per alcun tempo. Indi partiti poi saccheggiando, e ardendo il tutto, occuparono le spatiose campagne attorno il gran fiume Volga, dal quale tratto'l nome, chiamaronsi Vulgari, e poi Bulgari. Delli quali con successo di tempo vna parte si leuò da Volga, & venne al Danubio, e quindi finalmente penetrò nella Tracia. Et del tépo quando ciò occorse sono varie opinioni de gli Scrittori : alcuni de' quali vo-

Bulgari natióne Slaua.

Da Volga sono detti Bulgari.

Also, in the book *Cronicon Carionis expositum et auctum multis et veteribus et …*Volume 1; Volume 7 on p. Johannes Carion, 1624 on p. 580 writes: Post hoc bellum noua gens Arctoa Bulgari quæ non procul a Byzantio abeft, accefferunt, primumque tunc celebrari nomen Bulgarorum coepit, quos geolocationtimo dictos effe a Bolga fluuio, cuius dontes funt non procul Livonia iin paludibus Mofcoviae. In translation: "After this war, the new people Arctic Bulgarians descended to Lower Moesia, not far from Byzantium, and the name of the Bulgarians began to be celebrated at that time, because they were called after the river Bolga, not far from Livonia and the marshes of Muscovy."

580   CHRONIC. CARIONIS

Mutháuia pacem à Romanis petit. Facta est igitur pax annos triginta.

Bulgaroru̅ mentio prima in hiftoriis.

Post hoc bellum noua gens Arctoa Bulgari ad Myfiam inferiorem, quæ non procul à Byzantio abeft, accefferunt, primumque tunc celebrari nomen Bulgarorum cœpit, quos exiftimo dictos effe à Bolga fluuio, cuius fontes funt non procul à Liuonia in paludibus Mofcouiæ. Adeo autem crefcit fluens verfus Orien-

Devayana is also sometimes called *Devapatha* and has exactly the same translation as the path of gods or immortal beings. *Devayana*, is an original Vedic concept described in the earliest Upanishads such as ***Chandogya, Brihadaranyaka, and Kausitaki Upanishad***. The verses associated with it describe how and under what circumstances liberated beings (*jivanmuktas*) travel this route and reach the highest world of Brahman, also known as Parandhama, and the experiences they go through during the journey. According to Vedic beliefs that path is solar and those who travel on this path reach this world and never return and are not reborn. It is mentioned in the ***Mundaka Upanishad*** in the verse associated with the famous saying, Satyameva Jayate: "***satyam eva jayate nanrtam satyena pantha vitato devayanah***." which means: "***Only the truth conquers, but not the lie. With the truth, the way of the immortal gods is laid.*** " The Upanishads [28] suggest that after death, human beings reach one of the three worlds mentioned in the Vedas: The Sun, the Moon, and the Underworld *(Patala)*. Those who achieve liberation (moksha) from the cycle of rebirths and death measures, through austerity and renunciation, go to the world of Brahman on the solar path of the immortals - *Devayana*. ***Brihadaranyaka Upanishad 6.2.15*** explains the process in some detail: *"Those who know this and those who contemplate the truth in the forests with faith, pass into the realm of light rays. From the region of light rays in the day, from the day in the two weeks of the waxing moon, from the two weeks of the waxing moon in the six months in which the sun travels to the north, and from these months in the world of the gods, from the world of the gods in the sun and from the sun in the lightning. Then the born mind (son of Brahma) goes to that world of lightning and leads them to the world of Brahman. In those worlds of Brahman, they live for very long periods. None of them return to Earth."*

This strange notion is perfectly clear and intelligible when we suppose that the long-lived fathers and first regents of the human race originally dwelt at the North Pole and that they, apotheosized and glorified in the imagination of later generations, in course of time became the gods worshiped by all the ancients. nations. And in the epics, ***Iliad*** (Ἰλιάς) and ***Odyssey*** (Ὀδυσσεία), the scholar ***Anton Krichenbauer*** finds two types of days repeatedly mentioned. In what he considers the older parts of the poems, the day (day-night) is the period of a year, especially when used to describe the life and exploits of the gods; in what he considers to be more modern, the term has its modern meaning as a period of twenty-four hours. He quotes ***Lepsius*** [29] as recognizing a similar "one-day year"; in Egyptian and other ancient chronologies; also, in the mention by ***Palaifatos*** and ***Suidas***. [30]

28. The Upanishads (Sanskrit: उपनिषद् Upanishad - truth, virtue) are Hindu scriptures that form the core of Vedanta teachings. These are ancient Sanskrit texts that contain some of the central philosophical concepts and ideas of Hinduism, some of which are common to religious traditions such as Buddhism and Jainism. These discussions are part of the sciences that seek to explain the content philosophically. The oldest Upanishads come from the pre-Buddhist era and the younger ones are from the Christian era. The Upanishads are between 700 and 500 BC. composed by forest ascetics as the concluding parts of the Vedas.

29. Karl Richard Lepsius (Latin: Carolus Richardius Lepsius) (23 December 1810 – 10 July 1884) was a pioneering Prussian Egyptologist, linguist, and modern archaeologist.

30. Beitrdge zur homerischen Uranographie. Wien, 1874: стр. 1-34. Comp. p. 68. The Suda or Souda (Medieval Greek: Σοῦδα, Romanized: Soûda; Latin: Suidae Lexicon) is a large 10th-century Byzantine encyclopedia of the ancient Mediterranean world, formerly attributed to an author called Soudas (Σούδας) or Souidas (Σουίδας). It is an encyclopedic lexicon, written in Greek, with 30,000 entries, many drawn from ancient sources that have since been lost, often from medieval Christian compilers.

In all such hitherto unnoticed testimonies we have not yet fully exhausted the list, where we have new and singularly indisputable evidence that in the thought of these ancient peoples the land from which the created gods and men sprang was the land in which, as in our supposed Polar Eden, only one day and one night filled the whole year. Even in the time of ***Herodotus*** (Ἡρόδοτος) the claim that there was a people who slept for six months was incredible *(IV, 24)*, so we can conclude from this that even at that time the pre-flood past was still obscured and incomprehensible. [31] Other Greek authors say that in the beginning, the North Star always appeared at the zenith.

31. Even the Bushmen of South Africa have a strange idea that the Sun did not shine on their land in the beginning. It was only after the children of the first Bushmen were sent to the [northern?] top of the world and launched the Sun that light was procured for this [subterranean] South African region. *Bushman Folk-lore,* by W. H. J. Bleek, Ph. D., Parliament Report. Capetown and London, 1875: p. 9. A similar myth was found among the Australian Aborigines.

When the long continuous dawn of thirty days is explicitly mentioned in Vedic literature or the series of thirty closely related dawns, the previous long night is also mentioned, so where the long night reigns, we must also find places where it is spoken and for the long day. The portion of the year remaining when the period of a long day, long night, long dawn, and long twilight is subtracted, will be characterized by alternating ordinary days and nights in which the whole day never exceeds twenty-four hours, although for a time the day may it increased at the expense of the night, and then in the next period the night at the expense of the day, but always within twenty-four hours, which leads to a variety of days and nights of different lengths. All these phenomena arise from a single astronomical condition, so if one of them is determined, the others are derived from it in a scientific way. Therefore, once the long duration of the astronomical dawn is proven, it is not necessary from an astronomical point of view to investigate the other pieces of evidence for the existence of long days and long nights in the oldest Vedic scripture *Rig-Veda*. But since we are talking about phenomena of millennia ago, and facts which, although handed down by tradition, have not yet been interpreted in the way we present here, in practice it is safer to regard the above astronomical phenomena as mutually independent and gather together these various pieces of evidence, bearing in mind their astronomical connection, until we can perceive the cumulative effect of the whole body of evidence supporting the above facts.

Thus in the **Rig-Veda**, *I, 32, 10, Vritra (Vala),* the eternal enemy of *Indra (Purandara)*, is swallowed up by long darkness (*dirgham tamah âshayad Indrashatruh*), and in the **Rig-Veda**, *V, 32, 5* there is a verse that speaks of *asûrye tamasi* (literally "sunless darkness"), which **Max Muller** translates as "terrible darkness". In spite of such passages, the struggle between *Vritra* and *Indra* was regarded as a daily rather than an annual theory, the validity of which has been examined in detail by **B.G. Tilak** in the discussion of Vedic myths. For now, suffice it to say that the above expressions would have no meaning in the darkness in which the movements of *Indra's* enemies were no more than a mere night lasting twelve or at most twenty-four hours. It must have been, in fact, a long and terrible sunless darkness, before which all the powers of Indra and the powers of his faithful companions paled.

But regardless of that legendary fight, there are other verses in the ***Rig-Veda*** that clearly indicate the existence of a night longer than the longest we know. In the first place, we often see Vedic bards calling upon their deities to save them from darkness. So, in the **Rig-Veda**, *II, 27, 14*, the poet says: "***Aditi, Mitra, as well as Varuna, forgive us if we have committed sins against you! Make me shine with great light free from fear, O Indra! Make the long darkness not fall upon us.***" The term used in the text for 'long darkness' is *dîrgâh tamisrâh*, meaning 'a continuous series of black nights (*tamisrâh*),' rather than the simple form "long darkness." But even if we accept the above translation of **Max Muller**, there was no eagerness to see the dispersal of the long darkness, and it would make no sense if that darkness never lasted longer than 24 hours. [32]

32. Hibbert *Lectures*, p. 231.

In the **Rig-Veda**, *I, 46, 6* the *Ashvins* (twins of the gods, probably connected with the constellation of Gemini, the stars *Castor* and *Pollux)* are asked to "***give the worshiper strength to pass through the darkness***"; and in the **Rig-Veda**, *VII, 67, 2* the poet declares: "***The fire began to burn, the end of the darkness was seen and the banner of the dawn appeared***." The term ***"end of darkness"*** (*tamasah antâh*) is quite special, or "*long darkness*" as if referring to the long winter nights and nothing more, but not the ordinary nights we now know in the temperate and tropical zones. As we have seen before, the longest winter night in these zones always lasts less than twenty-four hours, and that period of long night lasts, after all, as much as fifteen days in certain latitudes. It is therefore unlikely that the Vedic bards perpetuated the memory of those long nights by describing them as unhappy to the extent that they had to seek the help of the deities to guard from them. We find other passages which bear witness to the same impatience to see the end of darkness or the appearances of light, and this is not explained by the theory that the night to the Vedic bards was like death, not because they lacked one of the means possessed by a civilized man of the twentieth century to remove the darkness of the night by artificial means of illumination. Even the savages of our time are not in the habit of showing themselves so impatient as to do this to see the morning light again. Despite their apprehension, the Vedic bards were advanced enough to use fire. It is also said that not only humans but also gods lived in long darkness. Thus, in **Rig-Veda X, 124, 1** it is related that *Agni* remained "*too long in the long darkness*," which is the translation of *jyog eva dîrgham tama âshayishtâh*. Those two words *jyog* (long) and *dîrgham* are even less appropriate if the duration of darkness never exceeds the duration of the longest night in our winters. There is a hymn in the tenth book of the **Rig-Veda**, *X, 127* dedicated to the goddess of the night, and the sixth stanza of that hymn calls for the night to "become easily passable" for the worshiper (*nah sutarâ bhava*). In the *Parishishta*, which follows this hymn in the **Rig-Veda** and is known by the name of *Râtri-sûkta* or *Durgâ-stava*, the worshiper asks the night to be kind to him: "*Make us reach the other shore safe and untouched*!", he says. In the **Atharva-Veda**, *XIX, 47*, which paralyzes the above from *Parishishta*, the second stanza reads thus: "*All moving things find rest in it (the night), of which no end is seen. O vast and dark nights! May we meet your end without harm!*" And in the third stanza of the fifth hymn of the same book, the faithful pray to reach the shore without bodily injury, "*through all successive nights*" (*râtrim râtrim*). A priori, one question arises, namely why everyone was so impatient to reach the end of the night, as the poet announces that the end was not in sight. Was it because she was ordinary or because it is Artic Night? **Julius Caesar** (*Gaius Iulius Caesar*) in his work "**de Bello Gallico**" (*Gallic Wars*) said: "**The Gallic Celts keep birthdays and the beginning of months and years in such order that the day follows the night." Longer periods were counted in nights, as in the surviving English term fortnight meaning two weeks and the obsolete expression se'nnight meaning a week**". The *Laws of*

Hywel Dda (in the editions surviving from the 12th and 13th centuries) repeatedly refer to periods of nine days *(nawfed dydd),* rather than the "*eight nights*" that make up the current word *wydd.* [33] Such marvelous expressions as prevailed among the Celts at that time seem to be featured originating somewhere in the regions of the Arctic Circle.

33. Wade-Evans, Arthur (1909). *Welsh Medieval Laws.* Oxford University Press. Retrieved 31 January 2013.

Fortunately, the ***Taittirîya Samhitâ*** has preserved the oldest answer to these questions, so that we do not have to relate to the minds of modern commentators. In the ***Taittirîya Samhitâ****, I, 5, 5, 4* we find an analogous mantra or prayer, addressed to the night in these words: "*O Chitravasu! Make me see your end healthy and alive*". A little further (*I, 5, 7, 5*), the ***Samhitâ*** itself explains this mantra: *"Chitravasu means a night in ancient (purâ) times, where the Brahmins (priests) were afraid that it (the night) would not end."* Here we have an explicit assertion that the priests or the people used to fear that the night would not end. What does that mean? That she was unusually long. In his explanation of this passage ***Sâyana*** [34] also gave the common interpretation that the winter nights were long and that the priests hastened to see their end. But here we may also quote a passage in which ***Sâyana*** contradicts himself and show that he has there interpreted an important stanza carelessly. It is well known that the ***Taittirîya Samhitâ*** often explains the Mantras, and the explanations constitute the sections called Brahmanas. So, the ***Taittirîya Samhitâ*** is composed of Mantra and Brâhmana, of prayers and their explanations or interpretations. A statement of the priest's fears regarding that mode of dawn is found in the ***Brâhmana Samhitâ****.* Indian theologians have divided the Brahmanas into nine chapters. (I) *Hetu* or cause; (II) *Nirvachana* or etymological explanation; (III) *Nindâ* or criticism; (IV) *Prahamsâ* or prayer; (V) *Samshaya* or doubt; (VI) *Vithi* or law; (VII) *Parakriyâ* or others' works; (VIII) *Purâ-kalpa,* ancient rite or tradition; (IX) *Upamâna,* comparisons or analogies.

34. Sāyaṇa, also called Sāyaṇācārya; died 1387, was a Sanskrit scholar of the Mimamsa school from the Vijayanagara empire of South India, near present-day Bellary. An influential commentator on the Vedas, he flourished under King Bukka Raya I and his successor Harihara II. More than a hundred works are attributed to him, among which there are commentaries on almost all parts of the Vedas. He also wrote on a number of subjects such as medicine, morality, music, and grammar.

In his introduction to the commentary on the **Rig-Veda**, **Sâyana** mentions the first nine of these chapters as illustrating the eighth, the *Purâ-kalpa*, which he quotes in explanation of a passage from the **Taittirîya Samhitâ**, *I, 5, 7, 5*, of which before we spoke a little. According to **Sâyana**, the phrase "*once the priests feared that the night would not end*", is therefore found in the *Purâ-kalpa*, which would be said in the ancient and traditional history, which is part of the *Brahmanas*. It is not about *artavyada* ie. reasoning or explanation given by Brahmana herself. This derives from the name *Purya* found in the *Samhitâ* text, which indicates that part of the traditional Indian intelligence is preserved there. If this idea turns out to be true, the question naturally arises why the ordinary winter nights were long for the priests which caused them uneasiness only in ancient times, and why the prolonged darkness has ceased to arouse the same fears in the present generations. The winter nights in tropical and temperate zones are as long today as they were many millennia ago, and yet none of us, even the ignorant, feel any specialness in the dawn that ends the darkness of those long nights. It may be noted that in ancient times at those moments, the bards did not have the necessary knowledge to predict the appearance of the dawn in cases lasting several hours. But the weakness of that argument is evident when we look at the Vedic calendar, which at that time was so advanced that it resolved the relationship between the solar and the lunar year with sufficient accuracy. Therefore, **Sâyana's** explanation is not satisfactory and must be rejected. In ancient times, the Vedic bards were not afraid of ordinary winter nights. It was something else, something very long, so long, that, although it was known that they would not last forever, the patience that was exposed to the ordeal and the anticipation of the dawn became unbearable. It is quite logical that long nights could also have a strong effect on people psychologically. In short, it was the long arctic night, and the word *pura* indicates that the phenomenon dates back to ancient times known to the Vedic bards through tradition. It is also found in the expression "*The Way of the Gods*" in the Persian scriptures. Thus, in **Farvardin Yasht** *56-57*, the *Farvashis*, who corresponds to the Vedic *Pitris*, is said to have shown the way brought by *Ahura Mazda*, the way brought by the gods by the Sun and the Moon. It is said that the Sun and the Moon remained for a long time in the same place, not progressing due to the oppression of the *Devashis*, before the Farvashis showed their way to Mazda. Let me briefly mention that the term *Deva* (*Daevashi*) has a totally sporting connotation among the Persians, as well as the Indian *Asuri* who are synonymous with demons and darkness among the Zoroastrians, they have the opposite role, as bright deities or *Ahuri*. This phenomenon of inversion of terms will be explained also in the second volume. This explains that Ahura Mazda's path began just like *Devayana*, when the Sun was freed from demons and darkness. This represented the phase of the year when the Sun was above the horizon where the Persians once lived. A very clear picture of where the Sun was stopped before the *Farvashites* showed the way to Mazda, which evidently means that *Devayana* or Mazda's way was the phase of the year when the Sun was above the horizon, having previously been pursued for a time by the forces of darkness. As it exists today in Astrology a natal chart, through which astrologers give instructions for the life of the individual, where through the moment of birth you can see the position of the stars from where the predictions are made, in a similar way, it seems that there was also a mortal chart through which it was determined where he will go the individual's soul after death. So, one of the main markers was the one that showed in which half of the year the individual would leave the body. In the Upanishads, we have numerous quotations describing the path of the human soul depends on whether he died in the *Devayna* or *Pitriyana* period. This was especially important for yogis, ascetics, and holy men. So *Bhīṣma* of the epic **Mahabharata**, dying on his bed, waited for the *Devayana* phase to come. This is clearly and directly seen in the **Avesta, Vendidad, Fagard V**, *III,10*, where a question is asked what the follower of *Ahura Mazda* should do if death occurs in the house after the end of the summer, during the winter, and to that question *Ahura Mazda* answers:

dâtare ... ashâum frâ hama saciñte atha aiwi-gâme kutha tê verezyãn aête ŷôi mazdayasna, âat mraot ahurô mazdå, nmâne nmâne vîsi vîsi thrâyô kata uzdaithyãn aêtahe ŷat iristahe.

"O Creator of the material world, thou Light! If summer is gone and winter is here, what are the Mazda faithful to do? Ahura Mazda replied: "In every house, in every district, they will erect three rooms for the dead".

Regarding the performance of the *Dakhma* ritual, where the dead body should first be exposed to the Sun for burial, **Fagard VIII**, *II,9-10* states that:

aêtadha hê uzbaodhãm tanûm nidaithyãn bixshaparem vâ thrixshaparem vâ mâzdrâjahîm vâ vîspem â ahmât ŷat frâ vayô patãn frâ urvara uxshyãn nyåñcô apa-tacin us vâtô zãm haêcayât.âat ŷat hîsh frâ vayô patãn frâ urvara uxshyãn nyåñcô apa-tacin us vâtô zãm haêcayât aêtadha hê aête mazdayasna ahe nmânahe upa-thweresãn upa-thweresayãn, dva dim nara isôithe vîzôishtãm vîzvâreñtãm makhna anaiwi-vastra zemôishtve vâ zarshtve vâ upa-skañbem vîcicaêshva dim paiti ainghå zemô nidaithyãn ŷadhôit dim bâidhishtem avazanãn sûnô vâ kerefsh-hvarô vayô vâ kerefsh-hvarô.

144

9." And they shall let the lifeless body lie there, for two nights, or three nights, or a month long, until the birds begin to fly, the plants to grow, the hidden floods to flow, and the wind to dry up the earth".

10. "And when the birds begin to fly, the plants to grow, the hidden floods to flow, and the wind to dry up the earth, then the worshippers of Mazda shall make a breach in the wall of the house, and two men, strong and skillful, having stripped their clothes off, shall take up the body from the clay or the stones, or from the plastered house, and they shall lay it down on a place where they know there are always corpse-eating dogs and corpse-eating birds".

Considering that the corpse of the follower of *Mazda* had to be exposed to the Sun before it was left to be eaten by the eagles, why wait even a month unless it was a long and dark night? The description of the flying birds, the flowing waters, and the drying up of the moisture are clear markers that the coming of dawn and springtime are being described, and it seems that the dead body was kept in darkness until the Sun appeared above the horizon, which gives us the absolute right to continue with our hypothesis that at that moment the ancient Iranians or Aryans were at the North Pole or in the Arctic Circle. Then in the Avesta, Vendidad, at the end of **Fagard II**, in connection with the location of *Yima* and the construction of the *Vara* (similar to Noah's Ark, only it does not float and is fixed), the following celestial phenomenon is described:

39. dâtare gaêthanãm astvaitinãm ashâum cayô âat aête raocå anghen ashâum ahura mazda ŷô avatha â-raocayeite aêtaêshva varefshva ŷô ŷimô kerenaot.
40. âat aoxta ahurô mazdå, hvadhâtaca raocå stidhâtaca, hakeret zî irixtahe sadhayaca vaênaite starasca måsca hvareca.

145

39. O Maker of the material world, thou Holy One! What are the lights that give light in the Vara that Yima made?

40. Ahura Mazda answered: 'There are uncreated lights and created lights. The one thing missed there is the sight of the stars, the moon, and the sun, and a year seems only like a day.

This verse of the *Avesta* seems to possess a large enough capacity to justify the assumed hypothesis of the Polar Eden, where we have no further need to elaborate and quote other verses. We have ample reason and justification to proceed further in our investigation. We also have a clear tendency to posit the theory that all ancient and sacred science originated from this arctic habitat, from where it was then distributed, and over time it slowly began to lose its original glory, from which numerous schools arose afterward and routes as pale copies, until the time of the appearance of the Latin term *religare* (*religion = re-uniting*), which seems to be the most appropriate and specific today for the widespread Abrahamic religions and the various sects derived from these denominations, while modern science itself, unfortunately, it is left as a dead body without its spiritual essence and a half. In the next volumes much more, attention will be given to this question connected with the source of the sacred science which we know today by the general term either religion alone or science alone. Day and night are an integral part of the natural biorhythm. One cannot do without the other. The basic sense of Aryan dualism in no sense denies the unity within the principle. However, it is not theological dualism in the other supra-ontological sphere, because it is not equated with the later and degraded forms of dualism. The Vedic cult of the Aryans does not claim that it is good and bad that there are two fundamental poles of reality: one of God on the other side and the other of being on this side, the all-encompassing being that also tries to present itself as unique. The mission of the Aryan man is to confirm that truth which is opposed to the world: it's sealing in the tissue of life, in the tissue of the cosmos, in the tissue of nature. The Aryan man understands the tissue of the world, its rhythm, and its meaning by witnessing the disparity between the transcendent and the immanent. No matter how many abstract solutions are offered, they are all insignificant before the fact is postulated by the Aryan soul – that the world exists and that God exists above everything and beyond its limits. And so long as there is a world, and so long as there is a God and the Aryan who witnesses their existence, that they do not align, the metaphysical dualism will never be effectually touched. Its sacred purpose is to maintain equilibrium both within and without, liberating itself with the help of knowledge (the Vedas) and the path of enlightenment (*jyotish*), which, like a compass in the fog, shows the way of being as from the traps of cosmic illusion (*Maya*) and transitory materiality to be released. He follows the path that frees rather than the path that ensnares. Although the solar path of the gods is liberating, yet the poet in ***Rig-Veda X, 88, 14-16,*** in the verse itself wants to emphasize the importance of harmony and balance between these two opposing forces of nature:

वैश्वानरं विश्वहा दीदिवांसं मन्त्रैरग्निं कविमछा वदामः |
यो महिम्ना परिबभूवोर्वी उतावस्तादुतदेवः परस्तात ||
दवे सरुती अश्रृणवं पितृणामहं देवानामुतमर्त्यानाम |
ताभ्यामिदं विश्वमेजत समेति यदन्तरापितरं मातरं च ||
दवे समीची बिभ्रतश्चरन्तं शीर्षतो जातं मनसाविमृष्टम |
स परत्यं विश्वा भुवनानि तस्थावप्रयुच्छन्तरणिर्भ्राजमानः ||

vaiśvānaraṃ viśvahā dīdivāṃsaṃ mantrairaghniṃ kavimachā vadāmaḥ |
yo mahimnā paribabhūvorvī utāvastādutadevaḥ parastāt ||
dve srutī aśṛṇavam pitṛṇāmaham devānāmutamartyānām |
tābhyāmidaṃ viśvamejat sameti yadantarāpitaraṃ mātaraṃ ca ||
dve samīcī bibhṛtaścarantaṃ śīrṣato jātaṃ manasāvimṛṣṭam |
sa pratyaṃ viśvā bhuvanāni tasthāvaprayuchantaraṇirbhrājamānaḥ ||

14. We invoke the Sage with the holy verses, Agni Vaishvanara, the ever-enlightened One, who has surpassed both heaven and earth in greatness: he is God both below and above us.
15. I have heard mention of two paths, the path of Pitrayana (mortals) and the path of Devayana (gods). On these two paths travels every moving being, everything between the Father and the Mother.
16 These two united paths carry every traveler who is born from the head and thought out by the spirit.

- *Midsommar, Midnight Sun, and cult of the White Nights*

"Nach der pythagoraischen, orphischen und neuplatonischen Lehre brachte der Nordwind Leben der Südwind Tod, wohnten hinter dem Nordwind die Seligen und die Gotter als Schopfer und Erhalter der Welt, hinter dem Südwind aber die Verdammten und alle bosenöer asserstörenden Urmächte." W. Menzel, (June 21 or 26, 1798 – April 23, 1873) Die vorchristliche Unsterblichketislehre, 1870

"According to the Pythagorean, Orphic, and Neoplatonic teachings, the north wind brought life, the south wind brought death, behind the north wind lived the blessed and the gods as creators and preservers of the world, but behind the south wind the damned and all evil, destructive primeval powers".

At the poles themselves, the Sun rises and sets only once each year on the equinox. During the six months that the Sun is above the horizon, it spends days appearing to continuously move in circles around the observer, gradually spiraling higher and reaching its highest circuit of the sky at the summer solstice. The term *"Midnight Sun"* refers to the consecutive 24-hour periods of sunlight experienced in the north of the Arctic Circle and south of the Antarctic Circle. In some countries, this Arctic cult of the White Nights festival is celebrated in the winter phase of the year, when the Sun transits through the southern lunar *Pitrayana*, but from the aspect of the Antarctic Pole, this is a six-mount day period. This cult is associated with the movement of the Sun through the Northern Hemisphere through the solar *Devayana* path or the path of the Gods. The sun rises at the North Pole on the Spring Equinox, approximately March 21, and the sun rises higher in the sky with each advancing day, reaching a maximum height at the Summer Solstice, approximately June 21 and the presumed inhabitants of this region could see this phenomenon of nature directly with their own eyes, without any difficulty in astronomical calculations. In this period the forces of light and good are at their maximum. However, the calendar, which is based on natural rhythms, is in complete yin-yang balance and seems to have its maximum of solar energy when the Sun transits through the constellations of Cancer and

Leo, despite the fact that then the daily hours already begin to decrease and *vice versa* during the period when the daily hours begins to grow up after the point called Midwinter 21st of December begins the phase when the forces of darkness are at their maximum strength when the Sun transits through the constellations of Capricorn and Aquarius. When the Sun is at the point called Midsummer (Summer Solstice) the Sun at the North Pole is at its zenith and maximum and this phenomenon has been celebrated since ancient times including the Neolithic Age.

In the Slavic pagan world, this holiday was called Kupala, which can be translated as bathing (купање, капење, капење, купање, капиштец – water sanctuary for baptizing). This ritual of bathing in rivers, lakes, and oceans is because then the waters have a special magnetism and power. Then the external "fire" or heat in nature grows and therefore man has a natural need to cool and purify his body. In this summer part of the year, active elements are fire and air. *Kupala Night* (Belarusian: *Купалле*, Polish: *Noc Kupały*, Russian: *Иван-Купала*, Ukrainian: Івана *Купала*, *Купайла*), also called *Ivana Kupala*, is a traditional Old Slavic holiday that was originally celebrated on the shortest night of the year, which is on 21-22 or 23-24 of June (Czech Republic, Poland, and Slovakia) and in Eastern Slavic countries according to traditional Julian calendar on the night between 6 to 7 July (Belarus, Russia, and Ukraine). Calendar-wise, it is opposite to the winter holiday *Koliada*. The celebration relates to the summer solstice when nights are the shortest and includes a number of Slavic rituals. It involves herb collecting, bonfire lighting, and bathing in the rivers. [1] Kupala is also created by medieval chroniclers based on the name of the *Kupala Night* holiday deity (personification of the Midsommer spirit).

The name of the holiday was originally Kupala; a pagan fertility rite later adapted into the Orthodox Christian calendar by connecting it with St. John's Day which is celebrated on 24 June. [2] Eastern Christianity uses the traditional Julian calendar which is misaligned with the actual solstice; 24 June in the Julian calendar falls on 7 July in the more modern Gregorian calendar. [3] This holiday symbolizes the birth of the Summer Sun – Kupalo.

In the 4th century AD, this day was proclaimed the holiday of the birth of John the Baptist – the forerunner of Jesus Christ. As a result of the Christianization of the pagan feast, the name "*Kupala*" got connected with the Christian "Ivan". The Ukrainian, Belarusian name of this holiday combines "Ivan" (Joan/Johan/John, in this case, John the Baptist) and *Kupala*. The two feasts could be connected by reinterpreting John's baptizing people through full immersion in water. However, the tradition of *Kupala* predates Christianity. The pagan celebration was adapted and reestablished as one of the native Christian traditions intertwined with local folklore.

1. Tryfanenkava, Maryna A. 2001. *"The Current Status of Belarusian Calendar-Ritual Tradition".* In: FOLKLORICA - *Journal of the Slavic, East European, and Eurasian Folklore Association* 6 (2): 44-45.

2. Niżegorodcew (et alii), Anna (2011). *Developing Intercultural Competence through English: Focus on Ukrainian and Polish Cultures.* Warsaw: Developing Intercultural Competence through English: Focus on Ukrainian and Polish Cultures Anna Niżegorodcew, Yakiv Bystrov, Marcin Kleban Wydawnictwo UJ. p. 91

3. Megre, Vladimir (2008). *Rites of Love.* Ringing Cedars Press LLC. p. 231

We can conclude that Kupala (Midsommer) is associated with John the Baptist, while the Koledo holiday (Midwinter) is associated with Jesus Christ. The difference between these two holidays is exactly six months. It is also not a coincidence that John the Baptist was supposedly older than Jesus by exactly six months. *Luke 1:36* indicates that John was born about six months before Jesus. Also in the Quran, God frequently mentions Zechariah's continuous praying for the birth of a son. Zechariah's wife, mentioned in the New Testament as Elizabeth, was barren and therefore the birth of a child seemed impossible. As a gift from God, Zechariah (or Zakaria) was given a son by the name of "Yaḥyā" (Yaḥyā ibn Zakarīyā (Arabic: يحيى ابن زكريا, literally Yahya, son of Zechariah), or "John", a name specially chosen for this child alone. In accordance with Zechariah's prayer, God made John and Jesus, who according to exegesis was born six months later, renew the message of God, which had been corrupted and lost by the Israelites *(Lives of the Prophets, Leila Azzam, John, and Zechariah)*. And in fact, the most important characters in the Christian world Jesus Christ and John the Baptist also divide the year into two parts, the maximum and the minimum peak of the Sun. In Gogol's story The Eve of *Ivan Kupala* (also called Saint John's Eve). Another name for this Midsommer festival is *Vidovdan* among the Serbs. This holiday is apparently associated with the Old Slavic god Vido *(Svetovid, Sventovit)* converted in Saint Vitus in Catholic Christianity. This deity is none other than the Germanic Odin, whose older name is Wotan, i.e. *Vidan, Vedun.* In the second volume, I will focus more on this deity because he has a more complex nature since Odin is also associated with the winter solstice (Midwinter).

Midsummer is a celebration of the season of summer usually held on a date around the summer solstice. It has pagan pre-Christian roots in Europe. The undivided Christian Church designated June 24 as the feast day of the early Christian martyr St John the Baptist, and the observance of St John's Day begins the evening before, known as Saint John's Eve. These are commemorated by many Christian denominations, such as the Roman Catholic Church, Lutheran Churches, and Anglican Communion, as well as by freemasonry. In Sweden, the Midsummer is such an important festivity that there have been proposals to make the Midsummer's Eve the National Day of Sweden, instead of June 6. In Finland, Estonia, Latvia, and Lithuania, the Midsummer festival is a public holiday. In Denmark and Norway, it may also be referred to as St. Hans Day.

Saint John's Day, the feast day of Saint John the Baptist, was established by the undivided Christian Church in the 4th century AD, in honor of the birth of Saint John the Baptist, which the Gospel of Luke records as being six months before Jesus. [4] As the Western Christian Churches mark the birth of Jesus on December 25, Christmas, the Feast of Saint John (Saint John's Day) was established at midsummer, exactly six months before the former feast.

4. Hill, Christopher (2003). *Holidays and Holy Nights: Celebrating Twelve Seasonal Festivals of the Christian Year.* Quest Books. p. 163. See, Fleteren, Frederick Van; Schnaubelt, Joseph C. (2001). Augustine: Biblical Exegete. Peter Lang. p. 197. The cult of John the Baptist began to develop in the first half of the fourth century. Augustine is the first witness to a feast of the birth of John the Baptist, which was celebrated on June 24. This date was reckoned from Luke 1:36, according to which the angel Gabriel said to

Mary, 'And behold, your kinswoman Elizabeth in her old age has also conceived a son, and this is the sixth month with her,' and June 24 is precisely three months after March 25.

The midnight sun is a natural phenomenon that occurs in the summer months in places north of the Arctic Circle or south of the Antarctic Circle when the Sun remains visible at the local midnight. When the midnight sun is seen in the Arctic, the Sun appears to move from left to right, but in Antarctica, the equivalent apparent motion is from right to left. This occurs at latitudes from 65°44' to 90° north or south and does not stop exactly at the Arctic Circle or the Antarctic Circle, due to refraction. The opposite phenomenon, polar night, occurs in winter, when the Sun stays below the horizon throughout the day around the summer solstice (approximately 21 June in the Northern Hemisphere and 21 December in the Southern Hemisphere), in certain areas the Sun does not set below the horizon within a 24-hour period. Because there are no permanent human settlements south of the Antarctic Circle, apart from research stations, the countries, and territories whose populations experience the midnight sun are limited to those crossed by polar circles: the Canadian Yukon, Nunavut, and Northwest Territories; the nations of Iceland, Finland, Norway, Sweden, Denmark (Greenland), Russia; and the state of Alaska in the United States. The largest city in the world north of the Arctic Circle, Murmansk (Russia), experiences the midnight sun from 22 May to 22 July (62 days). A quarter of Finland's territory lies north of the Arctic Circle, and at the country's northernmost point the Sun does not set at all for 72 days during summer. [5] In Svalbard, Norway, the northernmost inhabited region of Europe, there is no sunset from approximately the 19th of April to the 23rd of August. The extreme sites are the poles, where the Sun can be continuously visible for half the year. The North Pole has midnight sun for 6 months from late March to late September, but in some places, as we saw earlier, the artic day can be even longer because of the latitude itself. Because of atmospheric refraction, and because the Sun is a disc rather than a point, the midnight sun may be experienced at latitudes slightly south of the Arctic Circle or north of the Antarctic Circle, though not exceeding one degree (depending on local conditions). For example, Iceland is known for its midnight sun, even though most of it (Grímsey is the exception) is slightly south of the Arctic Circle. For the same reasons, the period of sunlight at the poles is slightly longer than six months. Even the northern extremities of the United Kingdom (and places at similar latitudes, such as St. Petersburg) experience twilight throughout the night in the northern sky at around the summer solstice. Places sufficiently close to the poles, such as Alert, Nunavut, experience times where it does not get entirely dark at night yet the Sun does not rise either, combining effects of the midnight sun and polar night, for example where during the "day" it reaches civil twilight and at "night" only reaches astronomical twilight.

5. Nuorgam, Lapland, Finland — Sunrise, Sunset, and Daylength, May 2022. Also, *Great Soviet Encyclopedia.*

Other festivals following this lead have arisen using names such as White Night, Light Nights, or Nuit Blanche which may be held in the winter as opposed to the summer. Some cities use the French phrase Nuit blanche (or Nuits blanches, if the event is spread over more than one night). Some use the same words in their language: White Nights, La Notte Bianca (Italian), La Noche en Blanco (Spanish), Noaptea alba (Romanian), Nata e Bardhe (Albanian), Baltā Nakts in Latvian. Others invent their names, such as *Lejl Imdawwal* ("Lit Night") in Maltese, Virada Cultural in São Paulo, Taiteiden yö ("Night of the arts") in Finland, and Kulturnatten ("Night of Culture") in Copenhagen. Since the axial tilt of Earth is considerable (23 degrees, 26 minutes, 21.41196 seconds), at high latitudes the Sun does not set in summer; [6] rather, it remains continuously visible for one day during the summer solstice at the polar circle, for several weeks only 100 km (62 mi) closer to the pole, and for six months at the pole. At extreme latitudes, the midnight sun is usually referred to as a polar day. The White Nights are an all-night arts festival held in many cities in the summer. The original festival is the White Nights Festival held in Saint Petersburg, Russia. The white nights are the name given in areas of high latitude to the weeks around the summer solstice in June during which sunsets are late, sunrises are early and darkness is never complete. In Saint Petersburg, the Sun does not set until after 10 p.m., and the twilight lasts almost all night. The White Nights Festival in Saint Petersburg is famous for fireworks and Scarlet Sails, a show celebrating the end of the school year. Locations where the Sun remains less than 6 (or 7) degrees below the horizon – between 60° 34' (or 59° 34') latitude and the polar circle – experience midnight civil twilight instead of the midnight sun, so that daytime activities, such as reading, are still possible without artificial light on a clear night. White Nights have become a common symbol of Saint Petersburg, Russia, where they occur from about 11 June to 2 July, [7] and the last 10 days of June are celebrated with cultural events known as the White Nights Festival. In fact, the festivals of "White Nights" that are celebrated all over Europe today have their own ancient Arctic cult and story. Other phenomena are sometimes referred to as the *"Midnight Sun",* but they are caused by time zones and the observance of daylight saving time. For instance, in Fairbanks, Alaska, which is south of the Arctic Circle, the Sun sets at 12:47 a.m. at the summer solstice. This is because Fairbanks is 51 minutes ahead of its idealized time zone (as most of the state is in a one-time zone) and Alaska observes daylight saving time. (Fairbanks is at about 147.72 degrees west, corresponding to UTC−9 hours 51 minutes, and is on UTC−9 in winter.) This means that solar culmination occurs at about 12:51 p.m. instead of at 12 noon. If a precise moment for the genuine "midnight sun" is required, the observer's longitude, the local civil time, and the equation of time must be taken into account. The moment of the Sun's closest approach to the horizon coincides with its passing due north at the observer's position, which occurs only approximately at midnight in general. Each degree of longitude east of the Greenwich meridian makes the vital moment exactly 4 minutes earlier than midnight as shown on the clock, while each hour that the local civil time is ahead of coordinated universal time (UTC, also known as GMT) makes the moment an hour later. These two effects must be added. Furthermore, the equation of time (which depends on the date) must be added: a positive value on a given date means that the Sun is running slightly ahead of its average position, so the value must be subtracted. [8] As an example, at the North Cape of Norway at midnight on June 21/22, the longitude of 25.9 degrees east makes the moment 103.2 minutes earlier by clock time; but the local time, 2 hours ahead of GMT in the summer, make it 120 minutes later by clock time. The equation of time at that date is -2.0 minutes. Therefore, the Sun's lowest elevation occurs 120 - 103.2 + 2.0 minutes after midnight: at 00.19 Central European Summer time. On other nearby dates, the only thing different is the equation of time, so this remains a reasonable estimate for a considerable period. The Sun's altitude remains within half a degree of the minimum of about 5 degrees for about 45 minutes on either side of this time. When it rotates on its own axis, it sometimes moves closer to the Sun. During this period of Earth's rotation from May to July, Earth tilts at an angle of 23.5 degrees above its own axis in its orbit. This causes the part of Norway located in the Arctic region at the North Pole of Earth to move very close to the Sun and during this time the length of the day increases. It can be said that it almost never subsides. Night falls in Norway's Hammerfest at this particular time of year. The number of days per year with potential midnight sun increases the closer one goes towards either pole. Although approximately defined by the polar circles, in practice the midnight sun can be seen as much as 90 km (55 miles) outside the polar circle, as described below, and the exact latitudes of the farthest reaches of the midnight sun depend on topography and vary slightly year-to-year. Even though in the Arctic Circle the center of the Sun is, per definition and without refraction by the atmosphere, only visible during one summer night, some part of the midnight sun is visible at the Arctic Circle from approximately 12 June until 1 July. This period extends as one travels north: At Cape Nordkinn, Norway, the northernmost point of Continental Europe, the midnight sun lasts approximately from 14 May to 29 July. On the Svalbard archipelago farther north, it lasts from 20 April to 22 August.

6. "What is the Midnight Sun Phenomenon? Earth Phenomena, Planetary Science". Scribd.

7. H. Spencer Jones, *General Astronomy* (Edward Arnold, London, 1922), Chapters I-III

8. Trygve B. Haugan, ed. Det Nordlige Norge Fra Trondheim Til Midnattssolens Land (Trondheim: Reisetrafikkforeningen for Trondheim og Trøndelag. 1940)

Also, the periods of polar day and polar night are unequal in both polar regions because the Earth is at perihelion in early January and at aphelion in early July. As a result, the polar day is longer than the polar night in the Northern Hemisphere (at Utqiagvik, Alaska, for example, a polar day lasts 84 days, while the polar night lasts only 68 days), while in the Southern Hemisphere, the situation is the reverse — the polar night is longer than the polar day. Observers at heights appreciably above sea level can experience extended periods of the midnight sun as a result of the "dip" of the horizon viewed from altitude.

- ## *Midwinter, Polar Night, and the cult of Black Days*

"Identisch ist also Süden und Unterwelt auch hier wie bei unserer kosmischen Ausrichtung der Erdachse." - Dr. Hugo Winckler, Leipzig, 1901, Himmels- und Weltenbild der Babylonier als Grundlage der Weltanschauung und Mythologie aller Völker

So, the south and underworld are identical here as in our cosmic alignment of the earth's axis."

Dakshinayana or *Pitrayan* is the southern transit of the Sun. *Dakshinayana* (Sanskrit: दक्षिणायन) is the six-month period between the Summer solstice and Winter solstice when the sun travels towards the south on the celestial sphere. In the period after the Autumnal Equinox, the Sun began to sink into the ocean below the horizon and then the long twilight phase of 40 days began. ***Professor Nordenskjöld*** has recently referred to the case as follows: ***"On the 14 th / 4 th November the Sun disappeared and was again visible on the 3 rd Feb. / 24 th Jan"***. In other words, when the Sun begins to transit through the constellation of Scorpio, the Polar Night begins. During this period, the Orthodox Christian holiday *Zadušnica* (Remembrance) dedicated to the ancestors and dead souls begins, which corresponds to the Gaelic Samhain i.e., today's Halloween holiday. On the 13 th of November, darkness reigns supreme, so far as the sun is concerned, for seventy-six days. ***Captain Bedford Pim***, of the Royal Navy of Great Britain, makes the following statement: ***"On the 16th of March the sun rises, preceded by a long dawn of forty-seven days, namely, from the 29th of January, when the first glimmer of light appears"***. But as we saw from the first chapter the astronomers say that in England twilight has been observed when the sun was 21° below the horizon. To be entirely safe some have therefore taken 20° as the limit of solar depression, and reckoning with this datum, instead of the 18° before mentioned, have found that at the Pole the morning twilight would begin January 20th, and the evening twilight would cease November 21st.

According to this, the morning twilight begins exactly on the Christian holiday of Epiphany (The Appearance of God or the Water festival, South Slavic: *Vodici, Водици* or *Богојавление*) and that is the period when the Arctic begins to slowly dawn. The morning twilight Epiphany also known as Theophany in Eastern Christian traditions, is a Christian feast day that celebrates the revelation (theophany) of God incarnate as Jesus Christ. It is during the period when the Sun transits through the constellation of Aquarius and Pisces. Icons associated with the Epiphany clearly show these zodiac symbols.

Orthodox icon depicting a scene from the Epiphany where the symbols of the constellations of Aquarius (Uranus) and Pisces (Neptun) are represented below by the feet of Jesus Christ. As we can see it is still dark outside only a small light is seen from above as a sign from God that the light is coming.

The word Epiphany is from Koine Greek ἐπιφάνεια, *epipháneia*, meaning manifestation or appearance. It is derived from the verb φαίνειν, *phainein,* meaning "to appear". In classical Greek, it was used for the appearance of dawn, of an enemy in war, but especially for a manifestation of a deity to a worshiper (a theophany). In the Septuagint the word is used as a manifestation of the God of Israel *(2 Maccabees 15:27)*. In the New Testament the word is used in *2 Timothy 1:10* to refer either to the birth of Christ or to his appearance after his resurrection, and five times to refer to his Second Coming. Alternative names for the feast in Greek include τα Θεοφάνεια, *ta Theopháneia* "Theophany" (a neuter plural rather than feminine singular), η Ημέρα των Φώτων, *I Iméra ton Fóton* (modern Greek pronunciation), *hē Hēméra tōn Phôtōn* (restored classical pronunciation), *"The Day of the Lights"*, and τα Φώτα, *ta Fóta*, *"The Lights"*. These lights are actually the lights that herald the day when the Arctic Dawn slowly begins to arrive. [1]

1. Cf. Schaff, Philip (April 28, 2014). "History of the Christian Church, Volume II: Ante-Nicene Christianity. A.D. 100–325. § 64. The Epiphany". Christian Classics Ethereal Library. Retrieved January 21, 2018.

Seen from our Arctic perspective, despite the fact that after December 21, the day begins to slowly increase, the forces of darkness do not decrease until the appearance of the dawn, that is, the Christian holiday of Epiphany. In our people, there is a proverb that *"the night is blackest before the dawn"*. The sun does not yet appear in the Arctic until Spring when it triumphs over the night. Although after the daily minimum on the 21st of December, when the day slowly begins to grow, the Arctic Sun becomes visible on the 21-22nd.

At the Middle-Winter point, the Midwinter (Winter Solstice) festival took place where the forces of darkness and the underworld have their maximum strength, until the Epiphany holiday 19-20th of January when the light of the dawn as a new hope became visible again. This Midwinter holiday in pagan Scandinavia is known as Yule. Midwinter is attested in the early Germanic calendars, where it appears to have been a specific day or a few days during the winter half of the year. Before the adoption of the church calendar, the date of midwinter may have varied due to the use of a lunisolar calendar, or it may have been based on a week system tied to the astronomical winter solstice. [2] In the medieval Icelandic calendar it was the first day of Þorri, the fourth winter month, which corresponds to the middle of January in the Gregorian calendar. [3] According to **Snorri Sturluson's Heimskringla** (c. 1230), the pre-Christian holiday Yule was originally celebrated at midwinter, but in the 10th century, the king

Haakon the Good moved it to the same day as Christmas, about three weeks earlier. [4]

2.Nordberg, Andreas (2006). *Jul, disting och förkyrklig tideräkning: Kalendrar och kalendariska riter i det förkristna Norden*. Acta Academiae Regiae Gustavi Adolphi (in Swedish). Vol. 91. Kungl. Gustav Adolfs Akademien för svensk folkkultur.

3. Jansson, Svante (2011). *"The Icelandic calendar"* In Óskarsson, Veturliði (ed.). Scripta islandica. Vol. 62.

4. Snorri Sturluson (2007). *Heimskringla: History of the Kings of Norway.* Translated by Hollander, M. Lee.

Beginning in the 18th century, the term midwinter has sometimes been misunderstood as synonymous with the winter solstice. Yule (also called *Jul, Julblot, jól, jólablót, joulu,* "Yule time" or "Yule season") is a festival historically observed by the Germanic peoples. Scholars have connected the original celebrations of Yule to the Wild Hunt, the god Odin, and the pagan Anglo-Saxon *Mōdraniht* ("Mothers' Night"). *Mōdraniht* or *Modranicht* Old English for *"Night of the mothers"* was an event held at what is now Christmas Eve by the Anglo-Saxon pagans. The event is attested by the medieval English historian **Bede** in his eighth-century Latin work **De temporum ratione**. It has been suggested that sacrifices may have occurred during this event. Scholars have proposed connections between the Anglo-Saxon *Mōdraniht* and events attested among other Germanic peoples (specifically those involving the *dísir (souls, Slavic: dusi),* collective female ancestral beings, and Yule), and the Germanic *Matres and Matronae*, female beings attested by way of altar and votive inscriptions, nearly always appearing in trios.

In De temporum ratione, **Bede** writes that the pagan Anglo-Saxons:

Incipiebant autem annum ab octavo Calendarum Januariarum die, ubi nunc natale Domini celebramus. Et ipsam noctem nunc nobis sacrosanctam, tunc gentili vocabulo Modranicht, id est, matrum noctem appellabant: ob causam et suspicamur ceremoniarum, quas in ea pervigiles agebant. [5]

... began the year on the 8th calends of January [25 December], when we celebrate the birth of the Lord. That very night, which we hold so sacred,

they used to call by the heathen word Modranecht, that is, "mother's night", because (we suspect) of the ceremonies they enacted all that night. [6]

5. Giles, John Allen (1843). *The Complete Works of the Venerable Bede, in the Original Latin, Collated with the Manuscripts, and Various Print Editions, Accompanied by a New English Translation of the Historical Works, and a Life of the Author.* Vol. VI: Scientific Tracts, p. 178.

6. Wallis (1999:53). Note that the first element of the phrase matrum noctem is here translated with "mothers", whereas it is plural: a translation "mothers' night" is therefore more accurate.

This pagan Scandinavian holiday dedicated to the earthly or chthonic aspect of nature, i.e. to the Mothers, is connected to our Orthodox Christian feast – *Materici (Материцu)*. *Materice* is a Serbian holiday celebrated on the second Sunday before Christmas. [7] This is the greatest Christian holiday for mothers and women. This festival of celebrating the mothers is actually celebrating the Material aspect of the creation, where the earth and the water elements are active in this winter part of the year.

7. *Serbian celebrations and religious customs*; Bishop Nikolaj and Archdeacon Ljubomir Ranković.

Yule underwent Christianised reformulation, [8] resulting in the term Christmastide. Some present-day Christmas customs and traditions such as the Yule log, Yule goat, Yule boar, Yule singing, and others may have connections to older pagan Yule traditions. Cognates to Yule are still used in the Scandinavian languages as well as in Finnish and Estonian to describe Christmas and other festivals occurring during the winter holiday season. Yule is the modern version of Old Norse *Jól* and *Jólnir* is one of the names for Odin. Both words are cognate with Gothic ᚷᛁᚾᛚᛖᛁᛋ *(jiuleis);* Old Norse, Icelandic, Faroese, and Norwegian Nynorsk *jól, jol, ýlir;* Danish, Swedish, and Norwegian Bokmål *jul,* and are thought to be derived from Proto-Germanic *jehwlą.* [9] The etymological pedigree of the word remains uncertain, though numerous speculative attempts have been made to find Indo-European cognates outside the Germanic group, too. [10] The noun *Yuletide* is first attested from around 1475. [11]

8. "Winter Solstice/Yule". Vancouver Island University. 21 December 2019. Retrieved 9 July 2020. Yule is a festival historically observed by the Germanic peoples. Departing from its pagan roots, Yule underwent Christianised reformulation resulting in the now better-known Christmastide.

9. Bosworth, Joseph; Toller, T. Northcote (1898), p. 424; *An Anglo-Saxon Dictionary.* See, Hoad, T. F. (1996). *The Concise Oxford Dictionary of English Etymology.* p.550. Also, Orel Vladimir (2003). *A Handbook of Germanic Etymology. Leiden: Brill Publishers.* p. 205.

All languages from the Indo-European family have undergone great changes throughout history, some natural and some in intentional ways. But specially it is expressed between that branch that lives today in Western Europe which was under a very strong influence of the Roman Empire and later the Holy Roman Empire and the Catholic Church. Since these empires applied the maxim *divide et impera,* in their management doctrine was also the linguistic separation of the Indo-European family that could no longer understand each other, so the tribes through politics and foreign interests should have been put into mutual war and constant conflict. In that case, without the knowledge of today's so-called Slavic languages, it is difficult to decipher the name of this Scandinavian or German holiday known as Yule. Many sounds that form letters are missing in the languages of Western Europe that were strongly influenced by the Latin alphabet and language, so for the imitation of some Slavic letters through the Latin script, two letters are used to create a sound or one Slavic letter.

The Old English derivates *ġēol* or *ġēohol* and *ġēola* or *ġēoli*, indicate the 12-day festival of "Yule" (later: "Christmastide"), and the latter indicates the month of "Yule", whereby *ærra ġēola* referred to the period before the Yule festival (December) and *æftera ġēola* referred to the period after Yule (January). So, the true etymology and meaning of this word *ġēol* or *ġēohol* or Yule which is phonetically equivalent to the Slavic word *Đavo* also *Gjavo, Gaol, Gjaol, Ѓаво, Џаво, Ѓаол,* simply means "Devil", (or *Đavol*; Greek. *Διάβολος,* Old Slavonic *Діаволъ, Đa-Volos, Veles).* In Slavic mythology, the Devil is Volos or Veles the god of the underworld, symbolically depicted as a serpent or dragon who lives under the dragon in winter. Also, the Danish word for Devil is "*Djævel* (Islandic: Djöfull)."

Yule is attested early in the history of the Germanic peoples; in a Gothic language calendar of the 5–6th century it appears in the month name *fruma jiuleis*, and, in the 8th century, the English historian **Bede** wrote that the Anglo-Saxon calendar included the months *geola* or *giuli* corresponding to either modern December or December and January. [10] However, it is not by chance that the letter "**Y**" (Yule) was chosen as the name of this winter holiday in later periods, because it pictographically associates with the horned god, where the Devil himself is recognizable.

10. Simek, Rudolf (2007) translated by Angela Hall. *Dictionary of Northern Mythology*. Orchard (1997:187).

Yaldā Night (Persian: شب یلدا *shab-e yalda*) is an Iranian Northern Hemisphere's winter solstice festival celebrated on the "longest and darkest night of the year."[rs 1] According to the calendar, this corresponds to the night of December 20/21 (±1) in the Gregorian calendar, and to the night between the last day of the ninth month (*Azar*) and the first day of the tenth month (*Dey*) of the Iranian solar calendar.

In Zoroastrian tradition the longest and darkest night of the year was a particularly inauspicious day, and the practices of what is now known as *"Shab-e Chelleh/Yalda"* were originally customs intended to protect people from evil (*dew*s) during that long night, at which time the evil forces of Ahriman were imagined to be at their peak. People were advised to stay awake most of the night, lest misfortune should befall them, and people would then gather in the safety of groups of friends and relatives, share the last remaining fruits from the summer, and find ways to pass the long night together in good company. In the belief of the followers of the special ritual of Mithraism, the Cypress tree is the sun and the birth of Mithra. A tree that is always green and refreshing and is stable against cold and darkness. Therefore, cedar was a symbol of a radiant and life-giving seal and a sign of immortality, freedom, and stability against the deadly power. For this reason, on the night of the birth of Mithra, Iranians decorate the cypress and leave gifts at its feet and make a pact with themselves to plant another evergreen cedar for the next years.

Also, the Yule 12-day festival is identical to the 12 *navia* (netherworld) days. In Bulgarian folklore, there is the image of 12 *navies*, which also correspond to the twelve so-called *"Unbaptized Days"* in Orthodox Christianity exactly in the same winter period of the year. There is a belief among the Slavs that these navies sucked the blood of women who gave birth, while in the **Russian Primary Chronicle** the navies are presented as a demonic personification of the plague in Polotsk from 1092. [11] These forces of darkness are the same as the Wild Hunt from Scandinavian folklore.

Навь (*Nav*, Serbian: *Нав*, Slovene: Navje, Ukrainian: *Мавка, Mavka* or *Нявка, Nyavka*) is a phrase used to refer to the souls of the dead in Slavic mythology. The words *nawia, nav,* and its other variants probably come from Proto-Slavic *navъ-*, meaning "corpse", or "deceased". Other Indo-European languages include Latvian *nāve* ("death"), Lithuanian *nõvis* ("death"), Old Prussian *nowis* ("body, flesh"), Old Russian *navi* ("corpse, dead body"), and Gothic *N∧ΠS* (naus "dead body, corpse"). [12] *Nyavka* may be related to the Sanskrit word *Naraka*, which refers to the concept of hell in Hinduism, or to the Arabic word (النار, *al-nar*) which is synonymous with Jahannam (Arabic: جهنم,) or hell in the Qur'an. The term *nawie, nawki*, was used as a name for the souls of the dead. According to some scholars (namely *Stanislav Urbanjčikj*, among others), this word was a general name for the demons emanating from the souls of tragic and premature deaths, murderers, fighters, murdered and drowned dead people. They are said to have been hostile and unfavorable to humans, jealous of life. [13] According to folk tales, navies usually took the form of birds. The phrase *Nawia* or *Nav* was also used as a name for the Slavic Underworld, ruled by the god Veles, closed from the world, or by a living sea or river, according to some beliefs located deep underground. According to Ruthenian folklore, Veles lived on a marsh in the center of *Nav*, where he sat on a golden throne at the base of the Cosmic Tree, wielding a sword. The entrance to *Nav* was guarded by a dragon. [14] It was believed that souls would later be reborn on earth.

11. Kempinski, Andrzej (2001). *Encyklopedia mitologii ludów indoeuropejskich [Encyclopedia of mythology of Indo-European peoples]* (in Polish). Warszawa: Iskry

12. Razauskas, Dainius (2011). "Ryba - mifologičeskij Proobraz lodki" [The Fish as a Mythological Prototype of the Boat]. In: *Studia Mythologica Slavica* 14 (October). Ljubljana, Slovenija, pp. 296, 303

13. Strzelczyk, Jerzy (2007*). Mity, podania i wierzenia dawnych Słowian [Myths, legends, and beliefs of the early Slavs]* (in Polish). Poznań: Rebis.

14. Szyjewski, Andrzej (2004). *Religia Słowian [Religion of the Slavs]* (in Polish). Kraków: Wydawnictwo, "Nikolai Mihailov: Slavist, Slavist, Baltist (11.06.1967–25.05.2010)". In: *SLAVISTICA VILNENSIS* 2010 Kalbotyra 55 (2). p. 174

The Old New Year in Serbia is commonly called the Serbian New Year *(Српска Нова година / Srpska Nova godina),* and sometimes the Orthodox New Year *(Православна Нова година / Pravoslavna Nova godina)* and rarely Julian New *Year (Јулијанска Нова година / Julijanska Nova godina).* A traditional folk name for this holiday as part of Twelve Days of Christmas is Little *Christmas (Мали Божић / Mali Božić).* The holiday in North Macedonia is known as Old New Year (Macedonian: *Стара Нова година, romanized: Stara Nova godina*) or as *Vasilica* (*Василица,* "St. Basil's Day"). Late on January 13, people gather outside their houses, in the center of their neighborhoods where they start a huge bonfire and drink and eat together. So, this is the period of celebrating the Old Year, not the New Year. As we will see later in the fifth chapter, the New Year holiday was not originally celebrated by our ancestors in the winter phase, but in the spring, that is, exactly when the Sun would appear during the spring equinox of the Arctic region. And that is why it is completely illogical to celebrate the New Year first and then the Old Year. It is much more logical to initially have a forgiving celebration of the Old Year, and then prepare the ground for the arrival of the New Year. During the feast of *Vasilitsa (Saint Basil's day)* or *Surovica (South Slavic winter holyday)* or *Stara Godina (Old Year),* bread is kneaded and then a metal coin is placed inside. Then the bread is baked and the night is broken and shared in the family. It is believed that whoever will have the coin will have a material blessing. The bread and coin are symbols of the earth's elements. St. Vasili is actually the Christian version of the god Veles. The Christian festival known as *Vasilica* or Old Year (Serbian Old New Year) has all the chthonic elements in which the god Veles is celebrated, where people dress in fur, often as bears, or some horned animal known as *Kukeri* in Bulgaria. The Lithuanian and Latvian word for "Devil" is *"Velns"* and *"Velnias".* Velnias, also called Velinas, Vels, or Velns, in Baltic religion, is the god of the underworld, Lithuanian vėlės or Latvian velis (also synonym for "zombie"), is *"phantom of the dead."* He is a one-eyed, prophetic trickster capable of raising whirlwinds and leading the host of the dead through the skies. Velnias is akin in type to the Germanic Wodan or the Scandinavian Odin and is identical with the god *Patollo* (compare with Patala-loka, the Hindu lowest hell), or *Pickollos* (compare with the Slavic word *peklo, pekol, pakao* with the meaning of hell), of early Old Prussian and Lithuanian sources. Beelzebub (Hebrew: בַּעַל-זְבוּב Baʿal-zəḇūḇ) or Beelzebul is a name derived from a Philistine god, formerly worshipped in Ekron, and later adopted by some Abrahamic religions as a major demon. The name Beelzebub is associated with the Canaanite god Baal. In theological sources, predominantly Christian, Beelzebub is another name for Satan. He is known in demonology as one of the seven deadly demons or seven princes of Hell, Beelzebub representing gluttony. This is a well-known fact to all ethnologists and scientists who study folklore. The corresponding figure in Greek-speaking Thrace is known as Kalogeros "rod-carrier", also shortened to *cuci*, in former Yugoslavia known as *didi, didici* (grand-fathers, ancestors), in Bulgaria as *kuker* or *babushar, as momogeros* in Pontic Anatolia, in North Macedonia it is known as *babari* (grand-fathers, grand-mothers) or *mechkari* (man-bears). In Romania, this figure mostly appears together with a goat, known as *capra, turca or brezaia*. Kukers, also called *chaushis, babugers, stanchinaris, dervishes, old men, souris, babars, babris, surovars, kalogeros, köpek beys or jamalars*, are a carnival masquerade in Southeastern Europe. It is usually held at the beginning of Great Lent, most often on Sirni Monday, but in some areas, such as Western Bulgaria, it can also take place between Christmas and Epiphany. Kukeri is a divinity personifying fecundity. Sometimes in Bulgaria and Serbia, it is a plural divinity. In Bulgaria, a ritual spectacle of spring (a sort of carnival) takes place after a scenario of folk theatre, in which Kuker's role is interpreted by a man attired in a sheep- or goat-pelt, wearing a horned mask and girded with a large wooden phallus. During the ritual, various physiological acts are interpreted, including the sexual act, as a symbol of the god's sacred marriage, while the symbolical wife, appearing pregnant, mimes the pains of giving birth. This ritual inaugurates the labors of the fields (plowing, sowing) and is carried out with the participation of numerous allegorical personages, among which is the Emperor and his entourage. In this period according to Ayurveda medicine, the internal fire *(agni)* or heat is at maximum, while the outside fire is at minimum, so the internal sexual energy in this period is very potent. That's why chthonic symbols like snakes or dragons are always connected with fertility powers and great sexual energy. *Gjolomaris, jaolmaris (голомари, ѓаоломари)* from Macedonia, also known as *vasilicari, survari, golomari, stracinari* in this period of 12 unbaptized days also had a sexual dance ritual for fertility. This winter festival *Yule, Yeol, Gēol* or *Gēohol, Julblot, Jól, Jólablót, Joulu* also seems to be associated with the chthonic deity *Yaldabaoth, Jaldabaoth,* or *Ildabaoth.* In the Archontic, Sethian, and Ophite systems, Yaldabaoth is regarded as the malevolent Demiurge and false god of the Old Testament who generated the material universe and keeps the souls trapped in physical bodies, imprisoned in the world full of pain and suffering that he created. [15]

Kukeri or Babugeri from Bulgaria

15. Fischer-Mueller, E. Aydeet (January 1990*). "Yaldabaoth: The Gnostic Female Principle in Its Fallenness"*. Novum Testamentum. Leiden and Boston: Brill Publishers. 32 (1): 79–95.

Yaldabaoth is further identified with the Ancient Roman god Saturnus. [16] During this period, the Sun passes through the astrological sign of Capricorn, which is under the influence of the planet Saturn lord of the Earth element. Therefore, it is no coincidence that the Devil is often depicted with horns and a goat-like appearance, such as Baphomet. This holiday is also known as *Surva* among the South Slavs, and the name itself comes from the word *"surov"*, which means cruelty. It means the mercilessness of the cold winter.

16. This article incorporates text from a publication now in the public domain: *Arendzen, John Peter (1908). "Demiurge". In Herbermann, Charles (ed.). Catholic Encyclopedia. Vol. 4. New York: Robert Appleton Company.*

Yama (Devanagari: यम) or Yamarāja (यमराज), is a deity of death, dharma, the south direction, and the underworld who predominantly features in Hindu and Buddhist religions. According to the Vedas, Yama is said to have been the first mortal who died. By virtue of precedence, he became the ruler of the departed, and is called *"Lord of the Pitrs."* [17]

17. Shanti Lal Nagar: *Harivamsa Purana* Volume 1, p. 85

The Cernunnos-type antlered figure or horned god, on the Gundestrup Cauldron, on display, at the National Museum of Denmark in Copenhagen

Koročun or *Kračun* is one of the names of the Slavic pagan holiday Koliada (Koledo, Koleda). In modern usage, it may refer to the winter solstice in certain Eastern European languages and the holiday of

Christmas. Belarusian: *Карачун, Karačun*; Bulgarian: *Крачон, Kračon* or *Крачунек, Kračunek*, Macedonian: *Крачун, Kračun;* Old Russian*: Корочунъ, Koročunŭ;* Russian: *Корочун, Koročun* or *Карачун, Karačun*; Ruthenian: *К(е)речун, K(e)rečun* or *Г(е)речун, G(e)rečun*; Serbian*: Крачун, Kračun;* Slovak: *Kráčún;* Hungarian: *Karácsony*; Romanian: *Crăciun.* There are many interpretations of what this word means and it seems to me that the suggestions given are wrong. ***Max Vasmer*** derived the name of the holiday from the Proto-Slavic *korčunŭ,* which is in turn derived from the verb *korčati,* meaning to step forward. [18]

Gustav Weigand, Alexandru Cihac, and ***Alexandru Philippide*** offer a similar Slavic etymology, based on *kratŭkŭ* (curt, short) or *kračati* (to take steps). [19]

18. Max Vasmer, *Etymological Dictionary of the Russian Language*, Корочун.

19. Romanian *Etymological Dictionary*, Crăciun

On the other hand, ***Hugo Schuchardt, Vatroslav Jagić***, and ***Luka Pintar*** proposed a Romanian origin of the word, [20] as does also the ***Romanian Etymological Dictionary***, tracing its roots back to the Latin creatio,-nis. However, most probably, this word is a loanword with Slavic roots as in Romanian, as well as in Hungarian. [21]

20. *Archiv für Slavische Philologie,* 1886, Vol XI, pp. 526–7., , Vol II, p. 610., Vol II, p. 610.

21. Nay, Alain Du; Nay, André Du; Kosztin, Árpád (1997). *Transylvania and the Rumanians*, Alain Du Nay, André Du Nay, Árpád Kosztin, Matthias Corvinus Publishing, 1997.

My interpretation is that this word is closely related to the words like *черно, црно, карно (karno, charno, crno)* words that mean "black". Even in Turkic languages, *kara* means "black". Thus, *Karachun* means Black God. *Koročun* or *Kračun* was a pagan Slavic holiday. It was considered the day when the Black God and other spirits associated with decay and darkness was most potent. The first recorded usage of the term was in 1143 when the author of the ***Novgorod First Chronicle*** referred to the winter solstice as *"Koročun"*. It was celebrated by pagan Slavs on December 21st, the longest night of the year and the night of the winter solstice. The Black God in ancient Celtic and Gallo-Roman religion is known as *Cernunnos* or *Carnonos* and was a god depicted with antlers just like the Devil. The iconography associated with *Cernunnos* is often portrayed with a stag and the ram-horned serpent. [22]

22. Green, Miranda (2003-10-03). *Symbol and Image in Celtic Religious*

Chernobog (lit. "Black God") and *Belobog* (lit. "White God") are an alleged pair of Polabian deities. *Chernobog* appears in **Helmold's Chronicle** as a god of misfortune worshipped by the Wagri and Obodrites, while *Belobog* is not mentioned – he was reconstructed in opposition to *Chernobog*. Both gods also appear in later sources, but they are not considered reliable. Researchers do not agree on the status *of Chernobog and Belobog:* many scholars recognize the authenticity of these theonyms and explain them, for example, as gods of good and evil; on the other hand, many scholars believe that they are pseudo-deities, and *Chernobog* may have originally meant "bad fate", and later associated with the Christian devil. In Latin records, this theonym is noted as *Zcerneboch* and *Zcerneboth*. [23]

The twelfth-century German monk and chronicler *Helmold*, who accompanied the Christianization missions to the Elbe Slavs, describes in his Chronicle of the Slavs the cult of *Chernobog*:

Also, the Slavs have a strange delusion. At their feasts and carousals, they pass about a bowl over which they utter words, I should not say of consecration but of execration, in the name of [two] gods—of the good one, as well as of the bad one—professing that all propitious fortune is arranged by the good god, adverse, by the bad god. Hence, also, in their language they call the bad god Diabol, or Zcerneboch, that is, the black god. [24]

23. Alvarez-Pedroza, Juan Antonio (2021). *Sources of Slavic Pre-Christian Religion.* Leiden: Koninklijke Brill.

24. Gorbachov, Yaroslav (2017). "What Do We Know about *Čьrnobogъ and *Bělъ Bogъ". *Russian History*. 44 (2-3): 209–242.

The next sources that speak of Chernobog and/or Belobog appear only in the 16th century. Around 1530, a Dominican monk from Pirna, **Johan Lindner**, recalls the gods in his compilation. Although he lived in or near the Lusatian region (Lusitanian Serbia, now part of Germany), he probably only used written sources and monastic stories, and not field research, which quickly made his work unbelievable by many historians, including **Georg Fabricius** and **Petrus Albinus**. They believed that although his sources were numerous and varied, he used them uncritically. At the end of the 17th century, **Abraham Frencel** also mentioned the *Chernobog* in his list of the Lusatian Sorbs gods. This information is also considered unbelievable because it came into being late, when the Lusatian paganism was probably completely extinct and about half of the gods he mentioned are of Prussian origin. [25]

In the old Dutch Calendar, the mount of December is known under different names such as *wintermaand* ("winter month"), *midwintermaand* ("Midwinter month"), *sneeuwmaand* ("snow month" = French Republican Nivôse), Kerstmismaand ("Christmas month"), *Joelmaand* ("Yule month"), *wolfsmaand* ("wolves' month"), *donkere maand* ("dark month"). [26]

25. Strzelczyk, Jerzy (1998). *Mity, podania i wierzenia dawnych Słowian* (in Polish).

26. These archaic or poetic Dutch names are recorded in the 18th century and were used in almanachs during the 19th century. *Neue und volständige Hoogteutsche Grammatik of nieuwe en volmaakte onderwyzer in de hoogduitsche Spraak-Konst* (1768)

Serbia also we have a period of *Wolf days* like the Dutch *wolfsmaand* ("wolves' month"). Among the people, these days are also known as *Mratinci,* because St. Mrata was the patron saint of wolves. When it comes to this baptismal glory, the folk belief goes back to the distant past and the mythology of the ancient Slavs, so this holiday is associated with the wolf as a dangerous but also powerful opponent, and sometimes a protector. In the first volume of the **Ethnography of Montenegro**, **Pavle Rovinski** mentions the Mratin carnival on November 14. [27] In the second volume, it is written that before Christmas there are 6 weeks of fasting, which is called Christmas or Philip's, because it starts on the day of St. Apostle Philip (November 14, according to Julian). Although that fast began in Montenegro from that day, the last fat day after it was called *Mratinj pokladi,* named after St. Mratin ie Martin, which comes on November 12 (according to the Catholic calendar, November 11), and the fast itself is the Christmas or Mratin fast. The prevalence of the name *Martin in Montenegro is attributed to Western influence.*

27. Pavle Rovinski 1998, p. 115, 116.

This fictitious saint Mratin is the code name of the Slavic god Moran who is actually the god of death and the underworld. He is the husband of the goddess Morana who heralds the dark half of the year and is the opposite of her sister Vesna who heralds the summer half of the year, the warm and pleasant season. The name Moran or Morana itself is not difficult to understand because many words are formed from this name, such as the English *mortal*, or the Sanskrit word *mṛtyu* (मृत्य mRtyu) or the Latin *mortis. Mṛtyu-Māra* appears as Death in Buddhism or *Māra*, as a demon in Buddhist cosmology, the personification of Temptation. The name *Mora* among the Lusatian Serbs meant the goddess of diseases, and the goddess of death, among the Poles and Russians, a delusion, an apparition, an angry spirit, a nightmare, and a vampire, "demonic spirit", among Slovaks *Mara* is "disease"; in Proto-Slavic *"Mara"* means "appearance", "lie", "illusion", "ghost", in Serbian-Church Slavic *"Mora"* means "witch" or night-mare *(košmar)*. In one word, this is related to the Proto-Slavic *Morv*, which means "death" and to *merti* - "to die". Winter, Death, and Darkness – are the three attributes of Morana and Moran. As a goddess of winter, she was never a favorite among the ancient Slavs which can be understood considering the climate in which they once lived. Morana was a long and cold winter, a winter that could bring with it death in the form of hunger and unbearable cold, which could be the cause of diseases or pestilence of livestock. Because of this, her arrival was awaited with fear, and her departure was celebrated with excitement and joy. During this period when the *Wolf Days* begins, exactly in this period the Sun enters the constellation of Scorpio and then the night definitely begins at the North Pole. This sign of the zodiac is under the auspices of the planet Mars and in this case, it is the winter or cold Mars (in opposition to the male, positive, or fire Mars as a patron of the Aries sign of the Zodiac), where in Western Astrology it is identified with the aspect of Pluto, the god of the underworld. The Death card itself in the major arcana of the Tarot is also a Scorpio card. But I would still add that it is a deity of underground waters such as the river Styx, while Saturn in the sign of Capricorn is the supreme lord of the earth and the material aspect of the creation and the pick of darkness in the *Pitrayana* half-year period. A very large number of demons and rivers have this root in their name: *Morana, Murena, Morice, Marice, Mora, Morna, Moran, Moria……*

Pic 1. Death (XIII) is the 13th trump or Major Arcana card in most traditional tarot decks. The Death card usually depicts the Grim Reaper, the personification of Death and this card is associated with the planet Pluto and Scorpio zodiac sign in astrology. Pic 2. The Devil (XV) is the 15 trump or Major Arcana card. The Devil card is associated with the planet Saturn, and the correlating zodiac Earth sign, Capricorn.

The old Slavs believed that all winter calamities, snow, ice, frost, and death come from Morana. The wolf and the snake are always associated with chthonic elements in Indo-European myths. The Nordic god *Loki* can also be read as "the cunning one" - the lord of lies, but at the same time as *wolf, vlukos, vuko*, from where the connection with the Greek *"lycanthropus"* is clearly seen, that is, the Slavic mythical creature werewolf. ***Alexander Fomich Veltman*** *(Александар Фомич Велтман born July 8, 1800, St. Petersburg - January 11, 1870, Moscow)* is a forgotten Russian cartographer, linguist, archaeologist, poet and writer who was quite right when he noted there is a connection between Loki and the cunning wolf: ***"Вуко, разыгрывая въ этоыъ событіи роль лукаваго, духа лжи (Lokke; по Датски Lyffve— ложъ), и филологически обратись въ Ливонскаго...."****translation: "Wolf, playing in these events the role of a trickster, he is the spirit of lies (Lokke; in Danish Lyffve – ложъ - liar), and philologically turned to Livonian...."*

«Non igitur mirum, qnod recentiores Scandinavi diabolum pro *Lokio* illo ceperint. Hoc revera ita evenit ut in Islandia, ubi phrases multae perantiquis de Lokio fabulis, suam debent originem: sic: *Loka lygi* (лукавая ложь), *Loka daun* (лукавый духъ) и проч.» — «In Scandinavorum cantilenis, quae medio aevo originem debent, variis celebratur *Lokius* nominibus et cognominibus: *Lokke Leiemand* (чортова (лукаваго) волынка); Lokke-löye (лукавый, юла, шутъ).» Edda Saem. Lex. Mith. p. III.

Aleksandar Fomich Veltman, Аттила. Русь IV и V века, p.109

In Slavic languages, the word *"lukav"(лукав)* means someone cunning, and usually, in our folklore, the wolf has all the attributes of a deceitful being. Also, the wolf Fenrir, together with Hel and the World Serpent, is a child of Loki. Scholars have connected the month event and Yule period to the Wild Hunt (Slavic navies - a ghostly procession in the winter sky), the god Odin (who is attested in Germanic areas as leading the Wild Hunt and bears the name *Jólnir*), and increased supernatural activity, such as the Wild Hunt and the increased activities of *draugar* - undead beings who walk the earth. [28] This *draguar* creature seems to be identical to the *Drekavac* (literally "the screamer" or "the screecher"), also called *drekalo, krekavac, zdrekavac* or *zrikavac*, is a mythical creature in South Slavic mythology. The name is derived from the verb *"drečati"* ("to screech"). It was popularly believed to be visible only at night, especially during the twelve days of Christmas (called unbaptized days in Serbo-Croatian) and in early spring, when other demons and mythical creatures were believed to be more active. When assuming the form of a child, it predicts someone's death, while in its animal form, it predicts cattle disease. [29] Perhaps the name of this creature comes from the word *draco, drakula, dragon*, as it is also described as a reptilian creature, looking like a dog, but with a "snake-like" head and hind legs. The interested one can see the *drekavac* on the internet because there is an authentic video of such a creature that was killed by a hunter in Serbia in 1992. [30]

28. Simek (2007:180–181 and 379–380) and Orchard (1997:187). Simek, Rudolf (2007) translated by Angela Hall. *Dictionary of Northern Mythology.* Orchard, Andy (1997). *Dictionary of Norse Myth and Legend.*

29. Š. Kulišić; P. Ž. Petrović; N. Pantelić (1970). "Дрекавац". *Српски митолошки речник* (in Serbo-Croatian). Belgrade: Nolit. p. 110.

30. YouTube title: *DREKAVAC - Weird Creature On Balkan.* Before the war in early spring 1991, the so-called zdrekavac appeared in the village of Krvavica near Kruševca in Serbia. This contribution by Radio Television Belgrade attracted considerable attention.

The events of Yule are generally held to have centered on midwinter (although specific dating is a matter of debate), with feasting, drinking, and sacrifice (blót). Scholar Rudolf Simek says the pagan Yule feast "had a pronounced religious character" and that "it is uncertain whether the Germanic Yule feast still had a function in the cult of the dead and in the veneration of the ancestors, a function which the mid-winter sacrifice certainly held for the West European Stone and Bronze Ages." The traditions of the Yule log, Yule goat, Yule boar (*Sonargöltr*, still reflected in the Christmas ham), Yule singing, and others possibly have connections to pre-Christian Yule customs, which Simek says ***"indicates the significance of the feast in pre-Christian time"***. All these holy days are winter or *Pitrayana* transit holidays of the season conceded with the underworld and dead ancestors. In Chelan myths, Coyote belongs to the animal people but he is at the same time "a power just like the Creator, the head of all the creatures." while still being a subject of the Creator who can punish him or remove his powers. [31] In the Pacific Northwest tradition, Coyote *(Canis latrans)* is mostly mentioned as a messenger or minor power. More often than not Coyote in Native American mythology is a trickster, but always different. The role Coyote takes in traditional stories shares some traits with the Raven figure in other cultures. In some Greek myths, Hermes plays the trickster. He is also the patron of thieves and the inventor of lying. Also associated with this holiday is Odin, who has a triple nature and who is a mediator between the heavenly, earthly, and underground worlds, but as I said, we will pay special attention to Odin in the second volume.

31. Edmonds, Margot; Ella E. Clark (2003). *Voices of the Winds: Native American Legends.* Castle Books. p. 5

The Dutch philosopher **Baruch de Spinoza** denies anthropomorphism in religion. For him, the Devil is not human and should not be attributed to human traits or moral qualities. God is not exclusively good; his actions may seem evil to people from their limited perspective. But evil is also a part of God, its opposite does not exist, because its boundlessness has incorporated that into itself. [32] Our ancestors were not originally Dualists as we are portrayed but they respected the Triple Principle through which harmony and balance were maintained.

[32] The phenomenon of evil in philosophy from classical patristics to Baruch de Spinoza, Accessed 5.4/2013.

The polar night is a phenomenon where the nighttime lasts for more than 24 hours that occurs in the northernmost and southernmost regions of Earth. This occurs only inside the polar circles. The opposite phenomenon, as we have seen, the polar day, or *Midnight Sun,* occurs when the Sun remains above the horizon for more than 24 hours."Night" is understood as the center of the Sun being below a free horizon. Since the atmosphere refracts sunlight, the polar day is longer than the polar night, and the area that is affected by polar night is somewhat smaller than the area of the midnight sun. From this natural phenomenon and rhythm of nature, ancient cults developed, which even today have left their visible traces in Christianity itself. The polar circle is located at a latitude between these two areas, at approximately 66.5°. While it is a day in the Arctic Circle, it is night in the Antarctic Circle, and vice versa. Any planet or moon with a sufficient axial tilt that rotates with respect to its star significantly more frequently than it orbits the star (no tidal locking between the two) will experience the same phenomenon (a nighttime lasting more than one rotation period). The polar shortest day is not totally dark everywhere inside the polar circle, but only in places within about 5.5° of the poles, and only when the moon is well below the horizon. Regions located at the inner border of the polar circles experience polar twilight instead of the polar night. In fact, polar regions typically get more twilight throughout the year than equatorial regions. For regions inside the polar circles, the maximum lengths of the time that the Sun is completely below the horizon varies from zero to a few days beyond the Arctic Circle and Antarctic Circle to 179 days at the Poles. However, not all this time is classified as polar night since sunlight may be visible because of refraction. The time when any part of the Sun is above the horizon at the poles is 186 days. The preceding numbers are average numbers: the ellipticity of Earth's orbit makes the South Pole receive a week more of Sun-below-horizon than the North Pole (see equinox). As there are various kinds of twilight, there also exist various kinds of the polar night. Each kind of polar night is defined as when it is darker than the corresponding kind of twilight. The descriptions below are based on relatively clear skies, so the sky will be darker in the presence of dense clouds. Polar twilight occurs in areas that are located at the inner border of the polar circles, where the Sun will be on or below the horizon all day on the winter solstice. There is then no true daylight at the solar culmination, only civil twilight. This means that the Sun is below the horizon but by less than 6°. During civil twilight, there may still be enough light for most normal outdoor activities because of light scattering by the upper atmosphere and refraction. Street lamps may remain on and a person looking at a window from within a brightly lit room may see their reflection even at noon, as the level of outdoor illuminance will be below that of many illuminated indoor spaces. It occurs at latitudes between 67°24' and 72°34' North or South, when the Sun does not rise, only civil twilight is visible.

Northern Hemisphere:

68° North: December 9 to January 2
69° North: December 1 to January 10
70° North: November 26 to January 16
71° North: November 21 to January 21

72° North: November 16 to January 25

Southern Hemisphere:

68° South: June 7 to July 3
69° South: May 30 to July 11
70° South: May 24 to July 18
71° South: May 19 to July 23
72° South: May 14 to July 27

Sufferers of the seasonal affective disorder tend to seek out therapy with artificial light, as the psychological benefits of daylight require relatively high levels of ambient light (up to 10,000 lux) which are not present in any stage of twilight; thus, the midday twilights experienced anywhere inside the polar circles are still "polar night" for this purpose. The civil polar night period produces only a faint glow of light visible at midday. It happens when there is no civil twilight and only nautical twilight occurs at the solar culmination. Civil twilight happens when the Sun is between 0 and 6° below the horizon, and civil night when it is lower than that. Therefore, the civil polar night is limited to latitudes above 72° 34', which is exactly 6° inside the polar circle. Nowhere in mainland Europe is this definition met. On the Norwegian territory of Svalbard, however, civil polar night lasts from about 11 November until 30 January. Dickson, in Russia, experiences a civil polar night from December 6 to January 6. During dense cloud cover places like the coast of Finnmark (about 70°) in Norway will get a darker "day". On the Canadian territory of Pond Inlet, Nunavut, however, the civil polar night lasts from about 16 December until 26 December. During the nautical polar night period, there is no trace of daylight, except around midday. It happens when there is no nautical twilight and only astronomical twilight occurs at the solar culmination. Nautical twilight happens when the Sun is between six and twelve degrees below the horizon. There is a location at the horizon around midday with more light than others because of refraction. During the nautical night, the Sun is lower than 12° below the horizon, so the nautical polar night is limited to latitudes above 78° 34', which is exactly 12° within the polar circle, or 11.5° from the pole. Alert, Nunavut, the northernmost settlement in Canada and the world, experiences this from November 19 to January 22. Oodaaq, a gravel bank at the northern tip of Greenland and a disputed most northerly point of land, experiences this from November 15 to January 27. Its antipode (83°40′S 150°7′E) experiences this from May 13 to July 31. The Canadian territory of Eureka, Nunavut, experiences this from December 1 to January 10. Its antipode (79°58′S 94°4′E) experiences this from June 1 to July 11. The Norwegian territory of Svalbard Ny-Ålesund experiences this from December 12 to 30. Its antipode (78°55′S 168°4′W) experiences this from June 12 to July 1. The Russian territory of Franz Josef Land experiences this from November 27 to January 15. Its antipode (81°S 125°W) experiences this from May 25 to July 17. The astronomical polar night is a period of continuous night where no astronomical twilight occurs. Astronomical twilight happens when the Sun is between twelve and eighteen degrees below the horizon and astronomical night when it is lower than that. Thus, the astronomical polar night is limited to latitudes above 84° 34', which is exactly 18° within the polar circle, or five and a half degrees from the pole. The only permanent settlement on Earth above this latitude is Amundsen–Scott South Pole Station, the South Pole scientific research station, whose winter personnel are completely isolated from mid-February to late October. During the astronomical polar night, stars of the sixth magnitude, which are the dimmest stars visible to the naked eye, will be visible throughout the entire day. This happens when the sun is between 18° and 23° 26' below the horizon. These conditions last about 11 weeks at the poles. The South Pole, Antarctica experiences this from May 11 to August 1. The North Pole experiences this from November 13 to January 29. If an observer located on either the North Pole or the South Pole were to define a "day" as the time from the maximal elevation of the Sun above the horizon during one period of daylight, until the maximal elevation of the Sun above the horizon of the next period of daylight, then a "polar day" as experienced by such an observer would be one Earth-year long. [33]

33. Burn, Chris. *The Polar Night.* The Aurora Research Institute. Retrieved 28 September 2015. "Time and Date.com.

Chapter IV
Śveta-Giri

"On Mount Meru, the Sun and the Moon orbit from left to right (pradakshinam) every day, and so do all the stars." "By its brightness, the mountain conquers the darkness so that the night is scarcely distinguishable from the day….' the day and the night together form a year for the inhabitants of that place." - *Vanaparvan, Mahabharata ch. 163, verse. 37, 38; ch 164, verse. 11, 13.*

We can literally translate the Sanskrit term *Śveta-Giri* (श्वेतगिरि *śveta-giri*) as "*Holy Mountain*" or *Sveta-Gora* on Slavic, from *śveta* > "*света*" or *"holy"* and *giri* > "*gora*" or "*гора*" - "*mountain.*" This chapter will be dedicated to this mystical prototype mountain. Comparative mythology is the systematic comparison of myths from different cultures. It moves towards discovering the main themes that are common in myths from different cultures. In some cases, comparative mythologists use the similarities between different mythologies to prove that those mythologies have common sources. This common source may be a common source of inspiration (a certain natural phenomenon that inspired a similar myth in different cultures) or a common "proto-mythology" that diverges into the different mythologies we find today. Interpretations of myths in the 19th century could often be compared, looking for a common origin for all myths. However, today's scholars are unfortunately suspicious of comparative approaches, avoiding overly general or universal statements about mythology. One exception to this new trend is **Joseph Campbell's (1904-1987)** book **"The Hero with a Thousand Faces"** from 1949, in which the author claims that in all heroic myths we have one and the same main theme and one and the same template, and we can freely place this author himself in that school of mythologists who prefer the inner or psychological side of the myth. This "monomyth" theory is not supported by the traditional teaching of mythology. However, for our search, it turns out that we have enough solid arguments to dispute this belief and we also have enough evidence to offer an alternative option, which will leave free space for the readers themselves to come to their own conclusion. We will begin now with an investigation of the cosmological worldview of the ancient peoples and their idea of sacred geography. *"**Heaven and hell are within us, and all the gods are within us. This is the great realization of the Upanishads in India in the ninth century BCE. All the gods, all the heavens, the whole world are in us.**"* - Joseph Campbell, *The Power of Myth*

- ### *Japanese tradition*

According to the most ancient texts, Japan is the center of the earth. - W. E. Griffies

According to the earliest cosmogony of the Japanese, as given in their most ancient book, the *Koji-ki*, [1] the creators and first inhabitants of our world were a god and goddess, *Izanagi* and *Izanani* by name. These, in the beginning, we quote from **Sir Edward Reed**, "*standing on the bridge of heaven, pushed down a spear into the green plain of the sea, and stirred it round and round. When they drew it up the drops which fell from its end consolidated and became an island. The sun-born pair descended onto the island, and planting a spear in the ground, point downwards, and built a palace around it, taking that for the central roof pillar. The spear became the axis of the earth, which had been caused to revolve by the stirring round*". [2]

1. Speaking of this work, M. Léon de Rosny calls it l'un des monuments les plus authentiques de la vieille littérature japonaise, and says, "Nous devons non seulement à cet ouvrage la connaissance de l'histoire du Nippon antérieure au vii. siècle de notre ère, mais l'exposé le plus autorisé de l'antique mythologie sintauïste. Il y a même ce fait remarquable, que les dieux primordiaux du panthéon japonais, mentionnés dans ce livre, ne figurent déjà plus au commencement du *Yamato bumi*, qui est postérieur seulement de quelques années à la publication du *Ko ji ki*. Ces dieux primordiaux paraissent oubliés, ou tout au moins négligés, dans les ouvrages indigènes qui ont paru par la suite." *Questions d'Archéologie Japonaise*. Paris, 1882: p. 3. An English translation of the Ko-ji-ki, by B. H. Chamberlain, has just appeared in *Transactions of the Asiatic Society of Japan*, vol. v.

2. Sir Edward J. Reed, *Japan,* vol. i., 31.

This island, however, was the Japanese Eden. Here originated the human race. Its name was *Onogorojima, "The Island of the Congealed Drop".* Its first roof pillar, as we have seen, was the axis of the earth. Over it was *"the pivot of the vault of heaven."* [3] **Mr. Reed,** who has no theory on the subject to maintain, says, *"**The island must have been situated at the Pole of the earth.**"* [4] In like manner, with no idea of the vast anthropological significance and value of the datum, **Mr. Griffis** remarks, *"**The island formed by the congealed drops was once at the North Pole, but has since been taken to its present position in the Inland Sea**."* [5] Here, then, is the testimony of the most ancient Japanese tradition. Nothing could be more unequivocal. *Izanagi's* divinely precious spear of jade, [6] like the transverse jade -tube of the ancient Shu King, [7] is an imperishable index, not only to the astronomical attainments of prehistoric humanity but also to humanity's prehistoric abode.

3. Léon Metchnikoff, *L'Empire Japonais.* Genève, 1881: p. 265.

4. Ibid. Our interpretation of ancient cosmology and of the true Eden location at once brings light into the whole system of Japanese mythology. In the following, extracted from Mr. Griffis, no one has ever before known what to make *of "the Pillar of Heaven and Earth" "the Bridge of Heaven"* the position of primitive Japan *"on the top of the globe"* and at the same time at *"the center of the Earth"*: The first series of children born were the islands of Japan. Japan lies on the top of the globe. ... At this time heaven and earth were very close to each other, and the goddess Amaterazu being a rare and beautiful child, whose body shone brilliantly, Izanagi sent her up the Pillar that united heaven and earth, and bade her rule over the high plain of heaven. ... As the earth-gods and evil deities multiplied, confusion and discord reigned, which the sun goddess (Amaterazu), seeing, resolved to correct by sending her grandson Ninigi to earth to rule over it. Accompanied by a great retinue of deities, he descended by means of the floating Bridge of Heaven, on which the divine first pair had stood, to Mount Kirishima. After his descent, heaven and earth, which had already separated to a considerable distance, receded utterly, and further communication ceased. According to the most ancient texts, Japan is the center of the earth."

5. McClintock and Strong, *Cydopadia,* vol. ix., p. 688. Art. "Shinto."

6. Émile Burnouf, "La pique céleste de jade rouge."- *La Mythologie des japonais d'après le Kokŭ-si-Ryakŭ*. Paris, 1875: p. 6.

7. "He examined the pearl-adorned turning sphere, with its transverse tube of jade, and reduced to a harmonious system the movements of the Seven Directors." Legge's Translation in *The Sacred Books of the East*, vol. iii., p. 38. Professor Legge once examined this passage in my presence and found unexpected corroboration of the interpretation which identifies "the transverse tube of jade" with the axis of heaven.

• *Chinese tradition*

The rationalistic genius of the matter-of-fact Chinese is apparent even in the way in which they conceived their primitive history; and in this respect, as in many others, it brings them into nearer relations with the best modern science than belong to the other Oriental races. - *Samuel Johnson* (of Salem).

It is through this wonderfully pure seer [Lao-tse], as it appears to me, that we ascend to the primitive revelation of truth given to this ancient people. - *William Henry Channing*

Approaching this theme, a reviewer of **Shin Seen Tung Keen** a "**General Account of the Gods and Genii**" in twenty-two volumes offer the following observations: "**All nations have some tradition of a Paradise, a place of primeval happiness, a state of innocence and delight. The Taoists** [1] **are by no means behind in referring to an abode of lasting** *bliss, which, however, still exists on earth. It is called Kwen-lun.*" [2] In another article, by a student of Chinese sources, it is stated, "This locality, being the abode of the gods, is Paradise; it is round in form, and like Eden, it is the mount of assembly". [3] Like the Gan-Eden of *Genesis* it is described as a garden, with a marvelous tree in the midst; also, with a fountain of immortality, from which proceed four rivers, which flow in opposite directions toward the four quarters of the earth. [4] In the language of the writer first quoted in this chapter, "*Sparkling fountains and purling streams contain the far-famed ambrosia. One may rest on flowery carpeted swards, listening to the melodious warbling of birds, or feasting upon the delicious fruits, at once fragrant and luscious, which hang from the branches of the luxuriant groves. Whatever there is beautiful in landscape or grand in nature may also be found there in the highest state of perfection. All are charming, all enchanting, and whilst Nature smiles the company of genii delights the ravished visitor.*" [5] Where, now, is this Paradise mountain located? At the North Pole. The sentence before those last quoted reads as follows: "*Here is the great pillar that sustains the world, no less than 300,000 miles high*". This world-pillar, or axis of the earth, is sometimes conceived of as slender enough for the use of a climber. Thus, we read, "*One of the Chinese kings, anxious to become acquainted with the delightful spot, set out in search of it. After much wandering he perceived the immense column spoken of, but trying to ascend it, he found it so slippery that he had to abandon all hopes of gaining his end and endeavor by some mountain road which was rugged in the extreme to find his way to Paradise*. When almost fainting with fatigue, some friendly nymphs, who had all the time from an eminence compassionated the weary wanderer, lent him an assisting hand. He arrived there, and immediately began to examine the famous spot." [6]

---

1. "Die Secte der Tao-sse hat die Sagen and religiösen Gebräuche des alten China's noch am Meisten aufbewahrt." Lüken, *Traditionen des Menschengeschlechtes,* p. 77. "Lao-tse abounds in sentences out of some ancient lore, of which we have no knowledge but from him." Samuel Johnson, *Oriental Religions*—China. Boston, 1877: p. 861.

2. *The Chinese Repository* vol. vii., p. 519.

3. *The Chinese Recorder and Missionary Journal*, vol. iv., p. 94. Compare Isaiah xiv. 13, 14.

4. Liiken, *Traditionen des Menschengeschlechtes,* p. 72.

5. *The Chinese Repository,* vol. vii., p. 519.

6. *The Chinese Repository,* vol. vii., p. 520.

Such a pillar connecting the earth with an upper Paradise, and affording a means of access thereto, necessarily recalls to mind the analogous conception set forth in the *Talmud*: *"There is an upper and a lower Paradise. And between them, upright, is fixed a pillar; and by this, they are joined together, and it is called The Strength of the Hill of Sion. And by this Pillar on every Sabbath and Festival the righteous climb up and feed themselves with a glance of the Divine majesty till the end of the Sabbath or Festival, when they slide down and return into the lower Paradise."* [7]

In this conception, we have a twofold Paradise, one celestial and one terrestrial. Among the Chinese, we find the same. The upper is situated in the center or pole of heaven, the lower directly under it, at the center or pole of the northern terrestrial hemisphere. The Pillar connecting them is of course the axis of the heavenly vault.

7. Eisenmenger, *Entdecktes Judenthum*, Bd. ii., p. 318. (English translation, vol. ii., p. 25.) Compare Schulthess, *Das Paradies*, p. 354. Also the story of Er, the Pamphylian, in which we have the same *"column, brighter than the rainbow, extending right through the whole heaven and through the earth;"* here also the spirits visiting the earth are allowed seven days before ascending. Plato, *Republic,* 616. Also the Chaldæo-Assyrian conception of "the celestial and terrestrial Paradises, supposed to be united by means of the Paradisaic Mount itself." *The Oriental and Biblical Journal*. Chicago, 1880: p. 293. Also, the Greek idea: "Sehr merkwürdig ist, was Pindar (Olymp., ii., 56 f.) von den Seligen sagt. Wenn sie nämlich auf der Insel der Seligen sich befinden, steigen sie zum *Thurme des Chronos* empor. Dieser Höhentendenz entspricht nun die alte Vorstellung

vom Naturcentrum am Nordpol und so führen uns denn auch die griechischen Dichter auf einem langen Umwege doch zuletzt nach Nysa, wo uns die griechischen Künstler alle Wonnen des dionysischen Himmels aufthun." Menzel, *Die vorchristliche Unsterblichkeitslehre*, ii., p. 10. Finally, the Japanese idea in Griffis, *The Mikado's Empire*, p. 44.

We quote: *"Within the seas, in the valleys of Kwen-lun, at the northwest is Shang-te's Lower Recreation Palace. It is eight hundred le square, and eighty thousand feet high. In front, there are nine walls, enclosed by a fence of precious stones. At the sides, there are nine doors, through which the light streams, and it is guarded by beasts. Shang-te's wife also dwells in this region, immediately over which is Shang-te's Heavenly Palace, which is situated in the center of the heavens [the celestial pole], as his earthly one is in the center of the earth (the terrestrial pole)."* [8]

There can be no mistaking this use of the term "center" for pole, for the Chinese astronomers expressly state, "The Polar star is the center of heaven". [9] Elsewhere, instead of *Kwen-lun* being a *World-Pillar* in the "valleys" or "plain" or "mound" of the terrestrial Paradise, we find it described as a stupendous heaven-sustaining mountain, marking the center or pole of the earth: "The four quarters of the earth incline downwards. On this vast plain or mount, surrounded on all sides by the four seas, arise the mountains of *Kwen-lun*, the highest in the world according to the Chinese geographers: *"Kwen-lun is the name of a mountain; it is situated at the northwest, fifty thousand le from the Sung-Kaou mountains, and is the center of the earth. It is eleven thousand le in height (Kang-he)."* [10] The significance of the foregoing with respect to the location of Paradise cannot be doubtful.

8. The Chinese Recorder, vol. iv., p. 95.

9. The Chinese Repository, vol. iv., p. 194. Compare Menzel: "Der Polarstern heisst Palast der Mitte." *Unsterblichkeitslehre, Bd. i, p. 44.*

10. The Chinese Recorder, vol. iv., p. 94.

- *Hindu or East Aryan tradition*

"The reader cannot have failed to be struck, as the first explorers of Sanskrit literature have been, with the close analogy, - we might even say the perfect identity, of all the essential features of the typical description of Mount Meru in the Puranas with the topography of Eden in the second chapter of Genesis. The garden of Eden (gan-Eden), the garden of God (gan-Elohim, Ezek. xxviii. 13), which is guarded by the anointed and protecting Cherub (Ezek. xxviii. 14, 16), is placed, like the garden of the delight of the gods of India, on the summit of a mountain, the holy mountain of God (har qodesh Elohim (Ezek. xxviii. 14, 16), all sparkling with precious stones (Ibid.) [1]*"* – Lenormant.

In what kind of a world lived the ancient Brahman? And what was his conception of the location of the cradle of the race? One of the oldest of the elaborate geographical treatises of India is the **Vishnu Purana**. Taking this as a guide, let us place ourselves alongside one of the ancients of the country, and look about us. First, we will look to the South, far down the Indian Ocean. What was supposed to lie in that direction? To begin with their distribution of the different quarters of the world among the gods, this is the quarter belonging to Yama, the god of the dead:

> *"May he whose hands the thunder wield*
> *Be in the East thy guard and shield;*
> *May Yama s care for the South befriend,*
> *And Varun s arm the West defend;*
> *And let Kuvera, lord of gold,*
> *The North with firm protection holds."* [2]

North is upwards *(uttarat),* south is downwards *(adharat).* [3] Hence the abode and kingdom of *Yama* is not only to the south, but also below the level of India, i. e., on the under hemisphere, or, as **Monier Williams** locates it, in "the lower world". [4] All Hindu literature is full of similar references. The exact time required for the soul's journey was supposed to be four hours and forty minutes. [5] In this direction, evidently, we shall vainly seek paradise. Let us turn to the North and "ascend."

1. The continuation of the passage is as follows: "Jehovistic writer does not say so in Genesis, but the prophets are express in this respect. The tree of life grows in the midst of the garden *(bethoch haggan)* with the tree of the knowledge of good and evil *(Gen. ii. 9; iii. 3),* exactly like the tree Jambu, in the center of the delightful plateau which crowns the height of Meru. A river goes out of Eden to water the garden, and from thence it divides and forms four arms (Gen. ii. 10). This corresponds in the most precise manner with the way in which the spring Ganga, after having watered the "Celestial Land", or the "Land of Joy" at the summit of Meru, forms four lakes on the four counterforts of this holy mountain, whence it afterward flows out in four large rivers toward the four cardinal points."

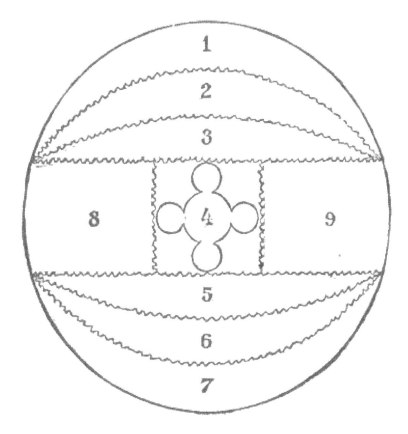

1. Uttarakuru. *5. Harivarsha.*

2. Hiranmaya. *6. Kimpurusha.*

3. Ramyaka. *7. Bharata (India).*

8. Ketumala. *9. Bhadrisva.*

4. SU-MERU in Ilāvṛta.

2. Griffiths, *Ramayana, ii. 20.*

3. Zimmer, *Altindisches Leben.* Berlin, 1879: p. 359.

4. Yama: "one of the eight guardians of the world as regent of the South quarter, in which direction in some region of the lower world is his abode called Yama-Pura; thither a soul, when it leaves the body, is said to repair, and there, after the recorder, Citra-Gupta, has read an account of its actions, kept in a book called Agra-Sandānī, receives a just sentence, either ascending to heaven, or to the world of the Pitris or being driven down to one of the twenty-one hells."—*Williams, Sanskrit Dictionary*, sub. "Yama."

5. "The soul is believed to reach Yama s abode in four hours and forty minutes; consequently, a dead body cannot be burned until that time has passed after death." W. J. Wilkins, *Hindu Mythology, Vedic and Puranic.* London, 1882: Art. "Yama". See, also, Muir, *Sanskrit Texts*, v. 284-327, and our references in "Homer s Abode of the Dead."

First, of course, we come to the Himalayas range, the *Himavat* of Indian geography. All that portion of the earth lying between this mountain range and the great ocean to the South constitutes one of the seven, or nine, "*varshas*" (continents) or divisions of the habitable (upper) hemisphere. Its name is *Bharata*. If now our ancient Hindu could proceed due North and cross the *Himavat*, which he does not think possible to mortals, he would find himself in *Kimpurusha,* an equally extensive but more elevated and beautiful *varsha*, extending northward till bounded by a second range of incredibly lofty mountains, the *Himakuta*. Still "ascending" or going North, until he had crossed this division and passed the *Himakuta*, he would enter *Harivarsha*, a still loftier and diviner country. This extends, in turn, to another boundary range, the *Nishadha,* crossing which one would come to *Ilâvrita*, the central *varsha* of all, which occupies the top as well as the center of the world. To the adequate description of the beauty and glory and preciousness of this country, no tongue is equal. In its center is situated the mount of the gods, *"Beautiful Meru"* is at the Pole, and around it revolves all constellations of heaven. It is the center of the habitable world. Continuing our imaginary journey across this divine country of *Ilâvrita* crossing of course this colossal central mountain, we should now begin to descend on the meridian opposite to that on which we ascended on the Indian side of the globe. The boundary of the central region on that side is the *Nila range*, then comes the *varsha* of *Ramyaka*; its farther boundary is the *Sweta range*, beyond which is the *varsha* of

Hiranmaya. Still descending, we cross this and the range which bounds it on the farther side, the *Sringin*, and we are in *Uttarakuru*, the last of the seven grand divisions of the earth, the one corresponding, in distance from Meru, to *Bharata*, or our starting-point. It, of course, is on the equatorial ocean, and here too we have only to cross this ocean in order to reach the underworld. The way in which the *varshas* are made to number "nine" is by subdividing the great central cross-section of the hemispherical surface, leaving *Ilâvrita* a perfect square on the top of the globe, the land descending eastward to the sea being called *Bhadrasva*, and the corresponding country to the West being called *Ketumala*. To assist the reader to a clearer conception of this sacred geography we give herewith two cuts, one of which presents in outline the side-aspect of the Puranic earth, and the other a flat polo-centric projection of its upper hemisphere. Having now answered our first question, and showed in what kind of a world the ancient Hindu lived, we pass to the second "***What was his conception of the location of the cradle of the race***? "The question is answered the moment we say that in the Hindu conception and tradition man proceeded from Meru. His Eden-land was *Ilâvrita*. It was therefore at the Pole. How strange that **Lenormant** could have written the following, and still imagined that the true primeval Eden of the Hindu was anywhere else than at the terrestrial Pole! He says: "***In all the legends of India the origin of mankind is placed on Mount Meru, the residence of the gods, a column which unites the sky to the earth. At first sight, on reading the description of Mount Meru furnished by the Puranas, it appears overcharged with so many purely mythological features that one hesitates to believe that it has any basis in reality. To realize these descriptions, one must represent one's self in the center of a vast level and a very elevated surface, surrounded by various mountain ranges, a gigantic block, the axis of the world, raising its head to the highest point of the heavens, whence there falls upon its summit, on the North Pole, the divine Ganga, the source of all rivers, which there discharges itself into an ideal lake, the Mânasa-Sârovara. . . Meru, then, is at one and the same time the highest part of the terrestrial world and the central point of the visible heaven, the two having been confounded through ignorance [6] of the real constitution of the universe: it is also, at one and the same time, the north pole and the center of the habitable earth,***

Jambu-dwîpa, literally of the continent of the tree Jambu, the tree of life. Leaving the higher basin of the mountain in which its waters have at first collected the source, Ganga travels seven times around the Meru in descending from the abode of the Seven Rishis of the Great Bear, to empty itself afterward into four lakes placed on four summits adjacent to this vast pyramid, and serving as buttresses on its four sides. . . . Fed by the waters of the celestial Gangâ the four lakes in their turn feed four terrestrial rivers which flow out through the mouths of four symbolical animals. These four great rivers water as many distinct regions, . . . and discharge themselves into four opposite seas, to the east, south, west, and north of the central Meru. . . . The four lakes, the four rivers, and the four oceans are composed of different liquids, corresponding to the four castes, and this latter, with which are connected all the nations of the human race, are reputed to have set out from the four sides of Meru to people the whole earth." |7|

Map of Jambu-dvipa showing the mountains Sommer (Sumeru, Meru) and Illawurtkhund (Ilāvṛta)

6. Lenormant here follows the misleading arguments of Wilford in *Asiatic Researches*, vol. viii., pp. 312, 313.

7. The *Contemporary Review*, Sept. 1881: Am. ed., p. 39. Also, *Les Origines de l'Histoire*, tom. ii. I, ch. i. Compare *Essai de Commentaire des Fragments Cosmogoniques de Bérose*, Paris, 1871: pp. 300-328. Also, Muir, *Sanskrit Texts*, vol. ii., p. 139. In his *Indische Studien*, vol. i., p. 165, Weber speaks of the "Aryan Indians being driven by a deluge from their home, and coming from the North, not from the West (as Lassen, i., 515 will have it), into India."

A similar illustration of the power of a wrong pre-possession is given to us in the illustrious *Carl Ritter*, who after expressly declaring that "*the numberless Puranas and their most diverse interpretations by the Pundits teach that Meru is the middle of the earth, and itself literally designates its center and axis*, [8] thereupon in the coolest manner imaginable proceeds to identify the same sacred height with the mountains of Central Asia. Still worse is the procedure of *Mr. Massey*, who after locating the Garden of Eden on Mount Meru, and saying explicitly, "*The Pole, or polar region, is Meru*" and again, "*Meru is the garden of the Tree of Life*", nevertheless tells us that in equatorial Africa beasts first grew into men. [9] Happier is the inconsistency of *Mr. Lillie*, who, despite his adhesion to the flat-earth theory of Hindu cosmology, still incidentally speaks of "the blissful Garden" as "at the Pole." [10]

8. "Die zahllosen Puranas und ihre verschiedenartigsten Auslegungen durch die Pundits lehren, dass Meru die Mitte der Erde sei, und selbst wörtlich auch das Centrum, die Axe, bezeichne". *Erdkunde*, Bd. ii., p. 7. 2

9. *The Natural Genesis*, vol. ii., pp. 28, 162.

10. *Buddha and Early Buddhism*, London, 1882: p. 8.

• *Iranian or Old Persian Tradition*

Aus den Angaben ü ber die Paradiesstrome und den Lauf derselben erhellt nun auch, wo wir das Paradies selbst zu suchen haben, nämlich im ä ussersten Norden. – *(From the information about the Paradise Streams and their course, it is now also clear where we have to look for*

Paradise itself, namely in the extreme north). - Friedrich von Spiegel (1820 – 1905)

According to the sacred books of the ancient Persians all the five-and-twenty races of men which people the seven *"keshvares"* (continents) of the earth descended from one primitive pair, whose names were *Mashyoi* and *Mashya*. The abode of this primitive pair was in the *keshvare Kvanîras*, the central and the fairest of the seven. [1] Let us see if we can determine its location. As a key to the old Iranian conception of the world let us investigate the nature and location of the *"Chinvat Bridge."* This, like the *Bifrost* of the Northmen and the *Al Sirat* of Islam, is the bridge on which the souls of the dead, the evil as well as the good, leave this world to enter the unseen. [2] The investigation is in itself and for its own sake full of interest, for no writer on the ideas and faith of the Mazdaeans has ever professed to be able to tell either the origin or true meaning of the myth. Most interpreters have either carefully abstained from all attempts at explanation, or have suggested that it probably refers to the rainbow or to the Milky Way, or to both. [3]

1. Bundahish, ch. xv., 1-30.

2. This, "says Professor Rawlinson" is evidently the original of Mohammed s famous way extended over the middle of hell, which is sharper than a sword and finer than a hair, over which all must pass. *"Ancient Monarchies,* vol. ii., p. 339 n. Compare Sale's *Koran*, Prelim. Discourse, Sect. iv. Professor Tiele thinks "it was borrowed from the old Aryan mythology" and that it "was probably originally the rainbow." *History of Religion.* London and Boston, 1877: p. 177.

3. The Bridge of Souls cannot be always the Milky Way. . . . Supposing the myths which once belonged to the Milky Way to have been passed on to the Rainbow, the name of the former might also have been inherited by the latter." C. F. Keary, *Primitive Belief.* Lond., 1882: p. 292. Comp. pp. 286-294, 347. Also, Justi, *Handbuch der Zendsprache*. Leipsic, 1864: p. III *sub-voce* "Cinvant."

To dispose of these suggestions, let us raise a few questions:

1. Do we find in any part of the Avestan literature any evidence that the *Chinvat Bridge* possessed a curvilinear form?

None.

2. Straight, or curved as a whole, where its two ends are conceived of as on a common level?

No, for motion upon it in one direction is described as upward, and in the opposite direction as downward.

3. Where was the upper end?

In the heaven of Ahura Mazda, the Supreme God, to whose abode the bridge conducts good souls.

4. But where is this abode?

At the Northern Pole of the sky, as elsewhere shown.

5. Where is the earthward end?

It rests upon "the Daitik peak."

6. Is this peak in Persia?

No, it is part of a sacred mountain in Airyanəm Vaējah, the Eden of Iranian tradition.

7. And where is *Airyanəm Vaējah*?

"In the middle of the world."

8. In what *keshvare*?

In Kvanîras, the center of the seven divisions of the earth, and the one in which men and the good religion were first created.

9. And in what direction from Persia was *Airyanəm Vaējah* supposed to lie?

Far to the North.

10. What natural "center of the earth" is situated in that direction?

The North Pole.

11. What other evidence is there that the *Daitik* peak is at the North Pole?

The fact that the mountain of which this is simply "the peak of judgment" is Harâ-Berezaiti, around which the heavenly bodies revolve, and which, as all allow, answers to the north polar Su-Meru of the Hindus. [4]

12. Then the *Chinvat bridge* extends from the North Pole of the heavens to the North Pole of the earth: what is its shape?

It is "beam-shaped."

To quote the sacred book: ***"That bridge is like a beam, of many sides, of whose edges there are some which are broad, and there are some which are thin and sharp; its broadsides are so large that its width is twenty-seven reeds, and its sharp sides are so contracted that in thinness it is just like the edge of a razor. And when the souls of the righteous and wicked arrive, it turns to them that side which is suitable to their necessities."*** [5]

4. "Like the Meru of the Indians, Harâ-Berezaiti is the pole and center of the world, the fixed point around which the sun and the planets perform their revolutions." Lenormant, *"Ararat and Eden"* in the *Contemporary Review*, September 1881. Am. ed., p. 41.

5. Dādestān ī Dēnīg, ch. xxi., 2-9. West, *Pahlavi Texts*, ii., pp. 47-49. It is a curious coincidence that in Polynesian mythology Buataranga, "guardian of the road to the invisible world" is wife to Ru, "the supporter of the heavens." Gill, *Myths, and Songs of the South Pacific*. London, 1876: p.51. So, if Heimdallr's true station were at the top of the rainbow, his title "son of nine mothers" (Vigfusson and Powell, *Corpus Poeticum Boreale*, London, 1883, ii. 465) would have no such obvious significance as our interpretation gives.

The Chinvat bridge, then, is simply the axis of the northern heavens, the *"Pillar of Atlas"*, the Talmudic *"Strength of the Hill of Sion"* the column which in the Chinese legend the emperor vainly sought to climb! In solving this long-standing problem, we have at the same time unlocking the mystery which has hitherto attached to *Bifrost* and *Al Sirat*. [6] But in locating our bridge we have located the Persian Eden. And the location is unquestionably at the North Pole. More than this, we have made clear the fact that in the mythical or sacred geography of these ancient people the world of living men was originally the northern circumpolar hemisphere. The arrangement of the *keshvares* now becomes entirely clear. [7] Like the divinely beautiful *Ilâvrita Varsha* of the Hindus *"illustrious Kvanîras"* holds the central position. In its center, as in the center of *Ilâvrita* is the holiest mount in the world. Directly over it is the true heaven. In this central polar country North and South and East and West would have no application; but speaking from their own geographical standpoint as south of *Airan-vej*, the Persians located to the east of this holy central *Kvanîras* the *keshvare Savah*, to the west *Arzah*, to the south the *keshvares Fradadafsh* and *Vidadafsh*, and to the north *Vorubarst* and *Vorugarst*. [8]

6. One of the etymologies of Chinvat makes it the "Bridge of the Judge." (Haug, *Essays*, 2d ed., p. 165 n.) As among the ancient Assyrians, and some other peoples, the pole star has been styled "the judge of heaven," it is possible that we have here at once the origin of the name and a new identification of the position of the mythical "beam-shaped" bridge. It is interesting to note in this connection that Heimdallr, the Norse god who stands at the top of Bifröst, is also, etymologically considered, the "World-judge" or "World-divider." Menzel, *Unsterblichkeitslehre*, i. 134. In Plato (Repub., 614 ff.) the judge stands at the bottom of the column.—For grotesque survivals of the Bridge of Souls in folklore, see Tylor, *Primitive Culture*, Index.

7. The diagram attempted by Windischmann, *Zoroastrische Studien*, p. 67, is inconsistent with the *Bundahish*, ch. v.9. So, must be every attempt to arrange the keshvares on a flat earth.

The Earth of the Persians

8. Darmesteter transliterates the names as follows: "The earth is divided into seven Karshvares, separated from one another by seas and mountains impassable to men. Arezahi and Savahi are the western and eastern Karshvare; Fradadhafshu and Vidadhafshu are in the south; Vourubaresti and Vourugarsti are in the north; Hvaniratha (Kvanîras) is the central Karshvare. Hvaniratha is the only Karshvare inhabited by man (*Bundahish*, xi. 3)."—Darmesteter, *The Zend-Avesta,* vol. ii., p. 123 n.

This gives a map of the northern hemisphere which in a plane polo-centric projection may be represented as on the foregoing page, the polar center of course being occupied by *Harâ-Berezaiti*. It would be a fascinating task to reinterpret the whole Avestan literature and mythology in the new light of this recovered geography and cosmology, but this would require a book of itself. It is worthy of remark that the *Vendidad* expressly calls the earth round and apparently recognizes the existence of its two far-separated poles. [9] As we have seen, its *Chinvat bridge* or beam, which is also an idea so ancient as to be found in the Avesta itself (*Farg., xix., 30, et passim*), is the axis of the world, conducting good souls by an upward "flight" into the north polar heaven of *Ahura Mazda*, but the evil by a fall "headforemost" into the south polar hell. [10] *Airyanem Vaejah* or "Old Iran" was the most natural name in the world for the Iranians to give to the traditional birthplace of their race. [11]

9. The *Avesta* (Darmesteter), i., p. 205 ; ii., pp. 143, 144. Compare Windischmann's version of the *Farvardin Yasht*, i. 3 : "die beiden Enden des Himmels." *Studien*, p. 313.

10. Apparently through the passage forced through the earth by Aharman (Ahriman). See *Zad Sparam*, ch. ii., 3, 4, 5. West, *Pahlavi Texts*, vol. i., p. 161. Also *Bundahish*, iii. 13. Rhode, *Die heilige Sage des Zendvolks*, p. 235. Windischmann's translation of *Bundahish*, ch. xxxi. (in Darmesteter numbered xxx.), seems especially to support this idea: "Ahriman und die Schlange werden durch die Kraft der Lobgesange geschlagen und hiilflos und schwach gemacht. Auf jener Briicke des Himmels, auf welcher er herbeilief, wird er in die tiefste Finsterniss zuriicklaufen. . .. Auch dies ist gesagt : Diese Erde wird rein und eben sein: ausser dem Berg Cakat-Cinvar wird ein Aufsteigen und ein Hinabtragen nicht sein." *Zoroastrische Sttidien*, p. 117. Compare Plato's "chasms" with ways leading hellward and heavenward. *Republic*, 614.

11. F. C. Cook, *Origins of Religion and Language*. London, 1884: p.187.

But all attempts to find it "on the banks of the Aras" or "in the far-off lands of the rising sun" [12] are entirely useless. Equally mistaken is the gloss which merely makes it "primitively" the mythic land where the disembodied "souls of the righteous" are assembled by Ahura Mazda. [13] The same must be said of the assertion that "the real site of the *Airan-Vej* or *Airyanem Vaejah* in its ancient and original conception is to the east of the Caspian Sea and of Lake Aral." [14] By every particular of its description, it is identified with the *Daitik* peak, with *Harâ-Berezaiti*, the polar "river" the polar "tree" and the polar "center" of the upper hemisphere. It is simply the Arctic Eden of humanity remembered as it was before the Evil One entered, and "by his witchcraft counter-created winter and the worst of plagues." [15] This being the case we need not wonder that in a paper on "The Aryan Birth-place" read in January 1884, before the Royal Society of Literature, **Mr. C. J. Stone** expressed his strong doubt of the current doctrine that the cradle of the Aryans was the upper valleys of the Oxus. [16] The cradle of the whole Aryan family will, at last, be found to be in "Airan, the Ancient" - and this in the Arctic birthplace of man.

12. Darmesteter, *The Avesta*, i., p. 3.

13. Ibid., i, p. 15.

14. Lenormant, *The Contemporary Review*, Sept. 1881 (Am. ed.), p. 41. Pietrement, *Les Aryas*, locates it just east of Lake Balkach, in lat. 45-47. Grill is so bewildered by the number of attempted identifications that he pronounces the land a purely mythical one, and denies to the name all historic or geographic reality. *Erzvater*, i. 218, 219.

15. Fargard, i. 3. The passage continues "There are (now) ten winter months there, two summer months; and those are cold for the waters, cold for the earth, and cold for the trees." This reminiscence of the oncoming of the Glacial Age at the Pole also appears in the Flood legend of the American aborigines, particularly the Lenni-Lenapi, or Delaware Indians. Rafinesque, *The American Nations*. Phila., 1836: Song III.

16. See also Dr. O. Schrader, Sprachvergleichung und Urgeschichte. *Linguistisch - historische Beiträge zur Erforschiing des indogermanischen Alterthums*. Jena, 1883. Dr. S. formerly adhered to the theory of a Mid-Asian Aryan birthland, but has been led to abandon it. Still more positive and emphatic is Karl Penka, who boldly locates the original home of the Aryans in Scandinavia. See his *Origins Ariacæ. Linguistisch-ethnologische Untersuchungen zur ältesten Geschichte der Arischen Völker und Sprachen*. Vienna, 1883. Mr. John Gibb argues in the same direction, "*The Original Home of the Aryans*" in *The British Quart*. Review, Oct., 1884.

• Sumerian, Assyrian, and Babylonian Tradition

We have here, even to the most minute details, an exact reproduction of the Aryan conception of Mount Meru, or Albordj, with its accessories. Here is the abode of the heavenly hierarchy, located on the summit of the Kharsak, or sacred mount which penetrates the heavens exactly in the region of the Pole star. - Rev. O. D. Miller.

We have already seen that the prehistoric inhabitants of the Tigro-Euphrates basin, called by some Akkadians, by others Sumerians, by yet others Akkado-Sumerians, had like other Asiatic peoples their Mountain of the World, on whose top was the celestial Paradise, and around which sun, moon, and stars revolved. Our present task is to locate this mountain more exactly and to consider its significance for our hypothesis respecting the site of Eden. That the earth, as conceived of by these ancient people, was spherical is not at the present day questioned. With their ideas probably, no archaeologist was more familiar than the late *Francois Lenormant*, and he expresses himself as follows: "*The Chaldees, says Diodorus Siculus (lib. ii., 31), have quite an opinion of their own about the shape of the earth; they imagine it to have the form of a boat turned upside down, and to be hollow underneath. This opinion remained to the last in the Chaldaean sacerdotal schools; their astronomers believed in it, and tried, according to Diodorus, to support it with scientific arguments. It is of very ancient origin, a remnant of the ideas of the purely Akkadian period*.....Let us imagine, then, a boat, turned over; not such a one as we are in the habit of seeing, but a round skiff, like those which are still used under the name of Kufa on the shores of the lower Tigris and Euphrates, and of which there are many representations in the historical sculptures of the Assyrian palaces; the sides of this round skiff bend upwards from the point of the greatest width, so that they are shaped like a hollow sphere deprived of two-thirds of its height [?], and showing a circular opening at the point of division. Such was the form of the earth according to the authors of the Akkadian magical formulae and the Chaldean astrologers of after years. We should express the same idea in the present day by comparing it to an orange of which the top had been cut off, leaving the orange upright upon the flat surface thus produced. The upper and convex surface constituted the earth properly so called, the inhabitable earth *(ki)* or terraqueous surface *(ki-a)* to which the collective name *kalama*, or the countries, is also given." [1]

It is well known that in minor details **Diodorus** is often found not altogether trustworthy. He was not a critical reporter. While, therefore, in the above quotation he has undoubtedly preserved to us one of the ancient Chaldaean similes, [2] by the use of which the true figure of the earth was taught, I can but think that the statement as to the hollowness of the earth underneath is an unauthorized inference, suggested by the hollow boat, and made by the comparatively uninstructed Greek solely upon his own responsibility. It is true that, in the same work from which the above extract is taken, **Lenormant** endeavors to adjust Akkadian cosmology to such a notion of a hollow sphere, saying "The interior concavity opening from underneath was the terrestrial abyss, *ge*, where the dead found a home (*kur-nu-de, ki-gal, aralli*). The central point in it was the nadir, or, as it was called, the root, *uru* the foundation of the whole structure of the world; this gloomy region witnessed the nocturnal journey of the sun." [3] But nothing can be more evident on examination than that this attempt involves the writer in at least three inconsistencies:

First, if the sun visits the interior of the earth at night, its proper orbit cannot be round and round the Mountain of the World to the northeast of Babylonia, as our author elsewhere represents.

Second, if *aralli,* the abode of the dead, is in the interior of the hollow earth, it cannot be to the northeast of Babylonia, as it is represented to be in the context.

Third, if the earth was conceived of as hollow, of course, its whole central portion was empty space; but according to this presentation, its central point was called the root, *uru*, the foundation of the whole structure of the world. Surely the foundation of the world can scarcely have been supposed to be mere emptiness.

1. *Chaldæan Magic, p. 150,* p. 150.

2. The figure was also used by the Egyptians, and other ancient nations. See Wilford, in *Asiatic Researches,* vol. viii., p. 274. Also articles and works on *"The Ark" and "Arkite Symbols."*

3. Ibid., p. 150. It is worthy of note that the expression "root" of the world, or "root-land" is applied to the same subterranean region of darkness in Japanese mythology. See "Shintoistn" by Griffis in McClintock and Strong's *Cyclopedia*, vol. ix., p. 688.

To a layman in these studies, this *uru* would much rather suggest the Antarctic *Tap-en-to* mountain of ancient Egyptian thought, the *Ku-Meru* of ancient India. But it is time to return to the Akkadian, or Akkado-Sumerian, a mountain of the gods. Again, we quote **Lenormant**: ***"Above the earth extended the sky (ana), spangled with its fixed stars (mul), and revolving round the Mountain of the East (Kharsak Kurra), the column which joins the heavens and the earth, and serves as an axis to the celestial vault. The culminating point in the heavens, the zenith (nuzkti), [4] was not this axis or pole; on the contrary, it was situated immediately above the country of Akkadia, which was regarded as the center of the inhabited lands, whilst the mountain which acted as a pivot to the starry heavens was to the northeast of this country. Beyond the mountain, and also to the northeast, extended the land of aralli, which was very rich in gold, and was inhabited by the gods and blessed spirits."*** [5] Here we have the "*Mountain of the East*" located, not in the east, but in the northeast. Elsewhere our author recognizes most fully the identity of this mount with the *Har-Moed* of *Isaiah xiv. 14*, and the difficulty of placing it anywhere but at the North Pole. [6] He adduces from the cuneiform texts no evidence whatever for a location to the "northeast" and seems to fix upon that direction only as a compromise of his own. "*Nous devons conclure*" (*We must conclude*) is his language.

4. Paku in the French edition.

5. Chaldæan Magic, p. 150.

6. Fragments de Bérose, pp. 392, 393.

His only reason for thinking of any other position than one due north appears to be a cuneiform expression which seems to make *Kharsak Kurra* at the same time "*the mountain of the sunrise*" [7] This, in reality, instead of being a reason for searching among the mountains to the east of Assyria or Babylonia, is, when rightly understood, precisely an additional reason for looking to the north. [8] One other statement in the extract calls for notice. The writer seems to have anticipated that his readers would inevitably locate a mountain, described as *"the column which joins the heavens and the earth, and serves as an axis to the celestial vault"* under the celestial pole; and believing that the cuneiform texts which locate the celestial pole directly over Akkad (or Akkadia), *"the center of the inhabited lands"* to be inconsistent with such a location, he introduces the remark that *"the culminating point in the heavens"* was *"not the axis or pole; on the contrary, it was situated immediately over the country of Akkadia, which was regarded as the center of the inhabited lands, whilst the mountain which acted as a pivot to the starry heavens was to the northeast of this country."*

7. The following from his latest account of the mountain will be valued: "La 'montagne des pays' est le lieu où résident les dieux. . . . Elle est située au nord, vient de nous dire Yescha' yâhoû; à l'est disent les documents cunéiformes, où l'expression accadienne *'garsag babbara* = assyriene *šad çit šamši*, 'la montagne du levant,' apparaît comme synonyme de l'accadien *'garsag kurkurra* = assyrien *šad matâti*; d'où nous devons conclure que c'est au nord-est du bassin de l'Euphrate et du Tigre qu'on la supposait placée. C'est elle qui vaut à l'orient, son nom accaclien de *mer kurra* et son nom assyrien de *šadû* signifiant tous les deux 'le point cardinal de la montagne.' Et le sens de ce terme est bien précisé par la variante accadienne mer *'garsag*, où ce mot, dont le sens 'la montagne' est incontestable, se substitue à son synonyme *kur*, dont la signification eût pu être douteuse."- *Les Origines de l'Histoire*, vol. ii., 1, p. 126.

8. See Menzel, *Die vorchristliche Unsterblichkeitslehre*, Bd. i., chapter entitled *"Der Sonnengarten am Nordpol"* pp. 87-93.

From so eminent an authority one naturally hesitates to differ; but inasmuch as **M. Joachim Menard**, in a work as recent as the one from which we have quoted while agreeing with **M. Lenormant** in making Akkad the traditional "center of the earth", differs from him in locating precisely in this central country "the mountain on whose apex the heaven of the fixed stars is pivoted," [9] we cannot avoid the conclusion that **Lenormant**'s distinction between the zenith of Akkad and the celestial pole is based upon a misapprehension, and is productive only of confusion. The solution to all difficulties is found the moment the mythological Akkad is made a circumpolar mother country, after which the Akkad of the Tigro-Euphrates valley was commemoratively named. [10] This supposition is made all the easier by three noteworthy facts: (*I*) that both the names Akkad and *Su-mir* (*Sumer compare with Su-Meru*) are not Assyrio-Babylonian, but loan - words from an older prehistoric tongue; [11] (*II*) that the etymological signification and appellatives of Akkad thoroughly identify it with the lofty country at the north polar summit of the earth; [12] and (*III*) that recently discovered tablets are compelling the Assyriologists to recognize two Akkads, one in the Tigro-Euphrates valley and one much farther to the North, though as yet none of these scholars have looked as far in that direction as to the Pole. [13]

9. ""Le pays d'Akkad est regardé, d'après les plus antiques traditions, comme le centre de la terre; c'est là que s'élève la montagne sur la cîme de laquelle pivote le ciel des étoiles fixes."- *Babylone et la Chaldée*. Paris, 1875: p. 46. ,

10. Compare the primitive name of Babylon, *Tin-tir-ki*, "Place of the Tree of life", Lenormant, *Beginnings of History*, p. 85.

11. "Il est certain que les mots Sumir et Akkad n'appartiennent pas à la langue assyro-chaldéenne. Ils sont propres à une langue antérieure; et nous savons, par les explications mêmes des Assyriens, que Akkad veut dire 'montagne.'"- *Ménant, Babylone et la Chaldée*. Paris, 1875: p. 47.

12. "Akkad is bovendien zeker een hoog land, geen lage vlakte bij de zee, zooals ook een glosse het door tilla, hoogte, verklaart." C. P. Tiele, *Is Sumer en Akkad hetzelfde als Makan en Melucha?* Amsterdam, 1883: p. 6. Compare last preceding note: Akkad = "montagne." Also Smith, *The Phonetic Values of the Cuneiform Characters*. London, 1871: p. 17.

If further proof were needed that the *Kharsak Kurra* of the earliest inhabitants of Mesopotamia was identical with the north polar World-Mountain of Egypt and the surrounding Asiatic nations, it would be found by investigating their conceptions of the region of the disembodied dead and their notion of a mountain of the rulers of the dead antipodal to the mount of the gods. The Akkadians, like the ancients generally, conceived of the realm of the dead as located to the South. Their underworld being simply the under or southern hemisphere of the earth, they could not place it in any other direction. In naming the cardinal points the Akkadians, therefore, called the South "the funereal point." [14] In this quarter was located the mount of the rulers of the dead. It was the under or south-polar projection of the earth. It corresponded with the south polar mount of demons in Hindu and in Egyptian thought. Even **Lenormant**, whose mistake in locating the mount of the gods in the East, logically leads to the mistake of locating this mount of the rulers of the dead in the West, still unconsciously gives evidence as to the true location by stating that it is" situated in the low-down portions of the earth." [15] And elsewhere he has told us that in the Akkadian language to descend and to go southward were synonymous expressions. [16] With **Professor Friedrich Delitzsch**, then, we locate the Akkadian *Kharsak Kurra* at the North. [17] Once make the primeval Akkad the equivalent of *Ilâvrita* in Hindu, or of *Kvanîras* in Iranian, mythology, all is perfectly plain and self-consistent. The primitive Akkad is now "the center of all lands" in the same sense in which *Ilâvrita* and *Kvanîras* are in their respective systems. As in both these systems, the mount of the gods is in the center of this central country, and so is *Kharsak Kurra*. *Su-Meru* and *Harâ-Berezaiti* and *Kwen-lun* are each exactly under the Pole star, having it in their zenith; the same is true of *Kharsak Kurra*. As every splendor of a divine abode crowns the top of all the former, so is the summit of *Kharsak* resplendent beyond description.

13. See Proceedings of the Society of Biblical Archeology, London, Nov.-Dec., 1881. "Mr. Pinches, in a further communication on the "Paris Tablet [in cuneiform characters, but supposed to be Cappadocian in origin], observes: The question of the original home of the Akkadians is affected thereby. ... As it seems that the country north of Assyria was also called Akkad, as well as the northern part of Babylonia, the neighborhood of Cappadocia as the home of the Akkadian race may be regarded as a very possible explanation, etc. "Brown, *Myth of Kirke*. London, 1883: p. 87. Finzi, in his *Carta del Mondo conosciuto dagli Assiri tracciata secondo le inscrizioni cuneiformi*, does not venture to locate either Akkad or Kharsak Kurra.

14. Chaldaan Magic, Eng. ed., p. 168, 169. Compare F. Finzi, *Ricerche per lo Studio del l'Antichita Assira*. Turin, 1872: p. 109 note 18.

15. "Située dans les parties basses de la terre." *Origines*, tom, ii, I, p. 134

16. The Beginnings of History, p. 313 n.4.

17. Wo lag das Paradies? p. 121.

As the sun, moon, and stars revolve around the Hindu and Iranian and Chinese mounts, so is *Kharsak* the point "on which the heaven of the fixed stars is pivoted." Moreover, from its top flows that Eden river, which, like *Ganga* and *Ardvî Sûra*, waters the whole earth. [18] Under these circumstances, the candid reader will probably be prepared to agree with the statement of ***Mr. Miller*** which we have made the motto of this chapter, and to say with ***Gerald Massey***, only with a better understanding than his, ***"The cradle of the Akkadian race was the Mountain of the World that Mount of the Congregation in the thighs of the North... The first mount of mythology was the Mount of the Seven Stars, Seven Steps, Seven Stages, and Seven Caves, which represented the celestial North as the birthplace of the initial motion and the beginning of time. This starting point in heaven above is the one original for the many copies found on the earth below. The Akkadians date from Urdhu, the district of the northern Mountain of the World."*** [19]

18. Of this celestial source Lenormant speaks as follows: ". . . et la fontaine divine Ghetim-kour-koû de la montagne des pays des Chaldéens. Cette dernière fontaine, dont le nom est accadien et veut dir 'las ource qui enveloppe la montagne sainte,' est dite 'fille de l'Océan,' marat apsi, et invoquée comme une déesse douée d'une personalité vivante, pareille a celle que revêt chez les Iraniens Ardvîçourâ-Anâhitâ. L'existence chez les Chaldéens de la croyance à un cours d'eau mythique d'où procèdent tous les fleuves de la terre semble attestée par la mention d'une rivière (dont le nom est malhcurcuscment en partie détruit sur la tablette qui contient ce reseignement) laquelle est qualifiée d'umme nâ'rï 'la mère des fleuves.'" *Origines*, tom. ii. 1, p. 133. Compare Siouffi, *La Religion des Soubbhas ou Sabéens*, Paris, 1880, p. 7 n., where the Euphrates is represented as rising in a celestial Paradise (Olmi Danhouro) under the throne of Avatha, whose throne is under the Pole star.

19. A Book of Beginnings. London, 1881: vol. ii., p. 520.

• *Egyptian Tradition*

According to the Kamite legend related by Diodorus, Osiris and Isis lived to g-ether in Nysa, or Paradise. Here there was a garden wherein the deathless dwelt. Here they lived in perfect happiness until Osiris was seized with the desire to drink the water of immortality. Then he went forth in search of it, and fell. . . But an earlier couple than Osiris and Isis were Sevekh and Ta-urt, who as the two constellations of the seven stars revolving around the Tree, or Pole, was the primeval pair in Paradise. - *The Natural Genesis.*

Th3 mythical geography of the ancient Egyptians is yet too little known to allow us to hope for much light from this quarter on the question of the site of Eden. Even their cosmology is little understood, and their scientific attainments are by many inexcusably underestimated. So good a scholar as **Mr. Villiers Stuart** could recently write, *"The Egyptians had not attained to a sufficiently advanced point in science to solve the problem of how the sun in his daily course, having sunk behind the western horizon, returned to rise at the opposite quarter of the heavens."* [1]

Nevertheless, as we desire to test our hypothesis as far as possible by all most ancient traditions and myths, whether favorable or unfavorable, we must inquire whether anything can be ascertained as to the ideas of the ancient Egyptians touching the form of the earth and the theatre of man s first history.

The leading features of Egyptian cosmology, as interpreted by the present writer, are in perfect accord with the cosmological ideas of other ancient nations as described in chapter first of the present division. They may be briefly expressed in the six following theses:

1. That in ancient Egyptian thought the earth was conceived of as a sphere, with its *axis perpendicular* and its the North Pole at the top.

2. That in the earliest time *Amenti* was conceived of neither as a cavern in the bowels of the earth, nor as a region of the earth to the West, on the same general plane as the land of Egypt, but was simply the under or southern hemisphere of the earth, conceived of as just described.

3. That the *Tat pillar* symbolized the axis of the world (heaven and earth) upright in space.

4. That *Ta nuter*, whatever its later applications, originally signified the extreme northern or topmost point of the globe, where earth and heaven were fabled to meet.

5. That *Cher-nuter* was the inferior celestial hemisphere under arching *Amenti*.

6. That *Hes* and *Nebt-ha* (Isis and Nephthys) were respectively goddesses of the North and South poles, or of the northern and southern heavens. [2]

1. Nile Gleanings. London, 1879: p. 262. This is as bad as the declaration of Lauer: *"Und so glaube ich dass auch Homer nie daran gedacht hat, wie die Sonne wieder aus dem Westen in den Osten gelange." Nachlass.* Berlin, 1851: vol. i., p. 317.

2. In a brief communication published in The *Independent*, New York, Feb. 8, 1883, the critical attention of Egyptologists was respectfully invited to these theses. Since that time much new evidence of their correctness has come to light. See, for example, the new *Thesaurus Inscriptionum* of Brugsch, pp. 176, 177, *et passim.*

Assuming now, with **Chabas, Lieblein, Lefevre,** and **Ebers**, that the earth of the ancient Egyptians, like that of the ancient Asiatic nations, was spherical, what was their conception of its northern terminus? In the chapter first of this Part, some indication has been already given. But our present investigation demands a fuller answer to this question. Turning to the great work of **Brugsch** on the "**Geographical Inscriptions of the Old - Egyptian Monuments**" we find that the Egyptians considered the farthest limit in the North to be "the four pillars or supports of heaven." [3] The fact that these four supports of heaven, instead of being situated in four opposite directions from Egypt, are all in the farthest North, is very significant. It shows that though the people might speak of heaven as supported on four pillars, it is not to be inferred therefrom that they conceived of the earth as flat, and of the sky as a flat Oriental roof one story above it. [4] **Brugsch** himself, though writing upon the supposition that the Egyptians' earth was flat, avoids this mistake. His inference, coming from one who had a traditional wrong theory to support, is most interesting and valuable. He says*, "Inasmuch as these four supports of heaven, the northern limit of the earth as known to the Egyptians, nowhere else occur as the name of people, land, or river, it seems to me most probable that we have here in the designation of a high mountain which was perhaps characterized by four peaks, or which consisted of four ranges, from which peculiarity it received its name. Like all peoples of antiquity, at least all those whose literature has come down to us, the Egyptians conceived of the earth as rising toward the North, so that at last at its northernmost point it joined the sky and supported it."* [5]

3. "Die Ansicht von den Enden der Welt ist eine uralte and vielen Völkern gemeinsame. . . . Als die äusserste Grenze im Süden galt den Egyptern das Meer (*'Sar*) and der Berg *ap-en-to* oder *tap-en-to*, wörtlich 'das Horn der Welt;' als die äusserste Grenze im Norden dagegen 'die vier Stützen des Himmels.'" *Geographische Inschriften*, Bd. ii., p. 35. Compare Taylor's Pausanias, vol. iii., 255, bot.

4. Maspero, *Les Contes Populaires de l'Egypte Andenne.* Paris, 1882: pp. Ixi.-lxiii.

5. Geographische Inschriften, Bd. ii., p. 37.

In the Buddhist conception of Meru, we have precisely the four peaked, heaven-supporting mountain which **Brugsch** here describes: "Each of the four corners of the mountain-top has a peak seven hundred yojanas high". It is not impossible that in the four dwarfs which support the dome of the modern Buddhist temple we have a far-off survival of ancient Egypt's "*four supports of heaven.*" Certainly, the Buddhist temple roofs symbolize the circumpolar heaven, [6] and a recent author, touching upon the latter s mythological support, writes as follows:

"This prop passing through the earth and the heavens at the pole, indicated as we have seen by the Alpha of Draco, became the nail of the old astronomers, the point round which all nature revolved. Between earth and the celestial pole, the prop idea was again brought forward as the central column of a huge conical mountain, Mount Meru, guarded at each cardinal point by a mighty king. The four dwarfs propping up some of the columns in the old Buddhist temples are evidently these four kings. When the prop pierced the highest heaven, it was a spire called the tee, and in Nepal, it is confessedly in all the temples the symbol of Adi Buddha, the supreme, in his heavenly garden, Nandana grove." [7]

6. Koeppen, *Die Religion das Buddhas*, ii. 262.

7. Lillie, *Buddha and Early Buddhism*, p.50.

But returning from this merely curious question, we remind ourselves that we have seen reason to believe that the ancient Egyptians conceived of the earth as a sphere, with a heaven-supporting mountain in the extreme North. In the extreme South was another mountain, *"The Horn of the World"* represented as of incredible height (eight atur or stadia). [8] This corresponds so perfectly with the earth of the Puranas, with its *Su-Meru* and *Ku-Meru*, that we are irresistibly impelled to inquire whether the parallelism extends any farther. We take the question of the direction of the abode of the dead. All agree that in Indian thought the abode of the dead is in the South. So was it in the thought of the ancient Egyptians? The recently discovered epitaph of Queen Isis-em-Kheb, mother-in-law of Shishak, king of Assyria (circa 1000 B. c.), thus reads: ***"She is seated all beautiful in her place enthroned, among the gods of the South she is crowned with flowers. She is seated in her beauty in the arms of Khonsou, her father, fulfilling his desires. He is in Amenti, the place of departed spirits."*** [9]

8. See the first quotation from Brugsch above.

9. Villiers Stuart, *The Funeral Tent of an Egyptian Queen.* London, 1882: p.34.

Again, in the mythological earth of India, the abode of the dead, being the southern or under hemisphere, is looked upon as inverted. Viewed from the standpoint of gods and men, it is bottom upward, and its inhabitants move about head downward. [10] The same is true of *Amenti,* the Egyptian underworld, and of its inhabitants. [11] Again, in Hindu thought all deadly influences proceed from the South, the abode of death; all beneficent and life-giving influences from the North. The same is true in ancient Egyptian thought." It is curious "says the English editor of ***Lenormant's Chaldean Magic***" [12] "*it is curious that in Egypt all good and healing and life proceeded from the West, the land of the setting sun, and all evil from the East the land of its rising."* The statement is "curiously" incorrect. The North is the sacred quarter, and from the North come life and blessing. The North wind is the very breath of God. It "proceeds from the nostrils of *Knum* and enlivens all creatures." [13] It is one of the high prerogatives of the blessed dead to "breathe the delicious air of the North wind." [14]

10. The gods in heaven are beheld by the inhabitants of hell as they move with their heads inverted." Garrett, *Classical Dictionary* of India: Art. "Naraka."

11. See Brugsch, *Hieroglyphischcs Demotisches Worterbuch*, S. 1331, sub v. "Set" ,"Set-mati." Also, the chapter first of the present division.

12. Undoubtedly there are Egyptian texts in which the sun-god Ra is represented as going into "the land of life" at his setting (see Brugsch, *Thesaurus Inscriptionum Ægyptiacarum*, 1ste Abth., Leipsic, 1883: p. 29), but this is made quite intelligible by Menzel's "Sonnengarten am Nordpol" in his *Vorchristliche Unsterblichkeitslehre.*

13. Records of the Past, vol. iv., p. 67.

14. Ibid., p. 3. Compare the expression, "Give the sweet breath of the North wind to the Osiris," Book of the Dead (Birch), p. 170; also 311, 312. Gerald Massey remarks, "In Egyptian the *Meh* is the North, the quarter of the waters, and the name of the cool wind that breathed new life." *The Natural Genesis*, vol. ii., p. 168. The following very curious passage from the apocryphal *Book of Adam*, translated from the Ethiopic by Dillmann, shows that this ancient Egyptian idea survived to a very late period: "Als der Herr den Adam austrieb, wollte er ihn auf der Südgrenze des Gartens nicht wohnen lassen, *weil der Nordwind, wann er darin bläset, den süssen Geruch der Bäume des Gartens nach der Südgegend hinführt;* und Adam sollte nicht die süssen Gerüche der Bäume riechen, und die Uebertretung vergessen, und sich über das was er gethan trösten, und durch den Geruch der Bäume befriedigt die Busse für die Uebertretung unterlassen. Vielmehr liess der barmherzige Gott den Adam in der Gegend westlich vom Garten wohnen." Dillmann, S. 13.

That they may breathe it is the prayer of bereaved affection. [15] The *"Fields of Peace"* are at the North of the fields of *Sanehem-u*. [16] There is the proper home of the great god of whom the Nile poet sang:

> *"There is no building that can contain him!*
> *There is no counselor in thy heart!*
> *Thy youth delight in thee, thy children;*
> *Thou directs them as King.*
> *Thy law is established in the whole land,*
> *In the presence of thy servants in the North"*

Of the same god it is said:

> *He created all works therein,*
> *All writings, all sacred words,*
> *All his implements, in the North.* [17]

Yet no texts have been discovered which represent the earliest Egyptian ideas of the origin of man and the location of his birthplace. One proof, however, that man was conceived of as having proceeded from the *"Land of the Gods"* in the North appears in connection with the myth of the reign of Ra. In Egyptian mythology, the reign of Ra was like the primeval reign of Kronos; the myth of it was a reminiscence of the sinless Golden Age. [18]

15. "Dans le papyre Boulak No. 3, 4, 16, on souhait à un défunt: 'les agréables vents du Nord dans la ÂMHÎ.'"—Brugsch, *Dictionnaire Géographique*. Leipsic, 1879: p. 37.

16. *Records of the Past*, vol. iv., p. 122.

17. Ibid., p. 101.

18. Maspero, *Histoire Ancienne des Peuples de L'Orient*, p. 38.

But in those primeval and perfect days, men still dwelt in the country of the gods, which country, as we have seen, was in the highest North. And because they still occupied the heaven-touching mountain, the rebellion by which they forfeited their estate of blessedness is expressly described as "on the mountain" [19] an object not easily found in Egypt. The same teaching is further supported by the language of certain scholars, who, without any particular theory as to the location of Eden, have held that the hieroglyph ⊕ used in Egyptian texts as the determinative prefix to names designating civilized lands, is simply a pictorial symbol of primitive Eden divided by its fourfold river. [20]

18. " Während er, der Gott der das Sein selber ist, seines Königthums waltete, da waren die Menschen und die Götter zusammen vereint." Brugsch, *Die neue Weltordnung nach Vertilgung des sündigen Menschengeschlechts*. Berlin, 1881: p. 20. Naville, The Destruction of Mankind by Râ. *Records of the Past*, vol. vi., pp. 103 *seq*.

19. Sometimes this hieroglyph is accompanied by a character signifying "God" or "divine." In such connection Brugsch renders it heilige Wohnstatte." On other renderings, however, see the *Zeitschrift für ägyptische Sprache*. 1880: p. 25. See also *Ceramic Art in Remote Ages; with Essays on the Symbols of the Circle, the Cross and Circle, the Circle and Ray Ornament, the Fylfot, and the Serpent, showing their relation to the primitive forms of Solar and Nature Worship*. By John B. Waring. London, 1874: Plates 33-37.

The expression "The Four Corners of the Earth" can be traced back to Egyptian mythology and refers to a sacred place. The Egyptian sign ('niwt') was a circle divided into four parts and it is one of the oldest known hieroglyphs, dating back to the pre-dynastic period (The hieroglyph is derived from graphic depictions of enclosure walls, which were depicted on flattened stones (pallets) found near Abydos in Upper Egypt and date from the late fourth millennium BC.

A writer in the **Edinburgh Review**, said to be **Mr. Walter Wilkins**, remarks: ***"The Buddhists and Brahmans, who together constitute nearly half the population of the world, tell us that the decussated figure of the cross, whether in a simple or complex form, symbolizes the traditional happy abode of their primeval ancestors, the Paradise of Eden toward the East, as we find it expressed in the Hebrew. And, let us ask, what better picture or more significant characters, in the complicated alphabet of symbolism, could have been selected for the purpose than a circle and a cross? the one to denote a region of absolute purity and perpetual felicity, the other those four perennial streams that divided and watered the several quarters of it."*** [21] **Mr. Wilkins** claims that in the Egyptian hieroglyph above given we have the same symbol as in the Indian Swastika. It was, therefore, primeval Paradise which was commemorated by "the sacred circular cakes of the Egyptians, composed of the richest materials, of flour, of honey, of milk, and with which the serpent and bull, as well as the other reptiles and beasts consecrated to the

211

service of Isis and their higher divinities, were daily fed, and which upon certain festivals were eaten with extraordinary ceremony by the people and their priests." He continues, ***"The cross-cake, says Sir Gardiner Wilkinson, was their hieroglyph for civilized land/ obviously a land superior to their own, as it was, indeed, to all mundane territories; for it was that distant, traditional country of sempiternal contentment and repose, of exquisite delight arid serenity, where Nature, unassisted by man, produces all that is necessary for his sustentation."***

"Seal"(sharalica) made of linden wood from the 19th century. Popularly known as "poskurnik", it was used for coloring the Slavic cake and for cult bread. It is part of the collection of objects with customs (cult objects) of the National Museum in Leskovac.

Now compare this Egyptian ceremonial cross-cake with our "Celebration cake" or "Slavic Cake", which is still a traditional Serbian and Slavic cake that is made during celebrations and holidays. It is a symbol of hospitality and respect for the guest. It is customary for the housewife to bake a cake, which is then consecrated by the priest, poured with red wine, and broken into pieces for each member of the family present before lunch. It is a symbol of the body of Jesus Christ, and the wine with which the cake is poured represents his blood. That is why in the middle of the cake, as well as in four places along the edge, there is a seal with the letters *ИС ХС НИ КА* (Cyrillic), which is the Greek abbreviation meaning "*Jesus Christ wins*". Although this cake has an ancient tradition, today it is celebrated in the Christian spirit, but the term *NIKA* is also an ancient code itself, as well as the Latin code *I.N.R.I.*, and they will be demystified in the next volume when we talk about the *"Polar Christianity"*. Compare also the map of the Garden of Eden before the Flood from the 18th century and the coat of arms of Serbia that is still used today.

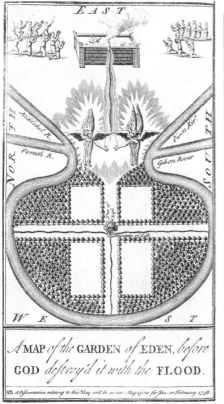 

Pic1: Map of the Garden of Eden before God destroy'd it with the Flood, 18th-century diagram showing the supposed layout of the Garden of Eden. The description in the Bible tells of a garden in a region called Eden with four rivers, an east-facing entrance, and the Tree of Knowledge of Good and Evil at the center. Once Adam and Eve had been expelled from the garden for eating the fruit of the tree, the entrance was guarded by cherubim and an Omni-directional flaming sword. This engraving first appeared in the Gentleman's Magazine in 1737. Pic.2. The coat of arms of Serbia with the four ocillas (ognjila), Hristofor Žefarović from Stematography 1741.

The symbol is known as Niwt (pronounced "nee-oot"), as a hieroglyph in Egypt

"This," says **Donnelly**, though arguing in favor of a mid-Atlantic island-Eden, *"this was the Garden of Eden of our race. ... In the midst of it was a sacred and glorious eminence, the Umbilicus Orbis Terrarium - toward which the heathen in all parts of the world, and in all ages, turned a wistful gaze in every act of devotion, and to which they hoped to be admitted, or rather to be restored, at the close of this transitory scene."* [22] Finally, if, as **Plato** *(Πλάτων)* represents, the story of lost Atlantis was received from Egypt and constituted a part of the priestly teaching of the dwellers upon the Nile, our next chapter will present us further evidence that the Eden and the antediluvian world of ancient Egyptian tradition were precisely where the tradition of other ancient peoples placed them, to wit, in the land of sacred memories in the far-off, faerie North.

21. The Pre-Christian Cross. *Edinburgh Review*, January 1870, p. 254. Zockler did not think the primitive character of this symbolism well established (*The Cross of Christ*, p. 35); but the moment Eden is identified with the "middle country" of the Pole the naturalness and primitiveness of the symbol become most easy of belief.

22. Donnelly, *Atlantis,* p. 322.

- *Hellenic tradition*

In the Centre of the Sea is the White Isle of great Zeus, There is Mount Ida, and our race's Cradle. *- Aeneas*

Respecting the origin of men there were among Greek writers, as ***Preller*** states, "very different opinions." Part of this diversity he ascribes to a difference in the natural environment of the first inhabitants: some, residing in the woody hills, would naturally think the first men came from these; others, inhabiting a valley, would more naturally think of their ancestors as having come out of the water. The Asiatic-Greek belief that the first of the human race were made out of trees he calls "quite peculiar." [1] What if it should be found that all these notions were merely fragments of old, old faith, according to which man originated on the mountain of all mountains, by the source of all waters, and under the tree of all trees!

1. Griechische Mythologie, i., pp. 56, 57.

However this may be, it is certainly very interesting to note that in the Greek myth of *Meropia*, or *Meropis*, ***Renan, Lenormant***, and others recognize the old Asiatic Meru. They hold that "the sacred expression *"Μεροπίς άνθρώποι"* originally meant the men sprung from Meru." [2] ***Stephanus*** has the same rendering in his ***"Thesaurus."*** In an advanced chapter of his ***"Origines de 1'Histoire"***, ***Lenormant*** expressed himself on this point as follows: ***"I have stated above, in agreement with M. Renan, that the sacred expression Μεροπες, as used among the Greeks to designate mankind, could not have originally been applied to them on account of their possessing the gift of articulate speech, as is pretended in the etymology of grammarians of late date, but as having proceeded from Meru."*** Such an explanation, the consequence of which is to carry back this name of the sacred mountain, the abode of the gods and the birth-place of mankind, to the most ancient period of Aryan unity, is corroborated, in a manner to my mind quite decisive, by the existence of myths which make the *Meropes* be a special and autochthonic population, of a date far back in the most ancient times, who lead a life of innocence and happiness, marked by extraordinary longevity (a feature in common with the Indian legends concerning *Uttara-Kuru*), under the government of a king, *Merops*, who is sometimes represented as preserving them from the Deluge in the same way as the Yima of the Iranians and assembling them around him to shelter them from the Flood, from which they alone escape. Meropis *(Μεροπις)* is today considered a fictitious island, mentioned by the ancient Greek writer ***Theopompus of Chios*** *(Θεόπομπος, c. 380 BC – c. 315 BC))* in his work ***Philippica***, which is only fragmentarily preserved through ***Aelian*** *(Κλαύδιος Αἰλιανός, c. 175 – c. 235 AD, Fragments see FGrHist 115 F 75).*

2. Lenormant, *Origines*, ii. i, p. 56.

This myth is usually localized on the island of Kos, which receives the name of *Meropeis*, *Meropis*, or *Merope*. But the island of Siphnos is also reputed to have been called *Meropia* in virtue of a similar tradition, and ***Strabo*** *(Στράβων)* speaks of a fabulous region of the name of Meropis, which was described by ***Theopompus*** *(Θεόπομπος)*, and which seems to have been placed near the country of the Hyperboreans. *Merops* is also given as a king of the Ethiopians; the most pious and most virtuous of men, the husband of Klymene the mother of Phaethon, and consequently anterior to the catastrophe of the conflagration of the universe, by which the first human race, that of the Golden Age, is often said to have been destroyed. Or else the same name is given to a prophet king of Rhyndakos, in Mysia, who also receives the very significant appellation of Makar, or Makareus, the happy. All this shows that the paradisaic myth of the *Meropes* was not peculiar to the island of Kos, but was current elsewhere in the Greek world, and had undergone more than one localization there." [3]

Plato's story of lost Atlantis, the island which the ocean-god Poseidon prepared for his son Atlas to rule over, is a fascinating picture of the ante diluvian world. Whether originating in Egypt, as claimed by ***Plato***, [4] or inherited as a part of the legendary wealth of the Hellenes, it is of special interest to us in the present discussion; and this for three reasons:

> First, we have elsewhere shown that in the oldest Greek thought Atlas belongs at the North Pole, and it is only reasonable to locate the kingdom of Atlas in the same locality.

Secondly, some authorities have unconsciously placed Atlantis in just this polar position by identifying its inhabitants as the "Hyperboreans." [5]

Thirdly, **Apollodorus** and **Theopompus** expressly call the lost land Meropia, and its inhabitants Meropes; i. e., according to the above authorities, "*issued from Meru*." [6]

3. Lüken, *Die Traditionen des Menschengeschlechtes*, p. 73. Bryant, *Analysis of Ancient Mythology*, vol. v., p. 157: "Pindar manifestly makes them [the Hyperboreans] the same as the Atlantians."

4. "It was a common practice with the Greeks to disguise their own ignorance of the purport of a foreign word by supplying a word of a similar sound and inventing a story to agree with it: thus Meru, or the North Pole, the supposed abode of the Devatas, being considered as the birth-place of the god, gave rise to the fable that Bacchus s second birth was from the thigh of Jupiter, because Meros, a Greek word approaching Meru in sound, signifies thigh in that language." J. D. Paterson, *"Origin of the Hindu Religion"* in *Asiatic Researches*. London, 1808: vol. viii., p. 51.

5. Reference is had to M. le Marquis de Nadaillac, who, being himself uncertain, says, "Que l'Atlantide ait été située vers le Nord, que ses limites aient été reculées vers le Sud, il est difficile de rien préciser et tous les hypothèses sont permises." *L'Amérique Préhistorique.* p. 186 Paris, 1883: p. 566. See Unger, *Die versunkene Insel Atlantis*. Vienna, 1860. Donnelly, *Atlantis: the Antediluvian World*. New York, 1882. A "conjectural map" is given in Bory de Saint Vincent, *l'Homme, Essai Zoölogique sur le genre humain*. The *Última Teoría sobre la Atlántida*, by D. Pedro de Novo y Colson, appended to the author's *Viajes Apócrifos de Juan de Fuca*, Madrid, 1881, pp. 191-223, has no independent value, being based on the *Studies* of M. Gaffarel. An extended essay by E. F. Berlioux, is entitled "Les Atlantes: Histoire de l'Atlantis et de l'Atlas primitif," appearing in the just issued *Annuaire de la Faculté de Lyon*. Paris, 1884, Première Année, Fasc. i., pp. 1-170.

The fabled country further resembles Eden in the difficulties that scholarship of every kind has found in giving it a location in harmony with all the data. These difficulties are so great that some learned writers have located it as far to the West as America, others as far to the East as in the Sea of Azof, or in Persia. Even of those who have sought a place for it in the mid-Atlantic, some have pushed it up and some down, until one of the latest writers says, "All hypotheses are permissible." [7]

6. "Ararat and Eden. *"The Contemporary Review*, Sept. 1881, Am. ed., p. 44. Compare Bryant, Analysis of Ancient Mythology. London, 1807 vol. v., pp. 75-92. Also, Samuel Beal: "It can hardly be questioned that the Buddhist cosmic arrangement is allied with Greek tradition as embodied in Homer." *Buddhist Literature* in China. London, 1882: p. xv.

7. "But, O Socrates, you can easily invent Egyptians or anything else!" Phaedrus, 275 B.

His illustrious countryman, **Monsieur J. S. Bailly**, a century ago, came nearer the truth, when, in view of the perplexities attending all other locations, he correctly placed his lost Atlantis in the Paleo-Arctic Ocean. Again, the antediluvian world was, of course, in the vicinity of lost Eden. But it is to be observed that in Hellenic tradition Deukalion is not a Greek, but an inhabitant of a country in the high North, a Scythian. Moreover, the Scythians, as we know from **Justin** *(Latin: Marcus Junianus Justinus Frontinus; c. second century)*, were considered a very much more ancient people than the Greeks; indeed, as the very oldest in the world. [8] Moreover, Scythia, like polar *Meru* and *Harâ-Berezaiti,* was conceived of as a lofty region from which all the rivers of the earth descend. [9]

8. "Scytharum gentem semper habitam fuisse antiquissimam."

9. The geographical indications of the great epic poem of the Mahabharata represent Meru rather as a vast and highly elevated region than as a distinct mountain, and make it supplies all the rivers of the world with water. This system is pretty much in conformity with that which Justin has borrowed from Trogus Pompeius, and according to which Scythia, the country of the most ancient of mankind, without having, properly speaking, any mountains, is higher than the rest of the earth in such a way as to be the starting point of all the rivers, *editiorem omnibus terris esse, ut cuncta flumina ibi nata*." Lenormant, *The Contemporary Review* Sept. 1881 (Am, cd.), p. 40.

All of which obviously connects the antediluvian *Deukalion* with the primitive country at the Arctic summit of the globe. Finally, in the Greek tradition, the first men lived under the beneficent rule of Kronos, father of Zeus, enjoying the blessedness of the Golden Age. But it is clear from Strabo and others that the seat of the Kronos kingdom was in the farthest North. [10] **Menzel** begins his chapter on *"The Isles of Kronos"* with these words: ***"The oldest of the Greek gods, Kronos, we must conceive of as enthroned at the North Pole."*** [11]

10. Pherecydes describes Kronos as dwelling in that part of heaven which is "nearest the earth" . i.e. the northern. Strabo, vii., 143, places him in "the home of Boreas." It agrees herewith that Sanchoniathon, as preserved in the Greek version by Philo of Byblos, places the seat of his power "in the middle of the lands" ... in "a place near springs and rivers, where henceforth the worship of heaven was established." Lenormant, *Beginnings of History*, p. 531.

11. Unsterblichkeitslehre, i., p. 93.

The Pelasgians are generally known to be the oldest ancient inhabitants of present-day Greece. For the Pelasgians, the ancient geographer **Strabo** *(Στράβων, 64 or 63 BC – c. 24 AD),* says: **"As for the Pelasgians, all the evidence points to there being an ancient people, who were spread throughout the territory of Hellas, especially among the Aetolians in Thessaly."** It is very likely that they never called themselves by that name, but that it is a pure Greek translation for the people who live by the sea or seafarers, that is, in a literal translation: *Πελασγός, Pelasgós* would mean – *Pomeranians* or *Pomorians (Поморјани,* people who live by the sea) in Slavic languages. Most likely, they are the mysterious Sea People, whom historical science has not yet fully illuminated them. **Ernst Klain** argued that the Ancient Greek word for "sea", *pelasgós*, and the Doric word *plagos* "side" (meaning plain) share the same root, *plāk-,* and that *pelag-skoi* would therefore be translated as *"Sea People",* where the sea is flat / sea plain / sea desert. This could relate to the maritime *marauders* called as "Sea People", in the Egyptian chronicles which until today represent a kind of unsolved mystery. The origin of the so-called Sea Peoples is undocumented. The Aegean or the White Sea (*Belo More, Бело Море*) was called by the Greeks *Αγαίως Πέλαγος:* "*Egéo Pélagos*" which means the Aegean Sea, but the word *pelagos* means "sea" and not "white" as many today try to derive and equate the word "*Pelasgians*" with "*Belazgians*" (white people, from the word *belo / бело).* This is clearly seen in the word archipelago or the area with a group of islands in a given body of water that is considered a physio-geographical unit. The term comes from the ancient Greek words *ἄρχι-,* "primary" and *πέλαγος* "sea"). The German Orientalist **Müller, Wilhelm Max** made this statement: **"In Egyptian history, there is hardly a problem of such great interest as the invasion of Egypt by the Mediterranean peoples, the facts of which are connected with the most important questions of ethnography and the** *primitive history of classical peoples."* - *(1888). "Notes on the "peoples of the sea" of Merenptah"*, on p. 147–154 and 287–289. However, we also see on old medieval maps that Peloponnese (Πελοποννησος) was also called Morea. The Moravian Despotism got this name after the medieval name for the Peloponnese which was called Morea [12], where supposedly according to folk etymology, the name was given by the crusaders because that area was overgrown with mulberry (Greek: Μωρέας or Μωριάς) which was used in the production of silk which then it was blooming. However, since the Slavic peoples also lived here, the possible etymology, as in the case of the Morlacs, has roots from the sea (*more, mare, море*). This etymology was even advocated by the Tyrolean (German) traveler, journalist, politician, and historian *Jakob Philipp Fallmerayer*. It should also be said that the ancient city of Pella (Πέλλα) the Macedonians was a port city connected to the Gulf of Thessaloniki by a navigable bay, but the port in the meantime became mud and since then the place no longer had access to the sea.

12. See Max Vasmer, Die Slaven in Griechenland, Verlag der Akademie der Wissenschaften, Berlin 1941). Also, in 1830: Geschichte der Halbinsel Morea während des Mittelalters. Teil 1: Untergang der peloponnesischen Hellenen und Wiederbevölkerung des leeren Bodens durch slavische Volksstämme (History of the Morea Peninsula in the Middle Ages. First part: the decline of the Peloponnesian Hellenes and the repopulation of the empty land by the Slavic peoples) Stuttgart)., 1835: Welchen Einfluß hatte die Besetzung Griechenland durch die Slaven auf das Schicksal der Stadt Athen und der Landschaft Attika? Oder nähere Begründung der im ersten Bande der Geschichte der Halbinsel Morea während des Mittelalters aufgestellten Lehre über die Enstehung der heutigen Griechen (What influence did the occupation of Greece by the Slavs have on the fate of the city of Athens and the countryside of Attika? Or, a more detailed explanation of the theory of the origin of today's Greeks, proposed in the first volume of the History of the Morea Peninsula in the Middle Ages.) (Stuttgart).

This very likely assumption becomes even more fascinating if we take into account of the fact that the Berbers of North Africa who themselves have many anthropological characteristics from the Indo-Europeans (corresponding to the Greek expression *Barbarians, βαρβαρος*, where the Pelasgians are also called Barbarians) also use the name *Mauri* (Seafarers), where the names of countries such as Morocco, Mauritania, and finally Mauritius are subsequently built from here, where we also find pyramidal structures similar to those of the Canary Islands, which are slightly and are known to the public today, and I will even venture to compare them even with the Maors of New Zealand, especially with their higher Ariki caste, of which we have already spoken. The Moors (Μαῦροι) by **Strabo (Στράβων),** who wrote in the early 1st century, as a native name, was also adopted into Latin, while he gives the Greek name for the same people as the Maurusi (Μαυρύσιοι).[13] The very name Mauri as a tribal confederation or generic ethnic designation seems to roughly correspond to the people known as Numidians in earlier ethnography; both terms are assumed to group early Berber-speaking populations (the earliest Tifinagh epigraph dates from about the third century BCE). The Berbers are Moors who are cited in the Chronicle of 754 during the Umayyad conquest of Hispania, and Moors became, from the 11th century, the catch-all term "Moors" (Spanish: *Moros*) in the documents of the Christian Iberian kingdoms referring to the Andalusians, North Africans, and Muslims. Naturally, over the centuries, there was a huge mix-up with the Ethiopians, that is, the Nubians, and already in the Middle Ages, until today, it seems that we can only see them as an ancient component of the Pelasgians. Of course, we can see the ancient Berbers as an Atlantic continuum that culturally influenced the creation of the Egyptian civilization, and by the way, here in North Africa, in the Maghreb region **[14],** we also find the Atlas mountain, which represents a toponym that seems to have been transferred from before - the subjugated homeland.

13. οἰκοῦσι δ᾽ ἐνταῦθα Μαυρούσιοι μὲν ὑπὸ τῶν Ἑλλήνων λεγομενοι, Μαῦροι δ᾽ ὑπὸ τῶν Ῥωμαίων καὶ τῶν ἐπιχωρίων "Here dwells the people called by the Greeks Maurusii, and by the Romans and the natives Mauri" Strabo, Geographica 17.3.2. Lewis and Short, Latin Dictionary, 1879 s.v. "Mauri.

14. The Maghreb (*al-Maġrib al-ʿArabī,* "western" is an area in Africa north of the Sahara and west of the Nile. From a geopolitical point of view, the area includes Morocco, Western Sahara, Algeria, Tunisia, sometimes Libya, and less commonly Mauritania. The Arab Maghreb Union contains all these states except for Western Sahara, due to its political status - for the Arab countries it is still a Moroccan province, and for others, it is temporarily occupied by Morocco. The local Arab-Berber population of the region has been referred to in Europe in the past as Moors. The Atlas is a mountainous region in northwestern Africa, located between the Atlantic Ocean and the Mediterranean Sea, and the Sahara Desert. It stretches across the states of Morocco, Algeria, and Tunisia. It is about 2,500 km long and 250 to 300 km wide. The highest peaks reach over 4,000 m. The Atlas Mountains are poor in water. The climate near the Atlantic Ocean and the

Mediterranean Sea in the lower parts is the Mediterranean, in the higher parts it is steppe, and on the southern side of the mountain, it is desert. The population is distributed in the coastal areas.

We have now interrogated not only natural and ethnological science but also the history, traditions, and myths of the eldest nations of the world. Nowhere have we found our hypothesis inadmissible; everywhere has it found remarkable confirmatory evidence. The aggregate of this evidence coming from such unexpected and entirely different sources is very great. It is so convincing that an advocate might well be content to leave the argument at this point, at least until some advocate of a different location shall have made out a better case than anyone has yet done.

All that is beautiful and rare seems to come from the North. *- Herodotus*

Chapter V
Aurora Borealis

उदु श्रिय उषसो रोचमाना अस्थुरपां नोर्मयो रुशन्तः |
कर्णोति विश्वा सुपथा सुगान्यभूदु वस्वी दक्षिणामघोनी ||

udu śriya uṣaso rocamānā asthurapāṃ normayo ruśantaḥ |
kṛṇoti viśvā supathā sughānyabhūdu vasvī dakṣiṇāmaghonī ||

The radiant Dawns have risen up for glory, in their white splendor like the waves of waters. She maketh paths all easy, fair to travel, and, rich, hath shown herself benign and friendly. We see that thou art good: far shines thy luster; thy beams, thy splendors have flown up to heaven. -
Rig Veda, Book VI, Hymn 64, Verses 1-2

The Aurora Borealis is a natural phenomenon that illuminates the northern hemisphere during the equinoxes, a magical effect of nature that has left no one indifferent. This northern light is named in honor of the Roman goddess of dawn - Aurora and of course the Hellenic name for the northern polar region *Borealis* or the god of the north wind - Βορέας, *Borei*. This imposing sight, where the magic color overflows and where the beautiful space colors are mixed with a greenish-purple glow, always caused a feeling of admiration and joy, where the ancient peoples experienced this phenomenon as the "*Dance of the Valkyries*", i.e. the Scandinavian fairies. The aurora near the magnetic field can be seen high above Earth, but seen from a greater distance, it illuminates the northern horizon with a greenish glow or sometimes a pale red color, making it appear as if the Sun is rising from an unusual direction. This light usually occurs during the equinoxes. It has been given many names throughout history. In Europe, during the Middle Ages, the Aurora Borealis was believed to be a sign from God. Its southern counterpart, the Aurora Australis (or southern light), has similar properties and is visible in the southern latitudes of Antarctica, South America, and Australia. This celestial glory and *leitmotif* of the Aryan myths will be the starting point for our further investigation. Most often, the term Aurora Borealis, that is, the northern light, refers to the amazing light that is usually observed at night and that occurs in the ionosphere. However, if we begin to research and analyze *Zorya*, the goddess of the dawn in Slavic mythology and folklore, we quickly come to the conclusion that this personified deity was conceived and experienced by our ancestors as the female creative energy of nature that also has a triple form. It turns out that the Dawn can be seen during the sunrise in the morning, the sunset in the twilight period, and also she can be nocturnal when it is absolute darkness of the pole. Many legends are explained in this way, to the extent that the dawn seems to represent everything to that Indo-European people. According to **Muir** [1], these hymns are among the most beautiful, if not the most beautiful; and the deity addressed by *Macdonell* is regarded as the most beautiful work of Vedic poetry, as in all other religious literature no more charming personage is found than the Dawn.

1. Muir: *Original Sanskrit Texts*, tom V, p. 181, Macdonell, *Vedic Mythology*, p. 46.

The Hindu goddess is also described as ore in red dawn shining from afar with "red rays of light", or she who "harnesses the red cows" as in the **Sama-Veda**. Dawn is "golden-colored" *(híraṇya-varṇā)* in the **Rig-Veda**, "golden-yellow" *(flāua)* in **Ovid's Amores**, and "golden-throned" *(khrysóthronos; χρυσόθρονος)* in the Homeric formula. In Latvian folk songs, Saule and her daughter are dressed in shawls woven with golden thread, and Saule wears golden sandals, which parallels the description of **Sapphō** *(Σαπφώ)* who depicts the dawn as wearing "golden sandals" *(khrysopédillos; χρυσοπέδιλλος)*. So much poetry and hymns are inspired by the dawn that really sometimes the question arises: can such a short phenomenon that happens every morning really leave such a strong impression on the soul of poets?

Dragoš Kalajic *(Драгош Калајић Belgrade, 1943 - 2005)* Serbian traditionalist, painter, journalist, and writer, in the introduction to the Serbian edition of Tilak's masterpiece **"The Arctic Home in the Vedas"** (1903), noted the following:

"We hope that the appearance of the Serbian-Croatian translation of the main work of B.G. Tilak will encourage the native, ethnologists to re-examine our national treasures of the traditions of our paganism in the light of the "Arctic theory". But from a doctrinal point of view, the contents of that treasury are not of first-class quality because the tradition in question is maintained in the domain of the third function, with appropriate censorship or misunderstandings and distortions. Unfortunately, we do not have a Slavic and Illyrian tradition that comes directly from the workshops of the first and second functions: it was lost under the blows of baptisms, war, genocide, and centuries of slavery. Finally, it was not fortunate that an inspired erudite, like Snorri Sturluson, could be born who could preserve such an eminent and reliable tradition. Despite the revealed shortcomings, the national treasures of the tradition contain an extraordinary wealth of themes and figures of Indo-European culture, as already noted by many researchers, from the golden and unsurpassed era of our ethnology, from Natko Nodilo to Čajkanović. In the Indo-European treasury of values, Serbian and Croatian folk traditions are distinguished by the dominance of the theme of the persistent and universal struggle between the forces of light and the forces of darkness. From a naturalistic point of view, the dominance and drama of the content of this theme cannot be satisfactorily explained by theories of dawn or theories of spring. The numerous folk expressions of the persistent and eager anticipation of the Dawn - which is often late, seized by the forces and princes of darkness and long-term imprisoned in the "underground" - do not correspond to the experiences of the solar cycles of the Balkan or Central Asian latitudes. For example, in the Croatian legend of the abduction and rescue of Dawn, the three-headed lord of the underworld kidnapped Dawn, and "Dawn has not yet dawned; people were sitting in the dark and cold, not doing their work, and Zorya was equally opposed to the Black God (Slavic: Cernobog, Celtic: Cerunus), not wanting to become his bride". "The solar hero-liberator, Svanimir [2], is in the world of darkness (tamnica, the dungeon), "The dawn is pale and faded, sunk in a heavy sleep."

2. In *Traditions of the Slavic Peoples* (selection and translation by Miroslav Smiljanić-Spasić), Belgrade, 1964.

We believe that there is no doubt that such and numerous similar dramas from the South Slavic traditions can only be brought with naturalistic optics to the experiences of the arctic conditions of life that are waited for months and where the dawn lasts for weeks. And the description of the city of *Svitogor*, to which the solar hero *Svanimir* returns victorious, contains, perhaps, the ancient memory of the Arctic or Hyperborean "eternal light": it is a city ***"that knows no night because it is governed by eternal light."***

Tilak's "Arctic" illumination of the ***Taittiriya Samhita*** period, which describes the circling of thirty forms of the Dawn around the polar horizon, evokes the Serbian personification of the Dawn, from the epic poem ***Marriage of Todor of Stalac*** *(Женидба Тодора од Сталаћа),* who ***"embroidered with gold everything on the pure silk"*** among the ***"thirty" girls"*** who ***"bleach white cloth"***. [3]

In these paintings and scenes, it is also clear that the fine and long-lasting "golden" embroidery and the persistent bleaching of the white cloth symbolize the very long dawns. Such long and precious dawn for the human eye can only be seen in the polar and circumpolar regions. We also find these thirty crystallizations of the dawn in the Bosnian poem about the fight of two solar heroes; "***With two green swords forged by one blacksmith***", "against *Leđanin Ban* and "*leđanskih crnih Laćmana*". [4] One of the two heroes previously fought against *Ledjanin Ban*: That Ledjanin Ban "*twelve times went out on the megdan (duel) - killed twelve captains*", "and" *the thirteenth Zdrinic*". One of the two heroes had previously fought against *Ledjanin Ban*: "*Seven times he went out on the megdan (duel) - sve na njemu mejdan ostanuo*". The battle is fought on "*Mount Vrtnik*", where thirty fires are burning.

3. Vuk Stefanović Karadžić, II, 82.

4. Jukić and Martić, I, 19

In the inspired exegesis of this poem, ***Natko Nodilo*** correctly noted that the death of the twelve captains and the thirteenth Zdrinič symbolized the annual decay of the visionaries and solar gods from winter, having correctly determined that the seven-time appearance on the battlefield of one solar hero marks the cycle of "advanced and beneficial months" in the year, although this cycle can also be marked by those months on the polar "day". However, his claim that Vrtnik mountain itself symbolizes the winter short day "joined by its thirty days in January" does not seem convincing at all, because in view of the December position on the Winter Solstice, the such association should be numerous to cover January. However, a such association has no confirmation in narrow or broad Indo-European tradition. Therefore, we should no longer be inclined to interpret the Vrtnik mountain and its "*thirty hearths*" or fireplaces in the light of the "Arctic theory" of Tilak, where the Vrtnik mountain (like Meru) is a sacred mountain, sanctified by the memory of the Arctic sacred space of the ancient homeland. sisters at dawn from the ancient scripture ***Taittiriya Samhita***. Otherwise, in the masterpiece of our Indo-European studies, in the ***Ancient Faith of the Serbs and Croats*** *(Stara Vjera Srba i Hrvata)*, ***Natko Nodilo*** successfully presented numerous links between the Vedic twins *Ashvins*, the Hellenic *Dioscuri* and the brothers from the Slavic mythology Pojezda and Prijezda, as analogies or isomorphic of their struggle against the sovereigns of darkness, the struggle for the light and liberation of *Zorya* (personification of the Dawn). However, ***Nodilo*** failed to convincingly explain the numerous folklore testimonies for the long-term captivity of the solar hero "down under", where there is "no Sun, no Moon, no white tribute, no hero", [5] and which sometimes lasts twelve months, and sometimes four years old. Namely, ***Nodilo***, lacking "Arctic" intuition, could only assume that those twelve months of darkness were twelve hours of the night and "if the knight's brother died in the 'fourth year with that, I guess, it was said that they go dark in the fourth hour of the day.

Under the light of the "Arctic theory", these numerous accounts of the months-long or long-term darkening of the South Slavic *Dioscuri* and *Zora* and her companions in the world of underground darkness (southern hemisphere) rather testify to the persistent memory of living conditions in the polar or near-polar homeland of the Indo-Europeans, therefore also the Slavs. Perhaps also frequent images of "glass hills"(which bring misfortune) those "petrified kingdoms", which folk tradition gives us, also preserve the memory of the catastrophic glaciation of the primordial homeland. Perhaps the stronghold of the struggle of the Serbian *Dioscuri* or *Ashvins, Pojezda and Prijezda*, "*Nebojša kula*" and "*Stojni Biograd*" (Belgrade – The White City) belong to the order of Indo-European fortresses, the last defenses against darkness and winter, which extend from Scandinavian via Iranian to Vedic traditions. Some of the numerous, possible, fruitful questions that ***Tilak's*** work provokes, open extraordinary cognitive perspectives toward the truths beyond the circle of emergence and disappearance. [6]

5. Vuk Stefanović Karadžić, II, 95.

6. Dragoš Kalajić, *Arkticka Pradomovina Veda*, Beograd, 1987. *Post scriptum, za domaće etnologe,* p.16-17

The dawn spoken of here is not the single-day dawn which we may observe in the tropics or the temperate zone, or, in other words, the day's victory of light over darkness, which is believed to have filled the spirit of the ancient bards with such awe that an extraordinary variety of myths.

Ushas or the Vedic dawn goddess is described in the hymns of the **Rig-Veda** with extraordinary stylistic richness, and what is more important for us, the physical form of the deity in the hymns is not in the least obscured by description and personification. Here, then, we have a good opportunity to prove the validity of our theory by showing, as far as possible, that the earliest description of the dawn is of a truly polar character. *A priori*, it does not seem likely that the Vedic poets could thus marvel at the short dawns of tropical or temperate zones, or that the delay of dawn could cause such uneasiness simply because the Vedic bards had neither electric lighting nor candles to light during the short night of fewer than twenty-four hours. But the hymns of the dawn have not been examined from that point of view. All the interpreters of the Vedas whether Eastern or Western, tacitly believed that the *Ushas* of the Rig-Veda could only be the dawns that we know in the tropical and temperate zones. It is quite natural that a ***Yāska*** or a ***Sâyana*** should think so, but even Western scholars have adopted this view, probably under the influence of the theory of the Central Asian origin of the Aryans. Hence several expressions which might have stimulated an inquiry into the physical or astronomical character of the Vedic dawn were either unknown or omitted from the

Vedic hymns to the misinterpretation of scholars who would have been able to throw more light on the subject had they not been influenced by arctic theory. We are essentially interested in such places, and we shall now see that, if we interpret them in common sense, they fully establish the polar nature of the Vedic dawn.

Canon Taylor, in his ***Origin of the Aryans*** *(1890),* summarizes the work done in recent years in this respect. *"It is,"* he says, *"a singularly destructive work,"* and he concludes his book by noting that ***"the tyranny of the Sanskritologist is now fortunately overcome, and it is proved that the immediate performance of philology must be systematically checked by the conclusions of prehistoric archaeology, anthropology, geology, and common sense".*** If it were not for this observation, it would be concluded that his book unnecessarily devalues the works of mythologists and philologists of the comparative method. In all fields of knowledge, old conclusions must always be called into question by new discoveries, but this is no reason to blame those who acted previously on the basis of insufficient data. Apart from this issue, one more important thing remains to be done. The discovery of the Vedic literature has given a new impetus to the study of myths and legends, but even the Vedas, which are admitted to represent the oldest documents of the Indo-Europeans, have hitherto been imperfectly understood. They became unintelligible as early as the age of the Brahmanas, several centuries before our era, and had it not been for the works of Indian grammarians, they would have remained hermetic books to this day. However, it is true that Western scholars have to some extent adopted Indian methods of interpretation and developed them with the help of facts illuminated through comparative methods. But no etymological or philological analysis can help us fully understand places that contain concepts and feelings alien to our universe. This is one of the main difficulties in the interpretation of the Vedas. Naturalistic theories can help us understand certain legends of that ancient collection. But it also contains passages which, in spite of their apparent simplicity, are entirely unintelligible on the basis of these theories, and in such cases, Indian scholars, such as *Sâyana* of the 14th century, are either content with a simple description of the terms, or they resort to distorting the texts in order to put those places into a framework that is understandable to them, and some Western scholars even go so far as to believe that these texts are inaccurate or forged. However, in both cases, there is no doubt that the Vedic texts are even more incomprehensible and therefore untranslatable.

Prof. Max Müller was fully aware of these difficulties; "The translation of the *Rig-Veda*," he notes in his introduction to the translation of the Vedic hymns, "*will be the task of the next century*" of scholars. But if the scientific discoveries of the last century have revived human history and culture in ancient times, it can be expected that they will provide a new key to the interpretation of the myths and Vedic passages believed to be the oldest beliefs of the Indo-Europeans. If man existed before the Ice Age and witnessed the tremendous changes brought about by glaciation, it is not absurd to suppose that in the oldest beliefs and chronicles of mankind there is some allusion, however hidden and remote, to these events.

The seventh chapter of the *Rig Veda* contains several hymns dedicated to the dawn. In one of them, the poet, having established earlier in the first two stanzas that the dawn raised its flag on the horizon with its usual brightness, explicitly says (third stanza) that between the first appearance of the dawn on the horizon and the birth of the Sun, a period of several days follows. Since this verse [7] is of great importance to our study, I will quote its verses here, inserting their literal translation:

तानीदहानि बहुलान्यासन या पराचीनमुदिता सुर्यस्य |
यतः परि जार इवाचरन्तुषो दद्रक्षे न पुनरयतीव ||

tānīdahāni bahulānyāsan yā prācīnamuditā sūryasya |
yataḥ pari jāra ivācarantyuṣo dadṛkṣe na punaryatīva ||

"Great is, in truth, the number of the Dawns which were a foretime at the Sun's uprising.
Since thou, O Dawn, hast been beheld repairing as to thy love, as one no more to leave him".

7. *Rig, VII, 76, 3,* (tânîdhâni bahulânyâsan ya prâchinamuditâ sûryasya — yatah pari jâr ivâcharantyuṣo dadṛkshe na punaryatîv).

B.G. Tilak, in translating this verse, has acted like **Sâyana** by separating the word *jâra-iva* in the Samhitâ text into *jâre* + *iva*, not *jârah* + *iva*, as **Shakala** did in the verse text; since the combination *jâre* + *iva* makes the comparison with *Ushas* (Dawn) more appropriate than that of *jârah*. Accordingly, these verses literally mean: ***"Indeed, there were many days before the rising of the sun, and where you are seen, O Dawn, as approaching to the lover, not as departing (woman) ".***

Tilak took *pari* from *yatah*, which means dawn comes after days. *Yatah pari*, is so complex, means "after what" or "about what". **Sâyana** agrees with a *dadrikshe*, and **Griffith** [8] translates *yatah* by "since." But such arrangements do not essentially change the meaning of the second half of the stanza, although the coincidence of *pari* with *yatah* allows us to regard the second verse as an adjective, which makes the meaning clearer.

8. Ralph Thomas Hotchkin Griffith (1826–1906) was an English Indologist, a member of the Indian Educational Service, and among the first Europeans to translate the Vedas into English. Lived in UK (Oxford) and India (Benares and Nilgiris).

In *IV, 52,* 1 it is said that the dawn must shine after its sister *(svasuh pari)*, and *pari*, with the ablative, does not necessarily denote the idea of distance, but is used in various senses, as, for example, in *III , 5, 10,* where we find the term *Bhrigubhyah pari*, which **Grassman** translates as "*in honor of Bhrigus,*" while **Sâyana** replaces *pari* with *paritah*, "about." Accordingly, in the stanza under consideration we may combine *pairs* with *yata* and interpret the expression in the sense of "after", "near" or "around those" (days). We must also not forget that the image implies a comparison between *jare* and something which we cannot obtain except by composing *yatah pari* as stated above. If we now analyze the stanza, we will find that it consists of three statements: one main and two adjectives. The main testimony says that those days were many. The demonstrative pronoun "you" *(tâni)* is accompanied by two basic testimonies: *yâ prâchînam* ... and *yatah pari* ... The first says that the days in question were mostly those that "preceded the rising of the sun." But if the days preceded the rising of the Sun, we can imagine that those days were darkness. That is why the poet adds in another relevant statement that although those days preceded the rising sun, they were such that "the dawn moved along or with them, like a lover, not like some indifferent woman." To sum up, the stanza establishes without any ambiguity that, on the one hand, there were many days *(bahulâni ahâni)* that took place between the appearance of the first rays of the morning and the rising of the sun, and on the other hand, on those days the dawn was faithfully observed, meaning that the whole period formed uninterrupted dawn that did not disappear. The sentence, as composed, does not justify any other interpretation, and we shall see to what extent it is intelligible to us. In the eyes of the interpreter, that stanza is a real puzzle. Thus, **Sâyana** does not understand how the word "day" *(ahani)* can be applied to the period of time before the rising of the Sun, because, he says, *"the name day (ahan) is used only to denote the period of time covered by dawn."* It seems that he also does not understand how it can be said here that between the first rays of the dawn and the rising of the Sun many days pass. This presented a great difficulty to **Sâyana**, so the only way out was to artificially change the meaning of the word to give it an intelligible meaning, an undertaking which was no problem for **Sâyana**.

The word *ahâni* meaning "day" was his only obstacle, so instead of taking it in the sense in it was used everywhere without exception, he reached for its root and interpreted it as a substitute for "light" or "shine." *Ahan* is derived from the root *ah* (or philological), "to burn" or "to shine," and from the same root is derived *ahan*, meaning "dawn." Etymologically, therefore, *ahâni* may mean "shine"; but it is a question of whether the word is used anywhere in that sense, and why we should reject the ordinary meaning of the word. We have already given the answer to **Sâyana**. According to him, the word "day" *(ahan)* was applied only to the period between sunrise and sunset. But this reasoning is not solid, for in the **Rig-Veda**, *VI, 9, 1,* ahan is applied equally to the dark as well as to the light period of time, for the stanza says, *"there is one dark and one light day."* This shows that the Vedic poets used the word *ahan* even when they spoke of the period without the Sun. [9] **Sâyana** knew this, so in his explanation of *I, 185, 4* he explicitly says that the word *ahan* can also include night.

9. *Rig-Veda*, VI, 9, 1, — (ahashcha kṛṣṇamahararyunam cha vi vartete rajasî vedyâbhih), as well as T.S. III, 3, 4, 1, (etadvâ anho rupam yadrâtrih), is explained in a similar way in T.S. VI, 3, 9, 1, the expression (shamahobhyâm) (1,3, 9, 1) through: (shamahobhyâmiti ninayatyahoratrabhyâmeva)

The real difficulty lay elsewhere in not being able to suppose that a period of several days could elapse between the first appearance of light and the rising of the Sun, and Western scholars seem to have experienced this difficulty. So, **Prof. Ludwig** basically adopts **Sâyana's** view and interprets the verse in terms of the many flashes of dawn, and that they appeared either before sunrise or if *prâchînam* is interpreted differently, "in the east" at sunrise. **Roth** and **Grassman** seem to have interpreted *prâchînam* in the same way.

Griffith translates *ahâni* as "morning" and *prâchînam* as "before". His translation of the stanza reads as follows: ***"Indeed, the number of mornings before the rising of the Sun is great; because thou art, O Dawn! You have been noted as going to meet your love, as (a woman) who does not wish to leave him any longer"***, but *Griffith* does not explain what he means by "*the great number of mornings that preceded the rising of the Sun.*" The case, therefore, boils down to this: the word *Ahan*, where *ahani* is the plural form, may be interpreted in its ordinary sense as **(a)** the period of time between sunrise and sunset; **(b)** a whole of one day and one night, in the sense of 365 days in a year; or as **(c)** a measure of time denoting a period of 24 hours, whether the Sun is above or below the horizon, as when we speak of a long arctic night of thirty days. Shall we then abandon all these meanings and interpret *ahâni* in the sense of "flashes" in the stanza in this question? The only difficulty is to understand the interval of several days which separates the appearance of the dawn flag on the horizon and the shrinking of the sun's disk above it, and this difficulty disappears if an adequate description of dawn is taken in the polar or circumpolar regions. Here is the real key to the meaning of that and other similar passages, which *Tilak* explains in detail in his book; and in the absence of such a key, many means have been used to make these passages intelligible to us. But for now, nothing like that is needed anymore. As for the word "days", we have already noticed that we often speak of a night of several days and a night of several months when describing the polar phenomena. In such terms, the words "day" or "month" simply means a measure of time equal to 24 hours or 30 days, so there is nothing unusual in the poet of the **Rig-Veda** stating that there were "many days between the first rays of dawn and the rising of the Sun". We have also seen that at the Pole it is possible to mark a period of 24 hours by revolutions of the celestial sphere or polar star so that the inhabitants of that place could call one complete revolution a "day". So, the verse in question *(VII, 76, 3)* explicitly describes the continuous dawn of several days, which is possible only in arctic regions.

But still, on that question, we have seen that the *Aurora* (Dawn) can be divided into periods of 24 hours, according to its rotation on the horizon. In such a case, we may speak very nicely of these divisions as being as many dawns during 24 hours, and asserting that there are as many passing as they come, as the verse, *I, 11, 3, 10,* discussed before, says. We can also say that as many dawns passed without the Sun rising, as in *II, 28, 9*, the stanza dedicated to the water deity *Varuna* who responded to the Christian saint *St. Nicholas*, in which the poet asks the deity for the following favor:

अव्युष्टा इन नु भूयसीरुषास आ नो जीवान वरुण तासु शाधि ॥
यो मे राजन युज्यो वा सखा वा सवपने भायं भीर्वे मह्यमाह ।

para ṛṇā sāvīradha matkṛtāni māhaṃ rājannanyakṛtena bhojam |
avyuṣṭā in nu bhūyasīruṣāsa ā no jīvān varuṇa tāsu śādhi ||

which literally means:

"Eliminate my debts (mistakes). Do it, O King! Not to be affected by the actions of others. Indeed, the many dawns have not yet fully spread. O Varuna! make us live to see them again." [10]

10. Rig-Veda, II, 28, 9 - para ṛiṇâ sâvîradha matkṛitâni mâham rajannayakritena bhojam avyuṣṭâ innu bhûyasîruṣasa â no dîvânvaruṇa tâsu shâdh

The first part of this stanza contains a prayer usually addressed to the gods, and there is nothing to add. The only expression to be discussed *is bhûyasih ushâsah avyushtâh* in the third verse. The first two words do not create any difficulties. They mean "many dawn". But *avyushtâh* is the negative particle of *vyushta*, where it is itself derived from *ushta* by the prefix *vi*. The difference between *usha* and *vyushta*, indicated by the division of dawn into three or five parts. *Vyushta*, according to the **Taittirîya Brâhmana** means "day", or before the *"branching of the dawn of the rising sun",* so the word *a+vi+ushta* means, "unaccompanied by the rising of the Sun". But **Sâyana** and others did not have in mind this distinction between *ushas* and *vyushti*; and even if they had, they could not have imagined the phenomenon of arctic dawn to last several days before the Sun's disc appeared on the horizon. The term *bhayasih ushâsah avyushtâh*, which literally means: *"many dawns have not risen or are not branched",* is, therefore, a mystery to these interpreters. Every dawn which they observed was normally followed by sunrise; and therefore, they could not realize how many "dawns" could be described as "unbranched." An explanation was therefore necessary, which was obtained by changing the passive participle of the last *avyushta* into a future participle; thus, the expression in question is rendered *"during the dawn (or days) which have not yet risen,"* or, in other words, *"during the dawn of the days to come."* But that explanation is "broken at the knees." If we wanted to talk about the coming days, the idea could be expressed more simply and briefly. The poet is evidently speaking of current events, so taking *vyushta* in its literal sense, we can easily and naturally interpret the expression that although there were many dawns, they did not become *vyushta*, meaning they were not followed by the rising sun and that *Varuna* had to protect worshipers in such circumstances.

Taittirîya Samhitâ, *IV, 3, 11,* expressly states that the dawns are thirty sisters, or in other words, that there are thirty of them and that they unite in five groups without stopping, all gathering in the same place and under the same flag. This entire *Anuvâka* dawn hymn may be said to consist of 15 stanzas which were used as mantras for placing certain sacred stones, called "dawn stones," on the sacrificial altar. There are sixteen stones that must be placed on the altar, and the *Anuvâka* in question gives 15 mantras that must be used at the proper time, while the sixteenth is noted elsewhere. The first stanza of the section, called *Anuvâka*, is used to lay the first stone of the dawn and speaks only of one dawn first appearing on the horizon. In the second stanza, however, two dawns "who are roommates in the same circle" are mentioned. In the third stanza, the third dawn is invoked, then the fourth, then the fifth. The five dawns are said to have five sisters each, rounding the total to thirty dawns. These "thirty sisters" *(trimshat svasârah)* are then described as "circling" *(pari yanti)* in groups of six, advancing towards the same goal *(nishkritam)*. Two stanzas further on, the worshiper seeks to convey to himself and his worshipers the same spirit of fellowship that reigns among these dawns or mornings. The last couplet of the *Anuvâka* summarizes this description by saying that the dawn, though it shines in different ways, is in reality only one. Throughout the *Anuvâka* there is not the slightest allusion to the rising sun or the appearance of its light, and the *Brâhmana* confirms this point by asserting: ***"There was a time when all was neither day nor night when I was in a state of indifference. Then the gods saw these dawns and set them, and then a light appeared; therefore, he for whom these (bricks of dawn) are laid will know the light and the end of darkness."*** The subject of this passage is an explanation of how and why the bricks of dawn were laid with these mantras, on successive days, but at a time when there were neither nights nor days.

A related remark, from the end of the *Anuvâka*, is that there is only one dawn, this is enough to prove that the thirty dawns mentioned in that text were continuous and not consecutive. But if it is necessary to find a more explicit statement, it is found in the ***Taittîriya Brâhmana***, *II, 5, 6, 5*. It is an ancient mantra, not a *Brâhmana* commentary, so the statement is as satisfactory as the stanzas previously quoted. The mantra addresses the dawns and says, ***"The dawns themselves are those who shone first, the goddesses create five forms; eternal (shashvatîh), they are not separated (avaprijyanti) and have no end (gamanti antam)"***. [11]

11. Taitt. Br., II, 5, 6, 5, — imâ eva tâ uṣaso ya prathamâ vyauchchan tâ devya shashvatîrnâvapṛijyanti na gamantyantam.

The "five forms" which are in question correspond to the division of the thirty dawns into five groups of six, the division made in the ***Taittirîya Samhitâ***, according to the mode of sacrifice *(shalahas),* or group of six days; so, it is explicitly said that the dawns that make up these five forms are continuous, connected or unbroken. In the ***Rig Veda, I, 152, 4,*** the garment of the lover of the dawn (literally maidens, *kaninam yâram*) is described as "one-piece" and "broad" *(anavaprigna and vitata),* so we read it in the light of the mantra of a moment ago, of the ***Taittîriya Brâhmana,*** leads to the conclusion that in the ***Rig-Veda*** itself the garment of the Solar Dawn, or the garment woven for the Sun by the Dawn as a mother *(cf. V, 47, 6),* is considered "wide" and "one-piece".

Translated into a common language, this means that the dawn described in the ***Rig-Veda*** was a long-lasting continuous phenomenon. In the ***Atharva-Veda*** [12] the dawns are described as *sachetasah* and *samîchîh*, which means that they go together and in harmony, not separately. The first term is found in the ***Rig-Veda***, but not the second, though it may be easily inferred from the fact that the dawns are described as *"gathered in the same circle."* ***Griffith*** translates *samîchîh* by *"close-knit group"* and interprets both words as follows:

> ***"The Shining One sent forth the dawns, the tight-knit group, pure, unanimous, shining in its domain."***

12. Ath. Veda, VII, 22, 2, — bradhnah samîchîruşasah samarayan arepasah sachetasah svasaré manyumattamâsh-chité goh.

In Ruthenian or Little Russian legends, the number of fairies *(boginki)* who are sisters is twenty-seven ("three times nine") or, in another version, they are thirty [13] which may correspond to those sisters who form the arctic dawn or else ecliptic division of 27 zodiacs (eg Nakshatras in Hinduism) and lunation.

13. Niedzielski, Grzegorz (2011). Królowie z gwiazd. Mitologia plemion prapolskich. *Sandomierz: Armoryka*, p. 166-169

All adjectives referring to the dawn clearly indicate an undivided, harmoniously acting group; and strange as it may seem, ***Griffith***, who otherwise translates correctly, does not understand the scope of this passage. With it, we have enough direct evidence to assert that it is a 'group', or, in ***Griffith's*** words, 'a closely compact group of thirty continuous dawns, spoken of in the Vedic hymns, and not the zone in the temperate and tropical zones, whether considered single or arranged in sequence.

It is interesting to examine how *Sâyana* explains the existence of several dawns amounting to thirty, before moving on to other statements. In his commentary on the *Taitiriya Samhitâ, IV, 3, 11,* he tells us that the first dawn referred to in the first stanza of the *Anuvâka* is that of the beginning of creation, (when all cannot be distinguished, according to the *Brâhmana*). Of the second dawn, in the second stanza, it is said to be ordinary dawn, the one that we observe every day. So far so good; but the number of dawns quickly outnumbers the types of dawn known to *Sâyana*, the third, fourth, and fifth stanzas of the *Anuvâka* describe three more dawns, so *Sâyana* is forced to finally explain that, although one, the dawn manifests different forms thanks to its yogic or mystical powers! But the five dawns are multiplied by the thirty sisters in the next stanza so that *Sâyana* concludes by adopting the explanation that thirty separate dawns represent thirty consecutive dawns of a month. But it is nowhere explained why these mantras speak only of the thirty *Mughrs* (Serbo-Macedonian: *mugri, мугри*) of a month, instead of the 365 *Mughrs* of a year. These explanations are not only contradictory but come into conflict, in the last verse of the *Anuvâka*, both with the *Brâhmana* or the explanation given in the *Samhitâ* itself and with the above passage extracted from the *Taittîriya Brâhmana.* But *Sâyana* was firmly convinced that the Vedic dawn was like what he and other Vedic interpreters such as *Yāska* [14] * observed in the tropics; and what is astonishing is not so much that he has given us so many contradictory explanations, but the fact that he has been able to suggest a considerable number of apparently plausible explanations to meet the requirements of the various mantras. In light of the progress made in the knowledge of the nature of the *Aurora Borealis* and the existence of man on earth before the last glaciation, we must not hesitate to accept a more intelligible and rational theory of the various places dedicated to the dawn in Vedic literature.

14. Once again.* Yāska was an ancient Indian grammarian and linguist (7th-5th century BC). Before Panini (7th-4th century BC), he is traditionally identified as the author of Nirukta, the discipline of "etymology" (explanation of words) within the Sanskrit grammatical tradition in India. Yāska is widely regarded as the precursive founder of the discipline of what would become etymology in both East and West.

Not a single dawn, whether in the temperate, or tropical zones, can appear to move like the sun, from east to west, above the observer in an upright plane. Therefore, the only circular motion possible is that which occurs along the horizon and cannot be observed anywhere except in the regions near the Pole. Dawn in the temperate or tropical zone is visible only briefly in the east before it is replaced by the glow of the rising Sun. Only in the polar regions, we can see the morning flames orbiting the horizon for several days, so if the circular movement of the dawn mentioned in *III, 61, 3* takes place, we must conclude from this that it is a phenomenon peculiar to the arctic regions, described above. Inappropriate for the description of dawn south of the Arctic Circle; on the contrary, if we suppose these expressions to refer to the polar dawn, they become not only intelligible but quite appropriate, since that dawn, after its diurnal rotation, must return to the point. from which she had left twenty-four hours earlier. Considering these passages, a single conclusion emerges: The **Rig-Veda** and the **Taittîriya Samihitâ** describe long continuous dawn divided into thirty periods of twenty-four hours, a feature found only in the polar regions. There are still a number of passages where the dawn is spoken of in the plural, especially when we address the morning deities, who follow not only one dawn, but also the plural dawns *(I, 6, 3; I, 180, 1; V, 76, 1; VII, 9, 1; VII, 63, 3)*. These passages have hitherto been interpreted as describing the appearance of deities after the successive dawns of the year. But the conclusion that we have just established now throws new light on these facts, starting from an examination of the various passages relating to the dawn in the **Rig-Veda**, the **Taittîriya Samihitâ** and the **Atharva-Veda Samhitâ**. By this, however, I do not mean to say that no reference to the dawn of the tropics and the temperate zone can be found in the entire **Rig Veda**. The Veda, which reports a 360-day year, certainly mentions the elusive dawn that precedes the days and regions south of the Arctic Circle. Most of these descriptions, after all, can be equally applied to long polar as well as short tropical dawns. Thus, both are living beings *(I, 92, 9)* or reveal the hidden treasures of darkness *(I, 123, 4)*. Likewise, the expression that the dawns come and go, and that every day a new sister comes after the missing one *(I, 124, 9)*, may equally be interpreted as a reference to successive dawns on several days rather than as an allusion to the *Aurora Borealis*, which lasts several consecutive days. These expressions, therefore, do not in any way lead us to the conclusion we reached earlier when considering the peculiarities of these *mugras*. What we want to prove is that *Ushas*, the dawn goddess, whose appearance was awaited with so much impatience and anxiety and who was the subject of so many hymns of Vedic literature, is not elusive tropical dawn, but a long-lasting circular *aurora*; so if we have been able to prove this on the basis of the above passages, it does not matter that elsewhere in the *Rig-Veda* there are one or more expressions referring to the common tropical dawn. The Vedic sages *Rishis* who sang these hymns must have been accustomed to these tropical dawns if ever they added the thirteenth month to ensure agreement between the lunar and solar year. But the *Ushas* was an ancient deity, whose attributes the *Rishis* came to know through oral tradition dating back to her origin; and the hymns of the dawn, such as we have today, faithfully described these qualities. After examining all the Vedic evidence in support of the polar theory, I will examine the question of how these ancient adjectives of the dawn goddess could have been preserved through the ages. For now, we will assume that these memories of the geographical origins of the Vedic people are preserved as hymns from three or four millennia ago. It follows from the preceding discussion that if the dawn hymns in the **Rig-Veda** are studied in the light of modern scientific discoveries and with the help of passages from the **Atharva-Veda**, the **Taittîriya Samhitâ** and the **Taittîriya Brâhmana**, we can establish the following results:

1. The dawn of the Rig-Veda was so long that several days elapsed between the first appearance of light on the horizon and the rising of the Sun that followed (VII, 76, 3); or, as stated in II, 28, 9, numerous dawns appeared one after the other before scattering at sunrise.

2. The plural used in addressing the dawn was not a form of respect, nor were the successive dawns of the year, but refers to the thirty parts of the dawn (I, 123, 8; VI, 59, 6; T.S., IV, 3, 11, 6).

3. Numerous dawns inhabited the same place, acted harmoniously, and never quarreled (IV, 51, 7-9); VII, 76, 5; AV, VII, 22, 2).

4. Thirty parts of the dawn were continuous and inseparable, forming a "tightly packed group" or "grouping" dawns " (I, 152, 4; T.Br., II, 5, 6, 5; A.V., VIII, 22, 2).

5. These thirty dawns, or thirty parts of the same dawn, revolved like a wheel, reaching the same goal every day, each dawn or part of the dawn following its destiny (I, 123, 8, 9; III, 61, 3; T.S., IV, 3, 11, 6).

Needless to say, these features apply to the polar zone. The last one is only found in areas very close to the North Pole. Therefore, we can safely conclude that the Vedic dawn goddess is of polar origin. But it should be added that, while the *Aurora* lasts from 45 to 60 days, the Vedic dawn, as described, contains only thirty parts of 24 hours, so this difference must be considered before accepting the conclusion that the Vedic dawn is an *Aurora Borealis* feature. This difference, however, is not very significant. We have seen that the duration of dawn depends on the power of atmospheric refraction and reflection of light; they, in turn, change depending on the temperature and other meteorological conditions. Therefore, it is not impossible that the duration of the dawn of the Pole, when the climate there was mild and pleasant, was not shorter than what we observe today when the climate is more severe. However, it is more likely that the dawn described in the *Rig-Veda* is not exactly the same as that seen by an observer located right at the North Pole. As we noted earlier, the North Pole is only one point, so if people lived near the Pole in ancient times, they must have lived a little further south of that point. By means of that explanation, it is quite possible to imagine the dawn of thirty days which, after the long arctic night of four or five months, turns like a point; and so far as astronomy is concerned, the description of the dawn as given in the Vedic literature has nothing improbable. We must also bear in mind that the Vedic dawn often lingered longer on the horizon, so her worshipers begged her not to be late for fear that the Sun would defeat her as an enemy *(V, 79, 9).* This shows that the dawn, although it usually lasted thirty days, sometimes exceeded that duration, so people at that time were eager to see the sunlight. This occurred on those occasions when *Indra*, the creator god, and friend of the dawn, had to break the chariot of the dawn and bring the Sun above the horizon (II, 15, 6; X, 73, 6) [15]

15. Rig Veda, II, 15, 6 — (vajjeṇan uṣasah sam pipéṣ — Rig, IV, 30, 8, etad gheduta
vîryamindra chakrath paunasyaim — striyam yaddurhâṇâyuvam vadhîrduhitaram divah).

There are other places where we find the same legend *(IV, 30, 8),* so today
it is assumed that the basis of that myth was the darkening of the dawn by
storm. But that explanation, like many others, does not satisfy us. The fact
that the storm rises at dawn would be a coincidence, so it can hardly be
taken as the basis of a legend. After all, the extension given in the legend
refers to the delay and not the eclipse of the dawn, and this supports our
polar theory, since the duration of the dawn is usually thirty days, but it
can vary in different places depending on the latitude, the climatic
conditions, and the thunderbolt of Indra was hence the need to end the
dawn spell and allow the Sun to rise. If the Vedic dawn is of polar origin,
the ancestors of the Vedic bards must have observed it not in the post-
glacial but in the pre-glacial era; and after all, we may wonder why we
find no references to it in the hymns a long time ago. Fortunately, they
preserve some clues to the time when those long dawns existed. The Vedic
poets were certainly aware of the fact that the mantras they recited while
setting the dawn stones could not be applied to the dawn as they
experienced it, so the **Taittiriya Samhitâ**, *IV, 3, 7* which explains the
Mantras, makes it clear that this description of dawn goes back to ancient
times *"when the gods (Devas) observed thirty dawns".* It is therefore
wrong to say that it is absent from the Vedic hymns without reference to
the time when those long dawns were visible.

• *The three faces of the Slavic goddess Zorya*

The goddess of the dawn without exception is respected and glorified by
all the so-called Indo-European peoples, but this cult can also be found
among other peoples who had civilizational contact with them. However,
Slavic myths, folklore, and legends further support and strengthen our
Arctic theory.

Dawn or "*Zorya*"; as we know is a female personified deity who appears
in many variants: Russian: *Zarya zaryanica*; Belorus: *Zara-zaranica,
Zorka-zaranica*; Ukrainian: *Zorya, Zorya-zoryanitsa, Zaria, Zara,*

Zaranitsa, Zorjushka, etc. She also appears as "*Klyuchnytsia neba*" or the heavenly key-keeper who opens the gates for the Sun to come out. Depending on the tradition, she may appear as a single entity, often called "*The Red Maiden*" or two or three sisters at once. What we said above about the Vedic goddess *Ushas* refers to the morning dawn, which is sung in the plural as 30 sisters. However, the triple division of the Dawn among the Slavs also indicates another different division. The etymological origin of the All-Slavic word "*zora*" and its variants come from the same root as the All-Slavic word *"зрѣтизірѣti"* ("to see, observe"), which originally probably meant "shine". The word *zara* may have originated under the influence of the word *žar* "heat" because it heralds the arrival of the Sun with its light. The all-Slavic word *zora* "dawn, aurora" (from Proto-Slavic *zoŗà*), and its variants, comes from the same root as the all-Slavic word *zrěti* ("to see, observe", from PS *жьrěti*), which originally may have meant "shine". The word *zara* may have originated under the influence of the word *žar* "heat" (PS *жарь*). Proto-Slavic *zoŗà* is connected to the Proto-Balto-Slavic *źori* (cf. Lithuanian *žarà, žarijà*), and the etymology of the root is very clear. [1] She lives in the palace of the Sun, opens the gate for him in the morning so he can set out on his journey across the sky, guards his white horses, and is often described as a virgin [2]. In the East Slavic tradition of *zagovory* (verbal folk magic), she represents the supreme power invoked by the practitioner. [3]

1. Graves Robert (1987). *New Larousse Encyclopedia of Mythology*: With an Introduction by Robert Graves. Gregory Alexinsky. p. 290–291.

2. Zarubin, L. A. (1971). "Сходные изображения солнца и зорь у индоарийцев и славян" [Similar images of the sun and dawns among the Indo-Aryans and Slavs]. Советское славяноведение [Soviet Slavic Studies] (in Russian). Moscow: Наука. 6: p. 70–76

3. Toporkov, Andrey (1995). "Zarya". *Slavyanskaya Mifologiya: Entsiklopedicheskiy slovar (in Russian)*. Moscow. p. 189

The word "*Zorya*" has become a loanword in the Romanian language as its the word for "dawn" (zori) and as the name of a piece of music sung by colinda tori *(zorile)*. Zorya shares the following characteristics with most goddesses of the dawn:

- She appears in the company of St. George and St. Nicholas (interpreted as divine twins like the Vedic *Ashvins*, Hellenic *Dioscuri*, and Lithuanian *Ašvieniai*,) [4]
- Red, gold, yellow, and rose colors
- She lives overseas, on the island of Buyan [5]
- Opens the door to the Sun [6]
- She owned a golden boat and a silver oar

4. Sańko, Siarhei (2018). *"Reflexes of Ancient Ideas about Divine Twins in the Images of Saints George and Nicholas in Belarusian Folklore". Folklore: Electronic Journal of Folklore. 72: 15–4.* In fact, the divine twins can be St. George, but also St. Dimitrius, which divides the year into two halves, summer, and winter. During Serbian slavery under the Turks, the Turks decided that their annual tax should be paid in two parts: on Gjurdjevdan or St. George's Day and on Mitrovdan or St. Dimitrius' Day. In the past, on St. George's Day, the hajduks left their winter quarters, and hiding places and went to the woods at the scheduled place to start again with guerrilla warfare. The people still remember the old saying „*Đurđev danak – hajdučki sastanak* (St. George's Day hajduk's meeting), *Mitrov danak – hajdučki rastanak* (St. Dimitris' Day haduk's separation)". According to the old Perisian religion, the deity Mithra was a judicial figure, protector of all-seeing truth, and guardian of cattle, harvest, and waters, and his month of glory corresponds to the period when the Sun transits through the sign of Libra. In the Zoroastrian calendar, the sixteenth day of the seventh month of the year is dedicated to and under the protection of Mithra. The Iranian civil calendar of 1925 adopted the Zoroastrian month names, and as such the seventh month of the year is called "Mihr". The position of the sixteenth day and seventh month reflects Mithras' rank in the hierarchy of deities; The sixteenth day and the seventh month are respectively the first day of the second half of the month and the first month of the second half of the year. The day on which the consecrations of the day-name and month-name intersect is (like all other such intersections) dedicated to the divinity of that day/month and is celebrated with Yashan (from Avestan Yasna, "Worship") in honor of that Deity. In the case of Mithra, this was Jashan-e Mihragan, or just Mihraga for short. There is no doubt that St. Demetrius is a Christian version of the ancient deity Mithras which was celebrated by the Aryans in Persia and India. If St. George is associated with the morning dawn, in that case, St. Dimitris is associated with the dusk, that is, the dawn that sends the Sun to the underworld. St. George is always depicted as a solar warrior with a red cloak, while St. Demetrius is the Lunar in a green robe on Orthodox icons. It is important to note that according to Tilak's calculations, before 6000 years the vernal equinox began with Ashvini or the constellation of Gemini, Castror and Polux. Mitrius (Latin: Mitrius; French: Mitre) is a Western Roman Christian saint of the 5th century, whose memory is commemorated on November 13. We also find here a reflection of this ancient deity in the Catholic church where Mitre (433–466) was a Catholic saint, who was born in Thessaloniki, Greece, and died in Aix-en-Provence According to the legend, Mitre, a

field worker living in Aix-en-Provence with Arvendus, was charged with witchcraft for making a miracle come true. He was beheaded. He then picked up his head and took it to a church in Aix, Église Notre-Dame de la Seds. On 23 October 1383, his relics were moved to the Cathédrale Saint-Sauveur in Aix-en-Provence. It is said that the right-hand column holding his tombstone had a shining hole in it, giving out a liquid good for curing eye sores. Saint Demetrius (or Demetrios) of Thessalonica (Greek: Ἅγιος Δημήτριος τῆς Θεσσαλονίκης, Hágios Dēmḗtrios tēs Thessaloníkēs), also known as the Holy Great-Martyr Demetrius the Myroblyte (meaning 'the Myrrh-Gusher' or 'Myrrh-Streamer'; 3rd century – 306), was a Greek Christian martyr of the early 4th century AD. Both St. Demetrius (Orthodox) and St. Mitre (Catholic) are a reflection of the ancient Aryan cult of Mithra.

5. Afanasyev, Alexander Nikolayevich (1865). Поэтические воззрения славян на природу: Опыт сравнительного изучения славянских преданий и верований в связи с мифическими сказаниями других родственных народов [Poetic views of the Slavs on nature: An experience of a comparative study of Slavic traditions and beliefs in connection with the mythical tales of other kindred peoples] (in Russian). Vol. 1. Moscow: Izd. K. Soldatenkova, стр. 81–85, 198.

6. Shedden-Ralston, William Ralston (1872). The Songs of the Russian People: As Illustrative of Slavonic Mythology and Russian Social Life. Ellis & Green, стр. 376

Zarubin (Иван Иванович Зарубин 1887 –1964), the Soviet expert on Iranian languages, made a comparison between Slavic folklore and Indo-Aryan **Rigveda** and **Atharvaveda**, where images of the Sun and its companions, the Dawns, have been preserved. These images date back to ancient concepts from the initially fetishistic (the Sun in the form of a ring or circle) to the later anthropomorphic. **Chludov's Novgorod Psalter** (Хлудовская псалтырь) of the late 13th century contains a miniature depicting two women. One of them, fiery red, signed as "morning Zora", holds a red sun in her right hand in the form of a ring, and in her left hand, she holds a torch resting on her shoulder, ending in a box from which emerges a light green stripe passing into dark green. This stripe ends in another woman's right hand, in green, signed as "evening Zora", with a bird emerging from her left sleeve. This should be interpreted as the Morning Zorya releasing the Sun on its daily journey, and at sunset the Evening Zorya awaits to meet the Sun. A very similar motif was found in a cave temple from the 2nd or 3rd century AD in Nashik, India. The bas-relief depicts two women: one using a torch to light the circle of the Sun, and the other expecting it at sunset. Some other bas-reliefs depict two goddesses of the dawn, *Ushas* and *Pratyusha*, and the Sun, accompanied by Dawns, appears in several hymns. The Sun in the form of a wheel appears in the Indo-Aryan ***Rigveda***, or the Norse ***Edda***, as well as in folklore: during the annual festivals of the Germanic peoples and Slavs, they lit a wheel which, according to medieval authors, was supposed to symbolize the sun.

Evening and morning Zoras from Chludov Psalter

Images similar to that of the Psalter and that of Nashik in India occur in various parts of the Slavic lands, e.g. on a carved and painted gate of a Slovak country estate (Očova village): on one of the pillars is carved the Morning Dawn, with a golden head, above her is a glow, and even higher is the Sun, rolling along a curved road, and on the other pillar is carved Evening Dawn, and above it is the Setting Sun. There are also eclipsed suns on this relief, probably dead suns appear in Slavic folklore. These motives are also confirmed by the Russian saying "The sun will not rise without the morning dawn". Such a motif is also found on the back of a 19th-century sleigh where the Sun in the form of a circle is in the palace and two Dawns stand at the exit and on a village folk shirt known as Rushnik from the Tver region where the Dawns ride up to the Sun on horseback, one is red and the other is green. One heralded spring and warmth, that is, the solar phase, while the other heralded autumn or cooling, that is, the lunar phase of the arctic night. In addition to the Artic theory, this place *Buyan* as the home of the goddess *Zorya*, is also a magical island of Slavic mythology and folklore. According to scholars, Lithuanian folklore attests to a similar dual role of the luminous deities *Vakarine* and *Ausrine*: [7] *Vakarine*, the Evening Star, sent the bed for the sun goddess *Saule*, and *Ausrine*, the Morning Star, lit the fire for her. as she prepared to travel another day. [8] In other accounts, *Ausrine* and *Vakarine* are said to be the daughters of the female Sun (*Saule*) and the male Moon (*Menes*), [9] and they take care of their mother's palace and horses. [10] In the Russian tradition, they often appear as two maiden sisters: *Zorya Utrenyaya* as the goddess of the morning dawn and *Zorya Vechernyaya* as the goddess of dusk. Each had to stand on a different side of the golden throne of the Sun. The Morning Dawn opens the gate of the heavenly palace when the Sun rises in the morning, and the Evening Dawn closes the gate when the Sun goes to the underworld or goes to rest. The seat of *Zorya* was to be located on the island of *Buyan*. [11]

7. Razauskas, Dainius. "Iš baltų mitinio vaizdyno juodraščių: Aušrinė (ir Vakarinė)" [From rough copies of the Baltic mythic imagery: The Morning Star]. In: Liaudies kultūra. Nr. 6 (2011), стр. 17-25, Also see Zaroff, Roman (1999). *"Organized Pagan Cult in Kievan Rus".* The Invention of Foreign Elite or Evolution of Local Tradition? [Organizirani Poganski Kult V Kijevski državi. Iznajdba Tuje Elite Ali Razvoj Krajevnega izročila?]. In: *Studia Mythologica Slavica* (2 May). Ljubljana, Slovenija. p. 54, 1844

8. Straižys, Vytautas; Klimka, Libertas. *"The Cosmology of the Ancient Balts".* In: *Journal for the History of Astronomy: Archaeoastronomy Supplement.* Vol. 28. Issue 22 (1997): p. 73

9. Razauskas, Dainius. "Dievo vaikaitis: žmogaus vieta lietuvių kosmologijoje" [God's grandchild: the human place in Lithuanian Cosmology]. In: Tautosakos darbai [Folklore Studies] nr. 42. 2011. стр. 131, 137 (and footnote nr. 17), исто види Laurinkienė, Nijolė. "Dangiškųjų vestuvių mitas" [Myth of the celestial wedding]. In: Liaudies kultūra Nr. 5 (2018). p. 25-33.

10. Andrews, Tamra. *Dictionary of Nature Myths: Legends of the Earth, Sea, and Sky.* Oxford University Press. 1998. p. 20

11. Shedden-Ralston, William Ralston *(1872). The Songs of the Russian People: As Illustrative of Slavonic Mythology and Russian Social Life. Ellis & Green. p. 375.*

In Polish folklore, there are three sister Zoras (*Trzy Zorze*): Morning Zorza (Polish: *Zorza porankowa* or *Utrenica*), Midday Zora (*Zorza południowa or Południca*) and Evening Zora (*Zorza wieczorowa or Wieczornica*), which appear in Polish folk charms and, according to **Andrzej Szyjewski,** represent a threefold division of the day. [12] They also function as Rozhanitsy: [13]

> *Zarze, zarzyce, three sisters.*
> *The Mother of God went on the sea, gathering golden froth;*
> *St. John met her: Where are you going, Mother?*
> *I am going to cure my little son.* [14]

> *Zorzyczki, zorzyczki,*
> *there are three of you*
> *she of the morning,*
> *she of midday,*
> *she of the evening.*
> *Take from my child the crying,*
> *give him back his sleep.* [15]

12. Szyjewski, Andrzej (2003). *Religia Słowian*. Kraków: Wydawnictwo WAM. p. 71

13. Grzegorzewic, Ziemisław (2016*). O Bogach i ludziach. Praktyka i teoria Rodzimowierstwa Słowiańskiego* [*On Gods and People. The practice and theory of the Slavic native religion*] (in Polish). Olsztyn.

14. Vrtel-Wierczyński, Stefan (1923*). Średniowieczna poezja polska świecka* [*Medieval Polish secular poetry*] (in Polish). Kraków: Krakowska Spółka Wydawnicza.

15. Czernik, Stanisław (1985*). Trzy zorze dziewicze: wśród zamawiań i zaklęć* [*Three Virgin Aurorae: Among Orders and Spells*] (in Polish) (2nd ed.). Łódź: Wydawn. Łódzki

> *Zorze, zorzeczeńki!*
> *You're all my sisters!*
> *Get on your crow horse*
> *And ride for my companion (lover).*
> *So he cannot go without me*
> *neither sleep nor eat,*

nor sit down, nor talk.
That I may please him in standing, in working, in willing.
That I may be thankful and pleasant to God and men,
and this companion of mine.[16]

16. "Wisła. *Miesięcznik Geograficzno-Etnograficzny.* 1903 T.17 z.3 - Wielkopolska Biblioteka Cyfrowa" [Vistula. *Geographical and Ethnographic monthly.* 1903 Vol. 17 z.3 – Greater Poland Digital Library]. wbc.poznan.pl (in Polish). Vol. 17. Retrieved 2019-12-25.

Another folk saying from Poland is thus:

Żarze, zarzyczki,
jest was trzy,
zabierzcie od mojego dziecka płakanie,
przywróćcie mu spanie. [17]

There is no problem here for us to understand the Morning Dawn (Polish: *Zorza porankowa or Utrenica*), or the Evening Zora (*Zorza wieczorowa or Wieczornica*) But it is quite unclear and illogical to us in this trilogy how the dawn can appear during the day was Midday Dawn. It is definitely a forgotten continuity of the ancient Arctic tradition, where the true meaning was gradually lost. But still, as we will see in some other Slavic traditions, we still have preserved the ancient traces.

17. "Dlaczego nie obserwujemy więcej komet?". Urania. 52 (4): 98–101. 1981.

The Ukrainian language also has words deriving from "*Zorya*": зірка (dialectal зіра "zira" and зіри "ziry") zírka, a diminutive meaning 'little star', 'starlet', '*asterisk*'; зірни́ця "zirnitsa" (or зірни́ці "zirnytsi"), a poetic term meaning 'little star', 'aurora, dawn'. [18]

In a saying collected in "Харківщині" (Kharkiv Oblast), it is said that "there are many stars (*Зірок*) in the sky, but there are only two Zori: the morning one (*світова*) and the evening one (*вечірня*)". In an orphan's lament, the mourner says he will take the "keys of the dawn" ("*То я б в зорі ключі взяла*"). [19] In a magical love charm, the girl invokes "three star-sisters" (or the "dawn-sisters"): [20]

18. Ukrainian-English Dictionary. Compiled by C. H. Andrusyshen and J. N. Krett, assisted by Helen Virginia Andrusyshen. Canada: Published for the University of Saskatchewan by University of Toronto Press. 2004 [1955]. p. 338.

19. Українська мала енциклопедія [*A little encyclopedia of Ukraine*]. У 8 т.[uk]. Том 2: Книжка IV. Літери Ж-Й. Буенос-Айрес, 1959. p. 512.

20. Toporkov, Andrei (2009). "*Russian Love Charms in a Comparative Light*". Charms, Charmers and Charming. pp. 121–144.

Vy zori-zirnytsi, vas na nebi tri sestrytsi: odna nudna, druga pryvitna, a tretia pechal'na

You dawn stars, you three sisters in the sky: one dull, the second welcoming, and the third sorrowful.

In a Slovene folksong titled "*Zorja prstan pogubila*" (Zorja lost her ring), the singer asks for mother *("majko"),* brother *("bratca"),* sister *("sestro")* and darling *("dragog")* to look for it. [21]

21. Štrekelj, Karl, ed. *Slovenske narodne pesmi*. V Ljubljani: Izdala in založila Slovenska matica. 1895. pp. 156-157.

According to **professor Monika Kropej**, in Slovene mythopoetic tradition, the sun rises in the morning, accompanied by the morning dawn, named *Sončica* (from *sonce*, 'sun'), and sets in the evening joined by evening dawn named *Zarika* (from *zarja*, 'dawn'). [22] These female characters also appear in a Slovenian narrative folk song about their rivalry. [23] F. S. Copeland also interpreted both characters as mythological Sun and Dawn, as well as mentioned another ballad, titled Ballad of Beautiful Zora. [24] Slovene folklorist **Jakob Kelemina** (sl), in his book about Slovene myths and folk tales, stated that a Zora appears as the daughter of the Snake Queen (possibly an incarnation of the night) in the so-called Kresnik Cycle. [25]

22. Kropej, Monika (5 May 2015). "*Cosmology and Deities in Slovene Folk Narrative and Song Tradition "Kozmologija in boštva v slovenskem ljudskem pripovednem in pesniškem izročilu*". Studia mythologica Slavica. 6: 121

23. Novak, Petra (17 October 2011). *"Najstnikom 'predpisana' slovenska bajčna in mitološka bitja"* [*'Prescribed' Slovene Mythical and Mythological Creatures for Teenagers*]. Studia mythologica Slavica (in Slovenian). 14: 327–341

24. Copeland, F. S. (1931). *"Slovene Folklore".* Folklore. 42 (4): 405–44

25. Copeland, Fanny S. *(1933). "Slovene Myths". The Slavonic and East European Review.* 11 (33): 631–651.

According to professor **Daiva Vaitkevičienė**, the Virgin Mary most likely replaced the deity Zaria in East Slavic charms. The Virgin Mary is also addressed as "*Zaria*" in Russian charms. [26] In a charm collected in Arkhangelsky and published in 1878 by historian **Alexandra Efimenko** (ru), the announcer invokes зоря Мария and заря Маремъяния, translated as "Maria-the-Dawn" and "Maremiyaniya-the-Dawn". [27] In another charm, the "Evening Star Mariya" and "Morning Star Maremiyana" are invoked to take away sleeplessness.

26. Vaitkevičienė, Daiva (2013*). "Baltic and East Slavic Charms".* The Power of Words: Studies on Charms and Charming in Europe. Central European University Press. pp. 211–236

27. Toporkov, Andrei (April 2018). *'Wondrous Dressing' with Celestial Bodies in Russian Charms and Lyrical Poetry".* Folklore: *Electronic Journal of Folklore.* 71: 207–216

A Russian myth speaks also of three Zorya's and their special task: [28]

There are in the sky three little sisters, three little Zorya's: she of the Evening, she of Midnight, and she of Morning. Unlike Polish songs of this Goddess and its appearance as Midday Dawn, now it is much easier for us to understand the Midnight Dawn because it is definitely about its form known to everyone as Aurora Borealis, which is a nocturnal phenomenon that is only visible at the poles and the Arctic circle. According to this, the tradition about the triple form of the dawn goddess must have originated exclusively from these extreme points of the earth. It is also very important to point out that in this Russian myth their duty is to guard a dog which is tied by an iron chain to the constellation of the Little Bear. When the chain breaks it will be the end of the world where this myth is probably connected also with the cataclysm and the world flood. And the north star or *Stella Polaris* is right on the tail of the Little Bear which is another confirmation of the Arctic tradition.

28. Graves, Robert (1987*). New Larousse Encyclopedia of Mythology*: With an Introduction by Robert Graves. Gregory Alexinsky. New York: Crescent Books, pp. 290–291.

Zara-Zaranitsa ("Dawn the Red Maiden") appears interchangeably with Maria (Mother of God) in different versions of the same *zagovory* plots as the supreme power that a practitioner applies to. She was also prayed to as *Zarya* for good harvests and health: [29] Ho, thou morning *zarya*, and thou evening *zarya*! fall upon my rye, that it may grow up tall as a forest, stout as an oak! Mother *zarya* (apparently twilight here) of morning and evening and midnight! as ye quietly fade away and disappear, so may both sicknesses and sorrows in me, the servant of God, quietly fade and disappear—those of the morning, and of the evening, and of the midnight!

Professor **Bronislava Kerbelytė** cited that in Russian tradition, the *Zorya's* were also invoked to help in childbirth (with the appellation "зорки заряночки") and to treat the baby (calling upon "*заря-девица*", or "*утренняя заря Параскавея*" and "*вечерняя заря Соломонея*"). [30]

29. Shedden-Ralston, William Ralston (1872). *The Songs of the Russian People: As Illustrative of Slavonic Mythology and Russian Social Life*. Ellis & Green. pp. 362–363.

30. Kerbelytė, Bronislava (2009). "*Folkloro duomenys - senosios raštijos žinių vertinimo priemonė*". Tautosakos darbai (in Lithuanian)."Заря-зарница, красная дѣвица / Утренняя заря Прасковья, Крикса, Фокса, / Уйми свой крикъ и дай младенцу сонъ. / Заря-зарница, молодая дѣвица, / Вечерняя варя Соломонѳя, Крикса, Фокса, / Уйми свой крикъ и дай младенцу сонъ

Zarya was also invoked as protectress and to dispel nightmares and sleeplessness:

> **Заря, зарница, васъ три сестрицы, утренняя, полуденная, вечерняя, полуночная, сыми съ раба Божія (имя) тоску, печаль, крикъ, безсонницу, подай ему сонъ со всѣхъ сторонъ, со всѣхъ святыхъ, со всѣхъ небесныхъ. [31]**

In another incantation, *Zarya-Zarnitsa* is invoked along with a "morning Irina" and a "Midday Daria" to dispel a child's sadness and take it away "beyond the blue ocean". [32]

In Belarusian folklore, she appears as *Zaranitsa (Зараніца)* or as *Zara-zaranitsa (Зара-Зараніца)*. In one of the passages, Zaranica is met by St. George and St. Nicholas, who, according to comparative mythology, function as divine twins, who in Indo-European mythologies are usually brothers of the goddess of the dawn: "Saint George was walking with Saint Nicholas and met Aurora". [33] In folklore, she also appears in the form of a riddle: [34]

31. "Русская народно-бытовая медицина" [Russian folk-medicine]: по материалам этнографического бюро князя В. Н. Тенишева / Д-р мед. Г. Попов. С.Петербург: тип. А. С. Суворина, 1903. p. 232

32. "Заря-зарница, красная дѣвица, утренняя Ирина, Дарья полуденная, прійдите, возьмите денной іфикъ и полуденный полу крикъ, отнесите его въ темные лѣса, въ далекіе края, за синія моря, на желтые пески, во имя Отца". "*Русская народно-бытовая медицина*" [*Russian folk-medicine*]: по материалам этнографического бюро князя В. Н. Тенишева / Д-р мед. Г. Попов. С.Петербург: тип. А. С. Суворина, 1903. p. 232.

33. Sańko, Siarhei (2018*). "Reflexes of Ancient Ideas about Divine Twins in the Images of Saints George and Nicholas in Belarusian Folklore".* Folklore: Electronic Journal of Folklore. 72: 15–40.

34. Shedden-Ralston, William Ralston (1872). *The Songs of the Russian People: As Illustrative of Slavonic Mythology and Russian Social Life.* Ellis & Green. pp. 349–350

Zara-zaranitsa, a beautiful virgin, was walking in the sky and dropped her keys. The moon saw them but said nothing. The sun saw them and lifted them up.

This is about the dew, which the moon does not react to and which disappears under the influence of the sun. [35] *Zara* is probably simply the goddess of the dawn and can be translated literally as "Dawn", and *Zaranica* is a diminutive and may indicate respect towards her. [36] In Belarusian tradition, the stars are sometimes referred to as *zorki* [37] and *zory*, such as the star Polaris, known as *Zorny Kol* ('star pole') and *polunochna zora* ('star of midnight'). [38]

35. Ibid. pp. 349–350.

36. Sańko, Siarhei (2018). *"Reflexes of Ancient Ideas about Divine Twins in the Images of Saints George and Nicholas in Belarusian Folklore"*. Folklore: Electronic Journal of Folklore. 72: pp. 15–40.

37. Moskalik, Michael. Janka Kupała: *Der Sänger des weissruthenischen Volkstums*. München/Berlin: Verlag Otto Sagner, 1961. p. 131

38. Avilin, Tsimafei (20 December 2008). *"Astronyms in Belarussian folk beliefs"*. Archaeologia Baltica. 10: 29–34.

Serbian historian **Natko Nodilo** noted in his study **The Ancient Faith of the Serbs and the Croats** that the ancient Slavs saw Zora as a "shining maiden" *("svijetla" i "vidna" djevojka),* and Russian riddles described her as a maiden that lived in the sky ("*Zoru nebesnom djevojkom*"). [39] As for the parentage of the Dawn, she is referred "in a Russian song" as "*dear little Dawn*" and as the "Sister of the Sun". [40]

39. Banov, Estela. "*Nodilova mitološka razmatranja kao arhitekst Pričama iz davnine Ivane Brlić–Mažuranić" [The mythological in the work of Vladimir Nazor and Ivana Brlić-Mažuranić (Slavic Legends and Tales of Long Ago)]*. Stoljeće Priča iz davnine Ivane Brlić-Mažuranić. Kos-Lajtman, Andrijana; Kujundžić, Nada; Lovrić Kralj, Sanja (ur.). Zagreb: Hrvatske udruge istraživača dječje književnosti, 2018. pp. 113-130.

40. Ralston, William Ralston Shedden. *The songs of the Russian people, as illustrative of Slavonic mythology and Russian social life*. London: Ellis & Green. 1872. p. 170

In the same book, **Nodilo** gives an interesting description of the dual form of the dawn as morning and evening, which is completely logical and understandable for our climate, but he also gives some kind of navigation for the third sister, which is completely incomprehensible for our geographical position, where he himself noted:

"Would not Trutin (Triton) be the same word that appears in the Greek divine names Τρίτων, Αμφιτρήτη, Τριτογένεια? The Greeks always had in mind some dark water when it comes to this ancient word, which is somewhat obscure in terms of meaning. In the first, in the initial mythology of the Hellenes, Triton is the obsolete Sun, which lies in the nocturnal open sea; Amphitrite is the night Dawn to him; and

***Tritogenija Zora*"** - *Nadko Nodilo, Ancient Faith od Serbs and Croats*, p. 90.

Nodilo then noted: "If out of kindness, and out of mercy to the people, who are called Milutin and Dragutin, in the fight with the Wolf, with the black Three-Headed (compare it with Greek. *Κέρβερος*, Latin. *Cerberus* - the three-headed demonic dog guarding the underworld from Greek mythology), the brothers bear personal knightly names: one is *Poyezda*, the rider, an older and solar brother, and the other, who rides next to him, *Prijezda*, the younger brother who is nocturnal and lunar. The Ashvinis, are the two horsemen, who are exactly the same in India. Under the name *Pojezda* and *Prijezda*, they represent three epics [41] songs, made by the heavenly heroes of the two dukes *Gjorge Smederevac*, that is *Poyezda* from Golubac city and *Todor Prijezda* from Stalac, while at the same time he installed the despot Gjorge on the throne of God Vido (Slavic variant for Odin, Wotan). The songs, despite all the recent transformations, are very old in their main content. If in them only *Poyezda* is mentioned, and *Priyezda* is celebrated, it completely coincides with the whole being of the two *Yaksins*, one of whom is far more significant and heroic than the other.

41. Vuk. ps., knj. II, 82-4.

The events of *Prijezda* are, in essence, the same as those of the villain *Jaksic*; and, almost all, agree on the being of the celestial rider. *Prijezda* kidnapped his wife, just as the other *Jaksic* forced him to return the sisters by force, or with the darkness from the lower chambers, the daughter of *Arap-aga* was brought out. For the sake of the woman, when he goes to battle, *Prijezda* "fastens his sword" and puts it on his horse "; which, on every occasion, is the knight's horse and the green sword of the old Warrior or *Yaksha*. With the kidnapped love, the hero "disappears through the clear sky - like a star through the field", and arrives at his court, when "the sun is setting", and "at midnight he married the girl". [42] This strange human wedding at midnight is God's wedding with the Midnight Dawn. The morning dawn is married to the Sun, according to our and Aryan mythology, and the evening dawn to *Prijezda*. *Prijezda* and Dawn are those of happiness because together they fall into the night; the darkened brides of God become *"sugjenik i sugjenica"*. [43] According to the poem, she is loyal to her husband, her usurper, she is chivalrous and radiant. All the pearls of the night and all the gold of the evening and the morning, with which the Aryans shower their triple dawn: her golden suit, and on her head "three garlands of pearls, the fourth of gold, around her neck three necklaces, two of gold, the third of pearl. "[44] He found Prijezda where **"zlatom veze, sve po čistoj svili"** (with gold ties, all in pure silk) [46]; and he found with her also thirty girls who **"belo platno bele"** (whiting white cloth) [46] **"Stara vjera Srba i Hrvata"**, p.76

42. 82, v. 38-9.

43. V. 88—94.

44. V. 55 - 9.

45. V. 61.

46. V. 46-7

The ingenious **Nodilo**, however, lacks knowledge of the arctic region and nature, himself tries to improvise, like **Sâyana**, providing some satisfactory and logical answer to the poem **Marriage of Todor of Stalac** *(Женидба Тодора од Сталаћа),* explaining: **"This bleaching and embroidery, as is known, is wedding preparation for the morning, according to the long-standing worldview of the Aryans. There are thirty maidens in our poem, for our dawn, besides being diurnal and annual, also refers to the moon, which rises and sets, as well as to the day and the year; with us, the day, the moon, and the year, dawn with the dawn, shine at the peak, and then fade in the dusk". "Stara vjera Srba i Hrvata"**, p.77 In another Slavic story from the East, the girl sits on the white-hot stone (Alatyr) on the island of Buyan, weaving red silk in one version, or Zorya with pink fingers, with her golden needle, weaves over the sky a veil of pink and "blood red" colors with a thread of "yellow ore" [36]. She is also depicted as a beautiful golden-haired queen living in a golden kingdom "on the edge of the white world" and rowing across the seas with her golden oar and silver boat. [47]

36. Kos-Lajtman, Andrijana; Horvat, Jasna. *"Utjecaj ruskih mitološki i menoknjiževnih elemenata na discurs Priče iz davnine Ivane Brlić-Mažuranić"* [*Influence of Russian*

mythological and oral literary elements on the dis-course of Priče iz davnine by Ivana Brlić-Mažuranić]. In: Zbornik radova Petoga hrvatskog slavističko kongresa. 2012. p. 160.

As we know the phenomenon of long and rotating dawns in the Polar or Circumpolar region where they draw the colorful landscape leaves no room for indifference or doubt that these old songs of ours reflect the paradise land that our ancestors walked on once upon a time.

• *Easter and Resurrection of the Sun*

"The Christian religion is a parody on the worship of the Sun, in which they put a man whom they call Christ, in the place of the Sun, and pay him the same adoration which was originally paid to the Sun." - Thomas Paine (American philosopher, political theorist, and revolutionary 1737-1809)

Easter in Slavic languages (*Velikden, Великден*) literally means "Great Day". Before getting into the essence of our problem, we will first try to clarify the picture with the help of etymology. In Greek mythology and religion, *Eos* (Ionic and Homeric Greek Ἠώς, *Ēṓs*, Attic Ἕως *Héōs* or Aeolian *Aΰēs, Aōs,)* is the goddess of the dawn, who rose every morning from her home on the banks of the river *Okeanos*, the world's river that found at the end of the world. [1]. The goddess of the dawn is sometimes depicted as eternally young, and ageless, and her coming as rebirth. She is ἠριγένεια "early-born" or "morning-born" as an epithet of *Ēṓs* in the ancient *Iliad*.

The proto-Greek form of Ἠώς or *Ēṓs* is reconstructed as αὐhώς / *auhṓs*, and in Mycenaean Greek as *hāwōs*. According to **Robert S. P. Beekes**, the loss of initial aspiration may be due to metathesis. [2] It is a cognate of the Vedic dawn goddess *Ushas*, the Lithuanian goddess *Aušrinė*, and the Roman goddess *Aurora* (Old Latin *Ausosa*), all three of which are also dawn goddesses. The word for dawn as a meteorological event is also preserved in Balto-Slavic *auṣtro* (lit. *aušrà* "dawn or morning light", a word that is close to Old Slavic word for morning or dawn, or Old Church

Slavic "*ustra*" meaning "morning" [3], in Sanskrit *uṣar* (dawn), or Ancient Greek αὔριον "tomorrow", or the modern Slavic words *jutar, sutar* or *utre, utro* (morning or tomorrow).

1. Boedeker, Deborah D. (1974). *Aphrodite's Entry into Greek Epic*. Brill. p. 77 (In Greek mythology, Ēós is described as living 'beyond the streams of river Okeanos at the ends of the earth).

2. R. S. P. Beekes, *Etymological Dictionary of Greek*, Brill, 2009, p. 492.

3. Lunt, Horace Gray. *Old Church Slavonic Grammar*. 7th revised edition. Berlin; New York: Mouton de Gruyter. 2001. p. 221. See also Pronk, Tijmen. "Old Church Slavonic (j)utro, Vedic uṣar- 'daybreak, morning'". In: L. van Beek, M. de Vaan, A. Kloekhorst, G. Kroonen, M. Peyrot & T. Pronk (eds.) Farnah: Indo-Iranian and Indo-European studies in honor of Sasha Lubotsky. Ann Arbor: Beech Stave Press. 2018. p. 298-306.

The derivative adverb, *huewsteros*, meaning "east" (lit. "dawn"), is reflected in Latvian *àustrums* ("east"), Avestan *ušatara* ("east"), Italic *austero* (cf. The same root seems to be preserved in the Baltic names for the northeast wind: lit. *aūštrinis* and lat. *austrenis, austrinis, austrinš*. [4] Also related to Old Norse *Austri*, described in *Gylfaginning* as one of the four dwarves guarding the four cardinal points (he represents the east), [5] and *Austrvegr* ("Eastern Way"), attested in medieval Germanic literature. [6] A common epithet associated with dawn in the **Rig-Veda** is *Diwós Dhuǵhtér*, meaning "*Daughter of Dyēus*", the Vedic sky god. The cognate forms arising from the formulaic expression appear in three traditions in Vedic, Greek, and Lithuanian, and we find her as "Daughter of Ζεύς / Διός" (probably related to *Ēós* in pre-Homeric Greek) and as "*Daughter of Dievas*" - the celestial god in Lithuanian folklore.

According to the etymology, we can now easily connect this goddess of the Dawn with the goddess *Ashtart* who was celebrated in the Middle East. She was also celebrated in Egypt, especially during the reign of the Ramesids, after the acceptance of foreign cults. The Phoenicians introduced her cult to their colonies on the Iberian Peninsula. *Astártē* was a goddess of both the Canaanite and Phoenician pantheons, derived from an earlier Syrian deity. She is noted in Akkadian as *As-dar-tú*, which is a form of *Ishtar*. [7] The name appears in Ugaritic texts as ʻ*Athtart*, in Phoenician as ʻ*Ashtart,* and Hebrew as *Ashtore*. Among the Akkadians,

Babylonians, and Assyrians, she is known by the name "*Ishtar*", which bears the epithet "Queen of Heaven." According to German-American philologist and comparative mythologist **Michael Witzel**, *Uzume* the dawn goddess in the Shinto religion of Japan is most closely related to the Vedic goddess *Uṣás*). [8]

4. Razauskas, Dainius. (2002) "*Correspondences to the Indo-Iranian Mythical Wind in Lithuanian Folklore* (Some Hints for a Deeper Investigation)". In: *Acta Orientalia Vilnensia*, 3: p. 44.

5. Shipley, Joseph Twadell. *The Origins of English Words: A Discursive Dictionary of Indo-European Roots.* Baltimore and London: The Johns Hopkins University Press. 1984. p. 237

6.Mallory, James P.; Adams, Douglas Q. (2006). *The Oxford Introduction to Proto-Indo-European and the Proto-*Indo-European World, p. 409, 432; West 2007, p. 219

7. K. van der Toorn, Bob Becking, Pieter Willem van der Horst, *Dictionary of Deities and Demons in the Bible*, p. 109-10.

8. Witzel, Michael (2005). Vala and Iwato: *The Myth of the Hidden Sun in India, Japan, and beyond*

We can connect all these forms and names to the Slavic "*istra" (spring, source = izvor, istok, извор, исток)* or "*east*", something that begins and ends in the sense of sunrise and the beginning of the day, but as we said before, the Sun at the North Pole is seen as rises from the south and it is not at all accidental that the source or spring (spring is also a word for the springtime period of the year) or the east (istek, istok, исток, извор, source, spring) of the Dawn and the Sun is exactly from this direction, because etymologically speaking the dawn goddess *Ôstara* among the Germans but also the word itself Balto-Slavic word *auṣtro* ("dawn or morning light") are closely related also connected with the word *austra* and *australis* which means southern direction, hence *Australis* in Latin – southern country, while the Slavic word "*jug*" (South) can perhaps be connected with *yuga* which means cycle and may indicate an annual cycle, i.e. the period when the Sun will again be born on Pole, and with that he will make a full circle. **Sermon Richard** noted in his book that the root goddess certainly comes from the root *austri*, which, if Germanic, would be cognate with Old English *Eostre* [9]. And the Latin word *austri* itself is phonetically identical to the term *australis* and unequivocally means the south, that is, the south side.

9. Sermon, Richard (2008). "*From Easter to Ostara: The Reinvention of a Pagan Goddess?*". Time and Mind. 1 (3): pp. 331–343

From the position of the Arctic, the south represented the path from which the dawn came and the Sun that started the long day. At the North Pole, every direction is south. On the Summer Solstice (~6/21) the Sun will be 23° above the horizon and will remain at 23° all day as it moves 360° around you. As the summer progresses, the Sun will continue to move in circles, gradually approaching the horizon, by the Autumnal Equinox on September 21st, the Sun will have traversed the entire horizon in an all-day moving sunset. As winter progresses, the Sun will disappear, then darkness will fall until next spring. So, at the North Pole, every direction is south. In Ukrainian, "south" is called "*пивдень*", if we separate the word *пив-день* means half-a-day, from which the word noon *(pladne, пладне)* is derived, because in that period of the day the Sun is in the south, while in the Latin language, apart from *australis*, there is also a word for the south side called *meridiem*, which is also a coinage of two words and has exactly the same meaning half-day or mid-day. In Latvian "south" is written as "*dienvidos*", where "*dien*" also means "day", while "*vidos*" can probably relate to the Slavic word "vid", which can finally be interpreted as seeing or seeing the day that began on Artic from the southern direction. The term *auṣtro*, or at least *easter*, appears to have been originally used for the southern side from which the Artic Sun appears to have risen, and in later stages, this expression was probably transferred to denote the eastern side, which also represents the source or rising of the Sun in our temperate and tropical latitudes. But in the Artic region, the south side is probably synonymous with the rising of the sun. However, what is perhaps crucial for our investigation is the very confirmation we have of the Old Church Slavonic word *oustru* (ustrŭ) which means "summer" in the sense of season. Of course, the word "summer" can mean the beginning of the warm period of the year (summer season or Leto in Slavic), but also in the past the word "**лѣто**" *(leto)* also meant a year, a word that we still use in the Slavic world today in the expression "**за многаа лѣта**" meaning *"for many years"* (literally: for many summers). We previously explained that in the past the Indo-Europeans divided the year into two halves, winter and summer. And here we have an obvious connection where the picture becomes even clearer that once in the past the beginning of the year or New Year was really celebrated during the spring, that is, the bright half–summer. Also, the Latin word for summer is *aestas* which is also a synonym for the year (*anus*). The German name for Austria, *Österreich*, derives from the Old High German *Ostarrîchi*, which meant "eastern realm" and which first appeared in the "*Ostarrîchi document*" of 996, but earlier in the past, this word Auster denoted the southern side, that is, the side from where the sun rose. We still have etymological remains that confirm this fact and it can easily be seen in the name of *Terra Australis* (Antarctica) i.e. the Southern Land.

And this in the North Pole, as early as February, the dawn began to wake up and break, while on March 21, exactly during the Spring Equinox, the sunrise began бand thus the day that lasted for six months began. So, the Sun rises in the south and not in the east. In the Arctic region, these dates change as we said due to the different latitudes. It is no coincidence that in the English language the word *Velikden* (Великден, Great Day) means Easter. Easter is essential "New Summer" or *"Ново Лето"* ((*Novo Leto*) which is also "New Year", started with the "day of the gods", the day when the Sun - *"Son of God"* will rise above the horizon (resurrection, Sol Invictus), and with that, the daytime half of the Arctic will begin. Etymologically, the English word Easter comes again from the German spring goddess *Ēostre*. Although she is led as the deity of spring, there is no doubt that she is the personification of the dawn, which is of course the bearer of spring and summer time (New Year). The name *Ēostre* comes from Old English: *Ēastre*, [10] Northumbrian dialect *Ēastro*, [11] Mercian dialect and West Saxon dialect (Old English) *Ēostre*, [12] Old High German: *Ôstara;* Old Saxon *Āsteron*. [13] By way of the Germanic month that bears her name (Northumbrian: *Ēosturmōnaþ*; West Saxon: *Ēastermōnaþ*; Old High German: *Ôstarmânoth*), she is the namesake of the holiday Easter in some languages. *Ēostre* is attested only by **Bede** [14] in his 8th-century work, ***De temporum ratione***, where **Bede** states that during *Ēosturmōnaþ* (equivalent to April), the pagan Anglo-Saxons held feasts in honor of *Ēostre*, but that this tradition it died out by his time and was replaced by the Christian Easter month, a celebration of the resurrection of Jesus.

14. Bede (Old English: Bǣda, Bēda 672/3 – 26 May 735), also known as Saint Bede, The Venerable Bede, and Bede the Venerable (Latin: Beda Venerabilis), was an English monk at the monastery of St Peter and its companion monastery of St Paul in the Kingdom of Northumbria of the Angles (contemporarily Monkwearmouth–Jarrow Abbey in Tyne and Wear, England).

By way of linguistic reconstruction, the matter of the goddess *Austrō* in Proto-Germanic has been studied in detail since the founding of Germanic philology in the 19th century by the scholar **Jacob Grimm** and others. Since the Germanic languages are descended from Proto-Indo-European, historical linguists traced the name back to the Proto-Indo-European dawn goddess from whom the common Germanic divinity of *Ēostre* and *Ôstara* originated. In addition, scholars have linked the goddess's name to various Germanic personal names, several place names (toponyms) in England, and, discovered in 1958, over 150 inscriptions from the 2nd century AD. relating to the *matronae Austriahenae*. So, the theonyms *Ēostre* or *Ēastre* (Old English) and *Ôstra* (Old High German) are cognates - linguistic sisters arising from a common origin. To repeat, they come from the proto-Germanic theonym *Austrō(n),* in the Baltic languages *auš(t)ra* (dawn, morning) The modern English word "east" (Slavic исток, *istok*) also derives from this root, through the Proto-Germanic adverb *aust(e)raz* ("east, towards the east") and here we must not bypass the Latin word *australis* meaning south instead of east. [15]

15. Kroonen, Guus (2013). *Etymological Dictionary of Proto-Germanic.* Page 43

According to linguist **Guus Kroonen**, Germanic and Baltic languages replaced the old formation *héwsos*, the name of the dawn goddess in Proto-Indo-European, also found in the Lithuanian deity *Aušrinė*. In Anglo-Saxon England, its spring festival borrowed, as we have said, its name from the month *Ēosturmōnaþ*, the West Saxon *Eastermonað*, [16] the equivalent of April, and then from the Christian holiday of Easter, which it eventually superseded. [17] In southern medieval Germany, the *Ôstarûn* festival similarly gave its name to the month *Ôstarmânôth* and to the modern festival of *Ostern* ("Easter", suggesting that a goddess named

Ôstara was also worshiped there. **[18]** The name of the month survives in 18th-century German as *Ostermonat*. An Old Saxon equivalent of the spring goddess called *Āsteron* can also be reconstructed from the term *asteronhus*, which is translated by most scholars as "Easter House" (cf. Medieval Flemish Paeshuys "Easter House"). The French historian **Einhardus** also writes in his ***Vita Karoli Magni*** (early 9th century AD) that after Charlemagne defeated and converted the mainland Saxons to Christianity, he gave German names to the Latin months of the year, which include the Easter month of **Ostarmanoth**.

16. Sermon Richard (2008). *"From Easter to Ostara: The Reinvention of a Pagan Goddess?"*. Time and Mind. 1 (3): 331–343

17. West, Martin L. (2007). *Indo-European Poetry and Myth.* p. 217–218

18. Simek Rudolf (1996). *Dictionary of Northern Mythology.* P. 255

Analogous to this, the question arises logically: Why exactly was the month of April or *Ostarmanoth* named in honor of the goddess of the dawn? The answer is more than clear, in that period the dawn of the Arctic or Circa-Arctic region was rising, and that tradition was later transferred and preserved in Europe during the age of migrations. In chapter 15 (***De mensibus Anglorum***, "The English Months") of his 8th-century **work De temporum ratione** ("*The Reckoning of Time*"), **Bede** describes the native month names of the English people. After describing the worship of the goddess *Rheda* during the Anglo-Saxon month of *Hrēþ-mōnaþ*, **Bede** writes of *Ēosturmōnaþ*, the month of the goddess Ēostre:

Eostur-monath, qui nunc Paschalis mensis interpretatur, quondam a Dea illorum quæ Eostre vocabatur, et cui in illo festa celebrabant nomen habuit: a cujus nomine nunc Paschale tempus cognominant, consueto antiquæ observationis vocabulo gaudia novæ solemnitatis vocantes.

Translation:

"Eostur-monath bears a name now translated as "Easter month," which was once called after their goddess named Eostre, in whose honor the festivals were celebrated in that month. Now they mark that paschal

(Easter) time by her name, calling the joys of the new rite by the time of the holy name of the old celebration". [19]

19. Giles (1843:179)

In his 1835 **Deutsche Mythologie, Jacob Grimm** cites comparative evidence to reconstruct a potential continental Germanic goddess whose name would have been preserved in the Old High German name of *Easter, Ostara*. Addressing skepticism towards goddesses mentioned by **Bede**, **Grimm** comments that "there is nothing improbable in them, nay the first of them is justified by clear traces in the vocabularies of Germanic tribes." Specifically, regarding Ēostre, Grimm continues:

"We Germans call April ostermonat to this day, and ôstarmânoth is still found in Eginhart (temp. Car. Mag.). The great Christian holiday, which usually falls in April or at the end of March, is preserved in the oldest High German, where the name ôstarâ remains ... mostly found in the plural because two days were kept at Easter. This feast of Ostarâ, like the [Anglo-Saxon] Eástre, must have signified in heathen religion some higher being, whose worship was so firmly rooted, that the Christian teachers tolerated the name, and applied it to one of their greatest feasts. [20]

20. Grimm (1882:290)

Grimm notes that "all the nations bordering on us have kept the biblical Passover; even **Ulphilas** writes ΠΛSRΛ, not ΛΠSTRΩ *(pasca not áustrô)*, though he must have known the word". **Grimm** states that the Old High German adverb *ôstar* "expresses movement towards the rising sun", as does the Old Norse term *austr*, and potentially also Anglo-Saxon ēastor and Gothic ΛΠSTR *(áustr)*. **Grimm** compares these terms to the identical Latin term *auster* and argues that the cult of the goddess may have centered around the Old Norse form, *Austra*, or that her cult may have already died out by the time of Christianization. **Grimm** notes that in the book *Gylfaginning* in the Old Norse **Prose Edda** testifies to a male being called *Austri*, whom he describes as a "spirit of light". **Grimm** comments that the feminine version would be *Austra*, yet that the High Germanic and Saxon peoples seem to have formed only *Ostarâ* and *Eástre*, feminine,

264

and not *Ostaro* and *Eástra*, masculine. **Grimm** further speculates about the nature of the goddess and the surviving folk customs that may have been associated with her in Germany: ***"Therefore, it seems that Ostarâ and Eástre was the divinity of the radiant dawn, of the rising light, a spectacle that brings joy and blessing, the meaning of which can easily be adapted to the day of resurrection of the Christian God. On Easter, bonfires were lit and according to a long-standing belief, at the moment when the sun rises on Sunday morning, he gives three joyful jumps, dances with joy... The water that is taken out on Easter morning is, like that of Christmas, holy and healing and here pagan notions seem to have been grafted onto the great Christian holidays. Girls dressed in white, who on Easter, in the annual time of returning spring, show themselves in the clefts of the rocks and mountains, suggesting the ancient goddess"***. [21]

21. Grimm (1882:291)

In the second volume of **Deutsche Mythologie, Grimm** again raised the subject of *Ostarâ*, speculating on possible connections between the goddess and various German Easter customs, and Easter eggs:

"But if we admit the goddesses, then, besides Nerthus, Ostarâ has the strongest claim for consideration. To what we said on p. 290 I can add a few significant facts. The pagan Easter had much in common with the May festival and the welcoming of spring, especially in relation to bonfires. Then, through many centuries, it seems that the so-called folk entertainment, connecting it with Christian reminiscences".

Grimm commented on further customs during Easter, including unique sword dances and certain cakes ("heathen-shaped pastry"). In addition, **Grimm** weighed a potential connection with the Slavic spring goddess *Vesna* and the Lithuanian *Vasara*. [22]

22. Grimm (1883:780–78)

The Christian holiday Easter is also synonymous with the holiday of Passover (Hebrew: פסח, *Pesach* – meaning "passing over" or "passing") and is an eight-day holiday celebrating the escape of the Jews from Egypt under the leadership of Moses. The holiday always falls in the spring, on Saturday, the 15th day of the month of Nisan, according to the Jewish calendar. However, this Jewish story is far from the true meaning of this holiday. Passover is actually the transition from the winter (night) to the summer half (day), and we explained that the word "summer" simultaneously means year, and the holiday itself means New Year or Easter.

• *Nowruz - Spring New Year*

"The first day of the official New Year [Nowruz] was always the day on which the sun entered Aries before noon" - *Muhammad ibn Muhammad ibn al-Hasan al-Tūsī (1201 –1274, Persian polymath, architect, philosopher, physician, scientist, and theologian.)*

Nowruz is the Persian-language term for the day of the Iranian New Year, also known as the Persian New Year. It begins on the spring equinox and marks the beginning of Farvardin, the first month of the Solar Hijri calendar (an Iranian calendar used officially in Iran and Afghanistan). The day is celebrated worldwide by various ethnolinguistic groups and falls on or around the date of 21 March on the Gregorian calendar. [1]

1. R. Abdollahy, Calendars ii. Islamic period, in Encyclopaedia Iranica, Vol. 4, London & New York, 1990.

The day of Nowruz has its origins in the Iranian religion of Zoroastrianism and is thus rooted in the traditions of the Iranian people; however, it has been celebrated by diverse communities for over 3,000 years in Western Asia, Central Asia, the Caucasus, the Black Sea Basin, the Balkans, and South Asia. [2] Presently, while it is largely a secular holiday for most celebrants and enjoyed by people of several different faiths and backgrounds, Nowruz remains a holy day for Zoroastrians, [3] Bahá'ís, and some Muslim communities [4]. The first day of the Iranian calendar falls on the March equinox, the first day of spring, around 21 March. In the 11th century CE, the Iranian calendar was reformed in order to fix the beginning of the calendar year, i.e., Nowruz, at the vernal equinox. As the spring equinox, Nowruz marks the beginning of spring in the Northern Hemisphere. [5] The moment at which the Sun crosses the celestial equator and equalizes night and day is calculated exactly every year, and families traditionally gather together to observe the rituals. Nowruz is the first day of Farvardin, the first month of the Iranian solar calendar.

2. "General Assembly Recognizes 21 March as International Day of Nowruz, Also Changes to 23–24 March Dialogue on Financing for Development – Meetings Coverage and Press Releases". UN. Retrieved 20 March 2017. Also, Kenneth Katzman (2010). Iran: U. S. Concerns and Policy Responses; General Assembly Fifty-fifth session 94th plenary meeting Friday, 9 March 2001, 10 a.m. New York.

3. Azoulay, Vincent (1 July 1999). *Xenophon and His World: Papers from a Conference Held in Liverpool in July 1999*

4. Isgandarova, Nazila (3 September 2018). *Muslim Women, Domestic Violence, and Psychotherapy: Theological and Clinical Issues. Routledge.*

5. "What Is Norooz? Greetings, *"History and Traditions to Celebrate the Persian New Year"*. International Business Times. Retrieved 1 February 2016.

The word *Nowruz* is a combination of Persian words نو *now* – meaning "new" – and روز *ruz* – meaning "day". A variety of spelling variations for the word nowruz exist in English-language usage, including *novruz, nowruz, nauruz and newroz.* [6] The very holiday or festival of New Year, as we see, is called "new day" and it seems that this is not at all accidental. If the ancient location of the best of all countries (according to the book *Vendidad*), the so-called *Airyanəm Vaējah* (Old Iran, Iranian Paradise) was really once located at the North Pole, then this name is quite logical, because then the new day began, which lasted for 6 months in full glory.

6. Elien, Shadi, "Is the Persian New Year spelled Norouz, Nowruz, or Nauruz?", The Georgia Straight, March 17, 2010.

7. *Vendidad 1.1 "The first of the good lands and countries which I, Ahura Mazda, created, was the Airyanem Vaejah, by the good river Daitya".* (translated by James Darmesteter). Also, Zoroastrian tradition knows at least two other terms that associate the Iranian people with a geographical region. The first is found in the Avesta specifically in the *Mihr Yasht. Vers Yt. 10.13* describes how Mithra reaches Mount Hara and overlooks the *Airyoshayana* (Avestan: airyō.šayana, 'Iranian lands'). Mount Hara is definitely the same as Mount Meru or Su-Meru of the Vedic, Buddhist, and Jain traditions.

Today in Europe we have a distorted calendar with distorted dates, but we are not the only ones, most calendars are incorrect. The calendar (Lat. *kalendae)* i.e. Slavic *"kolodar"* (circle) must always follow the natural rhythm and on the basis of that rhythm are built the celebrations and holidays which have above all religious or spiritual elements which in the end should also bring certain results. For that reason, distortion occurs today, which can be seen in the school year or the season itself, so some who were born in 1987 may be in the same class as those who were born in 1988. Also, we celebrate the New Year, then the Old New Year (*Vasilitsa* or *Serbian New Year*), which has absolutely no logic. Let's forget for a moment about this present-day calendar template and do some research on when the New Year was really celebrated among other Indo-European peoples.

We see that December (*Decembris*) which means the tenth (Lat. *decem* = 10) is now the twelfth month, then November (Lat. *Novembris*) which means the ninth (from (Lat. *novem* = 9) is now the eleventh month, October (Lat. *Octobris*) which means eighth (*octingenti* = 9) it is now the tenth month or September (*Septembris*) which means the seventh (*septis* = 7) is now the ninth month of the year. From here it is clear that we have a problem with a difference of two months. If we add those two months to the tenth month of December, then all fall into place in its natural and logical sequence. Thus, the month of February is the last month of the year. Let me first say that oriental scholars have advanced vague and uncertain conjectures about the age and character of the Vedas. ***Prof. Max Müller*** has divided the Vedic literature into four arbitrary periods, *Chandas, Mantras, Brahmna* and *Suttra,* and assigning two hundred years to each period he arrives at about 1200 B.C. as the latest date for the age and age when the Vedic hymns were composed. Against this linguistic method of determining the age of the Vedas, there is an astronomical method which, though condemned by European scholars as inaccurate and conjectural, may, if properly applied, lead us to good results. The *Vedas, Brahmanas,* and *Sutras* contain numerous allusions and references to astronomical facts. In the ***Rig-Veda,*** we have several sacrificial hymns. Now, no sacrificial system can be developed without knowledge of the months, the seasons, and the year. It appears that the Vedic Rishis (sages) or in Cambodia also known as Ruesi (Sanskrit: ṛṣi, Khmer: សាគិា) maintained their calendar by performing the appropriate round of sacrifices to the sacred fire that burned continuously in their houses; and as they were not only the sacrifices of the community but were also its time-keepers, these two functions seem to have merged into one by assigning the commencement of the several sacrifices to the leading days of the year on the natural ground that if sacrifices were to be performed, they had to be performed on the main days of the year. Therefore, *Samvatasarata* and *Yajna* (sacrifice) are considered convertible terms. Now let us examine the main parts of the year alias the sacrifice. The *savannah* or civil day, as its etymology indicates, was chosen as the natural unit of time and 30 such days made a month and 12 such months or 360 *savana* days made a year. Now, a month of 30 civil or *savana* days could not correspond to a lunar synodic month, and it was therefore necessary to omit a day in some of the *savana* months to ensure the coincidence of the civil and lunar months. Thus, the year of 360 Savannah days was practically reduced to a lunar year of 354 civil days or 360 *titis*. But further correction was necessary to bring the moon into line with the solar reckoning of time. Hence the commencement of the cycle of the seasons was the only means of correcting the calendar, and the ancient Aryans hit upon the device of the intercalary days or months for this purpose. The early Aryans had to determine the position of the Sun in the ecliptic by observing, each morning, the fixed star nearest to it. Under such a system, the year would naturally end when the Sun returns to the same fixed star. Accordingly, the solar year mentioned in the Vedic works must be considered sidereal and not tropical. The difference between a sidereal year and a tropical year is 20.4 minutes which causes the seasons to move back almost one lunar month every two thousand years. When these changes were first noticed, they caused surprise and were thought to portend some great calamity.

Another important point, relevant to our purpose, is when the year began. **Vedanga Jyotisha** makes the year (and *Uttrayana* also known as *Devayana*) begin with the Winter Solstice. But a closer examination shows that the Winter Solstice (21.10) could not have been the initial beginning of the annual sacrifices (and thus the year). The middle day of the annual Satra is called *Vishnuvan*, where *Vishnuvan* literally means the time when day and night are of equal length, if we assume that the year began with the Winter Solstice, *Vishnuvan* or the Equinox (Vernal Equinox) could never have its central day. If *Vishnuvan* was the central day of the year, the year must have begun sometime with the Equinox. We may therefore take *Devayana* as 'the passage of the Sun into the Northern Hemisphere, ie. north of the equator; and thus, we can say that the *Uttrayana or Devayana* had to begin with the Vernal Equinox. While describing the *Devayana* (path of gods) and *Pitrayana* (path of ancestors), the scripture *Śatapatha Brāhmaṇa* (II-I-3-3). clearly establishes that *Vasanta* (Rus. *Vesna*, lit. *Vasaru*, translated as Spring period), *Grishma*, and *Varsha* were the seasons of the Gods or Devas (Summer Semester). It is therefore impossible to claim that the *Devayana* - ever began with the Winter Solstice, because in neither hemisphere does the Winter Solstice mark the beginning of Spring, the first of the Deva seasons. It is difficult to determine the time when and why the beginning of the year was changed from the Vernal Equinox to the Winter Equinox when this change was made, but the *Devayana* must have gradually marked the first half of the New Year, i.e. the period from the Winter Solstice to the Summer Solstice especially since the word could be understood as "moving northward from the southernmost point."

All our current calendars are prepared on the assumption that the Vernal Equinox still coincides with the end of *Revati* (the star *Zeta Piscium*), and the current enumeration of the Nakshatras begins with *Ashvini* (corresponding to the head of Aries, including the stars β and γ of Arietis)., although the Equinox has now moved about 18° from *Revati*. This position of the Vernal Equinox was correct around 490 AD when the current system was probably introduced. Now let's see if we can trace the position of the Vernal Equinox among the fixed circle of stars. From **Varahamihira** [1], we know that before the Hindus began to make their measurements from the Vernal Equinox at *Revati*, there was a system in which the year began with the Winter Solstice in the month of *Magha*, and the Vernal Equinox was in the last quarter of *Bharani* or the beginning of *Kṛttikā* (the Pleiades). **Vedanga Jyotisha**, the oldest astronomical work in Sanskrit, gives the following positions of the Solstice and Equinox:

(1) Winter solstice at the beginning of Sravishta (astronomer: α to δ Delphini) known later also as Dhanishta (divisional).

(2) Vernal equinox at 10° from Bharani (astronomer: 35, 39, and 41 Arietis).

(3) Summer Solstice in the middle of Āśleṣā (astron. δ, ε "Āshleshā Nakshatra", η, ρ, and σ "Minchir" Hydrae)

(4) The Autumnal Equinox at 3° 20' of Vishākhā.

1. Varahamihira (c. 505 – c. 587), also called Varaha or Mihira, was an ancient Indian astrologer, astronomer, and polymath who lived in Ujjain (Madhya Pradesh, India). He was born in Kayata. Varahamihira's most important work is the Brihat Samhita, an encyclopedic work on architecture, temples, planetary movements, eclipses, timekeeping, astrology, seasons, cloud formation, rainfall, agriculture, mathematics, gemology, perfumery, and many other subjects.

From this data, astronomers calculated that the Sun occupied the upper position between 1269 BC. to 1181 BC. There are many passages in the ***Taittiriya Samhita*** and the ***Taittiriya Brahmana*** where *Kṛttikā* (the Pleiades) occupies the first place in the list of Nakshatras. We must therefore assume that the Vernal Equinox coincided with *Kṛttikā* when the ***Taittiriya Samhita*** was composed. The ***Taittiriya Brahmana** (I, 5, 2, 7)* says that the Nakshatras are the houses of the Gods and that the Nakshatras of the Devas begin with *Kṛttikā*. The ***Śatapatha Brāhmaṇa*** expressly states that the Sun was to be regarded as moving among the Devas and protecting them, when it turned towards the north, in the three seasons, spring, summer, and rains (the Hindu division of the seasons). This, therefore, immediately fixes the position of *Kṛttikā* at the beginning of the *Devayana* or Vernal Equinox at the time when these works were composed. The Vedas turns out to be twice as old as commonly assumed. The ***Taittiriya Samhita*** expressly states that the Winter Solstice fell then in *Maghā* (*Regulus*). From all this, we conclude that the *Kṛttikā* (Pleiades) coincided with the Vernal Equinox when the ***Taittiriya Samhita*** was composed (2350 BCE) while the Vedas are even older. The passage in the ***Taittiriya Samhita*** which states that the Winter Solstice fell in *Maghā* also refers to the Full Moon *Phalguni* and Full Moon *Chitra* nakshatra if the first days of the year. Now, since there obviously cannot be true beginnings of the year at intervals of one month, the passage must be understood as recording the tradition that these two days of the full moon were once regarded as the first days of the year. If the year began on the Winter Solstice with the *Phalguni* Full Moon, the Vernal Equinox must have been at *Mṛgaśīrā* (*Orion, λ, φ Orionis*). With the Vernal Equinox near the asterism of *Mṛgaśīrā*, the Autumnal Equinox would be at *Mūlā* which was so named because its achronic rising marked the beginning of the year. Again, with the Winter Solstice occurring on the day of the *Phalguni* Full Moon, the Summer Solstice fell on the *Bhādrapada* Full Moon, so that the dark half of *Bhādrapada* was the first fortnight in *Pitrayana*, understood as the commencement of the Summer Solstice. No other hypothesis can satisfactorily account for the devotion of the dark half of *Bhādrapada* to the Pitris. [2]

2. See in detail Tilak, Bal Gangadhar, *The Orion or the Antiquity of the Vedas*, 1893

Also, in the whole Europe in the past, the year was divided into summer and winter, i.e. *Devayna* or *Uttarayana* and *Pitriyana* or *Dakshinayna*. New Year or in German *Neu Jar*, is the same as *New Summer (Ново Лето)*, where summer also means year in this case, and *New Yar* etymologically itself is the equivalent of the Slavic god fire god Yarilo, converted later into Saint George the Dragonslayer in the time of Christianization, where the Dragon is a symbol of the chthonic winter period of the year – *Pitrayana* and St. George as a young solar knight - a symbol of fire sign Aries under the rule of war planet - Mars. Also, in astrology, the Sun is exalted in the sign of Aries. The Old Slavic god Yarilo is astrologically connected to the Roman god Mars and the Greek god Ares as it was celebrated in the early spring just as the Sun transits through the constellation of Aries. This is the first sign in the zodiac under the auspices of the planet Mars (Ares, Ram = Mar), which corresponds to the Vedic deity of fire – Agni (the Slavic word *Agan* or *Ogan* means "fire"), and that is the period when a sacrificial lamb (Lamb of God, Slavic: *agnec, jagne*) was ritually sacrificed in the spring. It is no coincidence that March is called Mars in French. The dawn (represented by Slavic Goddess Zarya) heralds the new day which started the New Year (Great Day or *Velikden*) with the beginning of the Aries constellation (represented by the Slavic God Yarillo).

• *The World Egg*

हिरण्यगर्भः समवर्तताग्रे भूतस्य जातः पतिरेकासीत |

स दाधार पर्थिवीं दयामुतेमां कस्मै देवायहविषा विधेम ||

In the beginning rose Hiranyagarbha, born Only Lord of all created beings.
He fixed and holdeth up this earth and heaven. - *Rig-Veda,*
Hiraṇyagarbha Sūkta 10.121

Hiranyagarbha (Sanskrit: *हिरान्यगर्भः*, literally "golden womb" or "golden egg") is the source of all cosmic creation or the manifested cosmos in Vedic philosophy, but also as an avatar of Vishnu in the ***Bhagavat Purana***. The concept of the golden womb is mentioned again in the *Vishvakarman Sukta* (*R.V. 10.82*). The *Nasadya Sukta*, the Hymn of Creation in the ***Rig-Veda*** *(10:129)* reports that the world began from the point or *bindu*, through the powers of heat. The earliest idea of the *"Cosmic Egg"* comes from some of the Sanskrit scriptures. The Sanskrit term for it is *Brahmanda* (ब्रह्माण्ड) which is derived from two words – 'Brahma' (ब्रह्मा) the 'creator god' in Hinduism and *'anda'* (अण्ड) meaning 'egg'. Certain Puranas such as the ***Brahmanda Purana*** speak of this in detail. The *Upanishads* elaborate that the *Hiranyagarbha* floated around in emptiness for a while, and then broke into two halves which formed Dyaus (the Heaven) and Prithvi (Earth). The ***Rig Veda*** has a similar coded description of the division of the universe in its early stages. This can also be considered as a correspondence with the "Big Bang" theory. In South Slavic riddles and children's folklore, the Sun is depicted as "the egg of God", the stars as eggs laid by the heavenly hen", while the starry sky is "a nest full of eggs". The world egg, cosmic egg, or mundane egg is a mythological motif found in the cosmogonies of many cultures that is present in Proto-Indo-European culture [1] and other cultures and civilizations. Typically, the world egg is a beginning of some sort, and the universe or some primordial being comes into existence by "hatching" from the egg, sometimes lying on the primordial waters of the Earth. [2] Eggs symbolize the unification of two complementary principles (represented by the egg white and the yolk) from which life or existence, in its most fundamental philosophical sense, emerges.

Jacob Bryant's Orphic Egg (1774)

The Orphic Egg in the ancient Greek Orphic tradition is the cosmic egg from which hatched the primordial hermaphroditic deity Phanes/Protogonus (variously equated also with Zeus, Pan, Metis, Eros, Erikepaios and Bromius) who in turn created the other gods. [3]

1. Leeming, David Adams (2010). *Creation Myths of the World: An Encyclopedia, Book 1.* ABC-CLIO. p. 144.

2. Anna-Britta Hellborn, "The creation egg", Ethnos: *Journal of Anthropology*, 1, 1963, pp. 63-105.

3. West, M. L. (1983) *The Orphic Poems.* Oxford: Oxford University Press. p. 205

The egg is often depicted with a serpent wound around it. Many threads of earlier myths are apparent in the new tradition. Phanes was believed to have been hatched from the World egg of *Chronos* (Time) and *Ananke* (Necessity) or *Nyx* (Night). His older wife Nyx called him Protogenus. As she created nighttime, he created daytime. He also created the method of creation by mingling. He was made the ruler of the deities and passed the scepter to Nyx. This new Orphic tradition states that Nyx later gave the scepter to her son Uranos before it passed to Cronus and then to Zeus, who retained it. The ancient Egyptians accepted multiple creation myths as valid, including those of the Hermopolitan, Heliopolitan, and Memphite theologies. Under the Hermopolitan theology, there is the Ogdoad, which represents the conditions before the gods were created *(Van Dijk, 1995)*. An aspect within the *Ogdoad* is the Cosmic Egg, from which all things are born. Life comes from the Cosmic Egg; the sun god Ra was born from the primordial egg in a stage known as the first occasion *(Dunand, 2004)*. In the **Kalevala**, the Finnish national epic, there is a myth of the world being created from the fragments of an egg laid by a goldeneye on the knee of Ilmatar, goddess of the air:

> *One egg's lower half transformed*
> *And became the earth below,*
> *And its upper half transmuted*
> *And became the sky above;*
> *From the yolk, the sun was made,*
> *Light of day to shine upon us;*
> *From the white, the moon was formed,*
> *Light of night to gleam above us;*
> *All the colored brighter bits*
> *Rose to be the stars of heaven*
> *And the darker crumbs changed into*
> *Clouds and cloudlets in the sky.*

In many original folk poems, the duck - or sometimes an eagle - laid its eggs on the knee of Väinämöinen. [4]

4. Martti Haavio: Väinämöinen: Suomalaisten runojen keskushahmo. Porvoo

The eggs were painted and decorated (Ukrainian: *пищанки*) in the spring, usually in red, which symbolized the Sun, heat, fire, and health, where the goddess Vesna brought them with her arrival. Eggs together with bread and wine were offered to the hosts of the house. The symbolism of rebirth - return to life also determines the symbolism of the use of the egg in the funeral rites: at the time of the funeral, chicken eggs (sometimes wooden or clay) were placed in the hands of the deceased, and they were also placed in the coffin, they threw him into a river, buried him in the ground, threw him into a fire, etc. In West-Slavic folklore, eggs are used throughout the year in the rites of the first plowing and sowing of the harvest, in livestock magic, as a healing agent; they threw it in the air during the sowing of flax and hemp, scattered the husk on the vegetable garden, etc. Among the Serbs, on the first plowing, an egg is broken from the forehead of the right ox or the plow, placed in the furrow, and the grain seed was blessed with it. Among the Balkan peoples, there was a series of beliefs about the egg as a symbol of fertility and the birth of new life. When the hen lays an egg with two yolks, it is a good sign for the household. The people say that it is a prediction that the housewife will soon become pregnant. To ease her labor pains, an egg was slipped through the shirt of the woman in labor. In a Kraishita in Serbia, three eggs were buried in the fields so that the harvest would be fruitful and good. There is also a custom where the egg is buried in an anthill as the household would prosper, to be industrious and numerous like the ants. The custom of "rolling eggs" was widely spread among Russians: for a whole week, young people had fun rolling the colored eggs on the ground. Eggs are also rolled on the graves of dead relatives when they go to greet them. Russian church teachings from the 17th century also tell us that all these ancient customs have nothing to do with Christianity, where among various church rules there is also a ban on "breaking eggs" because it is not a Christian custom *("Slovenian mythology - encyclopedic dictionary", Belgrade, 2001.)* The custom of breaking eggs existed for a long time in the East Slavic Easter tradition, and in ours, the South Slavic one, it has survived to this day. Coloring and decorating eggs *(пищанки)* was once, also, not only a general Slavic custom but a custom among all Indo-European Aryan peoples connected with the spring period and the awakening of nature. It is the beginning of the year, ie Easter. *Pisanka (Пищанка)* is a Ukrainian Easter egg, decorated with traditional folk designs using the wax resist method. The word *pisanka* comes from the verb *pisati*, "to write" or "to paint" because the designs are written (inscribed) with beeswax, not paint. According to many scholars, the art of decorating eggs with wax (batik) in Slavic cultures probably dates back to the pre-Christian era. They base this on the widespread nature of the practice and the pre-Christian nature of the symbols used. [5] There are no ancient examples of intact *pysanki*, as the eggshells of domesticated birds are fragile, but fragments of painted shells with wax-resistant decoration on them were unearthed during archaeological excavations in Ostrowek, Poland (near the town Opole), where remains of a Slavic settlement from the early Piast era have been found. [6]

5. Kilimnik, Stepan. *Український рик у народних доваях в историчкому обславленний*, том. III, Spring cycle. Winnipeg, Toronto: Ukrainian Research Institute of Volyn' p. 189-191

6. "Opole: *najstarsze polskie "pisanki" znaleziono na opolskim Ostrówku*". onet.pl. 31 March 2013.

As in many ancient cultures, Ukrainians (Russians) worshiped the sun god, Dazhbog (lit. *Giver God, Deus Donnor*). The sun was important - it warmed the earth and was thus the source of all life, but its glory and the cult of rebirth are due to the ancient arctic tradition. Eggs decorated with symbols of nature became an integral part of spring rituals, serving as good-natured talismans. In pre-Christian times, Dazhbog was one of the main deities in the Slavic pantheon; birds were the chosen creations of the sun god because they were the only ones who could approach him. People could not catch the birds, but they managed to get the eggs that the birds laid. Thus, eggs were magical objects, a source of life. The egg was also used during spring festivals - it represented the rebirth of the earth. Its shape itself reminds me of the belly of a pregnant woman, who was supposed to bring a new life. When the long, hard, and dark winter is over; the earth burst forth and gives birth again just as the egg miraculously burst forth bearing life. Therefore, the egg was believed to have special powers. [7] With the advent of Christianity, through a process of religious syncretism, the symbolism of the egg was changed to represent, not the rebirth of nature, but the rebirth of the man of God. Christians accepted the symbol of the egg and compared it to the tomb from which Christ rose. [8] With the adoption of Christianity in 988, the decorated pysanka was, over time, adapted to play an important role in the Russian rituals of the new religion. Many symbols of the old sun worship survived and were adapted to represent Easter and the resurrection of Christ. [9]

7. Manko, Vira. *The Ukrainian Folk Pysanka L'viv, Ukraine*: Svichado, 2005

8. Anne Jordan (April 5, 2000). *Christianity*. Nelson Thornes. Easter eggs are used as a Christian symbol to represent the empty tomb. The outside of the egg looks dead, but inside there is new life, which is going to break out. The Easter egg is a reminder that Jesus will rise from His tomb and bring new life.

9. Binyashevskyi, Erast. *Український Писанки* (Ukrainian Pysanky) Kyiv: «Art», 1968

No real *pysanki* have been found from the prehistoric periods of Ukraine because the eggshells do not preserve well. Ceramic cult eggs were discovered in the excavations near the village of Luka Vrublivetska, during the excavations of the Tripiliana site (from 5000-3000 millennium BC). These eggs were also decorated in the form of *torohkalci* (*torohkalci;* rattle with small pebbles used to scare away evil spirits). [10] Similarly, there are no actual *pysanki* from the Kievan Rus period, but stone, clay, and bone versions exist and have been excavated at many sites throughout Old Russia (modern Ukraine). The most common are the ceramic eggs decorated with the plant known as horsetail *(sosonka)* in yellow and light green on a dark background. More than 70 such eggs have been dug up across Ukraine, many of them from the graves of children and adults. They are thought to be representations of real decorated eggs. The Hutuls - a group of Russians who live in the Carpathian Mountains around western Ukraine - believe that the fate of the world depends on *pysanka*. If the custom of writing eggs continues, the world will exist. If for any reason, this ritual is abandoned, evil—in the form of a terrible serpent forever chained to a rock—will overtake the world. Every year the snake sends his minions to see how many *pysankas* have been written. If the number is small, the snake's chains are loosened and it is free to roam the earth causing chaos and destruction. If, on the other hand, the number of Easter eggs increases, the chains tighten, and good triumphs over evil for another year. [11]

10. Kirichenko, M.A. *Ukrainian National Decorative Painting Kyiv*: "Znannia-Press", 2008

11. Voropai, Oleksa. *Звичаї Нашого Народу* (*Folk Customs of Our People*) Kyiv: «Обериг», 1993.

More recent legends have blended folklore and Christian beliefs and firmly attached the egg to the Easter celebration. One of the legends refers to the Virgin Mary. She tells about the time when Mary gave eggs to the soldiers on the cross. She begged them to be less cruel to her son and she wept. Mary's tears fell on the eggs, marking them with dots of brilliant color. Another legend tells of when Mary Magdalene went to the tomb to anoint the body of Jesus. She had a basket of eggs with her to serve as breakfast. When she arrived at the grave and discovered the eggs, the pure white shells miraculously turned rainbow-colored. A common legend tells of the salesman Simon, who helped Jesus carry his cross on the way to Calvary. He left his goods by the side of the road, and when he returned, the eggs had turned into beautifully decorated Easter eggs. *Pisankas* were believed to protect households from evil spirits, disaster, lightning, and fire. The *pysankas* with spiral motifs were the most powerful, as demons and other unholy beings would be trapped in them forever. It was believed that the blessed Easter egg could be used to find demons hidden in the dark corners of your house. There were also superstitions regarding the colors and designs of Easter eggs. An old Ukrainian myth centered on the wisdom of giving Easter eggs to older people was given eggs with darker colors or a rich design, for their already fulfilled life. Similarly, it is appropriate to give the young eggs white as the dominant color, because their life is still a blank page. Girls often gave Easter cards to young men they loved and included heart motifs.

Milos S. Milojevic *(Милош С. Милојевић)*, in his book in which he collected rituals entitled ***"Songs and customs of the entire Serbian nation"*** *("Песме и обичаи укупног народа Србског")*, First Book:

> *У вече Ђурђева-дне удевају се у те дудуке пискови, који су направљени из врбових младица.Кад буде скоро око глувог доба ноћи, а негде и раније, момчад из целог села, пошто је се сабрала сва са својим дудуцима на један брег највишији, с ког се сво село види, одигра игру трипут уместо певајућиј и идући с десна на лево или за током сунца ове песме.*

> *On St. George's day, the duduk's (wind instrument), which is made of young willows, is singing. When it is almost nightfall, and sometimes even earlier, boys from the whole village, because they have gathered with their duduks on one bank, the highest, from where the whole village could be seen, played the dance three times instead of singing and going from right to left or for the sun in this song.*

> *Силни вељи Триглаву! Триглаву!*
> *Вишњи боже свесилни, Свесилни!*

Погледај нас нејачке Нејачке,
Твоје створе слабачке Слабачке,
Ми смо деца грешна ти Грешна ти!
Слаби мали нејачки Нејачки,
Удржи нас боже наш, Боже наш!
Боже богов великих, Великих!
Спаси наске и живи, И живи!
Дуго млого година Година.
Кад умремо узми нас
Узми нас Твојим светлим палатам' палатам

Strong and great Three-headed! Three-headed!
Vishnyi (Highest) God almighty, Almighty!
Look at us, little ones, Little ones,
Your weak creature, the weak ones,
We are children, you sinful, you sinful!
Weak little, helpless, helpless.
Keep us, our God, our God!
God of great Gods!
Save us and live, And live! Many, many years.
When we die take us,
Take us to Your bright palace 'palace.

This image is a clear indication of the way of celebrating the arrival of the New Year in the *Devayana* phase, i.e. the beginning of the year in the sign of Aries, the first sign in the zodiac. From all this, we can conclude that the cult of plastering and breaking eggs and celebrating the greatest Christian holiday, Easter (*Велигден* - Great Day), is a very old and ancient ritual in its original essence. This cult originates from the polar regions themselves, where after the long and dark night, spring began with the breaking of the dawn(s) which flared up gradually until the final triumph of the *Sol Invictus* and his victory over the black night. Enough proof is the ancient name of April or *Eostur-monath* dedicated in honor of the goddess of the dawn, and the mere breaking of the shell and the coming out of the yolk is a sufficient symbolic image that can be equated with the birth or resurrection of the Sun.

Chapter VI
Etnologia

"It is useless to speculate on this subject". - Charles Darwin

The location of the cradle of the human race is as much a problem for the ethnologist and anthropologist as it is for the theologian. The archaeologist, the zoologist, and even the biologist, if at all broad and philosophical in their inquiries, cannot ignore the high interest of the questions, was there for the human race one primitive center of distribution? and, if so, where was it located? Thirty years ago, the pretentious American work by *Nott* and *Gliddon*, entitled "*Types of Mankind*" [1] a work written in opposition to the doctrine of the unity of the human race, attracted unusual attention to the former of these questions. The teaching therein put forth was that there are very many types or varieties of men without genealogical connection with each other and that therefore a great number of primitive centers of distribution must be assumed. The avowed prejudices of the projectors of the work against certain races, particularly the African, would have rendered the influence of the work upon the scientific world extremely slight, had not contributions of some value from *Dr. S. G. Morton*, and Professor *Louis Agassiz* been incorporated with it. As it was, it gave European ethnologists the occasion to form and express very uncomplimentary conceptions of American representatives of ethnological research. [2] Fortunately, these crude beginners of the science have had no influential successors of their own sort in this country, and but obscure or half-hearted disciples in any other. [3] The polygeny of the race has at present no respectable support. Even the author of the latest and perhaps ablest of the works on the Preadamite Hypothesis remarks, *"The plural origin of mankind is a doctrine now almost entirely superseded. All schools admit the probable descent of all races from a common stock."* [4] To the second question, therefore, the attention of the scientific and archaeological world is steadily gravitating. Given one primeval point of departure for the race, where shall that point of departure be sought? The answers that recent biologists, naturalists, and ethnologists have given to this problem are hardly less numerous or less conflicting than the solutions proposed by theologians.

1. Philadelphia and London, 1854.

2. Such references as the following are not uncommon: "Unerlässlich bleibt die Behauptung eines einzigen Ausgangsortes sämmtlicher Menschenrassen, *im Gegensatze zur Anthropologenschule unter den Amerikanern, die vielleicht um ihr Gewissen über die vormalige Negersklaverei und den Rassenmord der Indianer zu beruhigen, in neuster Zeit über hundert Menschenarten, nicht Menschenrassen, überhaupt so viele geschaffen hat als Völkertypen sich aufstellen lassen,*" etc.—O. Peschel, in *Ausland*, 1869, p. 1110. Cited in Caspari, *Die Urgeschichte der Menschheit.* 2d ed., Leipsic, 1877, vol. i., p. 241.

3. See Simonin, *L'Homme Américain.* Paris, 1870: p. 12. A. Réville, *Les Religions des Peuples non-civilisés.* Paris, 1883: vol. i., p. 196.

4. Alexander Winchell, *Preadamites; or a Demonstration of the Existence of Men before Adam.* Chicago, 1880: p. 297. One of the latest and most authoritative criticisms and refutations of Agassiz s polygenism is found in Quatrefages, *The Human Race.* N. Y., 1879: chap. Xiv

Of these answers **Professor Zoeckler**, in late work, enumerates ten, each having the support of eminent scientific names. [5] In latitude, they range from Green land to Central Africa, and in longitude from America to Central Asia. Of the whole number, the two which seem to command the widest and weightiest support are, first, the hypothesis that "Lemuria" a wholly imaginary, now submerged prehistoric continent under the northern portion of the Indian Ocean was the "mother region" of the race; and, secondly, that it was in the heart of Central Asia. The former of these sites is the one supported by **Haeckel, Caspari, Peschel**, and many others. [6] Though less positive, **Darwin** and **Lyell** seem favorable to the same location or one in the adjoining portion of Africa. Most of the recent maps of the progressive dispersion of race over the globe have been constructed in accordance with this theory. [7] Perhaps the best popular summary of the arguments in its favor is that found in **Oscar Peschel's** "**Races of Men**". [8]

5. The Cross of Christ. Translated by Evans. London, 1877. Appendix iii., p. 389.

6. Ernst Haeckel, *The Pedigree of Man, and other Essays.* London, 1883: pp. 73-8o. Otto Kuntze, *Phytogeogenesis.* Leipsic, 1884: p. 52, note.

7. See Caspari's in *Die Urgeschichte der Menschheit,* at the close of vol. i.; Kracher's *Ethnographische Weltkarte in Novara Expedition*, Vienna, 1875 Winchell's in his *Preadamites,* p. I.

8. New York, *Appletons*, pp. 26-34.

But while biological speculation, especially in the hands of Darwinists, has strongly inclined toward the chief habitat of the ape tribes in its attempts to find man s primitive point of departure, comparative philologists, mythologists, and archaeological ethnographers have of late very strongly tended to place the cradle of mankind on the lofty plateau of Pamir in Central Asia. For these the eminent French anthropologist, **Quatrefages**, is well entitled to speak. We know [says this savant] that in Asia there is a vast region bounded on the south and south-west by the Himalayas, on the west by the Bolor mountains, on the north-west by the Alla-Tau, on the north by the Altai range and its off-shoots, on the east by the Kingkhan, on the south and south-east by the Felina and Kwen-lun. Judging of it by what exists in the present day, this great central region might be regarded as having included the cradle of the human race. In fact, the three fundamental types of all the races of mankind are represented in the populations grouped around this region. The negro races are the furthest removed from it but have nevertheless marine stations, in which they are found pure or mixed, from the Kiussiu to the Andaman Islands. On the continent they have mingled their blood with nearly all the inferior castes and classes of the two Gangetic peninsulas; they are still found pure in each of them; they ascend as far as Nepal, and, according to Elphinstone, spread to the west as far as the Persian Gulf and Lake Zareh. The yellow race, pure, or mixed here and there with white elements, seems alone to occupy the area in question. The circumference of this region is peopled by it to the north, the east, the southeast, and the west. In the south, it is more mixed, but it nonetheless forms an important element of the population. The white race, by its allophylian representatives, seems to have disputed the possession of even the central area itself with the yellow race. In early times we find the Yu-Tchi, the U-Suns, to the north of Hoang-Ho; and at the present day in Little Tibet, in Eastern Tibet, small islands of white populations have been pointed out. The Miao-Tse occupy the mountainous regions of China; the Siaputhes are proof against all attacks in the gorges of Bolor. On the confines of this area, we find to the east the Ainos and the Japanese of high caste, the Tinguians of the Philippine Islands; to the south the Hindus. To the southwest and west, the white element, pure or mixed, is completely predominant. No other region on the face of the globe presents a similar reunion of the extreme types of the human race distributed around a common center. This fact in itself might suggest to the naturalist the conjecture which I have expressed above, but we may appeal to other considerations. One of the weightiest of these is drawn from philology. The three fundamental forms of human language are found in the same regions and in analogous connections. In the center and the southeast of our area, the monosyllabic languages are represented by the Chinese, the Annamite, the Siamese, and the Tibetan. As agglutinative languages, we find, from the north-east to the north-west, the group of the Ugro-Japanese; in the south that of the Dravidians and the Malays; and in the west the Turkish languages. Lastly, Sanskrit with its derivatives, and the Iranian languages, represent, in the south and south-west, the inflectional languages. With the linguistic types accumulated around this central region of Asia, all human languages are connected, either by their vocabulary or their grammar. Some of these Asiatic languages resemble very closely languages spoken in regions far removed, or separated from the area in question by very different languages. Lastly, it is from Asia, again, that our earliest-tamed domestic animals have come. *Isidore Geoffrey-Saint Hilaire* entirely agreed on this point with *Bureau de la Malle*. Thus, considering only the present epoch, everything leads us back to this central plateau, or rather this vast enclosure. Here, we are inclined to say to ourselves, the first human beings appeared and multiplied down to the moment when the populations overflowed like a bowl which is too full and poured themselves out in human waves in all directions. [9] This view of the location of the first center of the race is very widely accepted. It has the support of many great names. To its establishment contributions have been made by scholars in a great variety of fields. Among them may be mentioned *Lassen, Burnouf, Ewald, Renan, Obry, D Eckstein, Hofer, Senart, Maspero, Lenormant*, etc. Perhaps the most important single treatise representing the view is *Obry's "Cradle of the Human Species"* a work of singular interest to every scholar. [10]

9. The Human Species, pp. 175-177. Quatrefages noteworthy suggestion as to the possibility of a modification of the above con clusion in consequence of the revelations of recent paleontological researches will be noticed in Part III., chapter 7.

10. Le Berceau de l'Espèce Humaine selon les Indiens, les Perses et les Hébreux. Amiens, 1858. See also Lenormant, *Origines de l'Histoire*. Paris, 1882: tom. ii. 1, pp. 41, 144, 145. (Translated in part in *The Contemporary Review*, Sept. 1881.) *Fragments cosmogoniques de Berose*, pp. 300-333. Renan, *Histoire générale des Langues Semitiques*, pp. 475-484. Wilford, *Asiatic Researches*, vol. vi., pp. 455-536, and the following volumes.

But the latest writers on the question are by no means confined to the two locations just mentioned. The difficulty of accounting for the first advent of human beings in America, without supposing in early times a closer land connection between the eastern and western hemispheres in the intertropical regions than now exists, has led not a few ethnologists to postulate a lost Atlantis, including perhaps the Canary and Madeira Islands, or the Azores, or located to the North or South of them, and to place in it the fountainhead of the streams of the population which colonized both the Old and the New World. [11] Another location lately advanced with great confidence and supported with remarkable acuteness and learning is that advocated by **Dr. Friedrich Delitzsch** in his valuable work entitled "*Wo lag das Paradies?* "[12] This site is on the Euphrates between Bagdad and Babylon. [13] In the author's construction, the "four rivers" are the great canal west of the Euphrates, called by the Greeks the Pallacopas, the Shat-en-Nil, and the lower Tigris and Euphrates. But despite the conceded ability of the plea, there seems at the present little prospect that it will secure acceptance among scholars.

11. Unger, Die versunkene Insel Atlantis. Vienna, 1860. An American work in advocacy of this theory is Ignatius Donnelly's *Atlantis: The Antediluvian World*. New York, 1882. In Europe, the hypothesis has been represented as largely abandoned. See Engler, *Die Entwickelungsgeschichte der Pflanzenwelt*. Leipsic, 1879 v i i., p. 82. But a new modification has since appeared in the work of M. Berlioux of Lyons: *Les Atlantes. Histoire de'l Atlantis et de l'Atlas primitif, ou Introduction a l'histoire de l'Europe*. Paris, 1883.

12. Wo lag das Paradies? Eine biblisch-assyriologische Studie. Mit zahlreichen assyriologischen Beiträgen zur biblischen Länder- und Völkerkunde und einer Karte Babyloniens. Von Dr. Friedrich Delitzsch, Professor der Assyriologie an der Universität

Leipzig. Leipsic, 1881. The author is a son of the well-known Biblical scholar Professor Franz Delitzsch, and is himself eminent as an Assyriologist.

13. Compare the language of his fellow-student in Assyriology, Professor Felice Finzi: "Mentre a cercare la culla degli Ariani dobbiamo volgerci ad Oriente, agli Uttara-Kuru degli Indiani, al mitico paradiso degli nomini del monte Meru, all' Airyanem Vaêdjô degli Irani, al regno di Udyana presso al Caschmir; mentre in qualche gruppo del sistema uralo-altaico dee forse indicarsi il centro di formazione della famiglia turanica, e la orografia del Caucaso potrà forse sola determinare il sito più opportuno per lo sviluppo delle tribù che se ne attestano autottone; i Semiti ci si mostrano figli di quella terra ove si sono svolte le pagine più belle della loro storia. È là forse in un angolo di questo paese ricco un tempo dello splendore di una natura lussureggiante che la tribù semita si formò."—*Ricerche per lo Studio dell' Antichità Assira.* Torino, 1872: p. 433.

The distinguished **Theodor Noeldeke**, in a recent review, while cordially praising the learning and ingenuity of the work, professes himself unmoved by its arguments. [14] Similarly a critic in this country writes: "Unfortunately for the theory so powerfully advanced, almost all the linguistic pieces of evidence by which it is supported are still of doubtful value, the etymology of the Babylonian names in most cases, and the reading in some, being disputed by high authorities in this obscure field of inquiry.

14. "Seine Ansicht zu begründen wendet er sehr viel Gelehrsamkeit und noch mehr Scharfsinn auf, aber ich fürchte umsonst. Nach sorgfältiger Prüfung muss ich festhalten an einer Lage des Paradieses in 'Utopien,' wie er etwas spöttisch sagt."—*Zeitsthrift der Deutschen Morgenländischen Gesellschaft*, 1882, p. 174.

Were the linguistic points proved, it would be hard to resist the power of the argument, in spite of various difficulties arising from the scanty text of *Genesis* itself? As it is, although all other solutions of the knotty Biblical problem may be subject to still graver objections, the following questions militate too strongly against **Professor Delitzsch's** solution: Why, if the stream of Eden is the middle Euphrates, is it left unnamed in the narrative, though it is certain that the Hebrews were perfectly familiar both with the middle and the upper course of that river? Why, if the Pison and Gihon designate the canals Pallacopas and *Shat-en-Nil*, are they said to compass lands that the canals only traverse? If the lower Tigris be meant by the Hiddekel, why is this river described as flowing in front of Assyria, which lay above the central Mesopotamian lowland asserted to be Eden? How should a writer familiar with the whole course of the Tigris deem its lower part a branch of the Euphrates? Why should Cush, a name which commonly designated Ethiopia, have been used by the narrator in a sense in which it nowhere else occurs in the Scriptures, without the least further definition? Why, on the other hand, is Havilah, if the Arabian borderland so well known to the Hebrews be meant, so fully described by its products? Who tells us that the gold, the bdellium, and the Soham of Babylonia were also characteristic of the adjoining Havilah? But whether these objections, in the present stage of Assyriological studies, be fatal to the theory of *Professor Delitzsch* or not, we have no hesitation in saying that his dissertation, amplified as it is by supplementary treatises on the ancient geography and ethnology of the Mesopotamian and neighboring countries, of Canaan, Egypt, and Elam, is a perfect treasury of knowledge, made most accessible by excellent indexes, and probably the most brilliant production in all Biblico-Assyriological literature" [15] At the present writing, the latest monograph upon the subject is the one just published in the *"Revue de l' Histoire des Religions"* from the pen of *M. Beauvois*. [16]

15. The Nation. New York, Mar. 15, 1883. See Lenormant s criticisms in *Les Origines de l'Histoire*, tom. ii.; and Halevy's in the *Revue Critique*, Paris, 1881, pp. 457-463, 477-485."

16. "L'Elysée Transatlantique et l'Eden Occidental," par E. Beauvois. Revue, Paris, 1883, pp. 273 ss. See also "L'Elysée des Mexicains comparé a celui des Celtes," by the same author, in same Review, 1884.

This locates the Eden of ethnic traditions in America and ascribes to the Celtic race no small influence upon the Greco-Roman mythology in the development of such ideas as those pertaining to the Gardens of the Hesperides, the Isles of the Blessed, etc. The site advocated is not new, though the line of argument is fresh and scholarly. The hypothesis that the cradle of the race is to be sought in America has before found advocacy at the hands of *J. Klaproth, Gobineau*, and others. That this, however, is not to be the last and only word on the subject is evident from the fact that, in a huge work just from the press, an English writer says: *"If there be an earthly original for the heavenly Eden, it will be found in equatorial Africa, the land of seething, swarming, multitudinous, and colossal life, where the mother nature grew great with her latest race; the lair in which the lusty breeder brought forth her black, barbarian brood, and put forth for them such a warm, welling bosom as cannot be paralleled elsewhere on earth. This was the world of wet and heaven of heat; the land of equal day and dark; that supplied the Two Truths of Uarti (Egyptian); the top of the world; the very nipple (Kepa) of the breast of earth, which is there one vast streaming fount of moisture quick with life. So surely as a topographical Meru is found in Habesh, so surely is the Earthly Paradise, the original of the mythical which was carried forth over the world by the migrations from Kam, to be found there, if at all."* [17] In fine, so resultless seem all discussions and investigations in this field that in his work on *"The Patriarchs of Humanity"*, *Dr. Julius Grill*, like *Noeldeke*, prefers to locate lost Paradise "in Utopia" and to deny to it all historic reality. [18] Evidently, the naturalists and the ethnologists, the comparative mythologists, and *Kultnrgeschichtschreiber*, have not yet solved the problem. Their "mother region" of the human race is as elusive and Protean as are any of the terrestrial Edens of theology, or of legend, or of poetry. Thus far, then, all search has been fruitless. Paradise is indeed lost. The explorer cannot find it; the theologian, the naturalist, and the archaeologist have all sought it in vain. Representative voices from every camp are heard confessing utter ignorance as to the region where human history began. "The problem," says *Professor Ebers,* remains unanswered."

17. *The Natural Genesis,* containing an attempt to recover and reconstitute the lost *Origins of the Myths and Mysteries, Types and Symbols. Religion and Language, with Egypt as the mouthpiece, and Africa as the birthplace.* By Gerald Massey. London, 1883: vol. ii., p. 162. It is impossible to understand how Mr. Massey reconciles the foregoing language with that used on p. 28 of the same volume, where he speaks of the crooked sword *Khepsh,* "that turned every way, and by its revolution formed the circle of Eden, or, as it was represented, kept the way of the Tree of Life, the Pole, where the happy garden was planted as the primary creation, which was the home of the primeval pair." But in the language of *The Nation* (June 26, 1884) the work is "an enormous conglomeration of facts set down with entire indifference to scientific principles of comparison, and, as far as the author s aim is concerned, absolutely worthless." *18.* "Der Ort, wohin die althebräische Ueberlieferung die Wiege des Menschengeschlechtes verlegt . . . ist also nicht auf der Erde gelegen, and gehört dem Bereich der Wirklichkeit nicht an."—Grill, *Die Erzväter der Menschheit.* Leipzig, 1875: Abth. I., p. 242.

Chapter VII
Stella Polaris

tad viṣṇoḥ paramaṁ padaṁ sadā paśyanti sūrayaḥ paśyanti sūrayaḥ
divīva chakṣur ātatam

"Sages always look towards the supreme abode of Lord Vishnu" - *Rig Veda 1.22.20*

Polar Star is a star close to one of the celestial poles, i.e. is located on the imaginary Earth's axis of rotation. The star at the North Celestial Pole is called the North Pole Star, and at the South Celestial Pole, it is called the South Pole Star. *Ursae Minoris (α Ursae Minoris / Alpha Ursa Minor)*, also known as the guiding star, is the brightest star in the *Ursa Minor* constellation. It is located very close to the North Celestial Pole and is currently the Pole Star. The North Star has had an important role in orientation since the Paleolithic until today. At the South Celestial Pole, there is no such bright star as at the North Celestial Pole. The brightest star is the *Sigma Octant* star, which is sometimes called the South Star. Unlike other stars in the sky, which seem to change their position in the sky during the night and appear to rotate around the celestial pole, the position of the North Star appears to remain unchanged. Knowing this, one can easily determine the direction of the corresponding pole of the earth, which can serve as an orientation. Due to the precession of the Earth's axis and the corresponding displacement of the celestial pole, in a period of one platonic year, for a duration of about 26,000 Earth years, different stars, science believes that can become also Polar Stars.

- ## *The Throne of God*

The shrine where motion first began? And light and life in mingling torrent ran, from whence each bright rotundity was hurled, The Throne of God, the Centre of the World. - *Pleasures of Hope, Thomas Campbell 1777-1844.* [1]

According to the Astronomical Institute of Moscow University [2], many ancient peoples attached special importance to the North Star because of its immobility. The Persians call it *"Commander of all Commanders"*, the Chinese use the name for her as *"Celestial Emperor."* In the medieval period, the North Star was also known as *Stella Maris* or *"Star of the Sea"* (due to its role in navigation at sea), as **Bartholomeus Anglicus** (*1272),* translated by **John Trevisa (1397).** In Mandaean cosmology, the North Star is considered auspicious and is associated with the *"World of Light"* ("heaven"). Mandaeans also known as Sabians [3] face north when they pray and the temples are also north-oriented. On the contrary, the south is associated with the world of darkness, [4] and *Stella Polaris* was the object of their worship, as she is worshiped today among the so-called Mandaeans or the Sabians along the Tigris and lower Euphrates.

1. The poet is speaking of the North Pole. The first three lines are illustrated by the closing chapters of Part third, above; the last sums up the facts to be set forth in the present chapter. A word from Menzel is here in place: "Nysa wird in vielen griechischen Mythen als im Central punkt bezeichnet von wo das Weltleben ausging und wohin es zuriickkehrt". Das ideale Nysa kbnnen wir nirgend anders als im Ausgangspunkte des Welt, im Nordpol suchen. *Die vorchristliche Unsterblichkeitslehre,* i. 65; also p. 42.

2. Schernberg State Astronomical Institute at Moscow University - *Ursa Minor Constellation*

3. Mandaism (Romanized: mandaiia; Arabic: مَنْدَائِيَّة, Mandāʾīya), also known as Sabianism (Arabic: صَابِئِيَّة, Ṣābiʾīyah), is a Gnostic, monotheistic, and ethnic religion. The Mandaeans revered Adam, Abel, Seth, Enos, Noah, Shem, Aram, and especially John the Baptist. The Mandaeans speak an Eastern Aramaic language known as Mandaean. The name "Mandaeus" is said to come from the Aramaic manda meaning knowledge. Within the Middle East, but also outside their community, the Mandaeans are more commonly known as Arabic: صُبَّة Ṣubba (singular: Ṣubbī) or Sabians. The term Ṣubba is derived from the Aramaic root associated with baptism, and the Neo-Mandaic is Ṣabi. In the Qur'an, the Sabians (Arabic: الصَّابِئُون, aṣ-Ṣābiʾūn) are mentioned three times, along with Jews and Christians. Occasionally, the Mandaeans are referred to as "Saint John's Christians." Mandaean cosmology is heavily influenced by Jewish, Babylonian, Persian, Egyptian, Greek, Manichaean, and other Near Eastern religions and philosophies.

4. Bhayro, Siam (2020-02-10). *"Cosmology in Mandaean Texts"*. Hellenistic Astronomy. Brill. p. 572–579.

Similarly, the Finns knew the North Star as *Taehti* - *"The Star on the Top of the Heavenly Mountain"*. In ancient Northern India, the star closest to the pole was known as *Grahadhara*, the *"Pivot of the Planets"*, representing the great ascetic Dhruva, and the Persian astronomer ***Al Biruni*** (973-1048 AD) said that among the Hindus of his time they were an incarnation of Dhruva himself. The ***Bhāgavata Purāṇa*** *(भागवतपुराण)*, also known as ***Srimad Bhagavatam*** or ***Srimad Bhagavata Mahapurana*** like other Puranas, discusses a wide variety of topics including cosmology, astronomy, genealogy, geography, legends, music, dance, yoga and culture. For the Pole Star we can say the following:

"Established by the supreme will of the Supreme Personality of Godhead, the Pole Star, which is the planet of Dhruva Maharaja, is constantly shining as the central pivot for all the stars and planets. The dormant, invisible, most powerful weather factor causes these lights to revolve around the North Star without ceasing. Here it is clearly stated that all luminaries, planets, and stars, revolve under the influence of the supreme weather factor. The time factor is another characteristic of the Supreme Personality of Godhead." *(Śrīmad-Bhāgavatam, 5 canto, 23.2)*

In the previous chapters, as an extract from the cosmological mythology itself, we managed to extract that above the *"World Mountain"*, which was in the upper world or the terrestrial paradise in the northern hemisphere, it was directly connected to *Stella Polaris*, i.e. the Polar Star, known in the Slavic world and as *Severnica* (North Star). As we have said the worldly mountain which is known by various names such as *Su-Meru, Harâ-Berezaiti, Kwen-lun,* or *Kharsak Kurra* was located directly under the Pole Star, which was at their zenith. Thus, the North Star or the Pole Star would represent the heavenly paradise, the throne of God, while the world mountain and the island itself would represent the terrestrial paradise. We have already reminded the reader that in the earthly heaven situated at the North Pole, instead of appearing to rise and set as in our latitudes, the stars had a horizontal circular motion from left to right around the observer. This appearance of the celestial bodies, of course, can be found nowhere else than at the North Pole. However, one star that seems to "never" rotate is the North Star. But is this true? The Earth's poles represent the end or extreme points of the Earth's axis, and ***B.G. Tilak*** itself proves that the position of the axis never changed concerning the Earth, even in the first geological eras. The poles and the Circumpolar regions were, moreover, once the same as they are now, although the past and present climatic conditions of those places may be completely different. But the earth's axis makes a small and slow movement around the ecliptic, causing what is called precession of the equinoxes and causing only the celestial poles to shift, but not the terrestrial poles. Thus, 7000 years ago, the Pole Star occupied a different position than it does now, but the Earth's pole remains the same. It appears that every 72 years it moves one degree, or 30 degrees every 2160 years. For example, 3000 years BC. the constellation Bootes stood to the left of Ursa Major or the Great Bear. The name of the constellation comes from the Greek word *Βοώτης Boótēs* "shepherd" or "plowman" (literally, "ox-driver"; from *βοῦς boûs* "cow"), regardless of the translation this image corresponds to the Ursa Major as a plow, drawn by oxen. This idea apparently comes from an agricultural society, where for a nomadic tribe Bootes would probably be a driver of a plowing cart. However, the brightest star of the Bootes constellation is Arcturus which at that time was where Stella Polaris is now and represented the North. Its older ancient Greek name was *Arctophlax* - "the guardian of the bears". The name Arcturus is Latinised from the Greek star name *Ἀρκτοῦρος (arktoyros)* meaning "the Guard". The Greek name is found in ancient astronomical literature, e.g. **Hesiod's Work and Days**, **Hipparchus's** and **Ptolemy's** star catalogs. The folk etymology connecting the star name with the bears (Greek: *ἄρκτος, arktos*) was probably invented much later. In this case, it is highly probable that we can connect the man and the bear with the Ursarite, the nomadic keepers of bears. It is a cult that was spread both in Europe and Asia, and even among the native Ainu in Japan, where instead of the dragon they still worship the bear as the main archetypal animal, and in the Balkans, this cult was mostly preserved between the Roma people and the Vlachs. Our peoples, including the Russians, have kept the famous bear dance for the public since ancient times, especially during the celebrations associated with the Solstices and Equinoxes. Without any doubt, this cult traces its roots at least from the Neolithic Age. It is a remnant of an old shamanic ritual associated with the movement of the Big Dipper and the changing of the seasons. The shaman carried a staff – the symbol for the Axis Mundi, the "*Pillar of the*

Heavens", while his control of the bear was a symbol of the control of cosmic law. Ursarite was banned in Germany in 1920 due to animal concerns. However, that cult survived in the Balkans until a decade ago. Now it is almost completely gone, not only because of animal concerns, but also because the stars began to shift, and the original meaning and essence began to be lost at that point. By following this path, we can go even further back in time to search for the mythology of the North Star. For example, around 9000 BC when the North Star was near the constellation Hercules. In addition, it is very reminiscent of the Swastika, at the moment of rotation, and Hercules is definitely connected to the mythology of the North Star through the story of the "*Apple of the Hesperides*". The *Hesperides (Greek: Εσπερίδες, Latin: Hesperides)* are the daughters of the titan Atlas and the goddess of the night Nikete. Let us recall that **Plato** *(Πλάτων, 428/427 or 424/423 – 348/347 BC)* placed the mythical island of Atlantis outside the *"Pillars of Hercules"* (Ἡράκλειαι Στῆλαι).

According to some Roman sources, [5] while on his way to the garden of the Hesperides on the island of Erytheia, Hercules had to cross the mountain that was once Atlas. They were also called the Atlantides (Ancient Greek: Ἀτλαντίδες, romanized: *Atlantídes*) from their reputed father, the Titan Atlas. Instead of climbing the great mountain, Hercules used his superhuman strength to break through it. These two mountains taken together have since been known as the *"Pillars of Hercules"*, although other natural features are associated with the name, in some versions, Hercules instead built the two to keep the sky away from the earth, freeing Atlas from his curse. Later, probably due to the transmission of toponymy from the north to the Mediterranean, the *"Pillars of Hercules"* is thought to be the phrase applied in antiquity to the ridges that enclose the entrance to the Strait of Gibraltar. **Herodotus** *(Ἡρόδοτος c. 484 – c. 425 BC)* informs us *(IV, 42)* that Pharaoh Neco, King of Egypt, ordered the Phoenician sailors to sail from Libya (Africa) and return through the *"Pillars of Hercules"* (Strait of Gibraltar). The sailors made the journey and returned after the third year. But **Herodotus** did not believe them because they reported such things when they returned (to him they were incredible), for example, while they were sailing through

Libya, how they saw the Sun on the right side. *Herodotus* could not believe that the Sun could be in the north, but he did not think that the incredible would happen which would later be regarded as unequivocal proof of the authenticity of that voyage. In the Hesperides myth, Hercules meets Atlas, who held the world on his shoulders. This is a clear picture of the World Axis or Axis Mundi. Hercules took his weight for a moment, causing the ground to shake as they exchanged. Bootes is the closest constellation to the constellation Hercules and is in line with precession. Perhaps we can extract something important for us, which is that this myth seems to tell of an unfortunate event that happened about 9000 years BC. when the earth's axis passed between these two constellations. An event that may have caused the earth to shake could probably refer to a strong earthquake or meteor impact that caused some sort of planetary catastrophe. According to *Critias (Κριτίας)*, the Hellenic deities of old divided the earth so that each deity could have his share; Poseidon accordingly, and to his liking, bequeathed the island of Atlantis. The island was larger than Ancient Libya and Asia Minor combined, [6] but was later submerged by an earthquake and became impassable, preventing travel to any part of the ocean. *Plato* claims that the Egyptians described Atlantis *"as an island consisting chiefly of mountains in the northern parts and along the coast, and embracing a great plain."* [7]

That movement of the earth's axis which causes the precession of the equinox is important from an archaeological point of view to the extent that it is responsible for the unequal annual seasons, mainly with the help of that argument the author in his work *"Orion and Researches in the Antiquity of the Vedas"* show that the Vernal Equinox was placed in the constellation Orion when some of the *Rig-Veda* lore was composed and that the Vedic literature indeed clearly shows that the position of the Vernal Equinox has subsequently changed down to the present times. [8]

5. Burkert, Walter (1985). *Greek Religion.* Harvard University Press. p. 210.52. Seneca, Hercules Furens 235ff.; Seneca, Hercules Oetaeus 1240; Pliny, Nat. Hist. iii.4.

6. Also it has been interpreted that Plato or someone before him in the chain of the oral or written tradition of the report, accidentally changed the very similar Greek words for "bigger than" ("meson") and "between" ("mezon") – Luce, J.V. (1969). *The End of Atlantis – New Light on an Old Legend. London:* Thames and Hudson. p. 224.

7."Atlantis - *Britannica Online Encyclopedia"*. Britannica.

8. B.G. Tilak, *Arctic Home og the Vedas, Biblioteka Istok-Zapad, Beograd 1987, p.37*

Accordingly, if anywhere in the world of ancient tradition we could find a statement of the belief that at the beginning of the world the motions of the heavenly bodies were different from our present motions, especially if we should be able to find a trace of the belief that the original motion of stars was in apparently horizontal orbits, this would certainly be the most striking and convincing and unexpected evidence that human observation of the starry sky began at the North Pole.

In *Sûrya Siddhânta, XII, 43* it is noted that: *"In both directions from Meru are the two polar stars (dhruva-tara), fixed in the middle of the sky...".*

Literally, the same thing we have now found from modern astronomy itself that there are two polar stars on Earth, *Polaris Borealis (Alpha Ursae Minoris),* the bright star of magnitude - 2, aligned approximately on its northern axis that serves as a prominent star in celestial navigation and the much dimmer star at magnitude-5.5 on its southern axis known as *Polaris Australis (Sigma Octantis).*

If the observer is at the North Pole, the first thing that will amaze him will be the movement of the firmament above him. In the temperate and tropical zones, we see stars rising in the East and setting in the West, with some passing overhead and others crossing the sky in an oblique trajectory. But to an observer who would be at the pole, the sky appears to rotate around it from left to right, rather as if an umbrella had been inverted overhead. The stars neither rise nor set, but follow circular orbits on horizontal planes, and the continuous turning is like a potter's wheel, for the whole duration of a six-month night. And the Sun, when it is above the horizon for the next six months, appears to orbit in the same way. The center of the firmament above the observer is the celestial North Pole, and what he sees will be the northern celestial hemisphere, while the invisible part below the horizon will form the southern hemisphere. As for east and west, the daily rotation of the Earth on its axis makes them orbit the observer from right to left, so that in one day the stars will go around the whole circle, parallel to the horizon, from left to right, and will not go out each day in the east, nor will they set in the west as in our temperate and tropical zones. An observer stationed at the North Pole, therefore, will see only the northern hemisphere revolving above his head, while the southern hemisphere with all its stars will always remain invisible, and the hemisphere will form its celestial horizon. To such an observer, the Sun entering the Northern Hemisphere during its annual orbit will appear to come from the South, and this idea will be expressed by the words recorded in the ancient writings, "The Sun rose in the South," however much it may appear to us this strange from our present position.

Now we happen to have traces of just such a belief. In the attractive fragments of ancient habits preserved in the pages of *Diogenes Laertius* we find the famous Greek astronomer *Anaxagoras (Ἀναξαγόρας, c. 500 – c. 428 BC)* attributed this extraordinary teaching: ***"In the stars, the beginnings revolved in a tolliform manner. "*** Now to have motion in a tolliform manner it means to turn again in the horizontal plane, like the θόλος, or "dome," of an astronomical observatory. *Anaxagoras* himself described the movement more fully when he said that this movement is not υπο - from below, but περί around the earth. *Anaximenes (Ἀναξιμένης ὁ Μιλήσιος; c. 586 – c. 526 BC)* seems to have had the same idea, for he is said to have compared the primitive revolution of the heavens to the rotation of a man's cap on his head. Another explanatory expression (we do not know whether it comes from *Anaxagoras* or from his reporter) is this: ***"In the beginning, the Polar Star, which is constantly visible, always appeared at the zenith, but then it acquired a certain declination".*** [9]

9. See "Des ficrits et de la Doctrine d Anaxagore" in *Histoire de la Academic des Sciences et Bdles Lettres de Berlin*. Berlin, 1755: vol. ix., p. 378 ff.

Here, then, as a doctrine of the ancient astronomers, we have the only idea that, at the beginning of the world, the celestial pole was at the zenith and that the revolutions of the stars were around a normal axis [10]. It is impossible to say what could have induced the astronomer to invent such a doctrine. On the other hand, if it was one of the interesting and apparently paradoxical traditions of the early post-Flood world, it is perfectly easy to see how imperishable and memorable the story was, especially among the star-loving Chaldeans and Babylonians, from whom the earliest Greek astronomers and scholars did not receive just a small part of their doctrines. [11] And the fact that the Chaldeans and probably the Egyptians had exactly this idea is not disputed at all. [12] Now another interesting question arises. When and under what circumstances this alleged "declination"; at the Pole was imagined to have happened? Was it gradual, or sudden? Let us now see how this diamond that marks and adorns the northern sky was observed by the ancient ancestors. As I said before, the *"Rainbow Bridge"* connected the earth with the sky, where the so-called God's court and border station from which it was determined where the soul will travel after death, whether in the higher or lower dimensions. If the Polar Eden is conceived as the supreme paradise on Earth, then this star is the supreme heavenly instance, it is the throne of the Almighty, which perfectly connects the terrestrial and heavenly paradise. We will now turn to stellar mythology, with which we will briefly depart from astronomical thought, in order to show the symbolism of the supreme star in the universe.

• *The Myth of Dhruva Mahārāja*

tad gaccha dhruva bhadraṁ te
bhagavantam adhokṣajam
sarva-bhūtātma-bhāvena
sarva-bhūtātma-vigraham

My dear Dhruva, come forward. May the Lord always grace you with good fortune. The Supreme Personality of the Godhead, who is beyond our sensory perception, is the Supersoul of all living entities, and thus all entities are one, without distinction. Begin, therefore, to render service unto the transcendental form of the Lord, who is the ultimate shelter of all living entities. Śrīmad-Bhāgavatam, Canto 4: "The Creation of the Fourth Order", 12, 5

The seven stars revolving around the North Star at the zenith are called as we have said *Saptarṣi-maṇḍala*. On these seven stars, (constellation *"Ursa Major"*) which form the highest part of our planetary system, live the seven sages: *Kaśyapa, Atri, Vasiṣṭha, Viśvāmitra, Gautama, Jamadagni and Bharadvāja. (Śrīmad-Bhāgavatam, 9 canto, 16.24)*. These seven stars are visible every night, and each of them makes a complete orbit around the North Star within twenty-four hours. Along with these seven stars, all other stars also orbit from east to west. The upper part of the universe is called the northern part and the lower part is called the southern part. Even in our ordinary affairs, while studying the map, we think of the top of the map as north. The Pole Star of the universe and its circle are also called the *Śiśumāra circle,* and there is the local planet of the Personality of Godhead *(Kṣīrodakaśāyī Viṣṇu)*. Before reaching there, the mystic passes through the Milky Way to reach *Brahma-loka*, and while going there he first reaches *Vaiśvānara-loka*, where the demigod controls the fire. In *Vaiśvānara-loka* yogis are completely cleansed of all dirty sins acquired while in contact with the material world. The Milky Way in the sky is here indicated as the path leading to *Brahma-loka*, the highest spiritual planet of the universe according to some books.

Every planet in the universe travels at a very high speed. From the statement in **Śrīmad-Bhāgavatam** it is understood that even the Sun travels sixteen thousand miles per second, and from the **Brahma-saṁhitā** we understand from the verse, *yac-cakṣur eṣa savitā sakala-grahāṇām,* that the Sun is considered to be the eye of the Supreme Personality of Godhead, who has and the specific orbit in which it orbits. Similarly, all other planets have their own specific orbits. But all of them together surround the North Star, or *Dhruvaloka*, where in myth Dhruva Mahārāja is at the apex of the three worlds. We can only imagine how exalted is the actual position of the devotee, and certainly, we cannot even imagine how exalted is the position of the Supreme Personality of Godhead. (*Śrīmad-Bhāgavatam /4/12/39*)

All the great sages mentioned in this verse have their planets near *Brahma-loka*, the planet where the creator Brahma resides along with the four great sages - *Sanaka, Sanātana, Sanandana* and *Sanat-kumāra*. These sages live in different stars known as the South Stars, which orbit the

North Star. The North Pole, also called as *Dhruvaloka* is the pivot of this universe and all the planets move around this Pole Star. After purification through the seven planets near *Dhruvaloka*, the water of the celestial Ganga flows through the cosmic paths of the demigods. Then it overflows the Moon *(Candra-loka)* and finally reaches the Lord's abode on top of Mount Meru - *Sumeru-parvata*.

Dhruva (Sanskrit: ध्रुव, Dhruva, lit. "unshakeable, immovable, or fixed") was an ascetic devotee of Vishnu mentioned in the **Vishnu Purana** and the **Bhagavata Purana**. [1] The Sanskrit term *dhruva nakshatra* (ध्रुव नक्षत्र, "polar star") has been used for Pole Star in the **Mahabharata**, personified as the son of *Uttānapāda* and grandson of *Manu*, even though Polaris at the likely period of the recension of the text of the **Mahabharata** was still several degrees away from the celestial pole. [2]

1. Linda Johnsen. *The Complete Idiot's Guide to Hinduism, 2nd Edition: A New Look at the World's Oldest Religion*. Penguin. p. 216.

2. Aiyangar Narayan (1987). *Essays On Indo-Aryan Mythology-Vol. Asian Educational Services*. p. 1

Dhruva was born as the son of King Uttānapāda (the son of Svayambhuva Manu) and his wife Suniti. [3] The king also had another son Uttama, born to his second queen Suruchi, who was the preferred object of his affection. Once, when Dhruva was a child of five years of age, he saw his younger brother, Uttama sitting on his father's lap on the King's throne. Suruchi, who was jealous of the older son from the first wife (since he - Dhruva - would be heir to the throne, and not Suruchi's son), cruelly scolded young Dhruva for his efforts to sit on his father's lap. When Dhruva protested and asked if he could not be allowed to sit on his father's lap, Suruchi berated him saying, 'Go ask god to be born in my womb. Only then will you have the privilege'. Suniti - being of gentle nature and now the lesser favorite wife - tried to console the distraught child, but Dhruva was determined to hear of his fate from the Lord himself. Seeing his firm resolve, his mother bade him farewell as he set out on a lonely journey to the forest. Dhruva was determined to seek for himself his rightful place and noticing this resolve, the divine sage Narada appeared before him and tried to desist him from assuming severe austerity upon himself at such an early age.

But, Dhruva's fierce determination knew no bounds, and the astonishing sage guided him towards his goal by teaching him the rituals and mantras to meditate on when seeking lord Vishnu. The one mantra which Narada taught and which was effectively used by Dhruva was *Om Namo Bhagavate Vasudevaya.* [4] Having been advised, Dhruva started his meditation and went without food and water for six months. The austerity of his *tapasya (penance)* shook the heavens and Vishnu appeared before him, but the child would not open his eyes because he was still merged in his inner vision of Vishnu's form described to him by Narada. [6] Vishnu had to adopt a strategy of causing that inner vision to disappear. Immediately Dhruva opened his eyes, and, seeing outside what he had been seeing all along in his mental vision, bowed down before Vishnu. But he could not utter a single word. Vishnu touched Dhruva's right cheek with his divine conch and that sparked off his speech. Out poured forth a beautiful poem praising Vishnu in 12 powerful verses, which together are called *Dhruva-stuti.* [5]

3. "The story of Dhruva". *Hindustan Times.* 25 January 2007.

4. *Ibid.*

5. *Ibid.*

Vishnu Purana gives a slightly different account here. When Vishnu was pleased with Dhruva's *tapasya* and asked him to ask for a varadāna (grant of wishes), he asked for the varadāna of knowledge of *stuti* (hymn). Other persons would have asked for worldly or heavenly pleasures, or for moksha at most, but Dhruva had no personal desire. Renunciation of all desires is regarded to be essential for eternal peace in Hinduism: this is the meaning of *Dhruva-pada.* That was the reason why the Saptarshis decided to give Dhruva the most revered seat of a star - the Pole Star. [6]

6. *Dhruva (story from Srimad Bhagavatam)*

Having spent a long time in Vishnu's remembrance he even forgot the objective of his *tapasya*, and only asked for a life in memory of Vishnu. Pleased by his *tapasya,* Vishnu granted his wish and further decreed that he would attain *Dhruva-pada*: the state where he would become a celestial body that would not even be touched by the *Maha Pralaya.* [7] *Dhruva* returned to his kingdom, to be warmly received by his family, and attained the crown at the age of six. He ruled for many decades in a fair and just manner. [8]

7. *"The Story of Dhruva: Dhruva's Eulogy of Viṣṇu* [Chapter 21]"

8. Ibid.

The powerful message of this myth also has its own archetypal dimension, where the child symbolizes sincerity and purity, which are virtuous and divine qualities and characteristics, but on the other hand, also the ascetic feat itself and the sublime and pure desire, or rather not aspiring to any desires or dreams for some personal gain and result, are the supreme essence and the most spiritual state to which we should strive. A child's soul knows no boundaries. This myth shows the direction and path towards which pure, sinless and righteous souls move, and that is the northern sky and its zenith – the North Star. Thus, at the end of the complete dissolution of the world, Dhruva Mahārāja will go directly to *Vaikuṇṭhaloka*, a spiritual planet in the spiritual sky. **Śrīla Viśvanātha Cakravartī Ṭhākura** *(c. 1626 – c. 1708)* comments in this regard that *Dhruvaloka* is one of the lokas (regions) like *Śvetadvīpa, Mathurā* and *Dvārakā*. They are all eternal places in the kingdom of God, which is described in the **Bhagavad-gītā** *(tad dhāma paramam)* and in the Vedas *(oṁ tad viṣṇohparamam padaṁ sadā paśyanti sūrayaḥ)*. The words *parastāt kalpa-vāsinām, "transcendental to the planets inhabited after dissolution"*, refer to the *Vaikuṇṭha* planets. In other words, Dhruva Mahārāja promotion to the higher celestial realms was guaranteed by the Supreme Personality of the Godhead. *(Śrīmad-Bhāgavatam 5/23/7)*

The Lord says, "You will not return to this material world, for you will reach *mat-sthānam*, My abode." *Dhruvaloka*, or the North Star, is therefore the abode of Vishnu or the Supreme. There is an ocean of milk on it, and in that ocean, there is an island known as *Śvetadvipa* (श्वेतद्विप *Śvetadvipa)* or the White Island (Holy Island). It is clearly stated that this planet is above the seven planetary systems of the *ṛṣis*, the Seven Sages and since this planet is *Viṣṇuloka*, it is worshiped by all the other planetary systems. The specific meaning of this planet is that even though the entire universe will be destroyed, this planet will remain, even during the destruction that takes place during the night of *Brahma*. There are two kinds of dissolutions, one during the *"Night of Brahma"* and one at the end of *Brahma's* life. At the end of *Brahma's* life, the chosen individuals return home, back to divinity. Dhruva Mahārāja is one of them. The Lord assured Dhruva that he would exist beyond the partial dissolution of this universe within the limits of time and space. Thus, at the end of complete dissolution, Dhruva will go directly to a spiritual planet in the spiritual sky.

Chapter VIII
Sakrālā Geogrāfija

II y a done beaucoup d apparence que les peuples du Nord, en descendant vers le Midi, y portent les emblems relatifs au physique de leur climat; et ces emblems sont devenus des fables, puis des personnages, puis des Dieux, dans des imaginations vives et pretes a tout animer, comme celles des Orientaux. – Jean Sylvain Bailly, Paris, France (1736- 1793) [1]

(It is therefore very likely that the peoples of the North, in descending towards the South, bear there the emblems relating to the physics of their climate; and these emblems have become fables, then characters, then Gods, in lively imaginations ready to animate everything, like those of the Orientals).

1. Among the predecessors of the Indo-European homeland, is the astronomer of the last French king, Jean Sylvain Bailly (1736 - killed on the guillotine in 1793). With great surprise and wonder, Bailly determined that these maps were created by very accurate observations from the region between the sixtieth and fiftieth degrees of north latitude. Bailly thought that it was the astronomical observations of some "unknown people" (he assumed Atlanteans), on the migration routes from the extreme north to the south. It is interesting that these findings also encouraged the royal astronomer to investigate the naturalistic meaning of the dramas of numerous mythological figures, from the ancient Egyptian, Hellenic and Scandinavian traditions, from Osiris, through Prosporpina and Adonis to Freyja and her husband. In all these mythological expressions of the tradition, Bailly was able to recognize clear traces of the memory of the Arctic primordial: "when we unite these traditions, often cloudy and confused, it is observed with astonishment that they all strive for the same goal that places their origins in the North". Jean Sylvain Bailly: *Lettres sur l'Atlantide de Platon et sur l'ancienne histoire de l'Asie pour servir de suite aux lettres sur l'origine des science, adressées* a M. de Voltaire par M. Bailly, Londres—Paris, 1779. See also, by the same author: *Histoire.*

To the first men, on the hypothesis of an Arctic Eden, the zenith and the north pole of the heavens were identical. Such an aspect of the starry vault the humanity of our late historic ages has never seen. Under such an adjustment of the rotating firmament, how regular and orderly would nature appear. What profound significance would of necessity attach to that mysterious unmoving Centrepoint of cosmic revolution directly overhead! As intimated, that polar center must naturally have seemed to be the top of the world, the true heaven, the changeless seat of the supreme God or gods: "And if, through all the long lifetime of the antediluvian world, this circumpolar sky was thus to human thought the true abode of God, the oldest postdiluvian peoples, though scattered down the sides of the globe half or two thirds the distance to the equator, could not easily forget that at the center and true top of the firmament was the throne and the palace of its great Creator. "The religions of all ancient nations signally confirm and satisfy this antecedent expectation. With a marvelous unanimity, they associate the abode of the supreme God with the North Pole" the center of heaven or with the celestial space immediately surrounding it. No writer on Comparative Theology has ever brought out the facts which establish this assertion, but the following outline of them will suffice for our present purpose…

- *The Hebrew conception*

In so pure and lofty a monotheism as that of the ancient Hebrews, we must not expect to find any such strict localization of the supreme God in the circumpolar sky as we shall find among polytheistic peoples. *"Do I not fill heaven and earth?"* is the language of Jehovah. Nevertheless, as the Hebrews must be supposed to have shared, in some measure, the geographical and cosmological ideas of their age, it would not be strange if in their sacred writings traces of these ideas were here and there discernible. Some of these traces are quite curious, and they have attracted the attention of not a few Biblical scholars, to whom their origin and rationale are entirely unsuspected. Thus a learned writer on He brews geography, after blindly repeating the common assumption that "the Hebrews conceived the surface of the earth to be an immense disk, supported, like the flat roof of an Eastern house, by pillars" yet uses such language as this: *"The North appears to have been regarded as the highest part of the earth s surface, in consequence, perhaps, of the mountain ranges which existed there."* [1] Another, touching upon the same subject, says *"The Hebrews regarded what lay to the North as higher, and what lay to the South as lower: hence they who traveled from South to North were said to go up/ while they who went from North to South were said to go down.*" [2]

In Psalm seventy-fifth, verse sixth, we read, ***"Promotion cometh not from the East, nor from the West, nor from the South.***" Why this singular enumeration of three of the points of the compass, and this omission of the fourth? Simply because heaven, the proper abode of the supreme God, being conceived of by all the surrounding nations, if not by the Hebrews themselves, as in the North, in the circumpolar sky, that was the sacred quarter, and it could not reverently be said that promotion cometh not from the North. [3] It would have been as offensive as among us to say that promotion cometh not from above. Therefore, having completed his negative statements, the Psalmist immediately adds ***"But God is the judge; He putteth down one, and setteth up another.***"

1. Rev. William Latham Bevan, A. M., in *Smith's Dictionary of the Bible, Art.* "Earth" vol. i., p. 633, 634 (Hackett's ed.). McClintock and Strong's *Cyclopedia,* Art. *"Geography"* vol. iii., p. 792.

2. McClintock and Strong, *Cyclopedia*, Art. "North" vol. vii., p. 185. The Akkadians had the same idiom. Lenormant, *Beginnings of History*, p. 313.

3. "A peculiar sanctity is attached to the North in the Old Testament records." T. K. Cheyne, *The Book of Isaiah.* London, 1870: pp. 140, 141. [See our cut: *"The Earth of the Hindus"* p. 152.]

A curious trace of the same conception appears in the book of Job, in the eighth and ninth verses of the twenty-third chapter. In ***Old Testament*** times, the Hebrews and the Arabians designated the cardinal points by the personal terms "before" for East, "behind" for West, "left hand" for North, and "right hand" for South. Thus Job, in the passage indicated, is complaining that he can nowhere, East or West, North or South, find his divine judge. [4] But, in speaking of one of these points, he adds this singular qualification ***"where God doth work".*** This is said of the left hand or North. It seems to be inserted to render peculiarly emphatic the declaration, ***"I go . . . [even] to the left hand where He doth work, but I cannot behold Him."*** If at first blush such an apparent localizing of the divine agency seems inconsistent with Job's splendid descriptions of God s omnipresence in other passages, it should be remembered that we, too, speak of the omnipresent deity as dwelling *"on high"* and address Him as *"Our Father which art in Heaven."* A natural counterpart to this idea of northern heaven would be a belief or impression that spiritual perils and evils were in a peculiar degree or manner to be apprehended from the right hand, or South, as the proper abode of demons, the quarter to which *Asmodeus* fled when exorcised by the angel. [5]

4. Adam Clarke, *Commentary, in loc.* The best explanation the oldest commentators know how to give is this There were more human beings and more intelligent ones North of Job's country than in either of the three other cardinal directions; especially was the North the seat of the great Assyrian empire; but God desires to reside and to work preeminently among men, hence the language of the text! Matthew Poole, in *Dietelmair and Baumgarten's Bibeliverk*, vol. v., p. 634.

5. Tobit, viii. 3. Compare *The Book of Enoch*, xviii. 6-16; xxi. 3-10.

We cannot positively affirm that such a belief consciously prevailed among the ancient Hebrews, but, holding the possibility in mind, we find passages of Scripture that seem to stand out in a new and striking light. Thus, in case there was such a belief, how great the force and beauty of the expression "Because [the Lord] is at my right hand [the side exposed to danger] I shall not be moved." [6] With this may be compared the confident expressions of the one hundred and twenty-first Psalm: *"The Lord is thy keeper: The Lord is thy shade upon thy right hand."* So also, in the ninety-first it is on the right hand that destruction is anticipated: *"A thousand shall fall at thy side, and [or even] ten thousand at thy right hand; but it shall not come to nigh thee."* Again, in the one hundred and forty-second, it is said *"I looked on my right hand, but there was no man that would know me: refuge failed me; no man cared for my soul."* Notice also the imprecation. *"Let Satan stand at his right hand"* (Ps. cix. 6), and the vision of Zechariah, where the great adversary makes his appearance on the right of the one whom he came to resist *(Zech. iii. i).* But as Satan here reveals himself from beneath and from the South, so to Ezekiel the true God reveals himself from above and from the North *(Eze. i. 4).* In that quarter was God s holy mountain *(Is. xiv. 13),* the city of the Great King *(Ps. xlviii. 2),* the land of gold *(Job xxxvii. 22, marg.),* the place where divine power had hung the earth upon nothing *(Job xxvi. 7).* [7]

Hence the priest officiating at the altar, both in the tabernacle and later in the temple, faced the North. According to the Talmud, King David had an Aeolian harp in the North window of his royal bed-chamber, by means of which the North wind woke him every night at midnight for prayer and pious meditations. [8] Probably it is not without significance that in Ezekiel's vision of the ideal temple of the future the chamber prepared for the priests in charge of the altar was one *"whose prospect was toward the North."* [9] *(Eze.xl. 46.)*

6. Ps. xvi. 8. The reference seems even more unmistakable since the next two verses speak of Sheol, or Hades.

7. "Im Norden sind die hochsten Berge, vor alien der heilige Gotterberg Is. 14, 13. ... Vom Norden her kommt in der Regel Jehovah." Herzog's *Real-Encyklopddie*, Art. "Welt" Bd. xvii., S. 678. "Like the Hindus, Persians, Greeks, and Teutons, . . . the Semitic tribes spoke of a mountain of their gods in the far North *(Is. xiv. 13; Eze. xxviii. 14)*; and even with the Jews, notwithstanding the counteracting influence of the Mosaic creed, traces of such a popular belief continued to be visible *(Ps. xlviii.),* the North being, e. g., regarded as the sacred quarter *(Lev. i. n; Eze. i. 4)*." Dillmann, in *Schenkel's Bibel Lexicon*. Leipsic, 1879: vol. ii, p. 49

8. "Daily from the four quarters of the world blow the four Winds, of which three are continually attended by the North wind; otherwise the world would cease to be. The most pernicious of all is the South wind, which would destroy the world were it not held back by the angel Bennetz." Quoted from the Talmud by Bergel, Studien *uber die naturwissenschaftlichen Kenntnisse der Talmudisten*. Leip sic, 1880: p. 84. Compare Dillmann, Das Buck Henoch, Kap. lxxvi. ; lxxvii. ; xxv. 5 ; xxxiv. ; xxxvi, W. Menzel, *Die vorchristliche Unsterblichkeitslehre*, Bd. ii., p. 35, 101, 168,345. See also p. 177 of this volume.

9. At first view it seems strange that in the Middle Ages, in Chris tian Europe, the North should have come to be regarded as the special abode of Satan and his subjects, and that on the north side of some churches, near the baptismal font, there should have been a "Devil s Door" which was opened to let the evil spirit pass to his own place at the time of the renunciation of him by the person baptized. The simple explanation of this is found in the fact that the people were taught that their old gods, whom they had worshiped when pagans, were devils. Compare Grimm, *Deutsche Mythologie*, p. 30,31. Conway, in his *Demonology and Devil Lore* (London, 1879: vol. ii., 115; i., 87), entirely misconceives the philosophy of the fact. A similar change seems to have occurred among the Iranians after Mazdeism had transformed their ancient Daevas from gods to demons. Hence, while in portions of the Avestan literature (generally the older) the heaven of Ahura Mazda is in the North, in other portions the North is the world of death and demons. See Bleek's

Avesta, i., pp. 3, 137, 143; ii. 30, 31; iii. 137, 138, et passim. Darmesteter, Introduction, p. lxvii., lxxx. Haug, *Religion of the Parsis*, pp. 267 ff.

- ### *The Egyptian conception*

The correspondence of the ancient Egyptian conception of the world and of heaven with the foregoing would be remarkable did we not know that Egypt was the cradle of the Hebrew people? The ancient inhabitants of the Nile valley had the same idea as to the direction of the true summit of the earth. To them, as to the Hebrews, it was in the North. This was the more remarkable since it was exactly contrary to all the natural indications of their own country, which continually ascended toward the South. As stated in a previous chapter, **Brugsch** says, ***"The Egyptians conceived of the earth as rising toward the North, so that in its northernmost point it, at last, joined the sky.*** [1] In correspondence herewith the Egyptians located their *Ta-nuter*, or "land of the gods" in the extreme North. [2] On this account, it is on the northern exterior wall of the great temple of Ammon at Karnak that the divinity promises to King Rameses II. the products of that heavenly country, *"silver, gold, lapis-lazuli, and all the varieties of precious stones of the land of the gods."* Hence, also, contrary to all natural indications, the northern hemisphere was considered the realm of light, the southern the realm of darkness. [3] The passage out of the secret chambers of the Great Pyramid was pointed precisely at the North Pole of the heavens. All the other pyramids had their openings only on the northern side. That this arrangement had some religious significance few students of the subject have ever doubted. If our interpretation is correct, such passages from the burial chamber toward the polar heaven intimated a vital faith that from the chamber of death to the highest abode of life, imperishable and divine, the road is straight and ever open. [4]

1. *Geographische Inschriften altagyptischer Denkmäler*. Leipsic,1858: n.ii., p. 37.

2. In one place Brugsch translates *ta-nutar-t mahti* "das nördliche Gottesland." *Astronomische und astrologische Inschriften*, p. 176.

3. "To the twelve great gods of heaven are immediately subjected the stars dispersed in infinite number through all the ethereal space, and divided into four principal groups

according to the four quarters of the world. They were then divided into two orders more elevated, the one filling the northern hemisphere and belonging to light, to the good principle, the other to the southern hemisphere, dark, cold, *funeste*, and to the somber abodes of Amenti." Guigniaut's Creuzer, *Religions de l'Antiquite*, vol. ii., p. 836. A very curious survival of the above conception is found in the Talmudic *Emek Hammeleck*. See Eisenmenger, *Entdecktes Judenthum*, Stehelin s version, vol. i., p. 181; comp. p. 255 ff.

4. The association of Set with the constellation of the Great Bear, reported by Plutarch and lately confirmed by original astronomical texts (Brugsch, *Astronomische Inschriften alttrgyptiscker Denkmaler*, Leipsic, 1883, pp. 82-84, 121- 123) seems at first view inconsistent with the south polar location of demons and destructive divinities. But the apparent difficulty is transformed into an all the stronger proof of the correctness of our theory when it is remembered that in the most ancient times Set "was not a god of evil" but the supreme world-sovereign from whom the Egyptian kings derived their authority over the two hemispheres. *"It was not till the decline of the Empire that this deity came to be regarded as an evil demon, that his name was effaced from the monuments, and other names substituted for his in the Ritual."* Renouf, *Religion of Ancient Egypt*, pp. 119, 120. The expression *navel or center of heaven*, as a designation for the northern celestial Pole, so common among ancient nations, would seem to have been current among the Egyptians also. Brugsch, Ibid., p. 122, 123. In the text as translated, however, there is some, obscurity. Compare p. 154.

- ## *The Conception of the Akkadians, Assyrians, Babylonians, Indians, and Iranians*

After what has been said in former chapters respecting the location of *Kharsak Kurra, Sad Matati, Har-Moed, Su-Meru,* and *Hâra-Berezaiti*, no further proof is needed that all the peoples above named associated the true heaven, the abode of the highest gods, with the northern celestial pole. [1] In each case, the apex of their respective mounts of the gods pierced the sky precisely at that point. To this day the Haranite Sabaeans, the most direct heirs of the religious traditions of the Tigro-Euphratean world construct their temples with careful reference to the ancient faith. [2] Their priests also, in the act of sacrifice, like all ancient priesthoods, face the North. [3] In the ***Rig Veda***, *ii., 40, I*, we read of the *amṛtasya nibhim*, the *"Navel of the Heavens"*. The same or similar expressions occur again and again in the Vedic literature. They refer to the northern celestial Pole, just as the expression *nābhir pṛhivyās*, "Navel of the Earth" *R. V. iii., 29, 4,* and elsewhere, signifies the northern terrestrial Pole. To each is ascribed preeminent sanctity.

1. "There can be no doubt that the "Heaven of Anu" was the particular limited celestial region, centering in the Pole star and penetrated by the summit of the Paradisaical Mount." Rev. O. D. Miller, *The Oriental and Biblical Journal.* Chicago, 1880: p. 173.

2. "L'église n'a que deux fenêtres et une porte qui est toujours ouverte du côté du sud, afin que celui qui y entre ait l'étoile polaire devant lui." N. Siouffi, *Études sur la Religion des Soubbas ou Sabéens, les Dogmes, leur Maeurs.* Paris, 1880: p. 118.

3. "Cette position de la victime permet au sacrificateur, qui a le morgno appuyé sur l'épaule gauche, de se placer, pour remplir son rôle, de façon qu'il ait la figure tournee vers l'étoile polaire qui couvre Avather, tout en ayant en même temps la tête de l'animal ā sa droite." Ibid., p. 112.

The one is the holiest shrine in heaven, the other the holiest shrine on earth. That no translator has hitherto caught the true meaning of the terms seems unaccountable. [4] In Buddhism, the heir and conservator of so many of the ancient ideas of India, the same notion of a world ruler with his throne at the celestial Pole lived on. [5] Very curiously, if we follow the authority of the **Lalitavistara**, the first actions and words ascribed to the infant Buddha on his arrival in our world unmistakably identify the North with the abode of the gods, and *its nadir* with the abode of the demons. [6] Even the modern relics of the non-Aryan aboriginal tribes of India, for example the Gonds, have retained this ancient ecumenical ethnic belief. [7]

4. In his heading to Hymn I., 185, 5, Grassman parenthetically conjectures that the Navel of the World therein spoken of may be "*im Osten*" but suggests no reason for its location in that or any other quarter. Not by accident, however, did the ancient bard elsewhere (X., 82, 2) place the abode of God "beyond the Seven Rishis" in the highest North.

5. "The omnipotence of Amitâbha is dwelt on in some fine gâthâs. In the center of heaven, he sits on the lotus throne and guides the destinies of mortals." Arthur Lillie, *Buddha and Early Buddhism.* London, 1882: p.128. Compare also p.7: "This Pole-star *(Alpha Draconis)* was believed to be the pivot round which the cosmos revolved. The symbol of God and the situation of Paradise got to be associated with this star."

6. "Le Lalitavistara, 97, rapporte ces paroles d'une maniére un peu différente: 'Je suis le plus glorieux dans ce monde, etc'. Ensuite, aprés avoir fait sept pas dans la direction du septentrion: Je serai le plus grand de tous les etrês, puis aprés sept pas dans la direction du nadir: Je détruirai le Malin et les mauvais esprits, je publierai la loi suprême qui doit éteindre le feu de l'Enfer au profit de tous les habitants du monde souterrain." Note to Professor Kern's *Histoire du Bouddhisme dans l'Inde. Revue de l'Histoire des Religions.* Paris: tom, v., nro. i, p. 54. Compare the less explicit account in Beal's *Romantic History of Buddha*, p. 44.

7. " In burying they lay the head to the South and the feet to the North, as the home of their gods is supposed to be in the latter direction. They call the North Deoguhr sometimes, and the South, Muraho, is looked upon as a region of terror; so the feet are laid towards Deoguhr in order that they may carry the dead man in the right direction." *Report of Ethnological Committee*, quoted in Spencer's *Descriptive Sociology*, Div. I., Ft. 3, A., p. 36

• *The Phoenician, Greek, Etruscan, and Roman Conception*

That the Phoenicians shared the general Asiatic view of a mountain of the gods in the extreme North that appears from *Movers* learned work upon that people. [1] The evidence that in ancient Hellenic thought, also, the heaven of the gods was in the northern sky is incidental but cumulative and satisfactory. For example, heaven is upheld by Atlas, but the terrestrial station of Atlas, as we have elsewhere shown, is at the North Pole. Again, Olympus was the abode of the gods; but if the now generally current etymology of this term is correct, Olympus was simply the Atlantean pillar, pictured as a lofty mountain, and supporting the sky at its northern Pole. [2] In fact, many writers now affirm that the Olympus of Greek mythology was originally simply the north polar *"World-mountain"* of the Asiatic nations. [3]

1. Die Pönizier. Bonn, 1841-56, vol. i., pp. 261, 414.

2. "Here the idea is that the gods reside above this mountain [*SuMeru*], which is, as it were, the support of their dwellings. This brings to our mind the fable of Atlas supporting the heavens; the same idea may probably be traced in the Greek Olympus (Sanskrit, *ālamba*, support)." Samuel Beal, *Four Lectures on Buddhist Literature in China.* London, 1882: p. 147. Compare Grill.

3. Compare A. H. Sayce, *Transactions of Society Bib. Archeology*, vol. iii., 152. - Even in the mathematical cosmos of Philolaos, though the *sedes deorum* seems to be placed in Hestia, at the center of the system, there is yet a steep way leading perpendicularly to the polar summit of the heavens, by means of which the gods and holy souls attain the diviner realm of all perfection: "Dii vero, quando ad pergunt, turn quidem acclivi via proficiscuntur sub summura qui sub coelo est fornicem (ἀψιδα), et immortales quae dicuntur animae, quando ad summum pervenerunt, extra progresses in coeli dorso consistunt, circumlataeque cum iis animabus, quae comitari eas potuerunt, loca supra coelum spectant, ubi pura et absoluta veritas, cognitio virtus, pulchritude, atque omnis omnino perfectio patet." Aug.Boeckh, "De vera indole astronomiae Philolaicas." *Gesammelte Kleine Schriften.* Leipsic, 1866: vol. iii., p. 288. Compare pp. 290-292.

In prayer, the Greeks turned towards the North, and from **Homer,** we know that when they addressed the "Olympian" gods they stretched out their hands "toward the starry heavens" Greek prayers, therefore, must have been addressed toward the northern heavens. Entirely confirmatory of this is the account **Plato** gives of *"the holy habitation of Zeus"* in which the solemn convocations of the gods were held, and which, he explains ***"was placed in the Centre of the World."*** [4]

That this center is the northern celestial Pole is placed beyond question by a well-known passage from **Servius Maurus** [5], where it is called the *"domicilium Jovis"* and where we are informed that the Etruscan and Roman augurs considered thunder and lightning in the northern sky more significant than in any other quarter, being *"higher and nearer to the abode of Jove."* [6] Countries in high northern latitudes shared in this peculiar sanctity. "Toward the end of the official or state paganism," says **M. Beauvois** ***"the Romans regarded Great Britain as nearer heaven and more sacred than the Mediterranean countries."*** [7] ***Varro*** and other Latin writers confirm this general representation so that all modern expounders of the old Etruscan religion unite in locating the abode of the gods of Etruria in the *Centre of Heaven*, the northern circumpolar sky. [8] ***Niebuhr*** and other authorities of the highest rank assure us that the Romans shared the same faith. [9]

4. Critias, 120.

5. Aeneid, ii, 693

6. "Et ideo ex ipsa parte significantiora essefulmina, quoniam altiora et viciniora domicilio Jovis" Compare Regell, "Das Schautempel der Augurn" in the Neite Fahrbücher der Philologie, Bd. cxxiii., pp. 593-637. "The Hawaiian soothsayer, or *kilo-kilo*, turned always to the North when observing the heavens for signs or omens, or when regarding the flight of birds for similar purposes. The ancient Hindus turned also to the

North for divining purposes, and so did the Iranians before the schism, after which they placed the devas in the North; so, did the Greeks, and so did the Scandinavians before their conversion to Christianity." A. Fornander, *The Polynesian Race*. London, 1878: vol.i., p. 240.

Proto-Etruscan ceramic. It is typical of the early phases of the Etruscan-Latium Iron Age (ninth to eighth centuries B.C.), The roof is decorated with a dense carved geometric design (swastikas, meanders, and angular motifs – Garden of Eden). From Castel Gandolfo, Montecucco area, tomb B, excavations of 1816-1817 900-850 B.C Ceramic mix, height 27 cm; base 29 cm x 30 cm Cat. 15407 Villanovan

7. Sacratiora sunt profecto Mediterraneis loca vicina coelo" Beauvois, in *Revue de l'Histoire des Religions*. Paris, 1883: p. 283. The statement is based upon expressions in the official panegyric of Emperor Constantine Augustus. Compare the following: "Diodorus Siculus speaks of a nation whom he calls the Hyperboreans, who had a tradition that their country is nearest to the moon, on which they discovered mountains like those on the earth, and that Apollo comes there once every nineteen years. This period, being that of the Metonic cycle of the moon, shows that if this could have been really discovered by them they must have had a long acquaintance with astronomy. Flammarion, *Astronomical Myths*. London: p. 88.

8. "Im Nordpunkte der Welt" K. O. Müller, *Die Etrusker*. Breslau, 1828: Bd. ii., pp. 126, 129. "Suivant eux, ceux-ci devaient habiter dans la partie septentrionale du ciel, á raison de son immobilité. C'est de la région polaire qu'ils veillaient sur toute la terre." A. Maury, in *Religions de l'Antiquite,* Creuzer et Guigniaut, torn, ii., p. 1217." La théologie étrusque, accueillant une doctrine que nous avons déjá recontrée á l'etat de rêve confus dans la théologie grecque, placait á l'extremé nord le séjour des Aesars ou dieux. Mais, tandis que l'Helléne se tourne vers les dieux pour les interroger, le Toscan imite leur attitude supposée, afin de voir l'espace comme ils le voient eux-mêmes. Ayant done le visage tourné vers le midi, il appelle *antica* la moitié méridionale du ciel" etc. A. Bouche-Leclercq, La Divination chez les Etrusques. *Revue de l'Histoire des Religions*. Paris, 1881: torn, iii., p. 326.

9. Der Wohnsitz der Gotter ward im Norden der Erde geglaubt." Niebuhr, *Römische Geschichte*, vol. ii., Anhang, p. 702. "It is well known that the Romans placed the seat of the gods in the extreme North." *The Oriental Journal*. Chicago, 1880: vol. i., p. 143. Niebuhr s remark, "Der Augur dachte sich schauend wie die Götter auf die Erde schauen" explains the somewhat unqualified and misleading statement of Professor Kuntze touching the rotary posture of the Roman in prayer. *Prolegomena zur Geschichte Roms. Oraculum, Auspicium Templum, Regnum.* Leipsic, 1882: p. 15.

- ### *The Japanese Conception*

We have already seen that in the Japanese cosmogony the down-thrust spear of Izanagi becomes the upright axis of heaven and earth. Izanagi's place, therefore, at the upper end of this axis can be nowhere else than at the North Pole of the sky. [1] But we are not left to inference. So inseparably was the Creator associated with the Pole in ancient Japanese thought that one of his loftiest and most divine titles was derived from this association. Writing of the primitive ideas of these people, one of our best authorities uses the following language: ***"I shall do the Ko-ji-ki, and the***

Shinto religion, and the Japanese philosophy, strict justice by saying that, according to them, there existed in the beginning one god, and nobody and nothing besides."

> Far in the deep infinitudes of space,
> Upon a throne of silence,

sat the god *Ame-no-mi-naka-nushi-no-kami*, whose name signifies *"The Lord of the Center of the World."* [2]

What this *"Center of Heaven"* is cannot well be doubtful to any careful reader of the present chapter.

*1.*See above, pt. iv., ch. 2.

2. Sir Edward J. Reed, Japan, vol. i., p. 27. Compare Léon de Rosny, in *Revue de l'Histoire des Religions.* Paris 1884: p. 208; also p. 211.

• *The Chinese Conception*

The oldest traceable worship among the Chinese is that of Shang-te, the highest of all gods. It is believed to have existed more than two thousand years before Christ. Shang-te is usually and correctly described as the god of heaven. But his proper place of abode, his palace, is called Tsze-wei. And if we inquire as to the meaning and location of Tsze-wei, the native commentators upon the sacred books inform us that it is "a celestial space about the North Pole." [1] Here, as in Japan, and in Egypt, and in India, and in Iran, and Greece, the Pole is *"the center"* of the sky. A writer in the **"Chinese Repository"** quotes from authoritative religious books these declarations: **"The Polar star is the Centre of Heaven."** "Shang-te s throne is in Tsze-wei, i. e., the Polar star." Immediately over the central peak of *Kwen-lun* appears the Polar star, which is Shang-te's heavenly abode." "In the central place the Polar star of Heaven, the one Bright One, the Great Monad, always dwells." [2] In accordance with this conception, the Emperor and his assistants, when officiating before the *"Altar of Heaven",* always face the North. [3] The Pole star itself is a prominent object of worship. [4]

1. Legge, *The Chinese Classics*, vol. iii., Pt. i., p. 34 n. See further, Legge, *Spring Lectures on the Religions of China*, London, 1880, p. 175, and the not well understood prayer in Douglas, *Confucianism and Taoism*, London, 1879, p. 278. From these and other references it is plain that Confucians and Taoists alike identified the northern sky with the abode of God.

2. Vol. iv., p. 194. So, likewise in West Mongolian thought the celestial pole and the "apex of the Golden Mountain" are identical*: "Altan kadasu niken nara Tagri-dschin urkilka.* Apex mentis aurei, nomine Cardo Coeli, Stella Polaris." *Uranographia Mongolica. Fundgruben des Orients*, Bd. iii., p. 181.

3. See *English Translation of the Chinese Ritual for the Sacrifice to Heaven.* Shanghai, 1877: pp. 25, 26, 27, 28, 31, 48.

4. Joseph Edkins, *Religion in China*, p. 115. Compare G. Schlegel, *Uranographie Chinoise,* pp. 506, 507.

And how prevalent this localization of the abode of God at the Pole remains after four thousand years may be illustrated by the following incident narrated by **Rev. Dr. Edkins**: "I met on one occasion a schoolmaster from the neighborhood of Chapoo. He asked if I had any books to give away on astronomy and geography. Such books are eagerly desired by all members of the literary class….. The inquiry was put to him Who is the Lord of heaven and earth? He replied that he knew none but the Polestar, called in the Chinese language *Teen-hwang-tate*, the *"Great Imperial Ruler of Heaven."* [4]

4. Religion in China, p. 109. This title irresistibly suggests the Assyrian one, *Dayan-Same*, "Judge of Heaven." *Transactions Society Bib. Archeology*, iii. 206.

• *The Ancient German and the Finnic Conception*

Like the ancients, when praying and sacrificing to the gods, the pagan Germans turned their faces toward the North. [1] There, in the northern heaven, at the top of Yggdrasil, the world axis, stood the fair city of Asgard, the home of the Asen. The Eddas expressly says of it that it was built in the *"Centre of the World."* [2] At that point, whence alone the whole world of men is ever visible by night and by day, stood *Hlidskjálf*, the watchtower of Odin.

*1.*Jakob Grimm, "Betende und opferende Heiden schauten gen Norden." *Deutsche Mythologie*, Bd. 5., p. 30.

2. Grimm, "Im Mittelpunkte der Welt." *Deutsche Mythologie*, p. 778. The following is from the Prose Edda: "Then the sons of Bor built in the middle of the universe the city called Asgard, where dwell the gods and their kindred, and from that abode work out so many wondrous things both on the earth and in the heavens above it. There is in that city a place called Hlidskjálf, and when Odin is seated there upon his lofty throne he sees over the whole world, discerns all the actions of men, and comprehends whatever he contemplates. His wife is Frigga, the daughter of Fjörgyn, and they and their offspring form the race that we call the Æsir, a race that dwells in Asgard the old, and in the regions around it, and that we know to be entirely divine." Mallet, *Northern Antiquities*, p. 406. The expression, from that abode work out so many wondrous things" recalls to mind Job's description of the North as the place "where God doth work".

From this *"partie septentrionale du ciel"* he and Frigga, like the great gods of the Etruscans *(PRSEMR, Rassena, Russians), "veillatent sur toute la terre."* [3] Among the ancient Finns, the name of the supreme god was Ukko. In their mythology, he is sometimes represented as up bearing the firmament, like Atlas, and sometimes he is called *Taivahan Napanen*, the *"Navel of Heaven"*. As **Castren** shows, this curious title is given to him simply because he resides in the center or Pole of heaven. [4] In the great epic of this people, the **Kalevala**, the abode of the supreme God is called *Tähtela*, [5] which word simply means *"Place of Tähti"*, Esthonian, *Täht*, the Polar star."

We have not exhausted our materials in hand for the illustration of this point [6] but surely, we have presented enough. Reviewing this singular unanimity of the ancient nations, no thoughtful reader can fail to be impressed with its significance. No other explanation of it can be so simple and obvious as the supposition that the heaven which overarched the cradle of humanity was heaven whose zenith was the northern Pole.

3.Vide supra, p. 214 n. 2.

4. Castren, *Finnische Mythologie* (Tr. Schiefner), pp. 32, 33.

5. *Rune* II, 32, 36, 40.

6. See, for example, Gill, *Myths, and Songs of the South Pacific.* London, 1876: p. 17.

• How did the Biblical Eden come to be in the East?

Let us first remind the reader of the fundamental concepts related to the Biblical paradise. The Garden of Eden (Hebrew גַּן עֵדֶן) or the Garden of Eden - the biblical גַּן־יְהֹוָה, *gan-YHWH "Garden of God"* or *Gan-Eden*, is described in the biblical book of *Genesis, chapter 2-3*, as well as in the *Book of Ezekiel*. As the *"Garden of God"* (without the word Eden) it is mentioned in *Genesis 13, and in Ezekiel 31* the *"trees of the garden"* are mentioned. The *Book of Zechariah* and the *Psalms* also mention trees and water as referring to a temple, without mentioning the word Eden. The name "Eden" is thought to come from the Akkadian word *edinnu*, which comes from the Sumerian word *edin* meaning "plain" or "steppe". Today Eden is thought to be more closely related to the Aramaic word meaning *"fertile, spring, or well."* [1] The Hebrew word is also translated as "joy" in *Genesis 18:9-15*. Another interpretation links the name to a Hebrew word for "pleasure"; thus, the Latin version of the *Biblia Vulgata* reads *"paradisum voluptatis"* in *Genesis 2:8,* and the *Douay–Rheims* version of 1609 which follows has the wording "And the Lord God planted a paradise of pleasure". In Jewish eschatological books such as the **Talmud** and the **Kabbalah** [2] learned rabbis agree that there are two types of spiritual places, called the "Garden of Eden". The first place is earthy, rich in vegetation, and is known as the "lower Garden of Eden". The second place is heavenly, the abode of immortal souls, and is known as the "upper Garden of Eden," which no mortal is said to have seen. In modern Jewish eschatology, it is believed that history will be completed and that the final destination will be when all mankind will return to the Garden of Eden. Gan translates as garden, and the Rabbis distinguish between Gan and Eden. Adam is said to have lived only in Gan, while Edem is said to have never been witnessed by any mortal eye. Our main task is precisely the search for the lower Eden, that is, the terrestrial paradise, for which we hypothesize that it was once located at the North Pole.

1. Cohen, Chaim (2011). "Eden". In Berlin, Adele; Grossman, Maxine (eds.). *The Oxford Dictionary of the Jewish Religion,* pp. 228–229

2. Gan Eden – *Jewish Encyclopedia*; 2010.

Before concluding the present chapter, another point of considerable interest should be noticed. In reading the Edenic traditions of the ancient nations as given in Part fourth, the question may well have suggested itself to the reader "How is it that, with such perfect unanimity on the part of contemporary nations in respect to the north-polar position of the cradle of mankind, the traditions of the Hebrews alone should have placed it in the East? "In the facts just now reviewed, we have a key to this puzzle. The only word in *Genesis* which connects Eden with the East is Kedem *(Qedem)*. This term "properly means that which is before or in front of a person, and was applied to the East from the custom of turning in that direction when describing the points of the compass." [3] From *Gen. xiii. 14*, it would seem to have acquired this association with the East as early as the days of Abraham, but according to "the custom" of a particular time or people it could mean one point of the compass as well as another. It was simply the "front-country." In late historic times among the Hebrews it was the East, and accordingly the West was the country "behind" the North the "left hand" the South the "right" as before noticed. In Egypt, however, the usage was different, the "front – country" being either the North or the South, which we cannot certainly tell, as Egyptologists are divided on the question. ***Pierret*** thinks that it was South and that accordingly, the right hand was West and the left East. [4] ***Chabas*** and others, however, exactly reverse the meaning of the hieroglyphics translated as "right" and "left" and hold that in designating the points of the compass the ancient Egyptian faced the North.

3. Smith's *Bible Dictionary*, Art. "East."

4. *Dictionnaire l'Archeologie Egyptienne*. Paris, 1875: P- I 9 I Comp. pp. 116, 118, 187, 344, 351, 364, 371, 392, 399.

Among the Akkadians and Assyrians, if we may rely upon a questionable statement of ***Lenormant***, still another adjustment prevailed: the right hand was the North, the left the South, and the "front" direction, of course, the West. [5] In view of these facts, it is plain that anterior to the fixation of Hebrew usage, that is in pre-Abrahamic times, *Qedem*, or the "front country" may as well have meant the North as any other quarter. And there is much reason to suppose that it did have this meaning. We have seen that this was peculiarly the sacred quarter of the whole Asiatic and

Egyptian world. Toward it faced all earliest priesthoods and worshipers of whom we have any knowledge. [6] What so natural as that they should contemplate and designate the different quarters of the world from the standpoint of their normal posture in worship? And if once we assume that such was the usage of all the Noachidae anterior to their dispersion and that accordingly "the front-country" meant the North, all at once becomes plain. *Genesis* then unites with universal ethnic tradition in locating the cradle of mankind in the North. The record then reads, ***"And the Lord God planted a garden in the North country, in Eden."***

5. Fragments de Berose, p. 367; also, 380, 419. But compare *Chaldean Magic*, pp. 168, 169, where, by identifying the West with the point "behind the observer" he directly contradicts the account given in his Commentary on Berosus. The paragraph does not appear in the original French edition of the work.

6. "Even among the aborigines of America and Africa we are told that "the West is the left hand and the East the right." Massey, *The Natural Genesis*, vol. ii., p. 231.

And, in precise agreement herewith, it is down from the mountainous heights of this North country "from Qedem" that the descendants of Noah after time come into *"the plain in the land of Shinar"* (Gen. xi. 2). So is cleared up simultaneously another mystery, for how to bring the first colonizers of Shinar into the Tigro-Euphrates valley, from any probable Ararat by any probable ***"journeying from the East"*** or, as the margin gives it ***"eastwards"*** has always perplexed the commentator. [7] This interpretation harmonizes for the first time *Gen. ii. 8 with Eze. xxviii. 13*, both now referring to one and the same point of the compass, the sacred North. Again, the well-known difficulty of harmonizing the references to *"the children of Qedem"* found in the oldest of the Hebrew Scriptures, such as *Gen. xxix. I,* and *Job i. 3*, is solved at once by this interpretation. At the same time, it gives us a location for "the land of Uz" exactly corresponding with the explicit declaration of ***Josephus***: ***"Uz founded Trachonitis and Damascus; this country lies between Palestine and Coelosyria."*** [8] To most readers, this solution to the problem of the exceptional character of the Hebrew tradition will probably at once commend itself as eminently satisfactory. To some, however, it may seem a little difficult to believe that one and the same term could in successive ages have found application to different points of the compass. [9]

7. "Of course, this interpretation proceeds upon the common assumption that *Miqqedem* is translocative in signification, and that the land of Shinar was in the Tigro-Euphrates basin. On another note, I have indicated the possibility that the land of Shinar was in primeval Qedem, in which case *Miqqedem in Gen. xi. 2* should be translated precisely as in *Gen. ii. 8* "in the North country.""

8. Antiquities of the Jews, Bk. i., 6, 4.

9. See diagram illustrative of the discrepancy between Euphratean and Egyptian orientations in Brown, *Myth of Kirké*. London, 1883: p. 99. Comp. p. 101, bot. Mr. G. Massey, in his vast astrotypological medley, refers to the horizon-displacement, but affords no intelligible explanation. He says, "In making the change to a circle of twelve signs, the point of commencement in the North was e slewed round eastward. Hence the Akkadian Mountain of the World became the Mountain of the East. Mount Meru, the primordial birth place in the North, likewise became the Mountain eastward. This may be followed in the Adamah of the Genesis; and in the Book of Enoch it says, The fourth wind, which is named the North, is divided into three parts, and the third part contains Paradise. Thus Eden, which began at the summit of the Mount, and descended into the Circle of Four Quarters prepared by Yima, in the Avesta, against the coming Deluge, was finally planted in the twelfth division of the zodiac of twelve signs, as the garden eastward." *The Natural Genesis.* London, 1883: vol. ii., p. 263.

To such the following, written, of course, with no reference to our problem, will be of special interest: ***"The names of the four cardinal points, and, what is very remarkable, the hieroglyphic signs by which they are expressed, are in a certain measure the same in the Akkadian and Chinese cultures. This I intend to show in a special monograph upon the subject, but that which is here of importance to note is the displacement of the geographical horizon produced in the establishing of the hundred families. The South, which was so termed on the cuneiform tablets, corresponds in Chinese to the East, the North to the West, and the East to the South, making thus a displacement of a quarter of a circle. It would be interesting if, on examination of the Akkadian and Assyrian names, we could find that they in their turn denoted an early displacement of which only these traces remain to us."*** [10]

10. Terrien de Lacouperie, *Early History of the Chinese Civilization*. London, 1880: p. 29. On this curious matter Mr. T. G. Pinches threw some new light at a meeting of the Society of Biblical Archeology, Feb. 6, 1883. In May Mr. Terrien de Lacouperie read a paper before the Royal Asiatic Society, entitled "The Shifting of the Cardinal Points in Chaldea and China" which will appear in his forthcoming work on *The Origin of Chinese*

Civilization. Similar interchanges and identifications of the North and West are referred to by Menzel, *Die vorchristliche Unsterblichkcitslehre*, i., p. 101. See also *Asiatic Researches*, vol. viii., pp. 275-284.

Possibly the usage of ancient Egypt may enable us to put our solution in a yet simpler form. If we may accept the teachings of the learned **Maspero**, the Egyptians often reduced the four quarters or directions to two, using the term East in a sense sufficiently broad to include both East and North, and the term West in a sense sufficiently broad to include both West and South. [11] If, then, Moses, who in his education was an Egyptian, written in accordance with such a usage, it would be quite possible to use *Qedem* for a *"front-country"* in the North, and again, without embarrassment, to use the same term in speaking of the East. [12]

11. "J'ai exposé depuis longtemps dans mes cours au Collegé de France une theorie d'aprés laquelle les Egyptiens auraient divisé les quatre points en deux series groupées : Nord-Est, Sud-Ouest. . . . Ce n'est que par suite de la classification dont je viens de parler qu'on met souvent á l'Ouest les regions proprement situees au Sud, ou reciproquement au Sud les régions situées á l'Ouest. L'application de cette idée á l'Est nous méne aussi á croire que l'on a pu dire du *Tanoutri* qu'il était au Nord." (M. Maspero, in a letter to the author, under date of December 20, 1882.) This usage could hardly have arisen among any people not acquainted with the spherical figure of the earth. How easily it could arise among us is illustrated by Sir John de Maundeville, who, writing in A. D. 1356, located Paradise so far to the East of England that *he could no longer correctly describe the place by this term.* Thus, after speaking of the Terrestrial Paradise as situate far "to the East, at the beginning of the earth", he says, "But this is not that East which we call our East, on this half, where the sun rises to us ; for when the sun is East in those parts towards Terrestrial Paradise, it is then midnight in our parts on this half, on account of the roundness of the earth, of which I have told you before ; for our Lord God made the earth all round in the middle of the firmament." Wright, *Early Travels in Palestine.* London, 1848: p. 276. The nearest way to an Eden thus located would, of course, be north ward. Its location could therefore be described with equal correctness either by the term "eastward" or "northward." Still another interesting theory of its origin will suggest itself to the thoughtful student of such facts as those alluded to by Mr. Scribner in *Where did Life Begin?* pp. 32, 33.

12. Compare the arrangement of the winds on the ceiling of the Pronaos of the temple at Dendera. Brugsch, *Astronomische Inschriften altägyptischer* Denkmäler. Leipsic, 1883: pp. 26 bot., and 27 top.

Chapter IX
Axis Mundi

He is the god who sits in the center, on the Navel of the Earth; and he is the interpreter of religion to all mankind. *– Plato*

Students of antiquity must often have marveled that in nearly every ancient literature they should encounter the strange expression the *"Navel of the Earth."* Still more unaccountable would it have seemed to them had they noticed how many ancient mythologies connect the cradle of the human race with this earth's navel. The advocates of the different sites which have been assigned to Eden have seldom if ever, recognized the fact that no hypothesis on this subject can be considered acceptable which cannot account for this peculiar association of man s first home with some sort of natural center of the earth. Assuming, however, that the human race began its history at the Pole, and that all traditional recollections of man s unfallen state were connected with a polar Eden, the mystery which otherwise envelops the subject immediately vanishes. We have already seen that the term "navel" was anciently used in many languages for "center" and that the Pole, or central point of the revolving constellations, was the *"Navel of Heaven"*. But as to the celestial Pole there corresponds a terrestrial one, so it is only natural that to the term the *"Navel of Heaven"* there should be the corresponding expression the *"Navel of the Earth."* Beginning with Christian traditions, let us make a pilgrimage to the Church of the Holy Sepulcher at Jerusalem. There, in the portion belonging to the Greek Christians, we shall discover a round pillar, some two feet high, projecting from the marble pavement, but supporting nothing. If we inquire as to its purpose, we shall be informed that it is designed to mark the exact center or *"Navel of the Earth"*. [1]

1. As my own inspection of this monument was nearly thirty years ago, I have thought it well to make an inquiry as to its present state. The following, written under the date of Oct. 28, 1884, by my obliging friend, Dr. Selah Merrill, the United States Consul at Jerusalem, and well-known as an Oriental archaeologist, will be read with much interest: "The stone to which you refer still stands in the middle of the Church (Greek) of the Holy Sepulcher, and is called the Centre or Navel of the Earth. It is called a pillar, although it is not a pillar, a vase, conforming in its general shape to a large, tall fruit dish. The top is in the form of a basin, with a raised portion in its center; that is, in the bottom of the basin. I was told that at every feast bread was laid on this pillar. I am assured that it is called the Centre of the Earth only by the Arab or native Christians of Syria, and not by the Greeks proper; also, that every Greek church in Syria that is built after the form of this one has such a pillar in the center. Within two or three years past, an old church has been excavated a little distance north of the Damascus gate. In the Palestine Fund Report for October 1883, I wrote some accounts of this to supplement what had been written before by others. In the center of that church, there is a similar stone, but that is a real pillar. This church is no doubt very old and is popularly spoken of as the Church of St. Stephen. In my judgment, it stands on the site of an older church. "It seemed to me a little singular that this object should be called a pillar (*Amûd*), when it is only a vase, or vase-shaped; but as the tradition connected with it is very old, the name may have come down from the time when the object used for this purpose was actually a pillar or column." It is interesting to compare with the foregoing the description given by Bernard Surius, of Brussels, in the year 1646, particularly as at that time the "Oriental Greeks" seem to have had no scruple in calling the pillar the Centre of the Earth: "Omtrent het midden steckt eenen witten marmer-steen uyt, van twee voeten in syn vierkant, daer een rondt putteken in is, t welck soo de Oostsche Griecken seggen, het midden van den aerdt-bodem is." *Reyse van Jerusalem*. Antwerp, 1649: P- 664.

Early pilgrims and chroniclers refer to this curious monument, but its antiquity no one knows. [2] As usually described, it is a monument of the geo graphical ignorance of those who placed it there, a proof that they supposed the edge of the "flat disk" of the earth to be everywhere equidistant from this stone. It is a monument of primeval astronomic and geographic science.

2. Bishop Argulf, in his pilgrimage, A. D. 700, "saw some other relics, and he observed a lofty column in the holy places to the north of the Church of Golgotha, in the middle of the city, which at midday at the summer solstice casts no shadow; which shows that this is the center of the earth." Wright, Early Travels in Palestine, p. 4. As late as A. D. 1102, it still seems to have been outside the then-existing Church. Bishop Saewulf says, "At the head of the Church of the Holy Sepulcher, in the -wall outside, not far from the place of Calvary, is the place called Compos, which our Lord Jesus Christ himself signified and measured with his own hand as the middle of the world according to the words of the Psalmist, God is my king of old, working salvation in the midst of the earth." Ibid., p. 38. In 1322, however, it is described by Sir John de Maundeville as "in the midst of the Church." Ibid., p. 167. At one time in the Middle Ages, the spot seems to have been marked by a letter or inscription. Barclay, *City of the Great King*. Philadelphia, 1858: p. 370. See Michelant et Reynaud, *Itinéraries á Jerusalem*. Geneve, 1882: pp, 36, 104, 182, 230, etc.

Omphalos, Center of the World in the Catholicon Greek Chapel in the Church of the Holy Sepulcher in Jerusalem, Israel.

To find the true symbolical and commemorative character of this pillar, we need to remind ourselves of a tendency ever present and active among men. We have already alluded to the scores of "Calvaries" which have been set apart in Roman Catholic lands and hallowed as memorial mounts. Up the side of each leads a *Via dolorosa*, with its different "stations" each recalling to the mind, by sculptured reliefs or otherwise, one of the immortal incidents of the Passion. On the summit is the full crucifixion tableau, the Savior hanging aloft upon the cross, between two crucified malefactors. The spear, the reed with the sponge, the hammer, all are there, sometimes the ladder also; and nearby, the tomb wherein never man was laid. In the minds of the worshipers, it is a holy place. Even in our Protestant republic, on the shore of Lake Chautauqua, we have seen successfully carried out, in our own day, a complete reproduction of Palestine. Thousands have visited it to take object lessons in Sacred

Geography. From it, these thousands have gained clearer ideas of the relative positions and bearings of Hermon and Tabor and Olivet, of Kedron and Cherith and the Jordan, of Nazareth and Hebron and the Holy City, than else they ever would have had. What here has been done for purposes of instruction has elsewhere and often upon a greater or smaller scale, been done for purposes of direct religious edification, and for the gratification of religious sentiment. Now, just as Christians love to localize in their own midst their "Holy Places", so the early nations of the world loved to create miniature reproductions of Eden, the fair and sacred country in which man dwelt in the holy morning hours of his existence. [3] The traditional temple architecture of many early religions was determined by this symbolic and commemorative motive. This was eminently true of the sacred architecture of the Babylonians, Egyptians, Hebrews, and Chinese. [4] *Koeppen* assures us that "every orthodoxly constructed Buddhist temple either is, or contains, a symbolical representation of the divine regions of Meru, and of the heaven of the gods, saints, and Buddhas, rising above it." [5] *Lillie* says, *"The thirteen pyramidal layers at the top of every temple in Nepal represent the thirteen unchangeable heavens of Amitâbha."* [6]

3. "The Hindus generally represent Mount Meru as a conical figure, and kings were formerly fond of raising mounds of earth in that shape, which they venerated like the divine Meru, and the gods were called down by spells to come and dally upon them. They are called Meru-sringas, or the peaks of Meru. There are four of them either in or near Benares; the more modern, and of course the more perfect, is at a place called Sár-náth. It was raised in the year of Christ 1027. . . . This conical hill is about sixty feet high, with a small but handsome octagonal temple on the summit. It is said in the inscription that this artificial hill was intended as a representation of the worldly Meru, the hill of God, and the tower of Babel, with its seven steps or zones, was probably raised with a similar view and for the same purpose." Wilford in *Asiatic Researches,* vol. viii., p. 291.

4. Miller, "The Pyramidal Temple" in *the Oriental and Bib. Journal.* Chicago, 1880: vol. i., pp. 169-178. Also, Boscawen, in the same, 1884, p. 118. Perrot and Chipiez, *History of Art in Chaldea and Assyria.* London and New York, 1884: vol. i., pp. 364-398.

5. Die Religion des Buddha, vol. ii., 262.

6. Buddha and Early Buddhism, p. 51. We find the same symbolism even among the civilized aborigines of America. Thus *"the temple at Tezcuco was of nine stories, symbolizing the nine heavens",* Bancroft, *Native Races,* vol. iii., p. 184. Compare pp. 186, 195, 197; also 532-537.

With what astonishing elaboration this idea has sometimes been carried out may be seen in the Senbyoo temple in Mengoon, near the capital of Burmah. [7] That the natural features of the landscape were often utilized in producing these symbolic shrines and holy places is only what we should expect. "The Buddhists of Ceylon" as **Obry** states*, "have endeavored to transform their central mountain, Déva-Kuta (Peak of the Gods), into Meru, and to find four streams descending from its sides to correspond with the rivers of their Paradise."* [8] Again, in the "rock-cut" temples of Ellora, we have, in like manner, a complete representation of the Paradise of Siva. **Faber** develops the evidence of this practice among the ancients with great fullness, and with respect to the Hindus and Buddhists says *"Each pagoda, each pyramid, each montiform high-place is invariably esteemed to be a copy of the holy hill Meru"* the Hindu's Paradise. [9] From *"Records of the Past"* vol. x., p. 50, we see that the Egyptians had the same custom of building temples in such a manner that they should be symbolical of the abode of the gods.

7. See *Journal of the Royal Asiatic Society.* London, 1870: pp. 406-429.

8. Le Berceau de l'Espice Humaine, p. 118.

9. Origin of Pagan Idolatry. London, 1816: vol. i., p. 345. So an American writer says "Akkad, Aram, and all the other highlands of antiquity were but reproductions, traditionary inheritances from this primitive highland, this Olympus of all Asia. . . . Similar notions were associated at a later period with Mount Zion in Jerusalem, and with the Mohammedan Mecca and other sacred localities. Such ideas [as that they were respectively in the center of the world] are no indication of the ignorance of the ancients: they were symbolical and traditionary conceptions inherited from the sacred mount of Paradise." *The American Antiquarian and Oriental Journal.* Chicago, 1881: p. 312. Compare 1884, p. 118.

Rome the citadel mounts in their cities had quite as great religious as military significance. **Lenormant**, speaking of Rome and Olympia, remarks, *"It is impossible not to note that the Capitoline was first of all the Mount of Saturn and that the Roman archeologists established a complete affinity between the Capitoline and Mount Cronios in Olympia, from the standpoint of their traditions and religious origin*

(Dionysius Halicarn., i., 34). This Mount Cronios is, as it were, the Omphalos of the sacred city of Elis, the primitive center of its worship. It sometimes receives the name Olympos." [10] Here is not only symbolism in general but also symbolism pointing to the Arctic Eden, already shown to be the primeval mount of Kronos, the *Omphalos* of the whole earth. [11] Now, as Jerusalem is one of the most ancient of the sacred cities of the world, and, at the same time, the one where the tradition of the primeval Paradise was preserved in its clearest and most historic form, it would be strange if, in all its long history, no king or priesthood had ever tried to enhance its attractiveness and sanctity by making it, or some part of it, symbolize Earth's earliest Holy Land and commemorate man s earliest Theocracy.

10. Beginnings of History, pp. 151, 153.

11. Among the Romans no city, or even camp, was rite established and founded without a sacred *Umbilicus*. It "fiel in den Schnittpunkt des Decumanus und Cardo Maximus, d. h., wohin die *Via decumana*, sich mit der *Via principalis* kreuzt; dieser Schnittpunkt befand sich vor dem introitus Praetorii; da stand auch die *Ara castrorum*, da war der *Umbilicus* des Systems. Diesen *Umbilicus* nun finden vir in Rom noch in Mauerresten vorhanden am nordöstlichen Anfang des Forum wieder, welche Stelle als Umbilicus bezeichnetwurde." J. H. Kuntze, *Prolegomena zur Geschichte Roms*. Leipsic, 1882: p. 154. See notes below, on the cities of Cuzco and Mexico.

That the attempt was made is beyond doubt. To this day the visitor is shown the spot where, according to one tradition, Adam was created. [12] Not many feet away, under the custody of another religion, he finds the sacred rock-hewn grave in which at least the head of the first of men was buried. [13] In little Gihon, the name of one of the Paradise rivers still lives. The miraculous virtue of the Pool of Bethsaida was ascribed in early Christian legend to its being in subterranean contact with the Tree of Life, which grew in the midst of Paradise. [14] Christ's cross was said to have been made of the wood of the same tree. The very name, Mount Sion, is a memorial one. The Talmudic account of *"The Strength of the Hill of Sion"* shows that the Palestinian mount was named after the heavenly one, and not vice versa, as commonly supposed. The true sacred name of the Holy City is, therefore, not Sion (though it is often called by the heavenly appellation also), but *"Daughter of Sion."*

12. Murray's *Handbook for Syria and Palestine*. London, 1858: Pt. i., p. 164. Another account reads, "E de Iherusalem á Seint Habraham sunt. viii. liwes, e la fust Adam fourmé." *Itinéraires á Jerusalem, et Descriptions de lá Terre Sainte*. Rédigés en frangais aux X°, XI°,, XII°, siecles. Publics par Michelant et Reynaud. Geneve, 1882: p. 233.

13. See F. Piper, *Adams Grab auf Golgotha. Evangelischer Kalender*,1861: p. 17 ff. (illustrated). Philippe Mousket (A. D. 1241), in his descriptive poem on the Holy Places, makes it the tomb of both Adam and Eve:

> *"Et lá tout droit ú li ludeu*
> *Crucifiierent le fil Deu,*
> *Fu Adam, li premiers om, mis*
> *Et entierés et soupoulis,*
> *Et Eve, sa feme, avoec lui"* etc.

(Michelant et Reynaud, ut supra, p. 115.)

14. W. Henderson, *Identity of the Scene of Man's Creation, Fall, and Redemption*. London, 1864: p. 10.

She is simply a copy, a miniature likeness, of the true mount and city of God *"in the sides of the North."* So confident is **Lenormant** that Solomon and Hezekiah intentionally conformed their capital to the Paradisaic mount, and intentionally introduced in their public works features which should symbolize and commemorate peculiarities of Eden, that he uses the fact as an unanswerable argument against those imaginative critics who would place the composition of the second chapter of *Genesis* subsequent to the Babylonian exile. He says, ***"Another proof, and a very decisive one in my opinion, of the high antiquity of the narrative of Genesis concerning Eden, and of the knowledge of it possessed by the Hebrews long before the Captivity, is the intention so clearly proved by Ewald to imitate the four rivers which predominated in the works of Solomon and Hezekiah for the distribution of the waters of Jerusalem, which, in its turn, was considered as the Umbilicus of the Earth (Ezek.v.5), in the double sense of the center of the inhabited regions and source of the rivers. The four streams which watered the town and the foot of its ram parts one of which was named Gihon (I Kings i. 33; 38; 2 Chron. xxxii. 30, xxxiii. 14), like one of the Paradisaic rivers were, as Ewald has shown, reputed to issue through subterranean communications from the spring of fresh water situated beneath the Temple, the sacred source of***

life and purity to which the prophets (Joel iii. 1 8; Ezek. xlvii. 1-12; Zech. xiii. i, xiv. 8; cf. Apoc. xxii. i) attach a high symbolic value." [15]

15. "Ararat and Eden". *The Contemporary Review*, vol. iii., No. 27 l (Am. ed., p. 46).

In this citation, in addition to a strong assertion of the symbolical character of the topography and waterworks of Jerusalem, we have the location itself included in this symbolism. The city is said to have been the *Umbilicus* or *"Navel of the Earth",* for two reasons: first, because of its relation to surrounding countries [16] and, second, because of it containing the source of the rivers. In our last chapter, this last reason will become more significant than even the writer intended. At present we will only add that the true philosophy of this symbolical centrality of Jerusalem is found in two facts: first, the Hebrews had a tradition that primeval Eden was the *"Centre of the Earth"* [17] and, second, by styling Jerusalem the *"Navel of the Earth",* as they did, it was symbolically all the more assimilated to the primitive Paradise which in so many other ways it sacredly commemorated. Passing to the field of Hellenic tradition, we are told by all modern interpreters that the Greeks shared the *"narrow conceit and ignorance of all ancient nations"* and supposed their own land to occupy the middle of the "flat earth disk." And because of certain expressions in **Pindar** *(Πίνδαρος Latin: Pindarus; c. 518 BC – c. 438 BC)* and a passage in **Pausanias** *(Παυσανίας; c. 110 – c. 180)*, it is affirmed as a first principle in the geography of the ancient Greeks that Delphi was believed to be the exact topographical center point of the whole earth.

16. That this traditionally-given first reason for the appellation is not well founded is evident from the fact that the Hebrews had a "Navel of the Earth" farther to the North before ever they had possessed themselves of the site of Jerusalem (Judg. ix. 37).

17. In Origen, *Selectis ad Genesin*, we read, "Tradunt Hebraei lo cum, in quo Paradisum plantavit Deus, Eden vocari, et ajunt ipsum mundi medium esse, ut pupillam oculi". Compare Hershon, Talmudic Miscellany, p. 300.

Such a representation is far from satisfactory. For while the term *"Omphalos of the Earth"* was undoubtedly applied in a sense to Delphi, it belonged to it only as the name Athens belongs to many a town thus designated in America. It had other and older topographical connections and associations. We find traces of the same title in connection with

Olympos, with Ida, with Parnassos, with Ogygia, with Nyssa, with Mount Meros, with Delos, with Athens, with Crete, and even with *Meroë*. In the multiplicity of these localizations, the people seem to have lost the clue to the original significance of the conception and to have contrived crude etymological myths of their own for the explanation of what seemed to them a remarkable designation. [18] The moment we make the true original Omphalos of the Earth the North Pole and invest it with sacred traditionary recollections of Eden life, all this confusion becomes clear. The "center-stone" of Delphi, like the *Omphalium of the Cretans*, becomes merely a memorial shrine, an attempted copy of the great original. And if all the Olymps and Idas and Parnassos mounts were alike convenient repro ductions and localizations of the one celestial mountain of the gods at the North Pole, what wonder if we find each of them in some way designated as the *Centre of the Earth*. **Homer's** *"Omphalos of the sea"* Calypso's isle, has in like manner all the marks of a mythic-traditional north-polar Eden. Its name, Ogygia, connects it with far-off antediluvian antiquity. [19] It is situated in the far North, and Odysseus needs the blast of Boreas to bring him away from its shores on the homeward journey. Its queen, Calypso, is the daughter of Atlas; and Atlas proper station in Greek mythology, as elsewhere shown, is at the terrestrial Pole. Its beauty is Paradisaic, it is adorned with groves and "soft meadows of violets", so beautiful, in fact, that *"on beholding it even an Immortal would be seized with wonder and delight."* [20] Finally, identifying the place beyond all questions, we have the Eden "fountain" whose waters part into *"four streams, flowing each in opposite directions."* [21]

In Mount Meros we have only the Greek form of Meru, as long ago shown by **Creuzer**. [22] The one is the *"Navel of the Earth"* for the same reason that the other is. Egyptian *Meroë* (in some Egyptian texts *Mer*, in Assyrian *Mirukk*, or *Mirukka*), the seat of the famous oracle of Jupiter Ammon, was possibly named from the same *"World-Mountain."* This would explain the passage in **Quintus Curtius**, which has so troubled commentators, wherein the object which represented the divine being is described as resembling a *"navel set in gems."* [23]

18. "Á peine l'enfant [Zeus] venoit de naitre, que les Curétes le porterent sur l'Ida. Dans le trajet, le cordon ombilical se detacha et tomba au milieu d une plaine qui prit de lá le nom de ὀμφαλός, *nombril* (nom qu elle devoit avoir auparavant)." T. B. Emeric-David, *Jupiter; Recherches sur ce Dieu, sur son Culle*, etc., Paris, 1833, t. i., p. 248, referring to Callimachus, *Hymnus in Jovem,* v. 44; Diodorus Sic., v. 70.

18. See Welcker, *Griechische Gotterlehre*, i., 775 et seq.

19. Odyssey, v. 63-75. 8 Ibid.

20. Symbolik, vol. i., p. 537.

21. "Id quod pro deo colitur, non eandem effigiam habet, quam vulgo diis accommodaverunt: umbilico maxime similis est habitus, smaragdo et gemmis coagmentatus." Quintus Curtius, *De Reb. Ges.*, iv. 7, 23. See notes in Lemaire's ed., Paris, 1822; also, Diodorus Siculus, iii. 3. Capt. Wilford notices another coincidence: "The Pauranics say that . . . the first climate is that of Meru; among the Greeks and Romans the first climate was that of. Meroe." Wilford in *Asiatic Researches*, vol. viii., p. 289.

When the two doves of Zeus, flying from the two opposite ends of the world, determine the cosmic centralness of "Parnassos" it is of an antediluvian Parnassos that the myth is speaking. [24] It is that mount on whose polar top we have already found the *"domicilium"* of Zeus. *Nonnos*, in describing the symbolical peplos which Harmonia wove on the loom of Athene, says, *"First she represented the earth with its omphalos in the center; around the earth, she spread out the sphere of heaven varied with the figures of the stars…..Lastly, along the exterior edge of the well-woven vestment she represented the Ocean in a circle."* [25] That Delphi or the Phocian Parnassos is the *omphalos* here mentioned is far enough from credible. It is the Pole, and the manner in which the term is introduced shows that it was perfectly understood by every reader, and needed no explanation. The true shrine of Apollo was not at Delphi, but in that older earth-center of which *Plato* speaks in the motto prefixed to this section. His real home is among "the Hyperboreans" in a land of almost perpetual light, and it is only upon annual visits that he comes to Delphi. [26]

24. "Before this time "the time of the deluge of Deucalion" Zeus had once wanted to know where the middle of the earth was, and had let fly two doves at the same moment from the two ends of the world, to see where they would meet; they met on Mount Parnassos, and thus it was proved beyond a doubt that this mountain must be the center of the earth." C. Witt, *Myths of Hellas*. London, 1883: p. 140.

25. Lenormant, *Beginnings of History*, p. 549.

26. "Au début de l'hiver Apollon quitte Delphes pour le pays mystérieux des Hyperboréans, oú régne une lumieré constante, et qui échappe aux rigueurs de l'hiver." Maxima Collignon, *Mythologie Figuree de la Grece*. Paris, 1883: p. 96. See Alcaeus Hymn, referred to by Menzel, *Unsterblichkeitslehre*, i., p. 87. The present writer is not the first to be reminded here of polar Meru: "Bei ihnen (den Hyperboreern), wohnen beständig der Sonnengott Apollo und seine Schwester Artemis, wie auf dem indischen Meru ebenfalls Indra, der Lichtgeist und Sonnengott, wohnt." Dr. HeinrichLüken, *Die Traditionen des Menschengeschlechts, oder die Uroffenbarung unler den Heiden*. Minister, 2d ed., 1869: p. 73.

The remembrance of this fact would have helped the interpreters of **Pindar** *(Πίνδαρος, Latin: Pindarus; c. 518 BC – c. 438 BC)* out of more than one perplexity. [27] According to **Hecataeus** *(Ἑκαταῖος ὁ Μιλήσιος; c. 550 BC – c. 476 BC)*, Leto, the mother of Apollo and his sister Artemis, was born on an island in the Arctic Ocean, *"beyond the North wind."* Moreover, on this island inhabited by the Hyperboreans, Apollo is unceasingly worshiped in a huge round temple, in a city whose inhabitants are perpetually playing upon lyres and chanting to his praise. [28] So reports **Diodorus** *(Διόδωρος Diodoros Siculus; fl. 1st century BC, it., 47)*; and here with agrees to the imaginary journey of **Apollonius of Tyana** *(Ἀπολλώνιος ὁ Τυανεύς; c. 3 BC – c. 97 AD)*, a namesake of Apollo, who tells of his journey far to the North of the Caucasus into the regions of the pious Hyperboreans, among whom he found a lofty sacred mountain, the Omphalos of the Earth. [29] In the **Phaedo** we have a charming description of **Plato's** terrestrial Paradise. "In this fair region" **Socrates** *(Σωκράτης; c. 470–399 BC)* is made to say, ***"all things that grow trees and flowers and fruit are fairer than any here; and there are hills and stones in them smoother and more transparent and fairer in color than our highly-valued emeralds and sardonyxes and jaspers and other gems, which are but minute fragments of them: for there all the stones are like our precious stones, and fairer still. The temperament of their seasons is such that the inhabitants have no disease, and live much longer than we do, and have sight and hearing and smell and all the other senses in much greater perfection. And they have temples and sacred places in which the gods really dwell, and they hear their voices, and receive their answers, and are conscious of them, and hold converse with them, and***

they see the sun, the moon, and the stars as they really are." [30] If we ask as to the location of this divinely beautiful abode, every indication of the text agrees with our hypothesis. It is right under the eye when the world is looked at from its summit, the Northern celestial pole. [31] Viewed from the standpoint of Greece and its neighboring lands it is "above" it is "the upper Earth" the dazzling top of the "round" world. In it, moreover, is the *Navel of the Earth, μεσογαία,* inhabited by happy men. If anything is needed to disprove the common notion that geographical ignorance and national self-esteem first governed the ancient peoples in locating in their own country's "navels" of the earth, it is furnished by what is, in all probability, the oldest epic in the world, that of Izdhubar, fragments of which have survived in the oldest literature of Babylonia.

27. See *Olympian Odes,* iv., 74; vi., 3; viii., 62 ; xi., 10. *Nemean, viL, 33. Frag., i., 3, passim ; comp. Olymp., ii., iii.; Pyth., iv., etc.*

28. "The Dorian worship of Apollo was *primitively* Boreal." Humboldt, Cosmos (Bohn s ed.), ii., 511. Compare Pindar's expression in the second *Olympian Ode*: "the Hyperborean folk who serve Apollo."

29. "Cette montagne est sacrée; c'est l'ombilic du monde." Moreau de Jonnes, *L'Océan des Anciens,* p. 162. As to the Aegean Delos, the best explanation Keary can give is this: "Delos was after ward deemed to be the navel of the earth, because, being in special favor with Apollo, *it might be thought to stand under the eye of the midday sun*" (!) *Primitive Belief,* p. 183. Compare, on the other hand, Pindar's *Fragment* in honor of Delos, the Homeric *Hymn to Apollo,* and the Japanese myth of Onogorojima before described.

30. Phaedo, I I 0, III.

31. Εζ tis άνωθεν θεψto

These fragments show that the earliest inhabitants of the Tigro-Euphrates basin located in the *"Centre of the Earth"* not in their own midst, but in a far-off land, of sacred associations, where ***"the holy house of the gods"*** is situated, a land "into the heart whereof man hath not penetrated a place underneath the "overshadowing world-tree" and beside the "full waters". [32] No description could more perfectly identify the spot with the Arctic Pole of ancient Asiatic mythology. Yet this testimony stands not alone; for in the fragment of another ancient text, translated by ***Sayce*** in ***"Records of*** the Past" we are told of a *"dwelling"* which *"the gods created"* for the first human beings, a dwelling in which they *"became great"* and *"increased in numbers"* and the location of which is described in words exactly corresponding to those of Iranian, Indian, Chinese, Eddaic, and Aztec literature; namely, in the *"Centre of the Earth."* [33] In the Hindu Puranas, we are told over and over that the earth is a sphere, and that Mount Meru is its Navel or Pole. [34] But the expression *nabhi*, or "Navel" of the earth, is older than the Puranas, though the very meaning of Purana is "ancient."

The Naval of the Earth

32. A. H. Sayce, *Babylonian Literature*. London, 1878: p. 39. The Sunis of Northwestern Africa, in our own day, fix the center of the world outside their own territory "between themselves and the Soudan." R. G. Haliburton, *Notes on Mount Atlas and its Traditions*. Salem, Mass., 1883: p. 82

33. *Records of the Past*, xi., pp. 109 seq. George Smith, *Chaldean Account of Genesis*, 2d ed., p. 92. Lenormant, *Beginnings of History*, app., pp. 508-510.

34. "The convexity in the centre is the navel of Vishnu.", *Asiatic Researches*, vol. viii., p. 273.

Like the term *"Navel of Heaven"* it occurs in the hymns of the earliest Veda. But where was the sacred shrine to which it was applied? It was no holy place in Bactria or Punjab. Nothing tends to locate in India. On the other hand, the fifth verse of the one hundred and eighty-fifth hymn, mandala first, of the **Rig Veda**, seems most plainly to fix it at the North Pole. In this verse Night and Day are represented as twin sisters in the bosom of their parents Heaven and Earth; each bounding or limiting the other, but both kissing simultaneously the *Nâbhi* of the Earth. Now, everywhere upon earth, except in the polar regions, Night and Day seem ever to be pursuing and supplanting each other. They have no common ground. At the Pole and only where they may be said, with locked arms, to spin round and round a common point, and unitedly to kiss it from the opposite sides. [35]

संगच्माने विव्या समन्ते सवसारा जामी पित्रोरुपस्थे ।
अभिजिग्रन्ती भुवनस्य नाभिं द्यावा ... ॥
saṃghachamāne yuvatī samante svasārā jāmī pitrorupasthe |
abhijighrantī bhuvanasya nābhiṃ dyāvā ||

Together, young, with limited meetings, Twin sisters lying in their parents' bosoms, Together they love the center of the world. Protect us, Heaven and Earth, from terrible danger. *- Rig Veda, Mandala 1, Hymn 185 (trans. Grassmann, ii., 177.)*

This plainly is the meaning of the poet; and remembering all the legendary splendors of the polar mountain around which the sun and moon are ever moving, we must pronounce the figure as beautiful as it is instructive. [36]

35. The following versions may be compared: "Zusammenlcommend, die beiden Jungen, deren Enden zusammenstossen, die verbündeteten Schwestern in der beiden Aeltern Schosse, kussend den Nabel der Welt, schiitzt uns, Himmel und Erde, vor Gewalt." Ludwig, i. 182. "Going always together, equally young and of like termination, sisters and kindred, and scenting (sic) the navel of the world, placed on their lap as its parents; defend us, Heaven and Earth, from great danger." Wilson, ii., 188.

"Die Beiden Jungfraun an einander grenzend"
"Die Zwillingsschwestern in dem Schoss der Eltern"

"Die im Verein der Welten Nabel küssen"
"Beschirmt vor grauser Noth uns Erd und Himmel".

(Grassmann, ii., 177.)

Compare Rig Veda, i., 144, 3; ii., 3, 6, and 7; et passim. These two twin sisters are reminiscent of the pair from the old Slavic mythology, the pair Vesna - Morana, where the first is the personification of summer (spring) and life, while the other is winter and death.

36. A later poet borrowed the same idea:

> *"Around the fire in solemn rite, they trod,*
> *The lovely lady and the glorious god;*
> *Like Day and starry Midnight when they meet*
> *In the broadplains at lofty Meru's feet."*

(Griffith's Translation of *Kumara Sambhava*, or *The Birth of the War-God*. London, 1879.)

In perfect accord herewith, we find the bard asking, in another hymn, where the Navel of the Earth is; and in doing it he associates it as closely as possible, not with some central home shrine in his own land, but with the extreme *"End of the Earth"* an expression used again and again, in ancient languages, for the Pole and its vicinity. [37] Again, in another Vedic passage, the Navel of the Earth is located upon ***"the mountains"*** and this association points us to the North. [38] Still stronger evidence of its polar location is found in other hymns, where the supporting column of heaven the Atlas pillar of Vedic cosmology is described as standing in or upon the Navel of the Earth. [39]

37. The following is Grassmann s translation: "Ich frage nach dern aussersten Ende der Erde, ich frage wo der Welt Nabel ist" etc. *Rig Veda*, i., 164, 34; comp. 35.

38. Rig Veda, ix., 82, 3. 8

39. Ibid., ix., 86, 8; ix., 79, 4; ix., 72, 7, etc.

Finally, so unmistakable is the Vedic teaching on this subject that a recent writer, after asserting with all his teachers that the cosmography of the Vedic bards was "embryonic" and their earth a ***"flat disk"*** overarched by a solid firmament, which was "soldered on to the edge of the disk at the horizon" nevertheless, later, in studying one of the cosmogonical hymns of Dīrghatamas, the son of Mamata, reaches the conclusion that the singer knew both of the celestial and of the terrestrial Pole, and that, in seeking to answer the question as to the birth-place of humanity, he locates it precisely at the point of contact between the polar mountain and the Pole of the northern sky. [40] We have seen that according to Old-Iranian tradition also, the man was created in the "central" division of the earth. The primordial tree, which *"kept the strength of all kinds of trees"* was *"in the vicinity of the Middle of the Earth."* [41] The primeval ox, which stood by the Paradise river when the destroyer came, was *"in the Middle of the Earth."* [42] *Mount Taêra (Pahl.: Têrak),* the celestial Pole, and *Kâkad-i-Dâîtîk,* the mountain of the terrestrial Pole, are each described in similar terms: the one as the *"Centre of the World"* the other as the *"Centre of the Earth."* [43] The expression *Apâm Nepât,* the *"Navel of the Waters"* occurs in the Avestan writings again and again, and is always applied either to the world fountain from which all waters proceed or to the spirit presiding over it. [44]

40. The reader will no doubt be glad to see the exact language: "Le contact de la terre et du ciel, serait-il l'hymen mystérieux d'oiú l'humanité naquit? Le del, ce serait le pére qui engendre; la mére, ce serait la grande terre, ayant sa matrice dans la partie la plus haute de sa surface, sur les hauts monts; et ce serait la que lé pere féconderait le sein de celle qui est en meme temps, son épouse et sa fille. On a cru voir ce point de contact dont parle Dīrghatamas, *Outtânyah tchamwâh,* endroit septentrional oú les deux surfaces se touchent, au pôle nord, connu de l'auteur; l'étoile polaire se nommant *outtanapada.* Il est certain que la somme des connaissances positives collectionées par ce philosophe était relativement important." Marius Fontane, *Inde Vedique.* Paris, 1881: pp. 94, 200.

41. West, *Pahlavi Texts,* pt. i., p. 161.

42. West, *Pahlavi Texts,* pt. i., p. 162.

43. Ibid., pp. 22, 36. So, in consequence of the duality and opposite polarity alluded to in the context, "Hell is in the middle of the earth" at the South Pole, p. 19.

44. See Index to Darmesteter's *Zend-Avesta.* Compare the Vedic hymn (ii., 35), "An den Sohn der Wasser", *Apâm napât,* whose location is *"an dem höchsten Orte"* (v., 13, Grassmann). Compare quotation from Ritter, in part iv., chapter first, *supra.*

But as this world-fountain, *Ardvî Sûra*, is located in the north polar sky (see the last chapter), we have here also a recognition of a world - *omphalos*, inseparable from the ancient and sacred Paradise-mountain at the Pole. [45] The Chinese terrestrial Paradise is described not only as *"at the Centre of the Earth",* but also as directly under Shang-tee's heavenly palace, which is declared to be in the North star, and which is sometimes styled *"Palace of the Centre."* [46] Very probably the historic designation, "The Middle Kingdom" was originally a sacred name, [47] commemorative of that primeval middle country which the Akkadian called *Akkad*, the Indian *Ilâvrita*, the Iranian *Kvanîras*, and the Northman *Iðavöllr*. In the funeral rites of China, this supposition finds a cogent confirmation. [47]

46. In Kwen-lun is Shang-te's lower recreation palace. . . . Shangte's wife dwells in this region, immediately over which is Shang-te's heavenly palace, which is situated in the center of the heavens, as his earthly one is in the center of the earth. . . . The Queen mother dwells alone in its midst, in the place where the genii sport. At the summit, there is a resplendent azure hall, with lakes in closed by precious gems, and many temples. Above rules the clear ether of the ever-fixed, the polar, star." Condensed from the *Chinese Recorder,* vol. iv., p. 95.

46. Frédérik Klee, *Le Déluge*. Paris, 1847: p. 188, note.

47. "Quand je vous ai parlé des libations en usage a lá Chine, je vous ai dit, Monsieur, qu'on se tournait vers le pole septentrional pôur faire les libations en l'honneur des morts. En considérant la vénération de ce peuple pour ses ancêtres, on n'apergoit qu'une explication naturelle de cet usage; c'est de dire que les Chinois se tournent vers le pays du monde, oú ils ont pris naissance, et oil leur ancêtres reposent." Bailly, *Lettres sur l'Origine des Sciences et sui celle des Peuples de l'Asie*. Paris, 1777: p. 236. [48]

Passing to Japan, it is curiously interesting to note that the Ainos, who are supposed to have been the first inhabitants, are believed to have come into the archipelago ***"from the North"*** that their heaven is on inaccessible mountain-tops in the same quarter; [49] and that their name, according to some authorities, etymologically signifies *"Offspring of the Center"*. In burial, their dead are always so placed that when resurrected their faces will be set toward the lofty northern country from which their ancestors are believed to have come, and to which their spirits are believed to have returned. [51]

48. Griffis, *The Mikado's Empire,* p. 27.

49. "These [a mythological pair] were the ancestors of the Ainos. Their offspring, in turn, married; some among each other, others with the bears of the mountains [the Bear Tribe?]. The fruits of this latter union were men of extraordinary valor and nimble hunters, who, after a long life spent in the vicinity of their birth, departed to the far North, where they still live on the high and inaccessible table lands above the mountains; and, being immortal, they direct, by their magical influences, the actions and the destiny of men; that is, the Ainos." Ibid., p. 28.

50. Ai-no-ko. Ibid., p. 29.

51. It may not be devoid of interest to mention here that the Ainos bury their dead with the head to the South. . . . The Aino, to-day, as he did in ancient times, buries his dead by covering the body with matting, and placing it with the head to the South in a grave which is about three feet deep." *Notes on Japanese Archccology with es special reference to the Stone Age,* by Henry von Siebold, Yokohama, 1879, p. 6. Let no reader imagine this a meaningless rite of undeveloped savages. "From all these observations, as well as from the traditions of the Ainos, in which are ever-recurring laments for a better past; and from many peculiarities in their customs, we must conclude that the Ainos are to be classed with those peoples that have earlier been more richly supplied with the implements of civilization, but have become degraded through isolation. Prehistoric discoveries . . . favor this view. The pits found there for dwellings indicate that the Ainos came from the North to Yezo." Professor Brauns, of Halle. Translated from Memoirs of the Berlin Anthropological Society, in *Science,* Cambridge, 1884; p. 72.

Today, the Ainu people are almost on the verge of total extinction, because very few of this ethnic group have survived. They were at war with the Japanese for almost 1500 years. The Ainu are different from the Japanese, they are physically larger and stockier, have long beards and many of them do not have the slanted eyes that are typical of the Mongolic race. In the following volumes, we will get to know their history in more detail. This people have a distinctly strong cult of the archetypal totemic spirit of the bear.

Taking these facts in connection with those presented in chapter second of the preceding part, one can hardly evade the conclusion that, when *William Elliot Griffis (1843 - 1928)* informs us that the Japanese considered their country as lying at *"the top of the world"* and when others say that the Japanese once regarded their country as the *"Centre of the World"* [52] it is most probable that these writers have applied to the

Japan of to-day ideas which originally belonged to a far-distant prehistoric polar Japan, the primitive seat of the race, as it has lived on in these most ancient traditions of the Ainos. In Scandinavian mythology, we meet with a similar idea. In the Eddas, both *Asgard* and *Iðavöllr* are represented as in the *"Center of the World"* and at least one author, in explaining the reason for it, has come within a hair's-breadth of the truth, though missing it. **[53]**

Ainu man, 1890 from Hokkaido, Japan. He wears a sword in his belt and a ceremonial crown - サパウンペ, Sapaunpe, used during the iomante ritual and other religious practices.

52. "The Japanese in their *earlier separation* regarded their country as the centre and most important part of the world." J. J. Rein, *Japan, Travels and Researches*, English translation. London, 1884: p.

53. "Nos ancetres scandinaves placaient la demeure de leurs dieux, Asgard, au milieu du monde, c'est-á-dire au centre de la surface de la terre d'alors. Il est assez remarquable qu une telle idée n'est pas sans fondement, puisqu'il faut admettre, comme je crois l'avoir démontré, que l'Europe, l'Asie, et l'Amérique, unis vers le pôle nord, formaient avant le déluge un seul continent." Frédérik Klee, *Le Déluge*, Fr. ed. Paris, 1847 p. 188 n – But by clinging to "the highest mountains of Asia" as the centre originally meant, M. Klee loses the chief advantage of his supposed union of the continents at the Pole. The Teutonic *omphalos* of the world is preserved at Finzingen, near Altstädt, in Saxe-Weimar. See Kuhn and Schwartz, *Nord deutsche Sagen*. Leipsic, 1848: p. 215.

The ancient Mexicans conceived of the cradle of the human race as situated in the farthest North, upon the highest of mountains, cloud-surrounded, the residence of the god Tlaloc. Thence come the rains and all streams, for Tlaloc is the god of waters. The first man, Quetzalcoalt, after having ruled as king of the Golden Age in Mexico, returned by divine direction to the primeval Paradise in the North (*Tlapallan*) and partook of the draught of immortality. The stupendous terraced pyramid temple in Cholula was a copy and symbol of the sacred Paradise-mountain of Aztec tradition, which was described as standing *"in the Centre of the Middle-country"* [54] Some of the Mexican myths represent the mountain as now "crooked" or turned partly over. Among the ancient Inca subjects of Peru [55] was found the same idea of a *Navel of the Earth*, and even among the Chickasaws of Mississippi. [56]

54. *Im Centrum des Mittellands*. Lüken, *Traditionen*, p. 75; citing Clavigero, Storia del Messico, tom, ii., 13, 14. "Die Mexicaner opferten auf den höchsten Bergen weil sie glaubten, dass auf ihnen Tlaloc, der Herr des Paradieses wohne. Sie wurden einerseits als der *Mittelpunkt der Erde* betrachtet, andererseits aber als die Stätte, welche *dem Himmel am nächsten ist,* und ihm in näherer Berührung als die Erde selbst steht." Keerl, *Die Schöpfungsgeschichte*, p. 799. In like manner the national temple of Tlaloc and Vizilputzli, his brother, stood in the centre of the city of Mexico, whence four cause way roads conducted East, West, North, and South. In the centre of the temple was a richly ornamented Pillar of peculiar sanctity. Bancroft, *Native Races*, vol. iii., p. 292. The Quiche prayer to the "Heart of Heaven, Heart of Earth" would seem to rest upon similar conceptions of the true abode of God. *Popol Vuh*. Max Miiller, *Chips from a German Workshop*. New York, 1872: vol. i., p.335

55. "The center and capital of this great territory was Cuzco (i. e., navel), whence to the borders of the kingdom branched off four great highways, North and South and East and West, each traversing one of the four provinces or vice-royalties into which Peru was divided." *The Land of the Incas*, by W. H. Davenport Adams. London, 1883: p.20. In tne central temple here, too, there was a Pillar, plaéte dans le centre d'un cercle dans l'axe du grand temple et traversée oar un diamttré de Vest a Pouest. P. Dabry de Thiersant, *De l'Origine des Indiens du Nouveau-Monde et de leur Civilisation*. Paris, 1883: p. 125. Still more interesting is it to note that the pre-decessors of the Peruvians are reported to have had an idea of the work of the creation of the world as proceeding from the North to the South. Dorman, *Origin of Primitive Superstitions*. Philadelphia, 1881, p. 334

56. "Some of the large mounds left in Mississippi were called *navels* by the Chickasaws, although the Indians are said not to have had any idea whether these were natural mounds or artificial structures. They thought Mississippi was at *the center of the earth* and the

mounds were as the navel in the middle of the human body." Gerald Massey, referring to Schoolcraft, i. 311.

Thus, is all ancient thought full of this legendary idea of a mysterious, primeval, holy, Paradisiac Earth-center, a spot connected as is no other with the *"Centre of Heaven,"* the Paradise of God. Why it should be so no one has ever told us; but the hypothesis which places the Biblical Eden at the Pole, and makes all later earth navels commemorative of that primal one, affords a perfect explanation. In the light of it, there is no difficulty in understanding that Earth-center in Jerusalem with which we began. The inconspicuous pillar in the Church of the Holy Sepulcher symbolizes and commemorates far more than the geographical ignorance of the medieval ages. It stands for the Japanese pillar by which the first soul born upon earth is mounted to the sky. It stands for the *World Column* of the East-Aryans and the *Chinvat Bridge* of Iran. It stands for the law-proclaiming pillar of orichalcum in Atlantis, placed in the center of the most central land. It stands for that Talmudic pillar through which the tenants of the terrestrial Paradise mount to the celestial, and, having spent the Sabbath, return to pass the week below. It symbolizes *Cardo, Atlas, Meru, Harâ-Berezaiti, Kharsak Kurra*, every fabulous mountain on whose top the sky pivots itself, and around which all the heavenly bodies ceaselessly revolve. It perpetuates a religious symbolism that existed in its region be forever Jerusalem had been made the Hebrew capital, recalling to our modern world the *tabbur ha-aretz* of a period anterior to the days of Samuel. [57] In tradition, it is said to mark the precise spot "whence the clay was taken, out of which the body of Adam was modeled." It does so, but it does it in a language and method which were common to all the most ancient nations of the earth. It points not to the soil in which it stands, but to the holier soil of a far-away primitive Eden. [57]

56. Judg. ix, 37 (margin).

57. The genuinely scientific basis of this ancient symbolism is vividly shown in our above-given sketch-map of the actual relations of all the continents to the North Pole.

Chapter X

Trilokya

न मे पार्थास्ति कर्तव्यं त्रिषु लोकेषु किञ्चन ।

नानवाप्तमवाप्तव्यं वर्त एव च कर्मणि ॥ 3.22॥

na me pārthāsti kartavyaṁ triṣhu lokeṣhu kiñchana

nānavāptam avāptavyaṁ varta eva cha karmaṇi

In all the three worlds, O Partha, there is no responsibility for Me to fulfil; Nothing remains un-achieved or to be achieved. Still I continue in Karma. - *Bhagavat Gita 3.22.*

"There is no duty for me to do in all the three worlds, O Parth, nor do I have anything to gain or attain. Yet, I am engaged in prescribed duties."

Triilokya [1] is a chapter on the ancient three-tiered cosmogonic division of: upper, middle and lower world. Although we have previously mentioned the four-layer world division, I still think it is worth clarifying this once again for the reader. If we also divide the middle or earthly world into two parts, an upper and a lower world, it seems to fall into place in a logical sequence, and this alone will facilitate our search for the localization of the earthly paradise. We can divide this double terrestrial or mid-terrestrial division into solar and lunar halves, where the first will rule the northern hemisphere while the second the southern hemisphere. Pictorially and symbolically, this idea from today's perspective is also expressed in the very flags of modern countries, such as those today's countries that are influenced by the northern hemisphere, such as Finland, Norway, England, the Faroe Islands or Iceland (mainly the Christian northern European countries) highlight the solar symbol – the cross, while the Muslim countries of the southern hemisphere cultivate the lunar symbol shown on the flags of various countries such as Pakistan, Tunisia, Algeria, Malaysia, Saudi Arabia, Singapore, Turkey, Turkmenistan, Uzbekistan, etc.

1. Monier-Williams, Monier (1899). A *Sanskrit-English Dictionary.* p. 460, col. 1, entry for "[Tri-]loka" p. 462, col. 2, entry for "Trailoya." See also Blavatsky *Theosophical Glossary.* (1892), p. 336-7, entry for "Trailokya."

In the modern Western political concept, similar to the cosmogonic worldview of the ancient peoples, a similar three-part division of the world is made. The terms First, Second, and Third World were originally used to divide the nations of the world into three categories. The complete overthrow of the status quo after World War II, known as the Cold War, left the two superpowers (the United States and the Soviet Union) fighting for ultimate global supremacy. These forces created two camps, known as blocs.

The "Three Worlds" of the Cold War era, April-August 1975 are:

• *First World*: The Western Bloc led by the United States, Japan, the United Kingdom and their allies

• *Second World*: Eastern Bloc led by USSR, China and their allies

• *Third World*: non-aligned and neutral countries led by India and Yugoslavia

Today, the terms First and Third World are generally used to refer to developed and developing countries.

The three-part division from antiquity also has its own metaphysical basis that corresponds with the very energy qualities of these regions which, on the other hand, are closely related to the *Tri-Guna* philosophy that is adequately reflected by the spiritual concept of the holy trinity known among Hindus as – *Trimūrti*, or the Buddhist doctrine – *Trikāya* or the Old Slavic *Triglav*. We will now briefly enter into the three-part Ariosophic perspective of thought, to see how the ancient peoples of the East experienced the world, how we would acquire a clearer picture of what they meant by the term heavens or the upper world, in order to more easily locate our problem, about finding the polar paradise on earth. *Guna (Sanskrit: गुन)* is a concept in Hinduism, Jainism, and Sikhism that can be translated as "quality." The concept is originally notable as a feature of Samkhya philosophy. [2] The *gunas* are a key concept in almost all schools of Hindu philosophy. There are three *gunas*, according to this worldview, which have always been and continue to be present in all things and beings in the world. [3] Thus, every human, animal, plant, crystal or metal belongs predominantly to one of these *gunas*. These three *gunas* are called: *sattva* (kindness, calmness, harmony), *rajas* (passion, activity, movement) and *tamas* (ignorance, passivity, inertia, laziness). [4] All these three *gunas* are present in everyone and everything, with different proportions, according to the Hindu worldview. The interaction of these *gunas* defines the character of someone or something, of nature, and determines the progress of life. In the study of human behavior, guna means personality, the inherent nature and psychological attributes of an individual. [5]

2. guna. Monier Williams' *Sanskrit-English Dictionary*, Cologne Digital Sanskrit Lexicon, Germany. Also, Guna, *Sanskrit-English Dictionary*, Koeln University, Germany.

3. Larson, Gerald James, *Classical Samkhya: An Interpretation of its History and Meaning*. Delhi, 1969: Motilal Banarsidass, p. 37.

4. Alban Widgery (1930), *The principles of Hindu Ethics, International Journal of Ethics*, Vol. 40, No. 2, p. 234-237.

5. Theos Bernard (1999), *Hindu Philosophy*, Motilal Banarsidass, , p. 74–76. See Elankumaran, S (2004). *"Personality, organizational climate and job involvement: An empirical study"*. *Journal of Human Values*. 10 (2): 117–130 and Deshpande, S; Nagendra, H. R.; Nagarathna, R (2009). "A randomized control trial of the effect of yoga on Gunas (personality) and Self-esteem in normal healthy volunteers". *International Journal of Yoga*. 2 (1): 13–21.

> *Sattva* (Sanskrit: सत्व - means honesty) is a quality or guna of balance, harmony, goodness, purity, universalization, it has a holistic, constructive, creative and luminous nature that manifests itself with tranquility, peace and virtue. This guna brings the qualities of balance, balance, or yin-yang (- /+) harmony, and if a person develops these qualities, he or she more quickly attracts *Dharma* (righteousness) and *Jñāna* (knowledge). This is the guna which on the cosmological level in the "Sacred Geography" corresponds to the North Pole or *Terra Borealis* in which the spiritual and divine qualities of nature are present, where exactly in

this place the union and touch between the heavenly and terrestrial paradise occurs. *Sattva*, or *Sata* in the Pali language, is found in Buddhist texts, such as *Bodhi-sattva*. *Sattva* in Buddhism means "a living being, person or sentient being that has substance. Sattvic food: vegan, neutral flavors. This guna is associated with the god Vishnu विष्णु - the maintainer of life.

Rajas (Sanskrit: रजस् – means passion) is a quality that represents an activity, without any particular value and contextually it can be either good or bad. This is the *guna* of self-centeredness, selfishness, it has an individualizing, stimulating, driving, dynamic and temperamental nature that has a positive value (+) *yang*, it is a guna that has an earthly or human dimension in which the divine and demonic qualities are mixed. Geographically, it corresponds to "Middle Earth", that is, the Mediterranean and the belt that covers it up to the Equator - the imaginary circle that divides the planet into the northern and southern hemispheres. The latitude of the equator is 0°. This guna has a solar nature and is associated with the god Brahma ब्रह्मा - the creator of life.

Tamas (Sanskrit:तमस् – means darkness) is a quality of imbalance, disorder, chaos, anxiety, this guna has an impure and destructive nature, a guna that carries delusion, negativity, boredom or inactivity, apathy, extreme hedonism, carnal-animal gratification, inertia or lethargy, violence, malice, ignorance, and it is often translated as unknowing. It has a negative value (-) *yin* and is the *guna* that has a demonic dimension and qualities. Geographically this guna dominates in the Underworld or the South Pole (Down Under), *Terra Australis*. Food: blood food - meat, drugs, alcohol. This guna has a lunar nature and is associated with the god Shiva - शिव the destroyer of life.

A living being or substance is seen as the total result of the joint effect of these three qualities. According to the Samkhya school, no one and nothing is either pure *satva*, pure *rajas* or pure *tamas*. One's nature and behavior is a complex interaction of all these, with each guna in varying degrees. In some the behavior is predominantly *rajas* with significant influence of *sattvic guna*, in some it is *rajas* with significant influence of *tama guna*, etc. Let's not forget that Buddha was born, lived and died as a Brahmin (Hindu) and not as a Buddhist, while pre-chewed Vedism can be called Buddhism. In the image in the middle is *Buddha Amitābha* who is the representative of harmony, where his mudra joins the energies of both hands radiating universal peace and is adequate to Vishnu himself. On his left side is the bodhisattva *Avalokiteśvara* who is the solar male aspect and who has raised his right hand which has the function of giving (creation, birth) and is equivalent to Brahma.

The Buddhist Trinity - Trikāya

On his right is the bodhisattva *Mahāsthāmaprāpta* who raises his left which has the function of taking (dying, destroying). According to the **Amitayurdhyana Sutra** he is representative of the Moon and is adequate to the nocturnal principle corresponding to Shiva.

Our ancestors also believed in immaterial and heavenly worldly expanses that had the same hierarchical gradation, where in myths and legends and fairy tales we can often meet terms like "seventh heaven" and similar representations, which denote the highest world where the Highest sat on the throne, but also the spiritual world, which has both a deified and a demonic side, as we said, has its counterpart and reflection in the material world. The spiritual world has its analogy with the material world. Thus, the North Pole and its energy qualities and laws that rule in that sacred region coincide with the spiritual, i.e. God's world, and *vice versa*, the South Pole represents the zone where the laws of animal instincts and drives reign, it is the region of the demonic world of the flesh pleasures and base passions. Thus the northern archaic land *(Su-Meru)* represented the celestial, divine, or eagle hemisphere, where the god-like people live, while Antarctica represented the underground, dark or serpentine sphere of the southern land itself *(Ku-Meru),* where the people-beasts live, while the Mediterranean or the "borderline" is actually the "Middle Earth" or the Equator which represents the human dimension in which these two archaic forces of nature mix together. In this way, we have two diametrically opposed forces and laws: North-South or light-dark, while in the post-flood phase the tension is created between East and West, a conflict that in a geopolitical sense continues to this day.

In Central and South America, we also have a three-part division of the world, where the condor (eagle) represents the heavenly world of the spirit, the jaguar – the human world of passion, while the boa (snake) – represents the demonic and underground world. According to the **Atharva-Veda** and the Puranas, in the cosmological division of the Universe, there are 14 worlds, 7 heavenly or upper *(Vyahrtis)* and 7 lower or lower *(Pātālas).*

• The above seven heavenly worlds, including our earth are: *bhu, bhuvas, svar, mahas, janas, tapas, satya.*

• The lower seven underworlds are: *atala, vitala, sutala, rasātala, talātala, mahātala, pātāla.*

In different traditions, the three worlds carry different nomenclature, but the essence is the same. Somewhere that division may be as follows: *Swargaloka*, the land of gods; *Mrityuloka,* the middle kingdom of men;

and *Pataloka*, home of the Asuras, the fallen gods, and demons. Generally, in Vedic or later Hindu cosmology, the Universe and the world are divided into three loki:

• **Svarga-loka** (the world of the Devas, the good Gods, and the Heavens), or the North Pole

• **Prithvi-loka** or *Martya* (the earthly, human or mortal world) or the Equator

• **Patala-loka** (the world of Asuras, evil Gods or demons and the Underworld) or the South Pole.

In the mythology of Vedism or Brahmanism, the world of *Svaga-loka* has the following designations:

• *Svarga-* (heaven),

• *Trinaka-* (The world of the third god),

• *Triwisztapa* - (third kingdom),

• *Nakaprisztha-* (The world of the god at the top of the heavens).

Sometimes the names themselves vary depending on the scriptures, but the essence is everywhere the same. We must also not forget the hermetic maxim that reads: "As above, so below, as below, so above". In the same way, we can see this cosmological division through the "horizontal" or rather a microcosmic prism of our planet itself. According to the scripture **Śrīmad Bhāgavatam**, the cosmology, the Universe is represented as a tree, and the planets in this tree are like trunks, branches, and fruits, an image that associates with the *"Tree of Life"*, the famous template from the Kabbalah - Jewish mysticism. In the early stage of Jainism, an explanation of the nature of the Earth and the Universe is given, where a detailed hypothesis is presented for various aspects of astronomy and cosmology. Jainism does offer an interesting picture. And here according to the sacred Jain scriptures, the Universe is also divided into three parts – *Triloka* [6]:

• **Urdhva Loka** – the realms of the Gods or heavens.

• *Madhya Loka* – the realms of humans, animals, and plants.

• *Adho Loka* – the realms of infernal beings or infernal regions.

6. Raval, Mukundchandra G. (2016), *Meru: The Center of our Earth,* p. 81. See also Grimes, John A. (1996), A *Concise Dictionary of Indian Philosophy: Sanskrit Terms Defined in English,* p. 177

a) The upper world *(Udharva loka)* in Jainism is divided into different abodes and these are the realms of celestial beings (demigods) who are unliberated souls. The upper world is divided into sixteen *Devalokas*, nine *Graiveyakis*, nine *Anudishas* and five abodes of *Anuthar*. The 16 abodes of Devaloka are: *Saudharma, Aishana, Sanatkumara, Mahendra, Brahma, Brahmottara, Lantava, Kapishta, Shukra, Mahashukra, Shatara, Sahasrara, Anata, Pranata, Arana and Achyuta.*

- The 9 abodes of *Graivayak* are: *Sudarshan, Amogh, Suprabuddha, Yashodhar, Subhadra, Suvishal, Sumanas, Saumanas and Pritikar.*
- The 9 *Anudishis* are: *Aditya, Archi, Archimalini, Vair, Vairochan, Saum, Saumrup, Ark and Sphatik.*
- The 5 *Anutaris* are: *Vijaya, Vaijayanta, Jayanta, Aparajita and Sarvarthasiddhi.*

The sixteen heavens in *Devaloka* are also called *Kalpas* and the rest are called *Kalpatit*. Those who live in *Kalpatit* are called *Ahamindra* and are equal in grandeur. There is an increase in life span, the influence of power, happiness, the brightness of the body, purity in thought color, the capacity of senses, and range of clairvoyance in the celestial beings who dwell in the higher abodes. But there is a decrease in movement, growth, attachment, and pride. The higher groups reside in the 9 *Greveyakis* and the 5 *Anutari Vimans*. They are independent. Anuttara souls attain liberation within one or two lifetimes. The lower groups are organized as earthly kingdoms - rulers (like Indra), counselors, guardians, queens, followers, armies, etc. Above the anutary vimanas, at the pinnacle of the universe is the realm of liberated souls, the perfected omniscient and blissful beings, who are revered by the Jains. [7]

7. Schubring, Walther (1995), *"Cosmography",* in Wolfgang Beurlen (ed.), *The Doctrine of the Jainas,* Delhi: Motilal Banarsidass Publ. p. 204–246

b) The Middle World *(Madhya Loka)* is essentially our material planet consisting of 900 yojanas above and 900 yojanas below the surface of the earth. According to Jainism, it is inhabited by:

- Jyotishka devata (bright gods) - 790 to 900 yojanas up north. (North Pole)
- Tyryanch, [8] (Humans, animals, birds, plants) on the surface (Mediterranean, Equator)
- Vyantar devas (intermediary gods) – 100 yojanas below ground level.

Madhya Loka consists of many island continents surrounded by oceans, the first eight whose names are:

Continent: Island Ocean:

1. Jambūdvīpa Lavanoda (The Salt Ocean)

2. Ghatki Khand Kaloda (Black Sea)

3. Puskarvardvīpa Puskaroda (The Lotus Ocean)

4. Varunvardvīpa Varunoda (Ocean of Varuna)

5. Kshirvardvīpa Kshiroda (Milky Ocean)

6. Ghrutvardvīpa Ghrutoda (the ocean of milk with butter)

7. Ikshuvardvīpa Iksuvaroda (the ocean of sugar)

8. Nandishwardvīpa Nandishwaroda

Mount Meru *(Su-Meru)* is at the center of the world surrounded by *Jambūdvīpa,* in the form of a circle of 100,000 yojanas in diameter. The *Jambūdvīpa* continent has 6 mighty mountains, which divide the continent into 7 zones *(Ksetras)*. The names of these zones are:

1. Bharat Kshetra

2. Mahavideh Kshetra

3. Airavat Kshetra

4. Ramyak Kshetra

5. Hiranya vant Kshetra

6. Hemvant Kshetra

7. Hari Varsh Kshetra

The three zones viz. *Bharat Kshetra, Mahavideh Kshetra, Airavat Kshetra* are also known as *Karma bhoomi* as the practice of asceticism and liberation is possible and *Tirthankaras* preach the doctrine of Jainism. [8] The other four zones, *Ramyak Kshetra, Hiranya vant Kshetra, Hemvant Kshetra, Hari Varsh Kshetra* are known as *akarmabhoomi* or *bhogbhumi* because god-men live a sinless life of contentment and no special religion is required for liberation.

c) The lower world *(Adho Loka)* or Hades consists of a gradation like the seven heavens of the seven infernal regions, which are inhabited by demigods Bhavanpati and infernal beings. *Naraka* (Sanskrit: नरक) is the realm of existence in Jain cosmology characterized by the great suffering of souls. *Naraka* is usually translated into English as "hell" or "purgatory". Infernal beings live in the following nether regions:

1. Ratna prabha-dharma.

2.Sharkara prabha-vansha.

3. Valuka prabha-megha.

4. Pank prabha-anjana.

5. Dhum prabha-arista.

6. Tamah prabha-maghavi.

7. Mahatamah prabha-maadhavi

Buddhism, like Hinduism, has a rather interesting and complicated cosmological scheme where the three worlds break down into many subdivisions. Spatial cosmology in Buddhism depicts the diversity of the multitude of worlds embedded in the Universe. Spatial cosmology can also be divided into two branches. Vertical *(or cakravāḍa;* चक्रवाद*)* cosmology describes the arrangement of worlds in a vertical pattern, some higher and others lower. In contrast, horizontal *(sahasra)* cosmology describes the grouping of these vertical worlds into sets of thousands, millions, or billions. In vertical cosmology, in the Universe there are many worlds *(lokāḥ; Devanagari:* लोकाः*)* – that is, "spaces or realms" – arranged one after the other in layers. Each world corresponds to a mental state or state of being". A world, however, is not a location so much as the beings that make it up; it is sustained by their karma, and if the beings in a world die or disappear, the world also disappears. Similarly, the world comes into being when the first being is born into it. The physical division is not as important as the difference in mental state; humans and animals, although they partly share the same physical environments, still belong to different worlds because their minds perceive and react differently on those environments. The vertical cosmology is divided into thirty-three planes of existence and the expanses of the three worlds or dhātus, where each corresponds to a different kind of mentality or quality or guna.

These are the three celestial spheres or *Tridhātu* are:

• *Aūrūpyadhātu* (4 Realms) – it is the world of formlessness, the incorporeal realm inhabited by the four heavens, a possible rebirth destination for practitioners of the four stages of formlessness.

• *Rūpadhātu* (16 regions) – it is the world of form, mostly free of lower desires, inhabited by gods living in dhyāna (deep meditation which is the penultimate stage of yoga), a possible destination for rebirth.

• *Kāmadhātu* (15 regions) – it is the world of desires, typical of the lower passions, inhabited by hellish beings, preta (hungry spirits), animals, humans and lower demigods.

Then below them is *Manusaloka* – the human world, where then below our world follow the hellish dimensions known as *Narakas*. In some cases, all beings born in *Aūrūpyadhātu* and Rūpadhātu are informally classified as "gods" *(devāḥ)*, along with the gods of *Kāmadhātu,* even though the gods of *Kāmadhātu* differ more from those of *Ārūpyadhātu* than they do from humans. It should be understood that Deva is an imprecise term that refers to any being that lives in a longer and generally more cheerful state than humans. Most of them are not "gods" in the sense we have today, they have little or no concern for the human world and rarely ever interact with it; only the lowest *Kāmadhātu* gods correspond to the gods described in many polytheistic religions. The term *"brahmā; Brahmā"* is used both as a name and as a generic term for one of the higher devas. In its broadest sense, it can refer to any of the inhabitants of *Ārūpyadhātu* and *Rūpadhātu.* In a more limited sense, it may refer to an inhabitant of one of the eleven lower worlds of the *Rūpadhātu,* or in the narrowest sense of the three lowest worlds of the *Rūpadhātu.*

• *Manuṣyaloka* मनुष्यलोक – The human world

This is the world of humans and human-like creatures that live on the surface of the earth. Birth in this world is the result of the giving and moral discipline of the middle quality. This is the area of moral choice where destiny can be guided. The **Khana Sutta** emphasizes that this world presents a unique balance of pleasure and pain. It facilitates the development of virtue and wisdom to free the being from all cycles or rebirths. For this reason, rebirth as a human being is considered precious according to the **Chiggala Sutta**, and therefore life should be used wisely. The mountain rings that makeup Mount *Su-Meru* are surrounded by a vast ocean that fills most of the world. What is extremely important for us is the fact that the ocean is in turn surrounded by a circular mountain wall called *Cakravāḍa,* which marks the horizontal boundary of the world. In this ocean, there are four continents which are, relatively speaking, small islands in it. Because of the immensity of the ocean, they cannot be reached by ordinary seafarers, although in the past, when the kings of the *chakravatana* ruled, communication between the continents was possible with the help of a jewel called the *cakkaratana,* which the king and his entourage could use to flying through the air between continents. We will mention the four continents in the second volume of this book. The

Jambūdvīpaprajñapti is a Jain treatise on the *"Island of the Rose Tree"*, which contains a description of the continent of *Jambudvīpa* and the biographies of Ṛṣabha and King Bharata. Mount Meru is at the center of the world surrounded by *Jambūdvīpa*, in the form of a circle of 100,000 yojanas in diameter. There are two sets of Sun, Moon, and Stars revolving around Mount Meru; while one set is working, the other set is lying behind Mount Meru. [10]

10. B. H. Hodgson (1834). *"Remarks on M. Remusat's Review of Buddhism"*. Journal of the Asiatic Society of Bengal. Bishop's College Press. 3p 504. See also Pravin K. Shah. *"Jain Geography"*, *"Indian Cosmology Reflections in Religion and Metaphysics"*, Ignca.nic.in, archived from the original on 30 January 2012, retrieved 7 October 2010. Also, Schubring, Walther (1995), *"Cosmography"*, in Wolfgang Beurlen (ed.), *The Doctrine of the Jainas,* Delhi: p. 204–246. Ibid Cort, John (2010) [1953], Framing the Jina: *Narratives of Icons and Idols in Jain History* p. 90

A bas-relief in the famous ancient Ranakpur Jain temple in the state of Rajasthan, India. Jambudvipa carving, a Jain depiction of the terrestrial world with the sacred Mount Meru in the middle.

• *Narakas* – Infernal worlds

Naraka नरक or *Niraya* निरय is as in Jainism as in Buddhism the name given to one of the worlds of greatest suffering. These are areas of extreme suffering. As in other realms, a being is born into one of these worlds as a result of his karma and resides there for a certain time, until his karma has reached its full result, after which he is reborn in one of the higher worlds as a result of previous karma that has not yet matured. The mentality of a being in hell corresponds to states of extreme fear and helpless pain in humans. Physically, the *Naraka* regions are considered a series of layers extending below Jambudvīpa down into the earth. There are several schemes for counting these *Narakas* and enumerating their torments. One of the more common patterns is that of the eight cold and eight hot *Narakas*.

The Cold Infernal Worlds:

• *Arbuda*

• *Nirarbuda nirarbud*

• *Ataṭa* अतट

• *Hahava* हहव

• *Huhuva* हुहुव

• *Utpala utpal*

• *Padma* पद्म

• *Mahāpadma* महाप्म

Each life span in these Narakas is twenty times that of the one before it.

Hot Hell Worlds:

- *Sañjīva* संजीव

- *Kālasūtra* कालसूत्र

- *Saṃghāta associations*

- *Raurava/Rīrava*

- *Mahāraurava/Mahārīrava* महारूरव/महारीरव

- *Tapana/Tapana* तापन/तपन

- *Mahātāpana* महातापन

- *Avīci* अवीचि

In Norse mythology we see literally the same division of the three worlds:

• *Ásgarðr* - The Upper World, home of the god clan of the Æsir. The words: *áss, ǫss* or *ása*, are colloquially translated as "god", while "*garðr*" - "garden, city, fortress", where the 12th-century Icelandic poet Snorri Sturluson writes that Asgard is a very fertile land, where there is an abundance of gold and jewelry. The Assyrians were distinguished by strength, beauty, and talent. In the first poem of the work *Völuspá* of the **Poetic Edda**, many of the features of Asgard are mentioned, such as *Iðavöllr*, the place where the gods or the Aesirs met most often. It also describes *Yggdrasil*, a mythical World Tree that connects all of the nine worlds to Asgard located under one of its three roots. Asgard is made up of 12 realms, including *Valhalla, Trudheim, Breidablik.* Asgard is said by lore to be completely destroyed during the cataclysm known as *Ragnarök*, and later restored again after the restoration of the world. [11]

11. Boult, Katherine (1948). *Asgard and the Norse Heroes. Ann Arbor:* University of Michigan Library. стр. 21, 56–59, 72, 82–90, 121–123. Види исто "Asgard, Norse mythology". *Encyclopedia Britannica.*

• *Miðgarðr* – The middle world is also noted as *middangeard* in the Old English epic poem Beowulf, and has the same meaning as the Old Norse

358

word. The term corresponds to the Hellenic term Oikoumene corresponding to the inhabited world. The Gothic *Midjun-gards*; (midjun = middle, middle garden, city) is the name of "Middle Earth" or if you prefer *Tolkien's* fictional Middle-Earth, inhabited by the people in the early Scandinavian cosmology that answered to the Mediterranean. According to Edda lore, *Midgard* will be destroyed at *Ragnarok,* the great battle and doomsday. On that day, the great serpent *Jormungandr* will rise from the oceans and scourge the land. All the living world will be destroyed, and the land will sink into the seas, after which it will rise again, green and fertile. [12]

12. Orel, Vladimir E. (2003). *A Handbook of Germanic Etymology.* Leiden: Brill. p. 264, 462.

• *Útgarðar* - The Lower World, in English literally means: "Outyards". According to Norse orthography, *Útgarðar* can mean surrounded by the fortress of giants known as *jötnar,* who are enemies of the Asir and Vanir and are depicted as inhuman beings with negative traits. Although the term gigant or titan is sometimes used to clarify the word *jötunn* and its apparent synonyms in some translations and academic texts, where they can be described as too beautiful or as alarmingly grotesque. They are also led as old deities. Some deities, such as Skaði and Gerðr, who are married to Njörðr and Freyr, are described as jötnar. A similar parallel can be found between the Titans and the Olympian gods in Hellenic mythology. Here they are associated with Útgarða- Lokki, a large and negative giant involved in one of the myths concerning Þórr (Thor) and the other who competed in staged contests held in the nether worlds. These outer arenas contrasted with the putrid, inner cave where Útgarða-Loki was said to have lived when they were chained, according to the 12th-century text **Gesta Danorum**. [13] In another version of Norse mythology, Utgard is mentioned as the last of the three worlds connected to the World Tree - Yggdrasil representing the home of outer cosmic forces. Be that as it may, Útgarða-Loki, according to the name, is definitely connected with Lokki himself as an archetype, who in the myths plays the role of opposition and is always in a fight with the bright thunderer Thor (Þórr), who belongs to the god's clan, that is, the Aesirs. Loki in Old Norse loke, often anglicized as *louke* represents a chthonic deity in Norse mythology. According to some sources, Loki is the son of Fárbauti (jotun/giant) and Laufey (referred to as a goddess), and the brother of Helblindi and Býleistr. Loki was married to Sigyn and they had a son, Nari. From the Jotuna Angrboða, Loki is the father of Hel, the wolf Fenrir, and the world serpent Jörmungandr. Loki is also called as the father of Váli, in the **Prose Edda** it is said - *"Þá váru teknir synir Loka, Váli ok Nari eða Narfi"*. Nari is reminiscent of the Buddhist underworld Narka. According to the **Prose Edda**, Nari was killed by his brother Vali, who transformed into a wolf, and at the end of the passage in the poem *"Lokasenna"*, Vali became a wolf, which is very reminiscent of the Slavic chthonic god Veles, but also of the Vedic Vala – the brother of the demon *Vṛtra, (व:त्र,)* described as a snake or dragon fighting against the thunderer Indra who, among other things, bears the nickname *Purandar (पुॅदर,* breaker of fortresses) which definitely corresponds to the Slavic god Perun the Thunderer (Pol. *piorun* – thunder, blow, percussion) and the Scandinavian Thor.

13. Snorri Sturluson (1929) [1916]. "The Beguiling of Gylfi IX". The *Prose Edda.* Translated by Brodeur, Arthur Gilchrist. p. 21. Ibid. Snorri Sturluson (1929) [1916]. "The Beguiling of Gylfi XLVI-XLVIII". *The Prose Edda.* Translated by Brodeur, Arthur Gilchrist. p. 61–69. Same Snorri Sturluson (1936) [1923]. "Harbathsljoth". The *Poetic Edda.* Translated by Bellows, Henry Adams. p. 122, 130.

The so-called **"Book of Veles"**, which supposedly talks about ancient Slavic religion and history, today, in scientific circles (and among historians and linguists), has a generally accepted and widely documented position that it is a forgery, contains religious passages and historical records, interwoven with naturalism. The events mentioned in the book can be dated from the seventh century BC to the ninth century AD. According to **Yuryi Petrovich Miroljubov** *(Ю́рий Петро́вич Миролю́бов 1892-1970)*, a Russian émigré in the United States who is believed by many to be the real author, the book (specifically the birch plates) was allegedly found in the fall of 1919 by Colonel **Fyodor Arturovych Isenbek** while seeking refuge in Ukraine and coming across a ruined castle. He supposedly found these birch tablets hidden in it. Seeing them, he realized that something was written on them, so he took them and continued to wander through the country where the revolution was taking place. When the war ended, **Isenbek,** like many other like-minded people, left the country and went first to Turkey and then to Yugoslavia. In 1923, he offered the panels to the National Museum in Belgrade for a small fee, but he was turned down. Then he traveled to Brussels where he himself met *Miroljubov*. Allegedly, it took Miroljub 15 years to interpret the letter. Then *Miroljubov* went to the USA with the so-called Veles' book and gave the book to the Russian Museum in San Francisco. Since then, many experts have dealt with the book, including Shajan, Pešić, Kura, Lozko and Lesnoj. *The "Book of Veles"* is published in Serbian by the publishing house "Pesic and Sons". The book had several editions, and the 2000 edition mentioned that it was only the first part of the book and that this publishing house would publish the second part of the book with a translation of the remaining plates. I personally do not intend to be a lawyer for this book, as to whether it is true or a forgery, I would just like to briefly mention that the division of the world into three parts is also mentioned here. In the same way, we have a higher, middle and lower world, where in the book they are mentioned as *Prav, Jav* and *Nav*, and this is actually the only such mention among the Slavic peoples. Although this book may indeed be fiction, there is still no doubt as to whether the Slavic peoples had a three-part cosmological concept, and what is certain is that the term *Nav* or *Prav* itself is found in other places in the literature. We are already talking about the underworld – Nav, among the Slavs in the third chapter.

Concepts such as "Justice" and "Unjustice" *(Pravda and Krivda)* are noted in our traditions from the Balkans, which are briefly mentioned by Čajkanovic in his book *"Myth and Religion among Serbs"* from 1892 (p. 195, 276). The word Right is also a Law and among the Slavic peoples simultaneously signifies the right side (Russian: *правая сторона, the side of truth*), which is connected to the justice of God, the right hand of God, while among the Jews, as we have seen, it is opposite, the left side is equated with God and heaven, while the right hand is identified with Satan and hell. But in the New Testament, we come across these interesting passages:

1. Then I saw in the right hand of him who sat on the throne a scroll with writing on both sides and sealed with seven seals.

2. And I saw a mighty angel proclaiming in a loud voice, "Who is worthy to break the seals and open the scroll?"
3. But no one in heaven or on earth or under the earth could open the scroll or even look inside it.

- Revelation of the Holy Apostle John the Theologian 5. 1-3

Then in his book *" Fragments of the history of Serbs and Serbian-Yugoslav lands in Turkey and Austria"* (*Одломци историје срба и српских - југословенских земаља у турској и аустрији*) First Book, **Milosh S. Milojevic** (*Милош С. Милојевић 1840 —1897*) regarding the Old Slavic pagan supreme deity Triglav, which is the equivalent of the Indo-Aryan Trimūrti (*Trimurti* – three faces त्रिमूर्ति) from India, on p. 149 noted the following:

"Triglav or what is today's Holy Trinity, which was known by the Lithuanians under the name Trove or Troje, Trojstvo (Trinity), and was nothing else, where with its heads it signified: the power or strength over the forces of the upper or heavenly world, over the middle or earthly world and the lower or underground world, i.e. the world dead whom he could always revive and resurrect". [14]

14. Милош С. Милојевић, "*Песме и Обичаи Укупног Народа Српског"*, р. 149
"Узрастни и виши свију људских растова кипови богови, а на својим колима по тадањем српском веровању бораху се вечно за Србе и њихову народност. Триглав или то што и дан. св: Тројица, који и у Литоваца бјаше под именом Трове или Троје, Тројства, и није ништа друго био и са својим главама означавао, до: моћ или силу над силама, над гордим или небесним светом, над средним или земним светом и дољњим или подземним светом т.ј. мртвим којег је увек могао и оживити и ускрснути га".

Then **Milosh S. Milojević** in his work *"Songs and Customs of the Serbian People", First Book, Ritual Songs* published in Belgrade, 1869, recorded the following ritual song that was sung during St. George's Day where we find the following verse:

"The Vishnji Bog (The Highest God, Vedic: Visnu) sits in it (on the precious throne).
He looks at me from three sides.
On three sides of three worlds:

On the heavenly, under the heavenly,
And on the one under the ground".

The whole song is in the original Serbian language, the text in bold is the above text in English that we translated:

Град градила бела вила.
Бела вила Самовила: Од истока до запада,
Од запада до сјевера,
Од сјевера па до југа.
Град градила на градила!
По свом свету великоме,
По том зраку пространоме,
По том зраку трижди зраку.
Наградила направила!
Целог града од мерђана,
А зидове од биљура,
Јасне столе од алема,
А престоле од драгога.
У њем седи Вишњи Боже.
Он ми гледи на три стране.
На три стране у три света:
На небеског, под небеског,
И на оног под земљицом.
Свуда гледи свуда влада;
Свуда чини што ми треба.
Белу браду поглађује,
На Срба се насмехује.
Србину је свако добро,
Понајвеће веља снага.
Веља снага своја земља,
Та Инђија и Дунаво.
Црну браду поглађује,
На душмана попрекује.
На душмана Татарина,
Црна госта Манџурина

И Хобина љута звера,
Алемана и Хиндуша.
Црно гледа црње ради.
Црно ће јим вавек бити.
Рујну браду поглађује,
Плаветном се опасује,
Свима нама добро вели:
Свако добро и весеље.
И румено и плаветно,
И бијело пребијело,
Душманима црно добро
Црно добро и прецрно.

The song was obtained through: Mr. Ilije Spasojević, the teacher of the parish of Sirinićka in Old Serbia, was sent to us by Mr. Mihail Đorđević, teacher of Veliko-Očka in Old Serbia, Prizren Nahija. **[15]**

15. Milosh S. Milojevic, *"Songs and Customs of the Serbian People, First Book, Ritual Songs", (Песме и Обичаи Укопног народа Српског, Прва Књига, Обредне Песме),* Преко г. Илије Спасојевића учитеља жупе Сиринићке у Старој Србији, послао нам г. Михаил Ђорђевић учитељ Велико-Очки у Старој Србији призренској нахији. p.119.

The "Supreme God" *Вишњи Боже (Višni Boze),* which is mentioned in this precious folk and ritual song, looks on three sides, in three worlds, we can easily connect it with the Vedic supreme god Vishnu, worshiped by the ancient Aryans, as a sustainer and symbol of harmony, that is, the representative of the *sattva guna* that keeps the other two *gunas (rajas and tamas)* in balance. All three worlds are united in the Universal Tree, where the root is the underground world, the stem is the earthly world, and the crown is the heavenly world. From here it is clearly seen that our ancestors on the Helm Peninsula (Balkans) kept in mind the same three-world concept, as did other ancient peoples and civilizations around the world, and from all this, we can derive a key conclusion for our hypothesis, that the upper world is the world of the heavenly or sky people (gods), and once again our gaze is directed towards the distant north. Here is another excerpt from a poem from the same book on page 82, which describes the triple power of God as creator, sustainer, and destroyer:

Триглав бору највећем
Највећем.
Вишњем бору створ'оцу
Створ'оцу.
Силну бору Држ'оцу.
Држ'оцу.
И велику Рушиоцу
Рушиоцу.

From the same source from Zvornik, *Miloš* found and noted down several more songs, and I will present here just one more:

Sing songs for us to sing,
We sing!
Our god to celebrate
Let's celebrate:
We glorify the Triglav god
We glorify.
In three-headed three forces,
Three forces;
One is holding the earth
The Earth,
And that sky high
High.
The other creates all ours
All ours
The third destroys all ours
All ours.
Everything earthy is weakly
Weakly.
Glory is flowing to Triglav (Three-headed God)
To Triglav!
He fondles my girls
Caressing,
He gives gifts to heroes
He Gives.

Every girl is looking for Ryle
For Ryle
To them all for Traillo
For Traillo.
The medicine lasts for a long time
For a long time
Live healthy and happy
And happy… [20]

From Stana from Zvornik

20. Milosh S. Milojevic, *"Songs and Customs of the Serbian People, First Book, Ritual Songs"*, (Песме и Обичаи Укопног народа Српског, Прва Књига, Обредне Песме), From Stana from Zvornik. p. 83 (digital book):

Пјевај пјесне да пјевамо,
Пјевамо!
Наше боре да славимо
Да славимо:
Триглав бора вјеличамо
Вјеличамо.
У триглава три снаге,
Три снаге;
Јена држи зјемљицу
Зјемљицу,
И то њебо високо
Високо.
Друга ствара свје наше
Свје наше
Трјећа руши свје наше
Свје наше.
Свје ми зјемно нејачко
Нејачко.
Слава слива Триглаву
Триглаву!

.

Chapter XI
Mirovoe Dervo

"The Tree of Life,
The middle tree, and highest there that grew,
Sat like a cormorant."
John MILTON (1608-1674, Paradise Lost, Book IV, The Argument)

The *"World Tree"* is a fundamental and widespread mythic theme or archetype in many of the world's mythologies, religious or philosophical traditions and is closely related to the concept of the *"Tree of Life"*. The *"World Tree"* as a motif is present in many religions and mythologies, characteristic of Indo-European beliefs and traditions. This tree appears as *égig éő fa* in Hungarian mythology, *Ağaç Ana* in Turkish mythology, *Andndayin Ca'r* in Armenian mythology, *Modun* in Mongolian mythology, *Yggdrasil* in Norse mythology, *Irminsul* in Germanic mythology, *Iroko* in Yoruba religion, *Jianmu* in Chinese mythology, then in Hindu mythology as *Ashvattha* (Ficus religiosa) or the Holy Oak among the Slavs, Balts, Finns, etc. [1]

1. Farnah: *Indo-Iranian and Indo-European studies* in honor of Sasha Lubotsky. Lucien van Beek, Alwin Kloekhorst, Guus Kroonen, Michaël Peyrot, Tijmen Pronk, Michile de Vaan. Ann Arbor: Beech Stave Press. 2018

The *"World Tree"* in Russian is *Мировое Дерево*, where the word *"Mir"* (Мир) is translated as "Holy" but also as "World" and etymologically we can connect it with the mountain Meru or *Miru*, the *"Holy Mountain"* of the Aryans. In South Slavic languages *Mir* literally means "Peace." This tree is represented as a colossal tree that supports the sky, thus connecting the sky, the terrestrial world, and, through its roots, the underworld. It is strongly associated with the motif of the *"Tree of Life"*, which is the source of wisdom throughout the ages. The *"Tree of Knowledge,"* which connects with heaven and the underworld, and the *"Tree of Life,"* which connects all forms of creation, are both forms of the mundane or *"Cosmic Tree"* and are shown, as I have said, in different religions and philosophies around the world. In the mythology of different peoples and religious traditions, many symbols characterize the connection with God. Thus, the *"Tree of Life"* is one of the elements that characterize the development of life, respect for traditions and family values, and respect for commandments. It is believed that the *"Tree of Life"* is a kind of mythical symbol and cosmogonic-esoteric template that signifies the relationship between man and God, earth, and heaven. The tree carries a deep meaning, which cannot be understood by everyone.

In the center of the Garden of Eden, according to *Genesis iii. 3*, there was a tree exceptional in position, in character, and its relation to men. Its fruit was "good for food" it was "pleasant to the eyes", and "a tree to be desired." [2] At first sight, it would not perhaps appear how a study of this tree in the different mythologies of the ancient world could assist us in locating primitive Paradise. In the discussions of such sites as have usually been proposed, it could not; but if the Garden of Eden was precisely at the North Pole, it is plain that a goodly tree standing in the center of that Garden would have had a visible cosmical significance which could by no possibility belong to any other.

2. Was this "tree of knowledge" identical to the "tree of life "? Possibly. "The tradition of Genesis," says Lenormant, *Beginnings*, p. 84, "at times appears to admit two trees, one of Life and one of Knowledge, and again seems to speak of one only, uniting in itself both attributes *(Gen. ii. 17; iii. 1-7)."* Compare Ernst von Bunsen, *Das Symbol des Kreuzes bei alien Nationen*. Berlin, 1876: p. 5. To make the whole account relate to one tree it would only be necessary first to translate the last clause of ch. ii. 9 "the tree of life also in the midst of the garden, even the tree of knowledge of good and evil; "and then the last clause of *ch. iii. 22"* and now lest he continue to put forth his hand and to take of the tree of life" etc., for both of which constructions there are abundant precedents, if only the *gam* be rendered with the freedom used in some other passages. As to the first, see *I Sam. xvii. 40; xxviii. 3; Dan. iv. 10*; as to the second, the Hebrew grammars on the use of the future. Compare also *Prov. iii. 13, 1 8,* where *wisdom* is a tree of life.

Its fair stem shooting up as arrow-straight as the body of one of the "giant trees of California" far overtopping, it may be, even such gigantic growths as these, would to anyone beneath has seemed the living pillar of the very heavens. Around it would have turned the "stars of God" as if in homage; through its topmost branches the human worshiper would have looked up to that unmoving center-point where stood the changeless throne of the

Creator. How conceivable that that Creator should have reserved for sacred uses this one natural altar-height of the Earth, and that by special command He should have guarded its one particular adornment from desecration! *(Gen. ii. 16, 17.)* If anywhere in the temple of nature there was to be an altar, it could only be here. That it was here finds a fresh and unexpected confirmation in the singular agreement of many ancient religions and theologies in *associating their Paradise-Tree with the axis of the world, or otherwise, with equal unmistakableness, locating it at the Arctic Pole of the Earth.* [3]

3. "The Mythical Tree, like the Pillar and the Mount, is a type of the celestial Pole." Massey, *The Natural Genesis*, vol. i., p. 354. The arguments of Professor Karl Budde in favor of eliminating the Paradise-tree from the original Genesis account of the Garden of Eden betray a strange lack of insight. *Die biblische Urgeschichte.* Giessen, 1883: pp. 45-88. Even Kuenen refuses to entertain so arbitrary a notion, and M. Réville well exclaims, What would a Paradise be without *l'Arbre de Vie!*

That the Northmen conceived of the universe as a tree (the Yggdrasil) is well known to ordinary readers. Its roots are in the lowest hell, its mid-branches in close or overarch the abode of men, and its top reaches the highest heaven of the gods. It was their poetical way of saying that the whole world is an organic unity pervaded by one life. As the abode of the gods was in the north polar sky, the summit of the tree was at that point, it's base in the south polar abyss, its trunk coincident with the axis of heaven and earth. [4] It was, therefore, in position and nature precisely what an idealizing imagination magnifying the primitive tree of Paradise to a real World-tree would have produced. [5] But while most readers are familiar with this Norse myth, few are aware of how ancient and universal an idea it represents. This same tree appears in the earliest Akkadian mythology. [6] And what is precise to our purpose, it stood, as we have seen it before, at "the Centre" or Pole of the earth, where is ***the holy house of the gods.*** [7]

4. Menzel, Dieses Sinnbild entsteht ursprunglich aus der Vorstellung der Weltachse. *"Die vorckristkcke Unsterblichkeitslehre,* i. 70.

5. See *"Les Cosmogonies Aryennes"* par J. Darmesteter, *Reuve Critique.* Paris, 1881: pp. 470-476

6. "By the full waters grew the giant overshadowing tree, the Yggdrasil of Noise mythology, whose branches were of lustrous crystal, extending downwards even to the deep." Sayce, *Babylonian Literature*, p. 39. Compare Lepormant, Beginnings of History, pp. 83-107. Had Professor Finzi duly considered the Tree of Life in Akkadian tradition, he could hardly have felt "constrained" to ascribe the origin of the sacred tree of the Assyrian monuments to "Aryan, more particularly Iranian influences." *Ricerche per lo Studio dell'',* Antichitá Assira, p. 553, note.

7. "In Eridu a dark pine grew. It was planted in a holy place. Its crown was crystal white, which spread towards the deep vault above. The abyss of Hea was its pasturage in Eridu, a canal full of waters. Its station was the center of this earth. Its shrine was the couch of Mother Zikum. The (roof) of its holy house like a forest spread its shade. There were none who entered not within it. It was the seat of the mighty Mother". *Records of the Past*, ix, p.154

It is the same tree that in ancient Egyptian mythology closed the sarcophagus of Osiris, from which the king of Byblos caused the pillar of the roof of his palace to be removed. But this was only another form of the *Tat-pillar*, which is the axis of the world. [8] In the light of comparative cosmology, it is quite impossible to agree with **Mr. Renour** in his treatment of the tree in Egyptian mythology. It is neither the "rain cloud", nor the "light morning cloud", nor the "clear mist on the horizon". His citations of the texts happily show that under all its names the Egyptian Tree of Life is a true *"World Tree"*, whose trunk coincides in position and direction with the axis of the world; a tree whose branches reach to the sky where Bennu, the solar-bird, sits; a tree from whose northern polar tip, the "north wind" blows; a tree which, like the Norse Yggdrasil, produces heavenly rain which is life-giving like *Ardvî-Sûra* and which descends, not only on the fields of Lower Egypt but, like *Ardvî-Sûra*, to the Underworld itself, refreshing those "who are in *Amenti* " [9] Accordingly, the above-ground part of the Egyptian Yggdrasil, - like that of the Northmen's, stands at the Arctic Pole. The Phoenicians, Syrians, and Assyrians had each their sacred tree in which the universe was symbolized. [10] In the lost work of **Pherecydes** the former is represented as a "winged oak." [11] Over it was thrown the magnificent veil, or *peplos*, of Harmonia, on which were represented the all-surrounding Ocean with his rivers, the Earth with its *omphalos* in the center, and the sphere of Heaven varied by the figures of the stars. [12]

8. "Probably also at Memphis that he (Ptah) was represented as a pillar, beginning in the lowest and ending in the highest heaven, a conception doubtless alluded to that feature of the myth, as related by Plutarch, where the king of Byblos causes a pillar in his palace out of the tree that grew around the sarcophagus of Osiris. In fact, we have a depiction of Osiris as well as Ptah that fits this description. On a post, on which is carved a human figure, and which is covered with a garment, stands the so-called *Tat-pillar,* entirely made up of a kind of superimposed capitals, one of which has a rude face engraved upon it, interned, no doubt, to represent the shining sun. On the top of the pillar is placed the complete robe of Osiris, the horns of the ram, the sun, the ureus-adders, the double feather, all the emblems of light and sovereignty, and which, according to estimation, must have been intended to represent the highest heaven. (See the plate of Wilkinson, M., and C – 2d series, suppt. plate 25 and 33. No.5. Mariette. Abydos, I., pl. 16.) The *tat-pillar* is a symbol of endurance, and steadfastness. This representation of Osiris, for his rude and simple character, without a trace of art, proves that he was one of the oldest, where he must evidently have been regarded as a symbolic image as Lord of the length of time and of eternity. - Title, History of the Egyptian Religion, p. 45,47. See also G. Massey, The *Natural Genesis*, vol. i., p. 417, 418. 422; and Brugsch, *Astronomische und Astrologische Inschriften* p.72

9. See Renour, *"Egyptian Mythology, particularly with Reference to Mist and Cloud." Transactions of the Society for Biblical Archaeology.* London, 1884: pp. 217-220. A beautiful confirmation of our view is found in the important text in which "the abyss under the earth" *(die Tiefe unter der Erde)* is poetically expressed by the term "the cavity of the Persea *(die Höhle der Persea}.* Brugsch s version, from which the above German expressions are taken, may be seen in the *Zeitschrift für Aegyptische Sprache und Alterthumskunde.* Leipsic, 1881: pp. 77 ff. Surely no opening in an ordinary cloud could be called the subterranean deep.

10. "W. Baudissin is wrong in supposing it unknown to the Phosnicians." Lenormant, *Beginnings of History*, vol. i., p. 104 n.

11. But δρῦς was originally a generic term for the tree. See Curtius, *Etymologie*, s. v.

12. "This veil is identical with the starry peplos of Harmonia." Robert Brown, Jr., *The Unicorn*. London, 1881: p. 89. *The Myth of Kirké*. London, 1883: p. 71.

But as this self-interpreting symbol was furnished with wings to facilitate its constant rotation, it is plain that we have in it, not only a *World-Tree* but also one the central line of whose trunk is one with the axis of heaven and earth. [13] In the language of **Maury**, "It is a conception identical with the *Yggdrasil* of Scandinavian mythology." [14] That section of the tree, therefore, which reaches from the abode of men into the holy heavens rises pillar-like from the Pole of the earth to the Pole of the sky. Among the Persians, the legendary tree of Paradise took on two forms, according as it was viewed with predominant reference to the universe as an organic whole, or to the vegetable world as proceeding from it. In the first aspect it was the Gaokerena *(Gokard)* tree, or "the white Hom" (*Haoma* = Vedic *Soma*); in the second, the "tree of all seeds" the "tree opposed to harm." Of the former it is written, "Everyone who eats of it becomes immortal; . . . also in the renovation of the universe they prepare its immortality therefrom; it is the chief of plants." [15]

13. "Thus the universe definitively organized by Zeus, with the assistance of Harmonia, was depicted by Pherecydes as an immense tree, furnished with wings to promote its rotary motion, a tree whose roots were plunged into the abyss, and whose extended branches sustained the unfolded veil of the firmament decorated with the types of all terrestrial and celestial forms." Lenormant, *Beginnings of History*, p. 549. Compare Louis de Ronchaud, *"Le Péplos d'Athéné Parthérnos Revue Archéologique"*. Année, xxiii. (1872) pp. 245 seq., 309 seq. , 390 seq. ; xxiv. 80 seq. Also W. Swartz, "Das Halsband cler Harmonia und die Krone der Ariadne." *Neue Jahrbücher der Philologie*, 1883: pp. 115-127. This writer s view of the connection of the *Halsband* with the foot of the Yggdrasil is very curious and not wholly clear.

14. Religions de la Gréce Antique, iii. 253.

15. Bundahish, xxvii. Compare the *Vendidad*, Farg. xx.

Of the second we read, *"In like manner as the animals, with a grain of fifty and five species and twelve species of medicinal plants, have arisen from the primeval ox, so ten thousand species among the species of principal plants, and a hundred thousand species among ordinary plants, have grown from all these seeds of the tree opposed to harm, the many-seeded….When the seeds of all these plants, with those from the primeval ox, have arisen upon it, every year the bird (Kamros) strips that tree and mingles all the seeds in the water; Tishtar seizes them with the rain-water and rains them on to all regions."* [16]

Where stood this tree which, in its dual form, was at once the source of all other trees and the giver of immortality? Every indication points us to the northern Pole. It was in *Airyanəm Vaējah* [17] the Persian Eden, and this we have already found. It was at the source of all waters, the north polar fountain of *Ardvî-Sûra*. [18] It was begirt with the starry girdle of the zodiacal constellations, which identifies it with the axis of the world. [19] It grew on "the highest height of *Harâ-Berezaiti*, [20] and this is the celestial mountain at the Pole.

16. Ibid., xxvii. 2, 3.

17. Bundahish, xxix. 5.

18. Ibid., xxvii. Compare Windischmann: "Also der Baum des Lebens wachst in dem Wasser des Lebens, in der Quelle Ardvisura Anahita." *Zoroastrische Studien*. Berlin, 1863: p. 171.

19. Homa Yasht, 26. Haug, *Essays*, 2d ed., p. 182.

20. Yasht, IX. (Gosh.), 17. Compare *Bundahish*, xvm., as translated by Justi and Windischmann. See Grill, *Die Erzväter*, i., pp. 186191. Windischmann, *Zoroastrische Studien*, p. 165 seq. Spiegel, *Erânische Alterthumskunde*, i. 463 seq. It is by no means inconsistent herewith that, according to the Minokhired, the tree grows in the sea Var-Kash "am verborgensten Orte" since this statement has reference to the subterranean rooting of the tree in the lowest part of the Underworld. Kuhn, *Herabkunft*, p. 124.

Finally, although **Grill** mistakenly makes the *Chinvat Bridge* "correspond with the Milky Way and the rainbow" he nevertheless correctly discerns some relationship between *Chinvat* and the Persian Tree of Life. [21] By this identification we are again brought to the one unmistakable location toward which all lines of evidence perpetually converge. The Aryans of India, as early as in the far-off Vedic age, had also their *World-Tree*, which yielded the gods their soma, the drink which maintains immortality. As we should anticipate, its roots are in the Underworld of Yama at the hidden pole, its top in the north polar heaven of the gods, and its body is the sustaining axis of the universe. [22] **Weber** long ago expressly identified it with the World-Ash of the Edda; [23] and **Kuhn**, [24] **Senart** [25] and all the more recent writers accept without question the identification. Some of the late traces of it in Hindu art betray the ancient conception of the Pole as a means of ascent to heaven, a bridge of souls and of the gods, a stair substituted for the slippery pillar up which the Taoist emperor vainly sought to climb. [26]

21. Grill, Ibid. p. 191. Compare with the original Zend invocation in the Homa Yasht *"Amereza gayehe stuna"*, "O imperishable pillar of life", Haug, *Essays*, p. 177 n.

22. *Rig Veda*, x. 135, i; Atharvan Veda, vi. 95, I. See Kuhn, *Herabkunft des Feuers und des Gottertranks*. Berlin, 1859: p. 126 sec. J. Grill, *Erzväter*, i., p. 169-175. Obry, *Le Berceau de l'Espéce Huniaine*, pp. 146-160. Windischmann, *Zoroastrische Studien*, p. 176, 177. It is true that the roots of this divine *Aśvattha* are sometimes represented as in the heaven of the gods, and its growth downwards; but this is only to symbolize the emanation of nature and the life of nature from the divine source, as is clearly expressed in the opening verses of the fifteenth reading of the *Bhagavad Gita*. See the translation by John Davies London, 1882, p. 150; and for a parallel, M. Wolff, *Mubammedanische Eschatologie*, Leipsic, 1872, p. 197.

23. *Indische Studien*, Bd. i., p. 397.

24. *Herabkunft*, etc, p. 128.

25. *La Légende du Bouddha*, p. 240.

26. "In the Naga sculptures (Fergusson, *Tree and Serpent Worship*, pl. 27), the Tree of the Mount or Pole is identified at the bottom by one tree, and at the top by another, and between the two there is a kind of ladder, with a series of steps or stairs which ascend the tree, in the place of a stem. These denote the Tree of the Ascent, Mount, or Height, now to be considered as representing the Pole." G. Massey, *The Natural Genesis*, vol. i., p. 354.

Among the Greeks [27] it is more than probable that the "holy palm" in Delos, on which Leto laid hold at the birth of Apollo, represents the same mythical *World-Tree*. If so, and if we follow Hecataeus in locating the scene, we shall be brought to the Arctic Pole. [28] The eternally flourishing olive of Athene *(Euripides, Ion 1433)* seems also but another form of the holy palm, and this in some of its descriptions brings us again to the land of the Hyperboreans. [29] In the Garden of the Hesperides, the tree which bore the golden apples was unquestionably the *Tree of Paradise*; but following **Aeschylus** *(Αἰσχύλος Aiskhýlos; c. 525/524 – c. 456/455 BC),*

Pherecydes (Φερεκύδης, fl. c. 465 BC), and ***Apollodorus** (Ἀπολλόδωρος ὁ Ἀθηναῖος, c. 180 BC – after 120 BC),* we must place it in the farthest North, beyond the Rhipaean mountains. [30] Traces of the same mythical conception among the Romans are presented by ***Kuhn***. [31] The sacred tree of the Buddhists figures largely in their sculpture. An elaborate specimen representation may be seen on the well-known *Sanchi Tope.* One inconspicuous feature in the representation has often puzzled observers. Almost invariably, at the very top of the tree, we find a little umbrella. So universal is this that its absence occasions remark. [32] This little piece of symbolism has a curious value. In Buddhist mythological art, the umbrella symbolizes the north polar heaven of the gods, [33] and by attaching it to the tip of the sacred tree the ancient sculptors of this faith unmistakably showed the cosmical character and axial position of that to which it was attached.

But this cosmic tree was the mythical *Bodhi tree,* the Tree of Wisdom -

> ***"Beneath whose leaves***
> ***It was ordained that Truth should come to Buddh."*** [34]

27. Kuhn, *Herabkunft*, etc., pp. 133-137.

28. Menzel, *Unsterblichkeitslehre*, i. 89. Its "central" position with respect to the world of men is recognized by old Robert Burton in his *Anatomy of Melancholy*, New York, 1849, p. 292. Compare Massey: "The Tree of the Pole is extant in Celebes, where the natives believe that the world is supported by the Hog, and that earth quakes are caused when the Hog rubs itself against the Tree… At Ephesus they showed the Olive and Cypress Grove of Leto, and in it the Tree of Life to which the Great Mother clung in bringing forth her twin progeny. There also was the Mount on which Hermes announced the birth of her twins Diana and Apollo [sun and moon]. The imagery is at root the same as the Hog rubbing against the Tree of the Pole." *The Natural Genesis*, vol. i., p. 354. And again, the cosmical imagery of Hesiod: "Das leitende Bild eines Baumes, dessen Stamm sich von den Wurzeln erhebt und oben ausbreitet, tritt in den Worten der Theogonie v. 727: vom Tartarus aufwärts seien die Wurzeln der Erde und des Meeres, deutlich hervor." W. F. Rinck, *Die Religion der Hellenen.* Zurich, 1853: Bd. i., p. 60.

29. Nonnus, Dionysiac, xl. 443 seq. Lüken, Traditionen, p. 74.

30. Preller, *Gr. Mythologie,* i. 149. Völcker, *Mythische Geographie.* Leipsic, 1832: p. 134.

31. Herabkunft etc., pp. 179, 180.

32. James Fergusson, *Tree and Serpent Worship.* London, 2d ed., 1873: pp. 134, 135.

33. Lillie, Buddha and Early Buddhism. London, 1881: pp. 2, 19. A different study of the cosmical nature of this tree may be found in Senart, *La Légende du Bouddha.* Paris, 1875: pp 239-244.

34. Arnold, *Light of Asia,* Book vi.

Its location is in *"the Middle of the Earth."* [35] Notwithstanding his doctrine of an African origin of mankind, **Gerald Massey** says, ***"In the legendary life of Gautama, Buddha is described as having to pass over the celestial water to reach Nirvana, which is the land of the Bodhi Tree of Life and Knowledge. He was unable to cross from one bank to the other, but the spirit of the Bodhi tree stretched out its arms to him and helped him over in safety. With the aid of this tree, he attained the summit of wisdom and immortal life. It is the same Tree of the Pole and of Paradise in all mythology through. The Tree of the Guarani garden, the Hebrew Eden, and the Hindu Jambu-dwipa, are likewise the Tree of Nirvana. This final application of the imagery proves its origin. The realm of rest was first seen at the polar center of the revolving stars.***" [36]

The ancient Germans called their world tree the *Irmensul*, i. e., *"Heaven-pillar."* **Grimm** speaks of its close relationship with the Norse *Yggdrasil* and lends his high authority to the view that it was simply a mythical expression of the idea of the world s axis. [37] The same view was advanced still earlier by the distinguished Icelandic mythographer, *Finn Magnusen*. [38] How profoundly the myth affected medieval Christian art is illustrated in many places, among the rest in the sculptures on the south portal of the Baptistery at Parma. [39] It is also not without a deep significance that "in the medieval legend of Seth's visit to the Garden of Eden, to obtain for his dying father the Oil of Compassion, the *Tree of Life* which he saw lifted its top to heaven and sent its root to hell" [40] and that on the crucifixion of Christ, himself the:

"Arbor, quae ab initio posita est"

this cosmical Tree of the Garden died and became the *"Arbre Sec"* of a medieval story. [41]

35. "The Buddhists assert that this tree marks the middle of the earth." E. C. Brewer, *Dictionary of Miracles*. Philadelphia, 1884: p.314.

36. *The Natural Genesis,* vol. ii., 90. On the independence of the Buddhist cosmogony and cosmology Beal remarks, "But whilst we may regard Buddhism in the light of a reformation of the popular belief in India, we must bear in mind that the stream of tradition which reappears in its teaching, and may be traced in its books, is independent and probably distinct from the Brahmanical traditions embodied in the Puranas and elsewhere. At any rate, this is the case so far as the primitive question of creation and of the cosmic system generally is concerned. Mr. Rhys Davids has already remarked that the Buddhist archangel or god Brahma is different from anything known to the Brahmans, and is part of an altogether different system of thought (*Buddhist Suttas*, p. 168 n.). I am inclined to go further than this, and say that the traditions of the Buddhists are different from those of the Brahmans in almost every respect." Samuel Beal, *Buddhist Literature in China*. London, 1882: p. 146.

37. "Mir scheint auch die im deutschen Alterthum tief gegründete Vorstellung von der Irmensäule, jener altissima, universalis columna quasi sustinens omnia, dem Weltbaum Yggdrasil nah verwandt." J. Grimm, *Deutsche Mythologie*, p. 759. Compare pp. 104-107.

38. *Den aellre Edda.* Kjöbenhavn, 1822: Bd. ii., 61. Compare the following: "Yggdrasil has never been satisfactorily explained. But at all events the sacred tree of the North is, no doubt, identical with the *robur Jovis* or sacred oak of Geismar, destroyed by Boniface, and the Irminsul of the Saxons, the *columna universalis*, the terrestrial tree of offerings, an emblem of the whole world as far as it is under divine influence." Thorpe, *Northern Mythology*, vol. i., p. 155.

39. See F. Piper, *Evangelischer Kalender* für 1866, pp. 35-80 (illustrated). Also, Piper's "Baum des Lebens" in the same *Kalender* for 1863, pp. 17-94.

40. Gubernatis, *Zoölogical Mythology*. London, 1872: vol. ii., p. 411, note.
41. *The Book of Marco Polo.* Edition of Col. H. Yule. London, 1871: pp. 120-131. Notice particularly the picture on p. 127, which corrects Polo's blunder in confounding the Arbre Sol with the Arbre Sec, the bird at the top of the central and highest of the trees depicted conclusively identifies it with the World- tree of universal Aryan tradition. On this bird see Kuhn.

The *Paradise-Tree* of the Chinese Taoists is also a *World-Tree*. It is found in the center of the enchanting *Garden of the Gods* on the summit of the polar *Kwen-lun*. Its name is *Tong*, and its location is further denned by the expression that it grows *"hard by the closed Gate of Heaven."* [42] As in many of the ancient religions, the mount on which, after the Flood, the ark rested was considered the same as that from which in the beginning the first man came forth, it is not strange to find the tree on the top of the mountain of Paradise remembered in some of the legends of the Deluge. In the Taoist legend, it seems to take the place of the ark. Thus, we are told that *"one extraordinary antediluvian saved his life by climbing up a mountain, and there and then, in the manner of birds plaiting a nest, he passed his days on a tree, whilst all the country below him was one sheet of water. He afterward lived to very old age, and could testify to his late posterity that a whole race of human beings had been swept from the face of the earth."* [43] It is at least suggestive to find this same idea of salvation from a universal deluge by means of a miraculous tree growing on the top of the divine *Mountain of the North* among the Navajo Indians of our own country. Speaking of the men of the world before our own, and of the warning they had received of the approaching flood, their legends go on: *"Then they took soil from all the four corner mountains of the world, and placed it on top of the mountain that stood in the North; and thither they all went, including the people of the mountains, the salt-woman, and such animals as then lived in the third world. When the soil was laid on the mountain, the latter began to grow higher and higher, but the waters continued to rise, and the people climbed upwards to escape the flood. At length, the mountain ceased to grow, and they planted on the summit a great reed, into the hollow of which they all entered. The reed grew every night, but did not grow in the daytime; and this is the reason why the reed grows in joints to this day: the hollow internodes show where it grew by night, and the solid nodes show where it rested by day. Thus, the waters gained on them in the daytime. The turkey was the last to take refuge in the reed, and he was therefore at the bottom. When the waters rose high enough to wet the turkey, they all knew that danger was near. Often did the waves wash the end of his tail, and it is for this reason that the tips of the turkey's tail feathers are to this day lighter than the rest of his plumage. At the end of the fourth night from the time, it was planted the reed had grown up to the floor of the fourth world, and here they found a hole through which they passed to the surface."* [44]

42. Lüken *Traditionen*, p. 72.

43. The Chinese Repository, vol. viii., p. 517.

44. 1 W. Matthews, *"The Navajo Mythology"*. *The Am. Antiquarian*, July, 1883, p. 208. The difficulty of any interpretation of this cosmology other than the true is illustrated by the efforts of M. Reville. *Les Religions des Peuples Non-civilisés*. Paris, 1883: vol. i., pp. 271-274.

The opening sentence of the above citation gives us a topography exactly corresponding to Mount Meru, the Hindu *"Mountain of the North"* with its *"four corner mountains of the world"* in the four opposite points of the horizon. Moreover, in the Deluge myths of the Hindus, as in this of the Navajos, it was over this central mountain that the survivors of that world destruction found deliverance. However, as explained, the coincidences are remarkable. In Celtic tradition, the *Tree of Paradise* is represented by the tree which bore golden apples in Avalon. But Avalon is always represented as an island in the far North, and its "loadstone castle" self-evidently connects it with the region of the magnetic Pole. [45] In the ancient epic of the Finns, the **Kalevala**, we see the World-tree of other people. If any doubt could rise as to its position in the universe, the constellation of the Great Bear at its top would suffice to remove it. [46]

45. Menzel, *Unsterblichkeitslehre*, i. 87, 95; ii. 10. Keary, *Outlines of Primitive Belief*, p. 453. Especially see Humboldt s references to *"Monte Calamitico"* the mediaeval magnetic mountain in the sea to the north of Greenland. *Cosmos* (Bohn s ed.), ii. 659; v. 55. Also, *Le Cycle mythologique irlandais et la Mythologie celtique*. Par H. d'Arbois de Jubainville. Paris, 1884. Dr. Carl Schroeder, *Sanct Brandan*. Erlangen, 1871: pp. 57, in, 167, etc.

46. Erlangen, 1871: pp. 57, in, 167, etc. 2 The German translation by Anton Schiefner. Helsinfors, 1852: Rune x., 31-42. Compare Schiefner, *Heldensagen der minussinischen Tataren*, p. 62 seq. Traces of the same myth are found among the Samoans *(Samoa a Hundred Years Ago and Long Before*. By George Turner, LL. D. London, 1884: pp. 199, 201). Also, among the Ugrian tribes (Peschel, *Races of Man*, p. 406); and among many of the tribes of the American aborigines, and in Polynesia. See M. Husson, La Chaine Traditionnelle, *Contes et Légendes au point de vue mythique*. Paris, 1874: especially pp. 140-160. Massey, *The Natural Genesis*. "It was at the top of the Tree of Heaven the Pole that the Guaranis were to meet once more with their Adam, Atum, Turn, or Tamoi, who was to help them from thence in their ascent to the higher life. Here the Tree of Life becomes a tree of the dead to raise them into heaven. So, in the Algonkin myth, the tree of the dead was a sort of oscillating log for the deceased to cross the river by, as a bridge of the abyss, beyond which the Dog, as in the Persian mythos, stands waiting for the souls of the dead, just as the Dog stands at the Northern Pole of the Egyptian, and is depicted in the tree of the Southern Solstice, the Tree of the Pole which was extended to the four quarters." Vol. i., p. 404

Thus, the sacred trees, like the sacred waters, of every ancient people invariably conduct the investigator to lands outside the historic habitats of the peoples in question, and ever to one and the same primeval home-country, the land of light and glory at the Arctic Pole. [47]

47. Since completing the foregoing chapter I have seen the work entitled *Plant Lore, Legends, and Lyrics; embracing the Myths, Traditions, Superstitions, and Folk-lore of the Plant Kingdom.* By Richard Folkard, Jun. London, 1884. In the first three chapters the reader will find valuable supplementary reading on "The World-Trees of the Ancients" , "The Trees of Paradise" ,"The Tree of Adam" , "Sacred Trees of all Nations" etc. Other chapters treat of "Plant Symbolism", "Plant Language" and of the fabulous trees and miracle plants which play so important a part in the history of religious and scientific credulity. Should any reader thereof be inclined to claim that "the progress of science" has forever done away with such ignorant mediaeval mystagogy, he will do well to turn to *The Weekly Inter Ocean*, Chicago, Dec. n, 1884, in which, in an illustrated article entitled "The Tree of Life" we are informed that "science has now discovered in a most unexpected manner both the Tree and the River of Life." The former is the brain and spinal cord of man. "We do not mean that the brain merely looks like a tree or resembles one externally. We are not dealing with analogies. But we do mean that the brain and spinal cord are an actual tree. By the most rigid scientific examination it is shown to fill the ideal type and plan of a tree more completely than any tree of the vegetable kingdom. The spinal cord is the trunk of this great tree. Its roots are the nerves of feeling and motion branching out over the body. . . . The Tree of Life is planted in the midst of many others, for the heart is a tree, the lungs are a tree, and the pancreas, stomach, liver, and all those vital organs. The brain is its radiant and graceful foliage. The mental faculties are classified in twelve groups by the most recent scientific analysis. This Tree bears twelve kinds of fruit. . . . On each side of the Tree of Life is the great River of Life. Let us lay a man down with his head to the north, and his arms stretched to the west and to the east. The River of Life has its four heads in the four chambers of the heart, the two auricles and the two ventricles. The branches of this river pass upward to the head, the land of gold, eastward to the left and westward to the right arm and lung. But greatest of all the branches, The River, or Phrath, are the aorta and vena cava, reaching southward to the trunk and lower limbs. In branching over the body this river divides into four parts at seven teen different points. Two branches of the river form a network around the very trunk of the tree, and spread upward among its expanding branches. The blood is the Water of Life, and it looks as clear as crystal when seen through the microscope, the eye of science. It is three fourths water, and through this are diffused the red cells and the living materials which are to construct and to maintain the bodily organs." Had this article and its antique-looking illustration been found in one of the Church fathers, it would have afforded to a certain class of "scientists" great edification.

The "Tree of Life" is also used as an archetypal and hermetic template in Jewish mysticism known as Kabbalah, which dates back to ancient Mesopotamia (around the 18th century BC). In this concept is hidden a huge amount of wisdom and secrets related to the nature of the Universe and its connection with man, i.e. the secret relationship between the Microcosm and the Macrocosm. Kabbalah (Hebrew: קַבָּלָה = "giving, receiving") is a discipline and school dealing with the mystical aspects of Judaism, and it is a body of esoteric teachings intended to determine the spiritual meaning of the *Tanakh* (Hebrew Bible) and traditional rabbinical literature. According to Kabbalah, the *"Tree of Life"* represents the way to God. [48] The tree consists of three pillars: left-feminine, right-masculine, and a middle pillar that unites the two energies. It corresponds to the parts of the human body, with the highest sephirah corresponding to the head, the lowest to the feet, the middle to the plexus, etc. The *"Tree of Life"* is the basis of all Kabbalistic magical rituals. According to Kabbalah, the Bible hides all the secrets of the universe, but the right key is needed to make it completely understandable and clear.

48. Falcon, T. & Blatner, D. (2001), *Judaism for Dummies*, New York, NY: Wiley, John & Sons, Inc. p. 78.

Hilda Ellis Davidson comments that the existence of nine worlds around the *"World Tree"* Yggdrasil is mentioned more than once in Old Norse sources, but the identity of the worlds is never fully stated, although it can be inferred from various sources. Davidson comments that *"no doubt the identity of the nine worlds varied from time to time as emphasis changed or new images arrived." Davidson* says that it is not clear where the nine worlds are in relation to the tree; they could either exist above each other or perhaps be grouped around the tree, but there are references to worlds existing below the tree, while the gods are depicted in the sky, the rainbow bridge *Bifröst* connecting the tree to the other worlds. ***Davidson*** believes that ***"those who have tried to make a convincing diagram of the Scandinavian cosmos from what we are told in the sources have only added to the confusion"***. [49] ***Davidson*** notes parallels between Yggdrasil and shamanic lore in northern Eurasia: The concept of a tree rising through many worlds is found in northern Eurasia and is part of shamanic lore shared by many peoples of this region. This appears to be a very ancient conception, probably based on the North Star, the center of the heavens, and the image of the central tree in Scandinavia may have been influenced by it... Among the Siberian shamans, the central tree may be used as a ladder to ascend to the heavens. She then says that the notion of the eagle on the tree and the world serpent coiled around the roots of the tree have parallels in other Asian cosmologies. She goes on to say that Norse cosmology may have been influenced by these Asian cosmologies from a northern location. She adds, on the other hand, that it is confirmed that the Germanic peoples worshiped their deities in open forest clearings and that the sky god was especially associated with the oak, and therefore ***"the central tree was a natural symbol for them as well"***.

49. Davidson, Hilda Ellis (1993). *The Lost Beliefs of Northern Europe*, p. 69

Sidrat al-Muntaha (Arabic: سِدْرَة ٱلْمُنْتَهَىٰ, literally "The Tree of the Farthest Boundary") is a large Sidr tree [50] that marks the greatest boundary of the seventh heaven that no one can cross. It is called *Sidrat al-Muntaha* because the knowledge of the angels stops at that point and no one has gone beyond it except the Messenger of Allah. During Isra and Miraj, Muhammad traveled with the angel Gabriel to the tree (where the angel stopped), after which Allah taught Muhammad the five daily prayers. The Sidr tree, (also known as the Lote tree, the thorn of Christ, the *Jujube* tree or *Nabkh* whose botanical name reads - *Ziziphus spina-christi*, represents an ancient tree whose fruit was the first thing that the Prophet Adam ate when he was led to came down to the ground.
Sura 56, verses 27-34 reads:

وَأَصْحَابُ الْيَمِينِ مَا أَصْحَابُ الْيَمِينِ
فِي سِدْرٍ مَخْضُودٍ

وَطَلْحٍ مَنْضُودٍ
وَظِلٍّ مَمْدُودٍ
وَمَاءٍ مَسْكُوبٍ
وَفَاكِهَةٍ كَثِيرَةٍ
لَا مَقْطُوعَةٍ وَلَا مَمْنُوعَةٍ

27. And the people of the right - how blessed they will be!
*28. "They will be among the lot trees without thorns, (translated in the
Macedonian Koran: they will be among gardens with abundant fruit,
without thorns)*
29. and among the bananas, with fruits lined up
30. and among the frosts stretched out,
31. and near flowing water;
32. there will be various fruits:
33. shall neither cease nor be prohibited,
34. and on beds they will be raised!
— Quran 56:27–34 (Translated by Dr. Mustafa Khattab)

50. *Quran 53:14*

The commentary on the Qur'an entitled *Tafsīr al-karīm al-rahman fi tafsīr
kalām al-manān* by *Abd ar-Rahman ibn Nasir as-Sa'di*, while commenting
on **Qur'an** 53:14, for *Sidrat al-Muntaha* explains:

*"It is a very big tree (شَجَرَة - shajarah) which is outside the seventh
heaven. It is called Sidrat al-Muntaha because everything that ascends
from the earth and descends (from heaven) ends in it, including that
which descends from God, including waḥy (divine inspiration).
Alternatively, (it can be said that this name is because) it is the ultimate
end or the very end of the earth or the ultimate limit (إِنْتِهَاء - intihā'
which is one of the many Arabic words for the word "end") for the
knowledge of beings who they approach him, that is, his Existing Being
(as he is) above the heavens and the earth. Thus, it is al-Muntahā (End,
Limit) in terms of (all human) ways of knowing (عُلُوم - 'ulūm) or other
things besides. And God is best informed (about this matter). So
Muhammad saw Gabriel at that location (الْمَكَان - al-makān) which is in
the Domain of Pure and Beautiful, Exalted (Heavenly) Souls (مَحَلُّ الْأَرْوَاحُ
الْعُلْوِيَّةُ الْزَّوَكِيَّةُ الْزَّوَكِيَّةَ الْحَوْلُ الْأَرْوَاحُ الْعُلْوِيَّةُ الْوَكِيَّال -zakiyyah al-jamīliyyah)...*

383

The 19th-century English explorer **Richard Burton** claimed to have seen the ancient Sidr tree in the mosque that housed Muhammad's tomb in Medina. It was in the garden dedicated to his daughter Fatima. The fruit of the tree was sold to pilgrims and its leaves were used to wash dead bodies. [52]

51. Lambden, Stephen. (2009). *The Sidrah (Lote-Tree) and the Sidrat al-Muntaha* (Lote-Tree of the Extremity)

52. Burton, Richard Francis (1855). *"A Personal Narrative of a Pilgrimage to Al-Madinah and Meccah".* Project Gutenberg. p. 337

From all the so far presentation of the traditions of the most ancient mythological-cosmological and religious concepts, we gain insight that the tree itself represents a symbol for the atlas or the celestial pillar, which connects the earth and the sky, but at the same time represents a cosmogonic concept for the world itself and the universe as a whole. On the other hand, in a psychological sense, the *"Tree of Life"*, especially in the Kabbalah and similar Gnostic traditions, represents, among other things, the microcosmic aspect of the man himself, which are divided into three parts: legs (underground, roots), torso (middle world, pillar) and head (the heavenly world, the canopy) which are an analogy of the macrocosm. The human body can express the symbol of the world axis. Some of the more abstract *Tree of Life* representations, such as the sefirot in Kabbalism and the chakra system recognized by Hinduism and Buddhism, merge with the concept of the human body as a pillar between heaven and earth. Disciplines such as yoga and tai chi begin from the premise of the human body as *Axis Mundi*. The Buddha represents a world center in human form. [53] Large statues of meditating figures unite the human form with the symbolism of the temple and tower. Astrology in all its forms assumes a connection between human health and affairs and celestial-body orientation. World religions regard the body itself as a temple and prayer as a column uniting earth and heaven. The ancient Colossus of Rhodes combined the role of the human figure with those of a portal and skyscrapers. The Renaissance image known as the Vitruvian Man represented a symbolic and mathematical exploration of the human form as a world axis. [54]

53. Mircea Eliade (tr. Philip Mairet). *'Indian Symbolisms of Time and Eternity' in Images and Symbols.* Princeton, 1991. p.76

54. Chevalier, Jean and Gheerbrandt, Alain. *A Dictionary of Symbols.* Penguin Books: London, 1996. pp.1025–1033

However, the literal or physical existence of such an extremely huge tree that was planted in the paradise garden should not be ruled out at all, as it would have surrounded the whole on all levels: spiritual, psychological, and material. The ancient peoples, especially our Slavic ancestors, had a distinctly great cult of trees and for them, they were holy and sacred places. The oldest tree in the forest and the Middle Ages before Christianization and even after it was a sacred place, known as a holy tree or *"запис"* (*zapis*, record), where traditions were written down. The record tree was located in the center of the village and was the main cult place. His role is especially highlighted during the celebration of the village's glory - the vow when the villagers gathered at that place as if they were in church. That tree was a kind of natural temple. I would not rule out the possibility that the *"Tree in the Middle of Heaven"* may have been exalted as one of the giant Sequoias of California. The comparison is not made by chance. In the Miocene remains of Britain, conifers are especially numerous. And the most common of them is the giant pine *Sequoia Couttsiae*, which is closely related to the huge Sequoia gigantea in California. The almost allied form, *Sequoia Langsdorfii*, has also been discovered in the Hebrides (Scottish Archipelago). [53] From the width of the Sequoia forests of Mariposa County, California, to that of the Hebrides is a long step toward the pole; but we are not left to mere inference when we raise the question of whether the original starting point of this gigantic species of trees may have been still higher in the arctic regions. Miocene fossils at the highest available arctic latitudes tell their own story. Of the limited research that has been done on these fossils, ***Sir Charles Lyell*** noted:

"More than thirty species of conifers have been found, including several sequoias related to the giant Wellingtonia of California. . . . There are also beeches, oaks, poplars, walnuts, lindens, and even a magnolia, two cones that have recently been obtained, proving that this wonderful evergreen beauty not only lived but also ripened its fruit, within the Arctic Circle. Many lindens and oaks were large-leaved species, and flowers and fruits, in addition to huge amounts of leaves, have been preserved in many cases. . . . Even in Spitsbergen, at 12° from the pole, no less than ninety-five species of fossil plants have been obtained".

53. Nicholson, *Life-History,* p. 309

The vigor of Miocene-age plant life in these arctic regions struck the veteran geologist as something "truly extraordinary." We have a right, then, not only to draw a conclusion from the "abundance" and "extraordinarily ranked and luxuriant vegetation" of the Arctic regions in Miocene times, but also to learn a special lesson from the gigantic forms which linger on the American west coast. If the book of *Genesis* had described one of the trees of Eden as three hundred and twenty feet in height and thirty feet in diameter at the base, not only all the *Voltaire's* of modern history but until the discovery of California all the naturalists of the advanced anti-Christian variety, would not have put an end to the effort due to the unscientific or mythical *"Botany of Moses."* But *Sequoia gigantea* is a living, indisputable fact. Although not the oldest of conifers, it illustrates some of the earlier possibilities of plant life. It tells the botanist that growths once realized in great abundance are dying out, and unless perpetuated by human care will soon disappear from our globe forever. Its last surviving representatives in a state of nature, preserved to this day by certain fortunate local conditions and by their inherent longevity, are living witnesses betraying a distant world, witnesses whose testimony must be accepted by even the most incredulous of scientists. They tell of the distant dawn of man's day, they bear witness to the extraordinary life that characterized their distant native land. [54]

54. During the Tertiary period, sequoias "appeared all around the Arctic Zone"; (Asa Gray). Prof. J. D. Whitney finds evidence that one of the fallen trees in Placer County was over 2000 years old. See Yosemite's book; also Engler, *Entwickelungsgeschichte der Pflanzenwelt*. Leipsic, 1879-82: chap. i. and ii.

It is also worth noting that the Australian *Eucalyptus gigantea*, the only tree exceeding the Sequoia in height, is found in that very country, whose late living flora and fauna are more closely related to the northern species of the early world than any other. And if these last individuals of a dying race can maintain, under unfavorable biological conditions, a vigorous life through two millennia, which will declare it impossible for men of the time and place of the *Sequoia gigantea* to have averaged more than six feet in height, or reach an age exceeding our seventy years? As to the last point, it would take more than the combined lifetimes of two *Methuselahs* to observe the growth and death of a tree like those in California. The thought is not the incubation of the present writer; that's what the trees themselves told America's foremost botanist. [55]

55. We cannot look up at the huge and venerable trunks, which one crosses the continent to see, without wishing that these patriarchs of the grove had been able, like the long-lived fore-bearers of the Scriptures, to hand down to us the traditions through several generations upon centuries, and so say nothing of the history of their race. 1500 annual layers have been counted or satisfactorily made on one or two fallen trunks. It is probable that near the heart of some of the living trees may be found the circle recording the year of the Saviour's birth. A few generations of such trees could carry history far back. But the terrain on which they stand and the traces of recent geological changes and changes in the surrounding region testify that many such generations could not have flourished right here, at least in unbroken series. – Prof. Asa Gray, LL. D., *The Sequoia and its History. Proceedings of the American Association for the Advancement of Science*, 1872, p. 6. Methuselah is a 4,854-year-old. Great Basin bristlecone pine *(Pinus longaeva)* tree growing high in the White Mountains of Inyo County in eastern California. It is recognized as the non-clonal tree with the greatest confirmed age in the world. The tree's name refers to the biblical patriarch Methuselah, who ostensibly lived to 969 years of age, thus becoming synonymous with longevity or old age in many European languages including English.

The Devil's Tower, also known as the *Tree of Life* (Wooden Rock) by the Wyoming Indians, does not appear to be natural flesh, but a giant tree whose remains have long since been fossilized or petrified. A huge root network was discovered at its base. It's been around the web, Graham

Hancock, and other supposedly reliable researchers sharing this information. But no one confirms a reliable source, so the doubt remains. If it is not a big forgery, this is a real bomb that would make all history and prehistory textbooks obsolete. Devil's Tower is the first national monument of the United States, established on September 24, 1906, by President Theodore Roosevelt. A revolution that goes in the direction of the other history, as you know, the history that the Eden Saga tells for millennia.

Devils Tower (also known as Bear Lodge Butte) is a butte, possibly laccolithic, composed of igneous rock in the Bear Lodge Ranger District of the Black Hills, near Hulett and Sundance in Crook County, northeastern Wyoming, above the Belle Fourche River.

• The Miraculous Tree of the South Slavs

...едно дрво виданлија,
виданлија мајко нишанлија,
на врвот му сонце греит,
на средето му паун пеит,
во корен му змеот лежит.

...one tree vidanlija (all-seeing tree, Vedan's tree, Odin's tree),
vidanlija, o mother nisanlija (watchtower tree),
on the top sun is shining
in the midst of it a peacock sing,
in his root the dragon lies.

Tselakoski Naum, Debarca: rites, spells, and ritual songs

The *Axis of the World (Axis Mundi)* which connects the upper and lower parts is represented by objects reaching toward the sky. While the staircase, the throne, the pillar, the mountain, or the smoke represent the inanimate world, the tree with its eternal or renewing foliage as the axis of the world represents life itself. In static representations of the axis of the world as a tree, its top represents the space of the sky, and the root of the tree - is the lower world. The vertical connects two worlds in one object, unites them as parts that are in a harmonious or conflicting relationship, and enables mediation between the worlds. In mythical images and texts, the *"Axis of the World"* is dynamically represented as climbing or descending a tree or a mountain. The motifs of ascension, flight, and fall also show overcoming the vertical boundaries between the worlds, but often without materializing the axis as an object in space. Static and dynamic representation are combined, e.g. in fairy tales, in the motif where the eagle from the tree in the lower world takes the man who saved his birds in the upper world, as well as in the motif of climbing the "Tree of Ascension" or falling from a tree. Numerous books and studies by Slavic folklorists and ethnologists from the caliber of ***Afanasyev, Iliev, Sofrić,*** and ***Veselin Čajkanović*** to ***Gjordjević, Tolstoy*** and ***Agapkina*** have studied the beliefs and rituals associated with certain plants and different types of trees. In fairy tales, there are different types of trees of ascent to the higher worlds, trees of fertility, transformations, trees of knowledge and wisdom, etc. (*Parpulova 1980; Bošković-Stuli 1966*). The Holy Tree in Russian fables represents the *"Center of the World" (Shindin 1993: 116-11)*. In ritual songs of pagan origin, as well as in Christian-religious songs, a tree grew up to the sky, whose golden or silver branches covered the whole world, with miraculous fruits - pearls, ducats, gold coins, or *karagroshes*. In the poetry of the Balkan Slavs, *"The Tree of the World"* and *"The Tree of Fertility"* do not appear in epics and ballads, but in ritual and lyrical songs. Thus, different genres show a specific attachment to certain types of trees. The Slavs considered the oak as a miraculous tree, and the fir, the willow, the maple, the apple, the cypress, or the ash are less common. Not including all cases of the cosmic tree in Bulgarian mythology, **Ivanichka Petrova Georgieva** [1], writes: ***"Most often its species are oak, cypress, maple, primarily in oral art or fruit trees in ritual practice."*** *(1993: 40)*

This distinction in the poems is not consistent, but rather suggests a distinction between the mythic and magical layers of folk culture. The willow and the cypress, Mediterranean trees that are not typical of the continental regions, appear in the folklore of the Balkan Slavs (the cypress even among the Russians). Besides the common characteristic - the height to the sky - the very shape of the trees indicates some different characteristics of the *"Miracle Tree"*. In folk literature, from the nineteenth century, the *"Tree of the World"* in Slavic beliefs is considered oak. But other trees in folklore also have this function. Since the issue of reconstructing the plant code in folk culture is too complex, the interpretation of the original texts requires great care and caution. Sometimes the authors, supporting their thesis about the oak as a universal tree, cite examples in which elm, willow, beech, some huge tree also appears, which leads them to declare these trees as allomorphic forms. A number of interwoven oppositions require their individual and cross-examination. The poems show that the supposition of the Slavist **Nikita Ilyich Tolstoy** (1829-1910) [2], that "evergreen trees, firs and pines are *"Trees of Death"*, or 'trees of the other world' associated with the winter phase, while deciduous trees are the trees with the meaning of life and are related to the summer phase *(Raskovnik, 75-76: 65)* is well established. It is reasonable to add the contrast of form to this opposition - the evergreen tree is elongated and has no fruit, while the other has a canopy and real or symbolic fruits that it bears in the summer phase or Devayana half year. The observation of **Kiril Iliev Penushliski** (1912 - 2004) [3] that bigger and stronger trees are, grammatically speaking, male (oak, beech, pine), also leads to consideration of the genus of miraculous trees in the poems. Surprisingly, it turns out that it is not only the fertile female trees, but also what represents the *"Axis of the World"*. The importance of the grammatical gender of trees in the analysis of folk performances grows with the emphasis on these aspects in rituals and songs. Taking into account the appearance, emphasized properties, type of beings and actions associated with the archetypes of the tree, examples of the *"Cosmic Tree"* and *"Tree of Fertility"* will be discussed below. Among the Balkan Slavs, the cypress or Christmas tree, the elongated evergreen trees in the shape of a spindle, represent the *"Axis of the World"*. Even in proto-Slavic religion, the representation of the tree was also associated with other beings as archetypes. The symbolism of the tall, cosmic tree is connected and intertwined with animal symbolism. The researchers point out that certain creatures are found in certain parts of the tree, similar to what **Grimm** reports [4]: ***"Animals make noise on the tree and around the tree; the eagle sits on the top, the squirrel runs through the branches, then the four deer, and next to them snakes, rejoicing, descend to the root"***.

1. Ivanichka Petrova Georgieva (Иваничка Петрова Георгиева August 27, 1937, Kingdom of Bulgaria) is a prominent Bulgarian ethnologist, historian and long-time lecturer at the University of Sofia, professor at the Faculty of History.

2. Nikita Ilyich Tolstoy (Никита Ильич Толстой April 15, 1923, Vrsac, Kingdom of Serbs, Croats and Slovenes - June 27, 1996, Moscow, Russia) was a Soviet and Russian linguist and Slavist, folklorist, doctor of philological sciences, professor, academician of the Academy of Sciences of the USSR (from 1987 - 1984). He is the author of hundreds of works on the history of Slavic literary languages, Slavic dialectology, Old Slavic and Church Slavic languages, ethnolinguistics and lexicology. Great-grandson of Leo Tolstoy.

3. Kiril Iliev Penushliski (Кирил Илиев Пенушлиски November 15, 1912 - May 23, 2004) — prominent Macedonian folklorist, founder of this science in Macedonia. He was born in Thessaloniki on November 15, 1912. He completed primary education in his hometown, then high school in Skopje in 1931. In 1938, he graduated from the Faculty of Philosophy, Yugoslavian Literature group, and received his doctorate on the topic: "Stefan Verković - a collector of Macedonian folk works" (1956).

4. Grimm, Deutsche Myth., p. 664.

Even in the book of *A. N. Afanasiev "Poetic views of the Slavs about nature"*, the idea that the top and root of the oak are the abodes of the gods was presented. *Ivanov* and *Toporov* [5] establish the thesis about the oak as a tree in whose foot and roots lives Veles - the god of the underworld (the snake), and at the top - Perun (the eagle). In the transformations of folk beliefs and songs, some elements are lost, sometimes retaining only traces of antiquity. The arrangement of the animals next to the trees has a symbolic meaning. At the top of the tree in the lyrical and ritual songs there are birds, like heavenly beings: falcon, nightingale, peacock, sometimes the eagle also appears. These birds are also metaphorical names for the groom. The wedding elements of the symbolism of the tree and the creatures on it are sometimes very developed. The connection of two series of animals, one that pursues, fits into a parallel series in which the bridegroom and the bride (the male and female principles) are metaphorically represented.
The wedding symbolism of the song is close to the songs about the hero who planted a Christmas tree, opened the spring and left the girl, only to find her in full strength. *Katicić* supposes that the hero of the poem could be the divine person, St. George *(Katićić 1990: 80)* [6], but this thesis should be further supported by the connections between the wedding and St.George day texts. According to reconstructions of old Slavic beliefs, there was a dragon at the foot of the tree *(Ivanov and Toporov 1974: 5.36)*. *Milena Benovska* devotes her attention to the beliefs and legends about the dragon at the foot of the oak (1992: 131-143, 160). However, the dragon (and the snake) also appear under the fir or cypress in the songs of the southern Slavs and in the ballads of the eastern Slavs. In a Dalmatian poem, there is an angry dragon in the fir of Island of Šipan (Dalmatia), which tells the peregrine falcon in the branches not to build a nest above it

because it will release flames *(MH V, 14).* The substitution of divine and demonic beings occurs in various genres - riddles *(Toporov 1971),* fairy tales, ritual songs, etc.

5. Vladimir Nikolaevich Toporov (July 5, 1928, Moscow - December 5, 2005) - Soviet and Russian linguist and philologist. Doctor of Philology, full member of the Academy of Sciences of the USSR (1990). He was engaged in research in the field of Slavic studies, Indology, Baltic and Indo-European studies. One of the founders of the Moscow-Tartu semiotic school. Creator of the "master myth theory".

6. Radoslav Katičic (July 3, 1930 - August 10, 2019) was a Croatian linguist, classical philologist, Indo-Europeanist, Slavist and Indologist, one of the most prominent Croatian scientists in the humanities.

In the songs, the representation of the *"World Tree"* also occurs with human actors in new poetic plots. In several poems about the abduction of the girl Jana, the dragon lives at the root of the tree and the bird is at the top of the tall tree. In one poem from **Iliev's** collection of *"The Tall Tree",* the falcon watches the siege of the city of Buda [7], by Budim Yanka *(Iliev, 325).* A calendar poem from the same collection shows a slender tree with a falcon on top, and beneath the tree Turks (serpents) are strong janissaries. The poem ends with calendar blessings *(Iliev, 96),* although the variant is motifically reduced, the Turks as pseudo-historical beings replace the chthonic being of the older layers – the dragon, which is analogous to the inhabitants of the lunar or southern hemisphere which we can say is under Arabo-Islamic auspices.

7. In the era of the Ottoman invasion and conquest of the Balkans, it led to large migrations to the north in today's Hungary and Romania. Buda or Buda (Hungarian: Buda; German: Ofen) is the western part of the Hungarian capital Budapest, located on the west bank of the Danube. The name Budapest was created by combining the names Buda and Pest, which were united (along with Obud) in 1873. Count Istvan Szechenyi, a Hungarian politician, writer and historian, mentions this name in his book The World, published in 1831. The origin of the name Pest indicates a Slavic origin and is thought to be the root of the word peć (Bulgarian: пещт) and is related to the word cave.

In the Macedonian song, Budin Jana hides from the king who chases her to the Bogdanova smoky mountain, to the cypress tree at the root of which lies a dragon, and a nightingale sings at the top. When the whole mountain disappears, only that tree remains *(Miladinovci Bros., 167)*. The bird because of its aerial nature, especially the eagle that can fly high and live on the mountains, which is a graceful and proud archetype, a symbol of height and the sky corresponds to Perun himself, while the snake in winter hides in the depths of the earth, underground and because its venomous nature it always corresponds with the dead ancestors but also with fertility and its patron is the god Veles. Although the mentioned poems deviate from the mythical source, they indicate the miraculous properties of the girl, the forest and the trees and the reduced status of the pursuers (two emperors or Turks). In these poems, there is a bird at the top of the tree and a dragon at the root. The uniqueness of the tree is emphasized - it is the tallest, it is different - the only green among dry trees, the only one with a golden top or the only one that is not cut. In addition to these characteristics, it also stands out by opposing the words: many trees - one tree *(Shapkarev, 147)*. In the poems about the abduction of Jana, written in Macedonia, there are also variants in which instead of the cypress, the tall or thin tree, there is also the grown laurel. In the motif of the failed kidnapping, the tree has the power to protect, and the motif of hiding in the tree is also found in fairy tales. The three-part structure of the tree (top part - middle part - root) with the introduction of the third animal is not typical in the songs of the Balkan Slavs, but it is found among the Eastern Slavs. In Russian and Belarusian poems, there may be bees in the middle or at the top of the cosmic tree *(Potebnya 1887: 211-214, 220-221)*. Bees are definitely the representatives of light and the Sun which in turn corresponds to the middle sephirot *(Tipharet)* of the Kabbalistic pattern. In Russian songs of the groom, there is a nightingale at the top of the tree, a bee in the middle, and an ermine or snake at the *root (Ivanov and Toporov 1974: 23)*. **Vinogradova** cites a Russian wedding song in which bees, caterpillars and a beautiful girl are on a cypress tree *(Vinogradova 1982: 104)*. In Belarusian wedding songs - the maple with bees is a happy tree *(Ivanov and Toporov 1974: 251-252)*. In the songs of the Balkan Slavs, bees are found only in the allegorically Christianized representations of the paradise tree. In the harvest song from Debarca, *"Vidanlija's Tree"* the Sun is at the top, a peacock sings in the middle, and the dragon lies at the root. The song, which already has many traditions, ends with the resolution of the symbolic meanings - the Sun is the beloved one, the peacock is the brother, the dragon is a dear father *(Tselakoski Naum. 1989. "Prophylactic spells among the Balkan peoples in Macedonian folklore":20)* In addition to the two-part and three-part structure of the tall tree, there are also songs about the fir tree in which the number of beings in the tree is stated. In the calendar poem, with the boy's wishes to get married, a hunter is shown hitting the roots of the white fir tree and from there comes a girl - a dragon who teaches him how to bring her home and receive praise from his mother *(Iliev, 4)*. The importance of the fir tree as a wedding tree is as big as the place that in the wedding songs the bride is attached to the table in the Lazarus song for friends from the Leskovac region.

Две су јеле расле,
Једна другој говорила:
Расти јело да растемо,
Обе дари да прајимо.
Једна другој одговара
Расти јело, ја не могу,
У корен ми змија лежи.
Крши, врши гнезда праји.

Translation:

Two firs grew,
The one said to other:
Grow fir, let's grow
Let's make both gifts.
One tells to the other
Grow fir tree, I can't,
A snake lies at my root.
Breaks, making nests.

S. Dimitrijević, Folk songs of the Leskovac region, Volume 1, Leskovac, 1987, p. 13

The evergreen tree has the symbolism of eternal life, renewal, the fir tree is a Christmas tree for Catholics. Her function was later accepted by the Orthodox. In some epic and ballad songs and demonological legends, the Christmas tree is a fairy tree. The layered meaning of the fir throughout the history of folk culture is revealed by the belief that the soul of the dead goes to the other world through the trees. This belief in folk songs is evidenced by the motives for planting a fir tree on the grave. We know quite clearly why now the tree plays the role of an intermediary between the worlds in folklore. The second type of *Wonder Tree* is the canopy tree that covers the world and has the properties of a tree of fertility. It can be assumed that fertility was originally represented by vegetable fruits, and that valuables, silver, gold, money and pearls were later introduced into the representation of the fruit tree. Even the oldest records of songs about the miraculous tree date back to the time when the symbolism of precious metals already existed, so the texts themselves are not a reliable indicator of the antiquity of folk performances, since they unite several layers. Some illumination of some folklore motifs of the tree can be provided by magical-ritual procedures of cutting, decorating, planting, burning the tree, believing in the tree or working with the tree (sacrifice, visiting, sleeping). It is reasonable to assume that the ritual-magical decoration of the tree and sleeping under the tree could have been transformed to preserve the ritual traces in folk songs about the tree with *grosch* coins, gold coins, ducats as a tree of fertility. It is difficult to identify the functions of the decoration and the executors of the action, but in the performance of the carved, ritual-magical and mythical-poetic meanings are found for the *Miraculous Tree*. Because oral and ritual folklore are constantly permeated and transformed, the reconstruction of their original relationship is complex. The ornamental tree, as the tree of life, serves to magically encourage well-being. The pagan meaning of the decorated tree of life in the wedding ceremony symbolically represents and ensures fertility and wealth to the new family. By giving a wedding cake, with the godfather tree, good wishes for childbirth and happiness are ritually expressed to the newlyweds. The fruit of the apple is given the meaning of blessing, vows of fidelity and magical invocation of fertility. The apple appears in love songs with wedding symbols and in a series of wedding songs. In the Balkans, the apple is placed on the wedding flag, thrown, given *(Celakoski: 220, 224-7, 233; Agapkina 1994: 88-89)*. And in fairy tales, the connection between marriage and the motive for keeping or stealing the golden apple is very pronounced. ***Agapkina*** points to the rituals associated with fruit and within the annual cycle with the main function of encouraging the fertility of both plants and people.

In some poems, the apple appears as a mythical tree of life. The fruits of the quince, the apple, the orange, in addition to their vegetative symbolism of fertility, especially in the wedding meaning, with their bright color also indicate the sun, its life-giving warmth and radiance. **Benovska** presents the oak as a cosmic tree, and the apple as the *"Tree of Life" (1992: 132-141)*. In Greek mythology, Hera the wife of Zeus was the owner of the golden apple tree, located in the Garden of the Hesperides (daughters of Atlas). The garden was guarded by Ladon, a dragon with a hundred heads, so that no one had access to Hera's apples, which were considered sources of immortality. None but Hercules who managed to pick up a few apples, thus completing the eleventh task. The apple was also considered, in many cultures, a symbol of the life-giving sun. The solar god Apollo considered the apple a sacred plant. Perhaps the god's name Ἀπόλλων, seems to have the same linguistic root as apple.

Also, from the apple comes the name of the mythical island of Avalon *(The Isle of Apples),* where King Arthur retreated after being wounded in battle. Avalon (Latin: *Insula Avallonis*, Welsh: *Ynys Afallon, Ynys Afallach*; Cornish: *Enys Avalow*; literally *"Island of fruit or apple trees"*; sometimes spelled Avalon or Avilion - the legendary island found in Arthurian legend. The island is first mentioned by **Geoffrey of Monmouth** who calls it *Insula Avallonis* in Latin in **Historia Regum Britanniae** of 1136 *("History of the Kings of Britain")* as the place where King Arthur's sword Excalibur was made, and later where Arthur was taken to recuperate and heal when he was badly wounded at the Battle of Camlann. Since then, the island has become a symbol of Arthurian mythology, like Arthur's castle Camelot. In the later **Vita Merlini** (1150) the island is called *Insula Pomorum* (supposedly from the Latin *pōmus* "fruit tree", Serbian: *помаранџа*, pomarange means orange). In Old Welsh, Old Cornish, or Old Breton *aball* or *avallen,* meaning "apple tree," Welsh *afal*, from Proto-Celtic *abalnā*, literally "fruitful thing." The tradition of the "apple" island among the ancient Britons may also be related to Irish legends of an otherworldly island, the home of Manannán mac Lir and Lugh, Emain Ablach (also the Old Irish poetic name for the Isle of Man), where *Ablach* meaning "mansion of apple trees"[8] from Old Irish *aball* ("apple") which is similar to the Middle Welsh name *Afallach*, which was used to replace the name Avalon in medieval Welsh translations of the French and Latin Arthurian tales. All are related to the Gaelic root *aballo* "fruit tree" (found in the place name *Aballo* or *Aballone*) and come from the Proto-Celtic *abal-* "apple", which at the Indo-European level is related to English apple, our Slavic *јаболко, jabolka* or Latvian *ābele* etc.

Geoffrey's account (in *Taliesin's* narration of the story) indicates that a sea voyage was required to get there. ***Geoffrey*** dealt with the subject in more detail in the ***Vita Merlini***, in which he describes for the first time in Arthurian legend the enchantress Morgan (Morgen) as the chief of nine sisters (Moronoe, Mazoe, Gliten, Glitonea, Gliton, Tyronoe, Thiten and Thiton) who rule Avalon. ***Geoffrey's*** telling (in the in-story narration by Taliesin) indicates a sea voyage was needed to get there.

His description of Avalon here, attributed to the early medieval Spanish scholar ***Isidore of Seville*** (mostly derived from the section on famous islands in his famous work *Etymologiae, XIV.6.8 "Fortunatae Insulae"*), shows the magical nature of this island [9]:

"The island of apples which men call the Fortunate Isle (Insula Pomorum quae Fortunata uocatur) gets its name from the fact that it produces all things of itself; the fields there have no need of the ploughs of the farmers and all cultivation is lacking except what nature provides. Of its own accord, it produces grain and grapes, and apple trees grow in its woods from the close-clipped grass. The ground of its own accord produces everything instead of merely grass, and people live there a hundred years or more. There nine sisters rule by a pleasing set of laws those who come to them from our country." [10]

8. Hamp, Eric P. The north European word for 'apple', *Zeitschrift für Celtische Philologie*, 37, 1979, p. 158–166. Види кај Adams, Douglas Q. The Indo-European Word for 'Apple'. Indogermanische Forschungen, 90, 1985, pp. 79–82.

9. See Walter, Philippe; Berthet, Jean-Charles; Stalmans, Nathalie, eds. (1999). Le devin maudit: Merlin, Lailoken, Suibhne: textes et étude. стр. 125. Compare with Lot, Ferdinand (1918). "Nouvelles études sur le cycle arthurien". Romania. 45 (177): 1–22 (14). Спореди со Faral, Edmond (1993). *La Légende arthurienne, études et documents: Premiere partie: Les plus anciens textes*. Vol. 2 (reprint ed.). H. Champion. pp. 382–383. Also Cons, Louis (1931). "Avallo". *Modern Philology*. 28 (4): 385–394.

10. Vita Merlini. "By comparison, Isidore's description of the Fortunate Isles reads: "The Fortunate Isles *(Fortunatarum insulae)* signify by their name that they produce all kinds of good things, as if they were happy and blessed with an abundance of fruit. Indeed, well-suited by their nature, they produce fruit from very precious trees *[Sua enim aptae natura pretiosarum poma silvarum parturiunt];* the ridges of their hills are spontaneously covered with grapevines; instead of weeds, harvest crops and garden herbs are common there. Hence the mistake of pagans and the poems by worldly poets, who believed that these isles were Paradise because of the fertility of their soil. They are situated in the Ocean, against the left side of Mauretania, closest to where the sun sets, and they are separated from each other by the intervening sea." In ancient and medieval geographies and maps, the Fortunate Isles were typically identified with the Canary Islands.

In a poem from the **Erlangen manuscript**, the girl Jana sits under an apple tree in Constantinople, *"begging"* three doves for the emperor *(Erl, 10).* The beautiful Jana passes by an apple tree in the middle of Constantinople that has grown to the sky and agrees to be empress and give birth to a son and a daughter *(Simonović, 230).* In a poem from northeastern Bulgaria, a girl planted an apple tree that gave birth to heaven *(SevIz Blg 2, 972).* The wedding song talks about a golden apple with silver leaves on which a daisy flower blooms *(Iliev, 109).* In a poem from Prilep, an apple with a silver root and golden branches with gilded fruits from the bride's dream represents her and the children *(Miladinovci, 622).* In the wedding song, the golden apple from the laurel tree has the symbolism of fertility and the sun *(Shapkarev, 147).* The ritual decoration of a branch with apples and the motif of apples in ritual poetry often denote fertility. In the love songs, the bride wants to see the tree lover who is to come as the bridegroom. In the Lazar poems from **Sergiy Dimitrijević's** collection *(p. 53)* [11] there is a relatively rare replacement of a tall tree with a bird on top, with a fruit tree - the falcon on the apple symbolizes the groom - *"counting feathers to get married".* There are two wedding symbols taken out of their usual framework and brought together in the song of the spring ceremony by which the maidens are introduced into the circle of women ready for marriage. The application of the demonic code from the poem about the tall tree to the fruit tree is reflected in a poem from the collection of **Vuk Stefanović Karadžić** [12] in which the dragon in the root of an apple threatens the falcon to burn its nest *(Vuk 1, 664).* Another type of canopy tree is *Dafina*, a type of willow from the Mediterranean area (golden willow appears in North Russian wedding songs). The mythic consciousness, mirroring the space under the tree, includes a geographical concretization: the tree that grew up to the blue sky turns into silver for the Wallachian land and bears miraculous fruits *(Pirin 1, 906)*. The distribution of the roots of the cosmic tree, but also the canopy tree is often associated with *Karavlaska* (Black Wallachia).

11. Sergije Dimitrijević (Сергије Димитријевић March 12, 1912, Pirot - August 11, 1987, Belgrade) was a serbian (yugoslavian) lawyer, economist, historian and numismatist. Црнотравске и лесковачке народне песме ослободилачког рата и револуције, Београд, »Научно дело«, 1967.

12. Vuk Stefanović Karadžić (Вук Стефановић Караџић, pronounced 6 November 1787 (26 October OS) – 7 February 1864)was a Serbian philologist, anthropologist and linguist. He was one of the most important reformers of the modern Serbian language. For his collection and preservation of Serbian folktales, Encyclopædia Britannica labelled him "the father of Serbian folk-literature scholarship." He was also the author of the first Serbian dictionary in the new reformed language. In addition, he translated the New Testament into the reformed form of the Serbian spelling and language. He was well known abroad and familiar to Jacob Grimm, Johann Wolfgang von Goethe and historian Leopold von Ranke. Karadžić was the primary source for Ranke's Die serbische Revolution ("The Serbian Revolution"), written in 1829.

> *Там никнало д'рво дафиново;*
> *Корен пуштило Кара Влашка земља,*
> *Вис високо до Вишнего Бога.*
> *Клоне клонило свата Румелија;*
> *Листе листнало все кара-грошове;*
> *Цвјат е ц'фнало все дребен бисер;*
> *Род е родило все злати ябъ'лки.*

Translation:

> *A laurel tree grew there;*
> *Took root to the Black Wallachian land*
> *Go up high to the Most High God (Vishen Bog).*
> *Branch branch holy Rumelia;*
> *Leaves leafy all the kara-groshes (coins);*
> *Flower bloomed a small pearl;*
> *Yield borne all golden apples.*

The mythical geographical coverage is also found in the motif of the cypress root that reached the Black Wallachian land *(Miladinovci, 165)*. The improvisational nature of oral creation and the combinatorial possibilities of song can lead to a fusion of mythic and non-mythic layers, so that mythic geography can blend with reality. This is how the poem describes the small field with dwarf everlast *(Helichrysum arenariumand)* feathers, a golden bridge and a silver gate to the clear sky, a tree half the width of Sarajevo, with a leaf as far as Belgrade and the fragrance it gives reaches as far as Buda and Pest in Hungary. Although the motif of the miraculous great tree is far from the spirit of epic poetry, there are examples of epic transformations of ritual songs and motifs. In the variant, the **Shapkarev's** [13] Christmas tree (cypress) is replaced by the laurel. In the forest where they are fighting for Budin Jana, one tree stands out:

13. Kuzman Anastasov Shapkarev, (Кузман Анастасов Шапкарев), (1 January 1834 in Ohrid – 18 March 1909 in Sofia) was a Bulgarian folklorist, ethnographer and scientist from the Ottoman region of Macedonia, author of textbooks and ethnographic studies and a significant figure of the Bulgarian National Revival. Kuzman Shapkarev was born in Ohrid in 1834 now in North Macedonia. He was a teacher in a number of Bulgarian schools in Ohrid, Bitola, Prilep, Kukush, Thessaloniki, (1854-1883). In these towns he was especially active in introducing the Bulgarian language in local schools. He initiated the establishment of two Bulgarian high schools in Solun in 1882–1883. He wrote the following textbooks: "*A Bulgarian Primer*" (1866), "*A Big Bulgarian Reader*" (1868), "*Mother tongue*" (1874), "*Short Land description (Geography)*" (1868), "*Short Religion Book*" *(*1868) and others. Shapkarev criticized the dominance of eastern Bulgarian and even declared that it was incomprehensible in Macedonia. In his *Great Bulgarian Textbook (Golema balgarska chitanka)* from 1868, which he authored under the pseudonym "One Macedonian" (Edin Makedonets), he stated his intention to write in a language understandable to his compatriots, the Macedonian Bulgarians. He also announced a project of a dictionary that would contain translation from Macedonian into Upper Bulgarian and vice versa This activity was condemned by the Bulgarian press, which even accused Kuzman Shapkarev of advocating the existence of a separate Macedonian language and of a distinct history of the Macedonian people. Shapkarev was a contributor of many Bulgarian newspapers and magazines – "Tsarigradski vestnik" (Constantinople newspaper), "Gayda" (Bagpipe), "Macedonia", "Pravo" (Justice), "Savetnik" (Adviser), "Balgarska pchela" (Bulgarian bee) and others. Shapkarev was a collaborator of the revolutionary Georgi Rakovski and in the field of ethnography, he assisted the Miladinov Brothers. After 1883 he lived in Eastern Rumelia and Bulgaria –

in Plovdiv, Sliven, Stara Zagora, Vraca and Orhanie (Botevgrad). Along with his scientific and public occupation in Bulgaria he worked as a notary and a judge. From onwards 1900 he was a regular member of Bulgarian Academy of Sciences.

да бегаме димна гора.
Тамо имат многу древја,
многу древја јаорови,
едно дрво Дафиново,
на врфот му паун пеит,
на коренот змејот седи!

Translation:

let's run away to the smoky mountain.
There are many trees there,
many yew trees,
a one laurel tree,
on the top of it the peacock sings,
on the root the dragon lies!

Shapkarev, 147

The song from the **Miladinovci Bros.** collection begins lyrically:

Изникнало едно дрво
Едно дрво дафиново,
Колку лично, толку вишно;
Корено му по с' земја,
Вршенот по сино небе,
На вршенот паун пее
Дури пее, дур зборува:
„Слушајте малко големо,
Слушајте Турци, кауре!
Ка пее паун на дрво,

Translation:

A tree sprouted
A laurel tree,
As beautiful, as tall;
Rooted in the ground,
The top is in the blue sky,

402

The peacock sings at the top
He even sings, he even speaks:
"Listen a little big one,
Listen Turks, kaurs!
(In the Turkish Empire every subject who is not of the Muslim faith is
kaurin).
When a peacock sings in a tree…

Collection of Miladinovci, 383 song

From the top of the laurel tree, from the palace of Mavrojani, the *svastika* (sister-in-law) sees armies approaching. The Turks destroy the palace *(Miladinovci, 383 song)*. Under the tree up to the sky there are two girls, and above two ravens are crying because of the violent Turks *(Iliev, 74)*. The motif of spilled wine from which a tree grows often appears in poems about the *Miraculous Tree* in a dream. The cup is poured by a servant, a child or a girl (Jana or Neda), and in a late variant, far from the original forms - stars. From the spilled wine, the stars fell asleep, a tree appeared with its top to the sky, its root to the black earth and the fruit of the golden apple *(Pirin 1, 710)*. In the wedding song, a laurel tree grows from the wine with its root as far as *Karavlaska*, and its height as high as God *(Shapkarev, 147)*. The song sung at the table describes the fallen silver glass and the red wine, from which a tall tree grew that grows to the blue sky and bears miraculous fruits *(Pirin 1, 906)*. In a Lazarus song sung to the maidens for marriage, when Neda fell asleep, the wine watered the earth and a laurel tree rose with branches to the blue sky and leaves to the black earth, with yolks *(SevIz Blg 1, 272)*. A rhythmic song in a circle, also from northeastern Bulgaria, the slave girl Stanka fell asleep and dreamed that she was pouring wine from which a laurel tree grew.

In another song, Jana served for three days and three nights, fell asleep and a glass of wine was poured. There grew a laurel tree with white grosgrain leaves, flowers - yellow gold coins, gave birth to silver apples. When the beloved asks for at least one apple, the young man will give it to her, but he is not allowed, because they are counted as the rubies of the emperor. **Iliev** believed that the Savior's blood is symbolically represented by wine, but the verses themselves, which do not contain Christian elements, do not justify this. The Christianized versions (discussed below) do have similarities with these poems, but the symbolism of the pre-Christian tree of fertility was handed over to the new religious culture and the later poetic layer. However, *Iliev* is wrong when he says that there was no older, old faith layer, but Christianity introduced that motif into the folk song. According to this thesis, songs that do not feature Christ, the Virgin, or saints were probably later de-Christianized the original Christian songs. It is more likely that pagan motifs entered the Christianized variants, and some variants testify to the opposite trend, since elements of the Christian representation could return to songs in which there are no Christian figures. Related motifs of dreams, spilled wine, and the miraculous tree appear in both pagan and Christian poems. In the introductory part of the poem from the *Miladinovci*, more specifically *"Zbornik na Miladinovci"* – entitled *"Български народни песни"* *("Bulgarian folk songs" published in Zagreb, June 24, 1861)* the miraculous tree and the mother singing a lullaby to her child are shown with wishes to grow up.

Израстло ми дрво дафиново
Но стреде небо, на стреде земја;
И со вишина небо фтасало,
И со ширина земја покрило.
Под дрео ми је сирак Георгија;
С нога го лељат негова мајка
С нога го лељат, песма му пеит:
„Нани ми, нани сирак Георгија!
Ти да ми растиш и да порастиш
Та ке те пуштам на горна земја,
На горна земја на мирна земја,
Ти да ми видиш која доба је,
Али је есен, есен Митровден,
Ако је есен, есен Митровден.

Translation:

Laurel tree has grown
in the middle of the sky, in the middle of the earth;
And with the height it reached the sky,
And with the width covered the earth.

George is an orphan under the tree;
He is cradled by his mother
Caress him with feet, singing a song to him:
"Sleep, sleep orphan Georgia!"
May you grow and grow for me
So I'll let you go on higher ground,
On the upper ground of the peaceful land,
So you can tell me what season is,
But it is autumn, autumn Mitrovden (St. Dimitris day),
If it is autumn, autumn Mitrovden,

Collection of Miladinovci, song 249

Mother tells Georgia to grow and grow, to let him go to the upper world and bear fruit every season. This poem is a rare example of the tree as a path to the higher world. That motif is more developed in fairy tales, and here it is subordinated to the blessings for the child's growth. The expression of the mother's wishes is done by establishing the magical parallelism of the growth of the tree and the child. From the top of the laurel tree that has sprung up, the peacock gives advice to the hero who is "burning" for the girl *(Miladinovci, 380)*. The various genres in which the representation of the tree of life as a laurel tree is involved show two basic properties - it transcends the world and has symbolic fruits. The symbolism through which the barren tree bore "fruit" expresses the idea of fertility, although the tree represented is not fruit. In the poems, the fir, that is, the cypress, embodies the type of *"Cosmic Tree"*, while the apple and the laurel bear the meaning of the *"Tree of Life"*, which is often associated with wedding meanings.

The *Miracle Tree* of the old pagan faith, in the oral tradition of the Slavs in the Balkans, transferred some of its characteristics to the songs of a Christian character. In the contact of folk and Christian-ecclesiastical performances in songs, the two religious systems merged only in a few mythical performances. In the Christianized poems, one would expect a more significant presence of canonical written texts, but there are no biblical elements in them - the *Tree of Adam and Eve (the Book of Genesis)*, the *"Cosmic Tree"* from the *Book of Ezekiel (31)* or the dream of

Nebuchadnezzar *(the Book of Daniel, 4)* or the *Paradise Tree* of Revelation *(22:2)* which could bear fruit twelve times.

7. "Whoever has an ear, let him hear what the Spirit speaks to the churches - to the one who wins, I will give him to eat from the tree of life, which is in the middle of God's paradise." - Revelation of the Holy Apostle John the Theologian, 2.7

1. Then the angel showed me the river of the water of life, as clear as crystal, flowing from the throne of God and of the Lamb

2.down the middle of the great street of the city. On each side of the river stood the tree of life, bearing twelve crops of fruit, yielding its fruit every month. And the leaves of the tree are for the healing of the nations.

3.No longer will there be any curse. The throne of God and of the Lamb will be in the city, and his servants will serve him.

4.They will see his face, and his name will be on their foreheads.

5.There will be no more night. They will not need the light of a lamp or the light of the sun, for the Lord God will give them light. And they will reign for ever and ever.

The revelation of the Holy Apostle John the Theologian, 22.1-5

In poetic folklore, neither the motif of the series of medieval Apocrypha about the rivers flowing around (from) the Tree of Paradise *(Book of Enoch, Paul's Vision, Agapia),* nor the motif of the man climbing the silver and golden tree from the "story of the rich" , nor the motif of the birds of paradise on the tree, as well as the history of baptism, the tree of Christ's suffering *(Bonaventura, Orthodox Apocrypha).* In the Christianized poems, the Miraculous Tree (canopy or spindly tree), which is not geographically located, loses its name, and some animal inhabitants give way to saints, while the description is accompanied by a medieval Byzantine allegory, so that the poems contain two parts: display and interpretation. In some poems, the *Tree of Paradise* represents only the space where the saints are, while the action takes place elsewhere - on land or at sea. Thus, in a poem from the collection of ***Vuk Karadžic,*** St. Elijah awakens St. Nikola, who sleeps under the Paradise Tree, to go and transport the souls. They go to the mountain and make ships and transfer the souls from this world to the next, except for three souls who could not *(Vuk 1, 209).* ***Afanasiev*** explained that the saints in this poem replace the pagan deities – Perun and the ancient god of the sea *(1868: 293).* The most developed motif of the *Paradise Tree* in the folklore of the Balkan Slavs is a reworking of the apocryphal prayer *The Dream of the Virgin.* This apocryphal prayer is widespread in both East and West, but it has occupied a different place in the folklore of Orthodox and Catholics. In the folk song of the Croats and the Slovenes, the songs that depict the sufferings of Christ, about which the Virgin dreamed, are more developed, while in Serbia, Bulgaria and Macedonia, the image of a tree is more developed, which is rarely found among the Slavs of the western religion. About the motive of the mother's dream writes ***A. Veselovski (1876), N. Sumchov (1887), A. Potebnya (1887), V. Sakharov (1888), O. Bobler (1932), C. Vranska,*** in a separate chapter from the book ***"Apocrypha about the Mother of God and the Bulgarian folk song"*** (1940), ***V. Stojchevski Antic,*** *(1969),* ***J. Shetka** (1969),* ***L. Krechenbacher** (1975),* ***P. Stefanov** (1989).* ***Franić*** published the text of the apocryphal prayer in the journal of the Ethnographic Museum in Zagreb in 1935. These records, which were primarily concerned with the origin of Christian written sources in folk songs, do not emphasize the pre-Christian origin of some of their elements. To see it from that angle, it is worth turning to ritual, mostly calendar (Christmas) songs and wedding songs and rituals. ***Iliev*** accepts the theses of ***Potebnya** (1887: 224-226)* about the interweaving of the ideas about the *"Paradise Tree"* from the ***Sermon*** on the ***Panayot*** and other apocryphal and folk notions about the *"Miraculous Tree"* in the calendar poems *(Iliev 1892: 331).* The ritual decoration of trees and the singing of songs with the motif of a tree symbolizing abundance also belong to the same magical stimulation of fertility. The motif in the dream of poured wine from a cup, from which grows a tree with miraculous fruits, indicates the ritual pouring of wine and the penetration of rituals and poetry. Creatures arranged on the cosmic tree (fir or cypress) -

nightingale or bees at the top, snake or dragon at the bottom in the root, as animal hypostases of creatures from the old Slavic faith, in prose and poetic types represent traces that indicate an understanding of the vertical axis of the world. Birds and bees as creatures of the upper world appear in the representations of the spindly evergreen tree - cypress or fir, and in the motif of the laurel. The tree of paradise has golden branches, silver leaves, and wondrous fruits (of silver, pearls, and golden apples). In religious folk songs, the tree is given the attributes - table, tall, strange, personal, self-grown, and the name of the tree is lost, although it is the tree that covers the world with its canopy. An exception is the naming of the laurel tree *(Serbian Dialectological Collection 7, 255, No. 5),* which testifies to the mechanical taking of the name. The name of the *"God's Tree",* the medicinal plant *(Artemisia abrotanum* - named after the goddess Artemis, a plant that helped women) is also used by the Russians, it is not related to the tree from the songs. The use of this plant, also called the tree of the *Blessed Virgin Mary,* the herb of the Virgin, is also evidenced by the following entry in the spring celebration: *Drevo Jezusovo meću na Cvjetnicu u butaru, uz to dren, brišel, (ivy), fušpan i koju grančiču trešnjevu, ako trešnje več cvatu (ZNŽ 30, 2: 213).* In the poems about the *"Wonderful Tree",* Catholics only mention the tree they sleep under, while they do not name the tree they dreamed about. Unlike the songs of the Orthodox Slavs, they describe the ritual table and ritual objects under the tree. The motif of the saints at the table under the tree also appears among the Russians *(Katićic 1989: 78).* As Christmas songs, songs with the tree of paradise were most often performed. Even when the scribe did not indicate the origin of the song, it is possible, with great certainty, to assume that it is a song related to the celebration of Christ's birth. In the reconstructions of the proto-Slavic celebration of Christmas, the great importance of trees is pointed out, but the segments of this ritual complex are Christianized. In most poems, the Virgin dreams of a miraculous tree. In a rather religiously innovative version from the Sofia region *(Vatev, Vranska 1940: 154),* the Virgin sleeps in the church and dreams that in the middle of the church a miraculous tree has grown on the throne, and in the Harmanli region, she sleeps by the sea on a white stone *(SbNU 11, 4, Vranska 1940: 153).* In two Catholic versions she sleeps under a linden tree. The Virgin's dream is interpreted by the saints: Vasilije or Basilius

(Vuk 5, 226), Peter *(Iliev, 121)*, Ivan or John *(SbNU 6, 4)*, Elijah. In the songs, the Mother of God often learns the meaning of the dream on the way to heaven, and in some songs, she also goes from church to church. Tree descriptions and corresponding interpretations can be simple or complex, usually three-part. In the poem from *Vuk's* collection, the Mother of God dreams of a tall tree with spreading branches, and interprets the dream about Basilus as an announcement of Christ's birth and his mission:

> *Што ти расте украј срца дрвце,*
> *"То ћеш родити Христа Бога сина;*
> *"Што се дрвце широм раширило*
> *"И покрило с крај на крај свијета,*
> *"То ће свијет од гријеха спасити,*
> *"Што се дрвце к небу узвисило,*
> *"Са земље ће оцу Богу поћи*

Translation:

> *What tree grows near your heart,*
> *"You will give birth to Christ the Son of God;*
> *"As the tree spread wider*
> *"And covered from end to end of the world,*
> *"That will save the world from sin,*
> *"As the tree rose to heaven,*
> *"From the earth, it will go to the Father God*

Vuk Karadžić, 5, 226

In this song there is no tripartite description of a tree with trunk, branches and leaves or fruit, but only the universal power of Christ is proclaimed. In a Croatian poem from Dolno Zagorje *(Deželić, rkp MH I: 501-2)* Maria, asleep under a green linden tree, dreams that three trees grow from her heart, the top of which reaches the bright sky. Although the allegory in the Catholic hymns is not settled, it is likely that the three trees here are not the Adam, Eve, and Lord of the Baptism Apocrypha, but members of God's family. In the poem, on top of a tree, there is a golden table and the king of heaven holds a bloody sword in his right hand. In one poem, Mary dreams of Christ being caught, crucified, and placed in her lap. The seven-fold sword that pierces the heart represents the Jews *(Lahner, 6)*. Catholics celebrate the Immaculate Heart of the Mother of God (August 22). In the poem from Žganec's collection, Maria fell asleep under a green linden tree when she dreamed of a tree from her heart that sent veins on its black earth and branches on the gray sky, while at the top of the tree there were three heavenly birds. The Slovenian poems do not contain the motif of the dream and the heart at all but show a tree in the field, and its shadow, there is a table covered with white robes with a golden chalice from which three ruddy roses grow - the Heavenly Father, Jesus of Nazareth, Joseph, and Mary *(Strekkelj, 4928)*. The two songs sung in dance describe the golden apple tree below when the golden tables, the golden sprinkler, are God and Mary (and Peter, in the second song). The prayer calls for the three fallen apples to bring fertility to the fields, the mountains, and the village *(Štrekelj 5183, 5189)*. White-winged bees gather mead and God's guests. In folk beliefs, white bees symbolize special luck and appear in blessings. To reconstruct the origin of this song with various elements combined, a few more transitional "variants" would be needed. In the Virgin's dream, the tree represents the Lord. In some calendar variants the attribute of a "young" god is given. The exception is the song in which the tree does not represent God, but St. John the Baptist *(Iliev, 91)*. **Iliev,** from whose collection these verses originate in the text ***"The herbal kingdom in the folk poetry, customs, rituals and beliefs of the Bulgarians"***, expresses the opinion that the replaced character is John the Theologian, who was highly respected by the Bogomils *(Iliev 1892: 339)*. This song was sung on Ivanaden (St. John's day), when the cross was thrown into the water. The tree from the dreams is divided into three parts, so the allegorical interpretation is in three parts. In one poem, Saint Nedela (St. Sunday) dreams of a *"Miraculous Tree"*, but there is no interpretation, because the poem ends with the awakening of the saint *(Stoin, West Thrace, Bulgaria 73)*. Within the tripartite division, the tree is the Lord, the branches and leaves - saints, Christians, martyr children, unbaptized children, all Christians. The religious hierarchy took its simplified form in numerous variations. Deviating from the allegorical designation of the Christian god, church dignitaries and believers with pieces of wood appear in poems in which the branches denote churches, monasteries, icons. In some poems, the Virgin is replaced by saints, with Saint Nedela appearing paired with either Saint Nicholas or Saint Petka (Paraskeva). These poems testify to a partial breakdown of the oral tradition, but also to its addition of new details, in the description of the place where the saint sleeps, the description of the tree, the interpretation of its parts, the approximation of the heavenly and earthly spheres or the psychologization of the characters. Saint Nedela dreams the same dream in the Croatian poem *(Lahner 1926, 22)*. **Rusakiev's** record of the Bulgarians from Asia Minor presents Saint Nedela as she fell asleep in her father's yard, dreaming of the silver-gold tree that grows in the middle of the sea on the island *(Vranska 1940: 156)*. The elements of the Proto-Slavic representations of the *"Cosmic Tree"* are intertwined with Christian elements. In the version of the song from Thrace, a tree is described, but there is no interpretation, but St. Nedela descends in the new churches *(Stoin Trakia, 73)*. In a carol song from the Silvire region, Saint George addresses the saint "reprimandingly" - as if she herself did not come to the interpretation that the tree is the Lord and the pillars are the stars *(Stoin Trakia, 32)*. Saint John's dream by the blue sea is interrupted by Saint Nedela sprinkling him, and he is angry because in his dream he saw a tree with big branches and leaves, where the sky opened and the Pure Mother with Christ in her hands *(Crnushanov, 36)*. The motif of the opening of heaven in this poem shows a rare reconciliation of the "real" representation of heaven as a closed or locked space with the "oneiric" representation of the miraculous tree. This unusual connection of the two images leads to the abandonment of the allegorical representation of the Virgin and Christ and their direct presentation, as well as to the merging of two different folkloric-Christian representations. In one poem from Rhodope region in Bulgaria, there is neither a real nor a symbolic image of Christ, but only the introductory part of the poem about sleep and awakening is taken. Saint Nedela awakens Saint Nicholas to stand up and build churches by sprinkling him with September wine *(Arnaud's Rod: 27)*. In a calendar poem from northeastern Bulgaria, a self-grown tree, branches, and gilded leaves are dreamed of by Saint Nedela, and her dream, similar to the reduced status of the dreaming woman, is interpreted by a grammarian student *(Sevlz Blg 1, 206)*. In some songs, the time when saint fell asleep is determined. Sunday - on the eve of Sunday. In a Christmas or carol song *(koledo song)* from the Novozagorsk region, a girl appears instead of the Virgin or saints, and her dream is interpreted by a priest *(Vranska 1940: 157)*. The dream of Saint Nikolas, asleep between two fences, two roads, interprets St. Nedela, turning the three-part building into a two-part, one - the branches are angels, and the leaves are Christians *(Serb. Dialectological Collection 7, 255)*. The dream of Saint Nicholas, who fell asleep between two monasteries and two roads, is also interpreted by Saint Nedela - the wasps are the Jews and the bees are the Christians *(Ikonomov, 172, Yastrebov: 472)*.

Cvetana Vranska talks about the weakening of the religious character of the song about the dream of the Virgin and the popularization of the apocryphal story. She concludes that the motif of the Virgin's dream was mostly developed in the Bulgarian poems, but that the original meaning of the Apocrypha was completely lost in them *(Vranska 1940: 158)*. [13]

13. Tsvetanka Stoyanova Romanska-Vranska (Цветанка Стоянова Романска-Вранска is a Bulgarian folklorist and ethnographer. She was born on December 16, 1914 in Sofia in the family of the linguist Stoyan Romanski. Her older brother is the conductor Lubomir Romanski. In 1937, he graduated in Slavic philology at the "St. Kliment Ohridski" University of Sofia, and in 1937-1939 - doctoral studies at the Charles University in Prague. After returning to Bulgaria, he taught at the Sofia University, from 1963 he was a professor. In 1962-1969, he headed the folklore section at the Ethnographic Institute. He died on March 4, 1969 in Sofia.

The demythologizing of Christian concepts takes place on all levels of the presented reality - both in the depiction of space and in the relationships between characters of reduced status. In addition to replacing God with saints, and saints with ordinary people, religiosity is also lost by omitting the miraculous properties of the tree. This type of song breakdown, however, retains some elements of the Christian religion. At first glance, it is unusual that the motif of the paradise tree did not have much momentum in Catholic circles, but this can be explained by the strictness of the Catholic Church, which subjected the major holidays associated with the life of Jesus to strict control and discipline. The second type of *"Miraculous Tree"*, usually the fir, is associated with Easter and the symbols of Christ's suffering, in songs from Kosovo and Macedonia. In the book ***"Debarca", Naum Tselakoski*** mentions a song that was sung by women on a leisurely walk near the remains of the monastery of St. Jovan Bigorski on Easter - with a motif of tall pine trees, branches, and leaves with bloody eyelids. In the end, it is said that these are not drops of blood, but an honest communion *(Tselakoski: 161)*. Serbian Easter songs from Kosovo, which according to ***Jastrebov's*** testimony were sung in the square in front of the church, depict a sky-high Christmas tree that has bent its branches to the ground with green leaves, red flowers, and bees. The allegorical interpretation says that the Christmas tree is the *Gračanica* church, the leaves are the church books (priests), the red flowers are communions, and the bees are the people in the *church (Bovan, 153, Vukanovic: 154, Jastrebov: 117, Nushic)*. The red color of the flowers is the color characteristic of the Easter celebration. Only in ***Debeljkovic's*** variant, also from Kosovo, does the motif of the dream appear – Saint Nedela fell asleep in the lap of Saint Peter, he woke her up to show her communion and the people *(Debeljkovic, 34)*. From the circle of variants of the song about the fir trees, only this song was sung on St. Trinity (All Saints Day). Wreaths were woven and icons were decorated in the church on Trinity day. The meaning of bees as Christians is also found in other types of songs - Saint Paraskeva in one song asks the Mother of God about the flies around the *Paradise Tree*, and she explains that the tree itself is God, and that the flies are the unbaptized children *(Arnaud's Rod: 582)*. In the text on the spatial organization of Russian fables, ***Shindin*** cites the text about the Holy Mother of God who, in a dark forest under a cypress tree, dispelled flies and beasts with three rods *(1993: 117)*. In the ***Iliev*** variant *(91)*, the branches are monasteries, the silver leaves are icons, while the bees are God's Christians. In the above poem from Debar, the wasps at the root are Jews and the bees at the top are Christians *(Jastrebov: 453, Ikonomov, 172)*. In a Bulgarian poem, above the table is a golden tree in the middle of heaven with a basket on top *(Angelov-Vakarelski, 120)*. In the song of the ***Miladinovici*** brothers from Kostur (now town in Greece) Saint Nedela fell asleep in the lap of Saint Petka, and when she woke up she told a strange dream about a tall tree growing in the middle of the sea with two huge leaves - two books in the sky from which priests teach Christians to celebrate these saints *(Miladinovci, 35)*. The tree that grew on an island in the middle of the sea is a common motif in Russian folklore [14], but rarely appears among the Balkan Slavs.

14. In the section "The Green Oak at Lukomorje" Pushkin imagined it as an introduction to the poem "Ruslan and Lyudmila", which he started working on in 1817, when he was still a young high school student. It was only in 1828, when the poem was published in a new edition, that the reader became acquainted with the unusual poetic introduction. The poem is written in iambic tetrameter, closer to astrophic. At that time, it was this style of writing that was characteristic of poetic forms. Thoughts about characters from fairy tales, about the magic oak came to the author not by chance. His nanny Arina Rodionovna knew a huge number of fairy tales that she shared with her student. He heard these wonderful things from her. 33 heroes appear in the second synopsis of the folk tale recorded by Pushkin, probably by Arina Rodionovna. However, there they are siblings of the main hero, the prince, who is under the supervision of an unnamed uncle and, only after they have tasted mother's milk (mixed in bread), they remembered the connection. They first appear with him in 1828, in the famous preface "On the Lukomorye green oak" added to "Ruslan and Lyudmila": "And thirty beautiful knights; Clear water comes out of the waters; and their sea uncle is with them." To this day, the 35 magical stanzas attract literary critics and researchers of Pushkin's legacy. They are trying to solve the riddle of whether there really was a land called Lukomorye which is described as magical. Some have concluded that such a country and territory existed on old maps of Western Europe in the 16th century. It was an area in Siberia, on one side of the river Ob. However, from a symbolic point of view, we can definitely connect the name Lukomorye with some island and coastal country. Pushkin has always been attracted by history. Old names of towns and villages are often mentioned in his work. It reminds contemporaries that our roots go back to the distant past and must not be forgotten. Of course, in some of the next volume, this mysterious land called Lukomorye will be discussed in more detail, which represents a post-flood echo in which I believe archaic symbols from the pre-cataclysmic cycle of the Garden of Eden are preserved.

In a modern record of Saint Paraskeva wakes Saint Nedela to see how the righteous lushes are the first to climb the tree in heaven, while the wrong ones are the first to fall into hell *(Blg.bal, 552)*. This new "nation" joins the dream motif of the eschatological notion of rewarding the righteous and punishing the sinners. Some of the songs with the miraculous tree represent the heavenly genre of the scene - under the gilded tree of the world, Mary sews parsley and episcopal gloves *(Miladinovci, 39), and* Saint Paraskeva is looking for the keys to heaven. Unlike the combination of the "oneiric" representation of the miraculous tree and the "real" image of paradise in the mentioned poem from the collection of **Crnushanov**, in which the allegorical meaning of the tree as Christ is translated into its real appearance, preserving the basic idea of the motif, completely is lost.

Lacking the oneiric appearance of the tree and the allegorical interpretation of the dream, it fits, only with its miraculous properties, from the poem about the dream of the Virgin in the representation of the locked paradise. This is how two different folkloric representations of heaven come together. The poem from northeastern Bulgaria shows a tree with gilded branches and gilded leaves underneath when the church was built by God for young people to marry, children to be baptized and old people to sing *(SevIzBlg 1, 208)*. The choice of a place for the church under the miraculous tree is proof of God's grace. The *"Tree of the World"* and the *"Tree of Life"* of Slavic mythology handed over elements for the appearance of Christian representations, as well as some symbolic inhabitants (bees, birds), but in the new, monotheistic framework, the meaning of these elements was changed and they were subordinated of the church. Seen from a ritual point of view, these songs were performed in the pre-Christian era during the major holidays (today Christmas, and Easter). While the canopy tree that covers the world, the Mediterranean-Byzantine laurel, took over the functions of the willow or the oak, in depicting and invoking abundance, retaining some elements of the older poems (poured wine, dream), the spindly tree - the Mediterranean cypress or the Slavic fir they lost the demonic "dwellers" (the dragon and snakes) and the animal dwellers at the base of the tree. Only in the roots of the tree, in some poems, wasps are identified with Jews as harmful creatures. Folklore Christianity introduced a new, allegorical interpretation of parts of the tree, subordinated to the hierarchical notion of the unity of God, church dignitaries, and Christians. The development of songs about the *"Paradise Tree"* as the *"Tree of Life"*, especially in the Bulgarian and Macedonian regions, led to the demythologization of the united Christian and pre-Christian layer and introduced more naive elements into the popular view of the saints and their community. The loss of the properties of holy persons, the disappearance of the dream motif, and the miraculous qualities of the tree represent the last stage of the decay of the old mythical notions. In the beliefs of many peoples, the tree is a theophany, an image of the cosmos, a symbol of life, a central point of the world, and an allegory of nature that is constantly renewed. That is why it is a symbol of the cosmos.

- ## *Sanctuary Tree – Zapis*

"Култ дрвета и биљака једини је од старих култова са којим се црква, нарочито наша православна, брзо и безусловно измирила, тако да он данас у њој има нарочито своје место и своју симболику….. Колико је наша црква показала мало интересовање да ратује против старинског култа дрвета, најбоље се види из чињенице да у култу светога дрвета, записа, у адорирању његовом и приношењу жртава њему, узимају учешћа и свештеници. Све то учинило је да је култ дрвета и биљака у нашем народу и данас још необично свеж и јак". – Dr. Veselin Čajkanović (1881- 1946, Myth and Religion of the Serbs 1976, Cult of trees and plants among old Serbs, p.7).

"The cult of trees and plants is the only one of the old cults with which the church, especially our Orthodox, reconciled quickly and unconditionally so that today it has a special place in it and its symbolism…. How little interest our church has shown in waging war against the ancient cult of the tree, is best seen from the fact that in the cult of the sacred tree - zapis, priests also take part in adoring it and making sacrifices to it. All that made the cult of trees and plants in our nation still unusually fresh and strong today".

A *zapis* (Serbian Cyrillic: *запис*, Serbian pronunciation: literally "inscription"; plural: *zapisi* (записи) is a sacred tree in Serbian tradition, protecting the village within whose bounds it is situated. [1] A cross is inscribed into the bark of each *zapis*. Most of these trees are large oaks. Prayers are offered to God under the crown of the zapis, where church services may also be held, especially during village festivals observed to supplicate God for protection against destructive weather conditions. In settlements without a church, ceremonies such as weddings and baptisms were once conducted under the tree. Folk tradition maintains that great misfortune will befall anyone that dares fell a zapis. According to Serbian scholar *Veselin Čajkanović*, the zapis is inherited from the pre-Christian religion of the Serbs, in which it had been used as a temple.

1. Agapkina, T. A. (2001). "Запис". In Svetlana Mikhaylovna Tolstaya and Ljubinko Radenković (ed*.). Словенска митологија: енциклопедијски речник [Slavic Mythology: Encyclopedic Dictionary]* (in Serbian). Belgrade: Zepter Book World. pp. 189–90

The selected tree becomes a *zapis* through the rite of consecration performed by a Serbian Orthodox priest, in which a cross is inscribed into its bark. The *zapis* are chosen from large trees, primarily oaks, but also elms, ashes, beeches, pear trees, and hazels. A large cross, often made of stone, may be erected beside the *zapis*, and the surrounding area may be fenced. The *zapis* is inviolable: it is believed that great misfortune will befall anyone that dares fell it. Climbing it, sleeping under it, and picking its fruits and twigs, are also forbidden. Even the branches and fruits that fall from the tree should not be collected. A village may have more than one *zapis*: the main one in the settlement or near it, and several others in the village's fields, [2] usually chosen so that they surround the settlement. The *zapis* play an important role in rites connected with the festival known as krstonoše, meaning "cross-bearers", which is publicly celebrated within the village to supplicate God for protection against destructive weather conditions, as well as to ensure a good harvest. Not all villages celebrate krstonoše on the same day, but it usually falls between Easter and the eve of St. Peter's Fast. Some villages have abandoned this festival. Krstonoše commences with villagers gathering at the church and forming a procession headed by a cross, an icon, and church banners. The procession walks a closed line around the settlement, encircling as much of the village's territory as possible, and then returns to the church. [3]

2. Čajkanović, Veselin (1994). "Запис". *Речник српских народних веровања о биљкама [Dictionary of Serbian Folk Beliefs about Plants]* (in Serbian). Belgrade: Serbian Literary Guild. pp. 271–2.

3. Vuković, Milan T. (2004). "Литије – крстоноше". *Народни обичаји, веровања и пословице код Срба [Serbian Folk Customs, Beliefs, and Sayings]* (in Serbian) (12 ed.). Belgrade: Sazvežđa. pp. 136–7.

On its way, the procession stops by each *zapis* and at some crossroads, where the priest chants prayers. The cross inscribed in the *zapis's* bark is renewed, and the tree is censed. In eastern Serbia, a small hole is bored into the trunk and filled with cooking oil and incense. The service on this festival is held under the crown of the main *zapis*, or in the church after the procession returns. During the service, the priest and the man elected for the host of the krstonoše (cross barrier) hold together a round loaf of bread, rotate it three times counterclockwise, and break it into two halves. One half is given to the priest and the other to the man who will host the following year's krstonoše. A feast for the participants in the procession may be prepared under the main *zapis* and they may also dance the kolo there. A sheep used to be sacrificed under the tree so that its blood spilled on the trunk and roots. Some villages and hamlets in Serbia also observe a festival commemorating a disaster that has befallen the settlement, such as a flood, fire, or lightning strike. The festival is called the *zavetina*, the name being derived from the noun *zavet*, meaning vow. The service on the *zavetina* may be held in the shelter of the *zapis*. In settlements without a church, ceremonies such as weddings and baptisms were conducted under the crown of the *zapis*. People with health problems used to leave their clothes on the tree by night, believing this would help restore their health. In the regions of Pek and Zvižd, in eastern Serbia, a fire used to be built under the tree on the eve of Lent. In Gruža, money was lent under the *zapis*. In his study on the cult of trees among ancient Serbs, ethnologist **Veselin Čajkanović** states that the *zapis* are inherited from the Serbs' pre-Christian religion, in which it had been used as a temple. Prayers and sacrifices were offered under the crown of the *zapis*, as in a temple. A *zapis* is primarily selected from oaks, the trees associated with Perun—the thunder god of the ancient Slavic religion. A Serbian legend relates the story of a king who always prayed to God under a pear tree rather than in a church, saying, "the pear tree is my church." His prayers were so effective that he eventually became a saint. [4]

4. Čajkanović, Veselin (1973). *"Култ дрвета и биљака код старих Срба". Мит и религија у Срба: изабране студије [Myth and Religion of the Serbs: Selected Studies]* (in Serbian). Belgrade: Serbian Literary Guild.

A reverence towards trees, like that extended upon the *zapis*, has also been recorded in North Macedonia. During Easter, in the region of Gevgelija, the Eucharist was once given to selected pear trees. Each was surrounded with icons, after which a priest read from a Gospel facing the tree, sprinkled it with holy water, and then put the consecrated bread under its bark. In other areas, there was a custom of placing a cross, a fireplace, and a table made of stone by a tree on a hillock near a river or lake. After the Second World War, the celebration of village glory in addition to the *"Zapis-Tree"* was forbidden in some villages, so the whole ritual was moved to the churchyard. However, the belief that anyone who desecrates the *"Zapis-Tree"* will be punished and that a great evil awaits them is still very present in Serbia. Research by ethnologists in the field has shown that the villagers still know which tree is marked as a *"record / zapis"* and almost all adhere to the rule that it must not be damaged at any cost. Research in eastern Serbia shows how much respect there is for the sacred tree where not even the fallen bark of the tree was touched. In a village near Zajecar, there was a case where a tree that collapsed and fell on the road was not moved because it was a *"Zapis-Tree"*. The villagers of that place even built a new road, so that the sacred tree would not be moved. Although the celebration of the village vows next to the *"Zapis-Tree"* is no longer common, studies of this wonderful custom show how important the community once was. The sacred tree had a significant role in the religious life of the people and at the social level. Trials used to be held there because it was believed that in a holy place one must not lie, and thus had the opportunity to confess. In addition to the *"Zapis-Tree"*, meetings of the locals were held and decisions were made on important matters for the community. Thus, according to the belief that is still remembered in Serbia, the Second Serbian Uprising in 1815 was erected next to an oak tree, known by the name *"Takovski grm"*. The very name of the sacred tree says that the most important laws and rules were written on that tree, new things that the community needed to know. [15]

15. Čajkanović, Veselin (1994). "Record". *Dictionary of Serbian folk beliefs about plants.* Belgrade: Serbian literary association. p. 271-72. Čajkanović, Veselin (1973). "Cult of trees and plants among ancient Serbs". *Myth and religion in Serbs*: selected studies. Belgrade: Serbian literary association. See also Agapkina, T. A. (2001). "Record". Ed.: Svetlana Mihajlovna Tolstaia and Ljubinko Radenković. *Slavic mythology: an encyclopedic dictionary*. Belgrade: Zepter Book World. p. 189—190. Татьяна Алексеевна Агапкина (b. January 22, 1958 (1958-01-22), Moscow) is a Russian Slavic folklorist, ethnolinguist. Doctor of Philology. Leading Research Fellow, Department of Ethnolinguistics and Folklore, Institute of Slavic Studies, Academy of Sciences. Editor-in-Chief of the Indrik Publishing House (since 2000). Compare also

Vuković, Milan T. (2004). "Litius - cross bearers". Folk customs, beliefs and proverbs among Serbs (12 ed.). Belgrade: Constellation.

From everything stated so far, we can conclude that all these folklore elements related to the *Miraculous Tree* and the *Zapis Tree* of the Slavs from the Balkans and the Mediterranean region have their prehistoric and pre-flood Arctic origin, where these elements and memories from the old faith were skilfully inserted into the new religion of our people.

Chapter XII

Svētā Hidrogrāfija

"And water flowed out of Eden to water the paradise, and then it separated into four rivers" - Old Testament, Genesis, 2:10.
The Messenger of Allah said: "Saihan, Ceyhan, Al-Furat and An-Nil are the rivers of Jannah (Islamic paradise)." - Riyad as-Salihin, Book 18, Hadith 46

وعنه رضي الله عنه قال: قال رسول الله صلى الله عليه وسلم : "سيحان وجيحان والفرات والنيل كل من نهار الجنة" ((رواه مسلم)

Septentrionalium Terrarum descriptio" [1595]. Atlantis pars altera

In the second volume, we will pay special attention and analysis to the medieval globes and mysterious maps that show the sacred geography and the polar continent, where the reader could gain additional insight into what we have just presented. But for now, just briefly as a supplement to the map. I am attaching an interesting mysterious map of the Dutch cartographer **Gerardus Mercator** (1512-1594), which was issued one year after his death by his son. Just above Scandinavia itself and Greenland, as we see from this map below is a vast circular continent through which flow the four mighty rivers mentioned in many ancient traditions. In the very title of the map, the Latin *Atlantis pars altera* is also noted, from where we learned that the author himself equates this country with *Plato's* own lost continent.

Svētā Hidrografija or Sacred Hydrography is a chapter that will show the idea of the circulation of heavenly water and how it flows to the earth and branches into four rivers that then feed the whole world with life. In the preceding chapters, we have presented the simple and natural interpretation suggested by the primitive circumpolar continent hypothesis. If the reader will kindly looks back he will see how easily that natural water system of that lost land of pleasures could become the only, according to tradition, a river that watered the whole country. The insurmountable difficulties of all previous attempts to identify the four rivers are too numerous to present here in detail. [1]

1. "We entirely agree with Delitzsch [the elder] that Paradise is lost, and the four streams are on this account a riddle which cries, "Where is Paradise?" the question remaining without an answer. "*Ebers, Aegypten und die Bücher Mose*, p. 30. See McClintock and Strong's *Cyclopaedia,* Arts. "Gihon"; "Pison"," Eden" etc. "Wherever there is a river-head that can be made to run on all-fours, even by assuming the existence of water-channels no longer extant, the Biblical Eden has been discovered, whether in Asia, Africa, Europe, or America." Gerald Massey, *The Natural Genesis*, vol. ii., p. 162. We may add that Mr. Samuel Johnson's suggestion (*Oriental Religions*; Persia. Boston, 1885: p. 253), to the effect that the "four rivers" of the Hebrew story consisted of two real rivers, the Tigris and the Euphrates, plus two imaginary "words, that simply mean flowing waters, and that were used as generic terms for the purpose of making up the number four, the conventional sign of completeness in all Eastern mythologies", is a characteristic specimen of the unscholarly and dogmatic caprice of pantheistic exegesis in the field of ancient religious ideas and their history.

In our interpretation the original river is from the sky; the division takes place at the heights of the Pole, and the four resulting rivers are the chief streams of the circumpolar continent as they descend in different directions to the surrounding sea. Does such a view find any support in the traditions of the ancient world? That it does will be clear to anyone who has carefully read thus far. Let us take the rivers of the Persian cradle of the race. Where do they rise? If the investigator of this question has made no previous studies in Comparative Sacred Hydrography, he will be surprised to find that in Persian thought, not only the Paradise rivers but also all the rivers of the whole earth, *have but one head spring and but one place of discharge.* This head-spring is the *Ardvî Sûra*, situated in heaven, the heaven of the Pole. ***"This heavenly fountain,"*** says the German Orientalist **Dr. Martin Haug**, summarizing the contents of the **Abân Yasht**, ***"this heavenly fountain has a thousand springs and a thousand canals, each of them forty days journey long. Thence a channel goes through all the seven keshvares, or regions of the earth, conveying everywhere pure celestial waters".*** [2]

2. Essays, 2d ed., p. 198. See Darmesteter's translation: "From this river of mine alone flow all the waters that spread all over the seven keshvares; this river of mine alone goes on bringing waters both in summer and in winter." *The Zend-Avesta*, Pt. ii., pp. 52-84

The following is an ancient invocation to *Anâhita,* the spirit of these heavenly waters*: **"Come before me, Ardvî Sûra Anâhita! come down from yonder stars onto the earth created by Ahura Mazda! They shall worship the handy lords, the rulers of countries, sons of the rulers of countries."*** [3] From its elevation the heavenly height is called *Hûgar*, i. e., "the lofty": *Hûgar*, the lofty, is the mount from which the water of *Ardvî Sûra* leaps down the height of a thousand men." [4] Again it is written, ***"Hûgar, the lofty, on which the water of Ardvî Sûra flows and leaps, is the chief of summits since it is that above which is the revolution of Sataves, the chief of reservoirs."*** [5] ***As all the rivers of the earth s seven regions, so all lakes and seas and the ocean itself, are from this one celestial fountain. "Through the warmth and clearness of the water, purifying more than other waters, everything continually flows from the source Ardvî Sûra."*** [6]

3. Haug, Ibid., p. 198. Darmesteter, Ibid., p. 73.

4. Bundahish (West), xii. 5. *The Zend-Avesta* (Darmesteter), ii. p. 54

5. Bundahish, xxiv. 17. When West (*Pahlavi Texts,* Pt. i., p. 35, note 6) uses the last clause of this quotation to show that the location of Hûgar is "probably" in the western quarter, his
argument rests upon two mistakes, both of which seem to be shared by all modern Avestan students. The first mistake is to suppose Sataves a different star from Tishtar (Tistrya); and the second is the notion that Tishtar was the star now called Sirius. The fact is that originally Satavaêsa and Tisrtrya were simply two designations for one and the same object, and that object was not our Sirius, but the Pole star. I say our Sirius, because there is evidence that this name also once belonged to a very different heavenly body, and to one situated in *"die Mitte des Himmels"* i. e., at the Pole. (Ideler, *Sternennamen,* p. 216.) Hûgar (Hukairya) is the heavenly height of the polar sky, high above Hâra-Berezaiti, whenever this term is applied, as originally, to the terrestrial polar mount. *Abdn Yasht,* 88. See Windischmann, *Zoroastrische Studien.* 171.

6. Bundahish, ch. xiii., 3. The chapter on Seas.

However, named, all waters are simply portioning of the same heaven-descending stream. "The other innumerable waters and rivers, springs and channels, are one in origin with those, so in various districts and various places they call them by various names." [7] Even plant sap, and blood, and milk, and all the seventeen kinds of liquid enumerated in the **Yashts**, are parts of the one cosmic current. "All these, through growth, or the body which is formed, mingle again with the rivers, for the body which is formed and the growth are both one." [8] Everything of a liquid nature, therefore, in the whole world is conceived of as proceeding from one source high in the north-polar sky. Whither is it tending? What becomes of it all in the end? Where do its myriad rills and rivers at last discharge? As according to the cosmological conception so often illustrated in these pages, all start from the zenith, we should naturally expect all to reunite at last in the nadir. This is found to be the fact. But in this nether gathering place the waters, now polluted from their contact with all the filth and vileness of the world, are not allowed to rest and accumulate. [9] This cesspool of the universe has an obvious bottom. By the various processes of straining, vaporizing, aeration, etc., the polluted waters are by Tishtar brought back distilled and purified, and are re-discharged into the zenith-reservoir which perpetually supplies the gushing streams of source Ardvî Sûra [10] Into such a marvelously complete cosmical circulatory water system did the Iranic imagination develop the primitive headstream of Eden. [11]

7. *Bundahish*, ch. xiii., 3. The chapter on Seas.

8. Ibid., xx. 33. *Raṇha*, the original Avestan name of the world river, became corrupted into Araṇhâm Arang Aring and finally into Arg. Windischmann, *Zoroastrische Studien*, pp. 187, 189.

9. Ibid., xxi. 2. Henry Bowman, in his *Eighteen Hundred and Eighty-one, or the End of the Aeon* (St. Louis, Mo., 1884, p. 36), gives the following remarkable interpretation to the heaven-descending river: "The throne of God is the apex, culmination, directly over the pole's axis, and so in the center of the city, corresponding to the tree of life, which in the old creation was situated in the center of the garden, from which proceeds the ELECTRICAL CURRENT, the pure river of the water of life, clear as crystal.

10. This underworld is the long-misunderstood "cave" in which, in the Vedic myth, the demons try to imprison the stolen rain-cows, so that the earth may be cursed with drought.

11. Ibid., xx. 4. *Vendîdâd,* v. 16-19. More fully and graphically described in *Dâdistân-î Dînîk,* ch. xciii. The ancient idea seems yet to survive in modern folk-lore: "In der Geschichte von Ikirma und Chuseima (in den Erzählungen der 1001 Nächte) sitzen zwei Engel der eine in Gestalt eines Löwen, der andere in der eines Stieres vor einer Pforte, Wache haltend und Gott preisend. Die Pforte, welche nur der Engel Gabriel öffnen kann, führt zu einem von Rubingebirgen umflossenen Meere, der Quelle aller Wasser auf Erden; aus ihm schöpfen Engel die Gewässer der Welt bis zum Auferstehungstage." *Justi, Geschichte des alten Persiens*, 1879, p.80.

Salsabil (Arabic: سلسبيل) is a term referring to a spring or fountain in Paradise, mentioned in the Qur'an and in some hadiths. In the Qur'an, the word is used once and refers to a spring or fountain in Paradise (Janet). The only Quranic reference is in *Surah Al-Insan*.

وَيُسْقَوْنَ فِيهَا كَأْسًا كَانَ مِزَاجُهَا زَنجَبِ

"There is a fountain called Salsabiil" - *Qur'an, Surah 76 (Al-Insan),* *verses 17-18.*

Baburnama Collection of the National Museum New Delhi: Do you notice the mechanism of the miller's Persian wheel?

The verse may refer to an earlier verse regarding the drink given to those who enter heaven. *"Salsabil"* is usually, but not always, considered to be used as a proper noun, rather than a common noun, in this verse (that is, the capitalized name of a specific water source). The common noun is used in Hindustani (the lingua franca of Northern India and Pakistan) to mean "bright, clear, sweet water", and in Persian for a pleasant drink. A *Sebil* or *Sabil* (Arabic: سبيل, romanized: *sabīl;* Turkish: *sebil*) is a small kiosk in the Islamic architectural tradition where water is freely supplied to members of the public. The four rivers like those described in *Genesis* can be found in hadiths. A hadith from the **Prophet Muhammad** reports that four rivers flow out of heaven: *Euphrates, Nile, Sayhān and Jayhān*; **Hosseinizadeh** emphasizes that the last two are not necessarily *Sayhun* (Sir Darya) and *Jayhun* (Amu Darya). The hadith narrated by **Ibn Abbas Tigris** also includes the rivers of Paradise, the *Sayhun* identified as Hinds and the *Jayhun* river as *Balkh*. In the hadith **Mi'raj Muhammad** testifies that four rivers of water, milk, wine and honey flow from the base of the *Sidrat al-Muntaha* tree. [12] But never, even in the most extravagant mythological embellishments of the idea, was it for a moment forgotten that the original undivided stream originated in the northern polar sky; and that its division above all into four earthly streams and rivers is on the sacred mountain which stands in the center of the Kvanîras, the central and circular keshvar (continent) of the whole habitable earth. [13]

12. Hosseinizadeh, Abdol Majid (15 December 2012). "The Four Rivers of Eden in Judaism and Islam". Al-Bayan: Journal of Qur'an and Hadith Studies. 10 (2): 33–47

13. Спореди со Spiegel, Erdnische Alterthumskunde. Leipsic, 1871; vol. i., p. 198-202.

But never, even in the most extravagant mythological adornments of the idea, was it for a moment forgot ten that the original undivided stream originates in the north polar sky; and that its division into earthly streams and rivers is on the holy mount which stands in the center of Kvanîras, the central and circumpolar keshvare of the whole habitable earth. [14] The various fragmentary allusions of the oldest Greek poets to *Okeanos* and the rivers would seem to imply the early existence, and perhaps early loss, of a similar Hellenic conception of the water circulation of the entire earth. Thus, according to **Homer's** familiar couplet, it is from *Okeanos*, in some application of the term, that "all rivers and every sea and all fountains flow." [15] *Euripides (Εὐριπίδης, c. 480 – c. 406 BC))* presents the same idea. [16] There is, therefore, one fountain of all the world s waters. The same conception is expressed by *Hesiod (Ἡσίοδος 750 and 650 BC)* in his *Theogony*, where all rivers, as sons, and all fountains and brooks, as daughters, are traced back to *Okeanos*. Then we have a constant descending movement of all waters until they reach the world-surrounding Ocean-river at the equator, beyond which is the Underworld. From this equatorial ocean, parting off from the southern or under the shore, new branches diverge and form the river system of the Hadean kingdom. Other Underworld rivers were perhaps conceived of as percolating through the earth and emerging to the surface in the lower hemisphere. There is at least some evidence that the Greeks, like the Persians, had this idea of inter-terranean water courses, and even rivers, resembling the circulation of the blood in the human body. [17] Sometimes these Under world rivers are represented as four in number, thus making the circumpolar water system of the Underworld a perfect counterpart of the Eden rivers at the summit of the upper hemisphere. [18]

14. Compare Spiegel, *Eränische Alterthumskunde*. Leipsic, 1871; vol. i., pp. 198-202.

15. *Iliad,* xxi. 195.

16. *Hippolytus*, 119.

17. *Bundahish,* viii. 4.

18. "Un der Unterwelt gab es ausser dem Styx noch drei Flüsse. Die Vierzahl entspricht derjenigen der vier Paradiesflüsse." - Wolf gang Menzel, *Die vorchristliche Unsterblichkeitslehre*, vol. ii., p. 6.

All, moreover, like those of the Persian Underworld, seem to be plunging forward and ever downward, until in the last glimpse which the imagination can catch they are seen streaming from the roof of the grot of the goddess Styx, and, as *Preller* expresses it *"falling thence, beneath the Earth, downward into the deep, deep Night."* [19] Here, then, we have a unitary water system, embracing the whole earth, and the remarkable Homeric and Hesiodic term, *ἀψόρροος* "refluent" may well imply that the

Underworld προχοη, or "outflow" [20] returns in nature's perfect order to feed its original fountain, thus conforming the whole, in every part, to the sacred hydrography of the Persians. [21] Granting this, one should locate the *Okeanos* fountain, not where **Preller** and **Welcker** and **Völcker** and the other mythographers have hitherto placed it, but in the farthest North, and in the sky. That this location was the original one is plain from all the local implications of the mythological accounts of the proper home of *Okeanos* and *Tethys*, and is further confirmed by many incidental pieces of evidence connected with such myths as those of the Eridanus, [22] the Achelous, the birth of Zeus, and particularly those of Atlas and his children. [23]

19. Preller, *Griechische Mythologie,* i. 29. Plato, in his cosmical sketch in Phaedo, makes the Hadean rivers pour into Tartaros.

20. Odyssey, xx. 65.

21. "Fountful Ida" corresponds almost perfectly to the Iranian Hûgar, down whose sides leap and flow the waters of Ardvî Sûra. Moreover, in its very name Lenormant and others see a root connect ing it with Ilavrita, the circumpolar paradisaic varsha of Puranic geography. It should be added that to Ilävrita corresponds significantly the Norse Idavöllr, or "plain of Ida" which is "in the middle of the divine abode." Mallet, *Northern Antiquities*, p. 409.

22. "Der Eridanus ist *ursprünglich* ein mythischer Fluss." Ideler, *Ursprung der Starnennamen*, p. 229. See especially Robert Brown, Jr. *Eridanus*. London, 1883.

23. Compare the like conclusion of Grill, *Die Erzväter der Menschheit*. Leipsic, 1875: pp. 222, 223. Grill also claims that the ancient Germans had a similar world-river, p. 223. I cannot help think ing that in the descending Ukko's stream and in the ascending Ämmä's stream of Finnish mythology we have traces of a like cosmic water circulation. See Castrén, *Mythologie,* p. 45. After reading the long note in *Buxtorfii, Lexicon Chaldaicum, Talmudicum et Rabbinicum,* Lipsiae, 1865, pp. 341, 342, one could also readily believe that we have here the true origin of the two movements or paths set forth in the omnifluent philosophy of Heraclitus: τήν όδόν, κάτω u τήν όδόν άvω. Again, "In the Edda all rivers derive their origin from that called *Ilver gelmer.*" *Asiatic Researches,* vol. viii., p. 321.

In the most ancient Akkadian, Assyrian, and Babylonian literature there are expressions that seem clearly to indicate the presence among these peoples of a precisely similar conception with respect to the waters of the world. [24] The same is true of Egyptian literature, but in both these cases, the data are as yet too meager to make them entirely conclusive in the argument. [25] We therefore pass them by, and close with a glance at the Eden river of the ancient Aryans of India. This, as already seen, is the heaven-born *Ganga*. The Vedas call it ***"the river of the three worlds"*** for the reason that it flows through Heaven and Earth and the Underworld. In Vedic times" the original source and home of the waters were thought to - be the highest heaven *(paramam vyoman)* the region peculiarly sacred to Varuna." [26]

24. Attention is only called to the ancient Akkadian hymn given by George Smith, *Assyrian Discoveries*, pp. 392, 393; to the exceedingly interesting article by Professor Sayce on *"The Encircling River of the Snake-God of the Tree of Life"* in The Academy, London, Oct. 7, 1882, p. 263; and finally to the instructive account of the Akkadian "mother of rivers" given in Lenormant's *Origines*, ii. i, p. 133, a citation from which has already been made on p. 171. See also Robert Brown, *The Myth of Kirké*, p. 110

25. "Die Aegypter wussten schon friihe von einem die Erde umfliessenden Strom." Grill, *Die Erzväter der Menschheit*, i., p. 277.

26. E. D. Perry, *Journal of the American Oriental Society*, 1882, p. 134. He adds in a foot-note, "In the Veda, water and all corre sponding terms, such as stream, river, torrent, ocean, etc., are used indiscriminately of the water upon the earth and of the aqueous vapor in the sky or of the rain in the air", Compare M. Bergaigne: "L'eau des riviéres terrestres est reconnue identique par sa nature et son origine á celle des riviéres célestes" etc., etc. *La Religion Védique*, tom, i., p. 256. See pp. 251-261.

This is clearly illustrated in scores of passages: for example, in the beautiful prayer for immortality, where the fourfold [27] head-spring of all waters is located in the sacred *Centre of Heaven*. [28] Sometimes the heaven-sprung stream is called the *Sindhu*, [29] sometimes the *Sarasvati*. [30] In the later ***Mahabharata*** its head-spring is placed in the heaven of Vishnu, high above the lofty Pole-star (Druva). On their descent, the ethereal waters wash the Pole-star, and the Seven Rishis (the Great Bear), and the polar pivot of "the lunar orb", [31] thence falling upon the top of beautiful Meru. ***"On the summit of Meru"*** says the ***Vishnu Purana***, is the vast city of Brahma, . . . inclosed by the river *Ganga*, which, issuing from the foot of Vishnu and washing the lunar orb, falls here [on the top of Meru] from the skies, and, after encircling the city, **[32]** divides into four mighty rivers, flowing in opposite directions. These rivers are *Sítá*, the *Alakanandá*, the *Chakshu*, and the *Bhadrá*. The first, falling on the tops of the inferior mountains on the east side of Meru, flows over their crests, and passes through the country of *Bhadraswa to* the ocean.

JAMBU DVIPA.

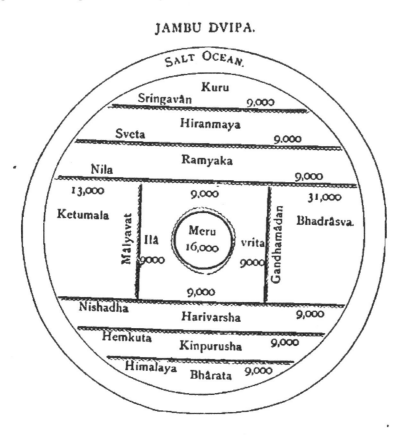

27. *Rig Veda,* ix. 74, 6.

28. *Rig Veda,* ix. 113,

29. Grassmann translates it:

> *"Wo Konig ist Vivasvats Sohn,*
> *Und wo des Himmels Heiligthum,*
> *Wo ewig stromt des Wassers Born,*
> *Da mache du unsterblich mich. "*

See the "Hymns to the Waters" generally, and particularly that ad dressed to *Apãm Napãt*, the "Navel of the Waters" R. V., ii. 35, comparing therewith the invocations to the "Navel of the Waters" in the Yashts. Darmesteter, *Zend-Avesta*, ii. 6 n., 12, 14, 20, 36, 38, 39, 71, 94, 102, 202. Windischmann, *Zoroastrische Studien*, pp. 177-186.

30. "Der vedische Inder redet von dem Sindhu κατ εξοχην, dem Einen himmlischen Strom oder Weltstrom, in dem er die Gesammtheit der atmosphärischen Dünste und Wasser als in Bewegung begriffener und die Erde rings umfliessender sich zur Anschauung bringt." Grill, *Die Erzväter der Menschheit*, Th. i., p. 197.

31. See the Vedic passages in Bergaigne, *La Religion Védique*, tom.i., pp. 325-328. Wilkins, *Hindu Mythology*. London, 1882: p. 102. In Indian cosmology the lunar sphere is concentric with and includes the earth sphere; hence water falling perpendicularly from the celestial to the terrestrial pole can yet on its way "wash the lunar sphere. So too a mountain at the North Pole, if only high enough, will reach to the "lunar sphere." Such, in fact, was the case with the Paradise mountain of Indian cosmology, and traces of the idea live on in the Talmud and in Patristic theology too plain for even Massey to render valueless: "Meru is shown to be the mount which reached to the moon and became a figure of the four lunar quarters. Hence the tradition that Paradise was preserved during, or was exempt from, the Deluge because it was on the summit of a mountain that reached to the moon (Bereshith Rabba, xxxiii.); which shows the continuation of the typical mount of the seven stars into the lunar phase of timekeeping, where the mount of the four quarters carried Eden with it." *The Natural Genesis* vol. ii., p. 244.

The *Alakanandá* flows south to the country of *Bharata*, and, dividing into seven rivers on the way, falls into the sea. The *Chakshu* falls into the sea after traversing all the western mountains and passing through *Ketumalá*. And the *Bhadrá* washes the country of the *Uttarakurus* and empties itself into the northern ocean." [33]

32. Here is probably the origin of the curious notion of the Sabaeans touching the Euphrates. Or was the borrowing on the other side? "Les Soubbas ont la certitude que l'Euphrate, qui, d'aprés eux, prend sa source sous le trône d'Avather (personnage qui préside au jugement des ames et dont le trône est placé sous l'étoile polaire), passait autrefois a Jerusalem." M.N. Siouffi, La Religion des Soubbas ou Sabéens. Paris, 1880: p. 7, note. Jehovah's city here takes the place of Brahma's.

33. The *Vishnu Purana*, Wilson s version, vol. vii., p. 120. Compare herewith the notions of the Chinese Buddhists: "With reference to this land of Jambu-dwîpa [the earth], the Buddhists say that in the midst of it is a center (heart), called the lake *A-nieou-to* (Anavataptu); it lies to the south of the Fragrant Mountains, and to the north of the great Snowy Mountains (Himavat). It is 800 li in circuit. In the midst of this lake is the abode of a Naga, who is in fact the transformed appearance of Dasabhumi Bodhisatwa (or of the Bodhisatwas of the ten earths). From his abode proceed four refreshing rivers, which compass Jambu-dwîpa. At the east side of the lake, from the mouth of a silver ox, flows out the Ganges River. After compassing the lake once it enters the sea towards the southeast. From the south side of the lake, from the mouth of a golden elephant, flows the Sindhu [Indus] River. After compassing the lake once it enters the sea on the southwest. On the west side of the lake, flowing from the mouth of a horse of lapis-lazuli, flows the river Foh-tzu (Vakshu, i. e., Oxus), which, after compassing the lake once, enters the sea on the northwest. On the north side of the lake, flowing from a crystal lion, flows the river Sida [Hoang-ho], which after making one circuit flows into the sea on the northeast." Beal, *Buddhist Literature in China.* 1882: p. 149.

Here, again, as our interpretation of *Genesis* requires, the four rivers traced back to their origin bring us to the summit of the earth at the Pole, to the one river which descends from the north polar sky. Curious confirmations of this primitive conception come even from the most distant continents. [34] Late Christian legend shows evident traces of it, for in *Maundeville's* description of the Paradise fountain he says, *"All the sweet waters of the world above and beneath take their beginning from that well of Paradise"* and again, "Out of that well all waters come and go" giving thus clear expression to the idea of unitary cosmic water circulation. [35]

So, again, in the apocryphal *"Revelation of the Holy Apostle Paul"* the angel who was showing the apostle the wonders of the heavenly city brought him to just such a World-river, whose spring was in heaven, but whose main body surrounded the earth. And he set me upon the river whose source springs up in the circle of heaven, and it is this river which encircled the whole earth. And he says unto me: *"This river is Ocean."* [36]

34. Thus in Africa, among the Damaras, "the highest deity is Omakuru, the Rain-giver, who dwells in the far North." E. B. Tylor, *Primitive Culture*, Am. ed., vol. ii., p. 259. So also, in America: "Die alten Mexikaner glaubten, das Paradies liege auf dem hochsten Berge, wo die Wolken sich versammeln, von wo sie Regen bringen, und von wo auch die Flüsse herabkommen." Lüken, *Traditionen*, i., p. 115. And this Paradise-mountain was in the farthest North. See the pathetic prayer to Tlaloc in Bancroft, *Native Races*, vol. iii., pp. 325-330.

35. Erlangen, 1871: p. 6l:

        "Vor dem sale stûnt ein brunne;

ûz dem vlôz milch und wîn
waz mohte wunderlicher sîn.;
ouch olei und honicseim darûz vlôz
daz an vier enden sich ergôz"

The editor (p. 105) connects this last line with the quadripartite river of Paradise, and the lines immediately following give it an un equivocally cosmical significance:

"Von dem selben brunnen,
haben die wurze saf gewunnen,
die got liez gewerden ie".

36. The Apocryphal Gospels, Acts and Revelations. Ante-Nicene Christian Library, vol. xvi., p. 483.

The Four Trees of the Cardinal Directions and the Four Rivers in *Codex Fejervary-Mayer*. Aztec Codex of central Mexico. It is currently kept in the World Museum Liverpool in Liverpool, England, having as its catalogue # 12014 M

Also in the highlands of Guatemala there is an extraordinarily beautiful body of water - Lake Atitlán. Many thought it could qualify as the center of the cosmos, and the Mayans who live there believe this to be true to this day. *Karen Bassie-Sweet*, of the University of Calgary, suggests that Lake Atitlan was the center of the four rivers that flowed to the cardinal directions and would represent the rivers or rivers/roads that radiated from a central point at the time of creation. These rivers were the *Samalá, Grijalva, Motagua,* and the *Chixoy* river, which the Maya also considered routes for their merchants who traveled by boat. [36]

11. Karen Bassie-Sweet, Maya Sacred Geography and the Creator Gods (Norman: University of Oklahoma Press) 2008: 239.

But in fact, this template model of the *Sacral Geograpy* originally originates, as we have seen, right from the *Heaven on Earth* - Arctic region.

• *Teologia*

Some have placed Paradise in the third heaven, some in the fourth, in the heavens near the moon, on the moon itself, on a mountain near the lunar sky, in the midst of the air, outside the earth, on the earth, under the earth, in a place which is hidden and separate from man. It was placed under the North Pole, in Tartarus, or in the place now occupied by the Caspian Sea. Others placed it in the extreme south, in the land of fire; others in the Levant, or on the banks of the Ganges, or in the island of Ceylon. It is set in China, or in an inaccessible region along the Black Sea; by others in America, in Africa, etc. - Bishop Huet.

Namely, symbolically speaking, the message of Christian teaching flows into the believer through the four heavenly rivers, from the four corners of the world, through the four evangelists, that is, the four gospels of the *New Testament*. Filled with sensory experience, the man was encouraged to turn sense impressions into contemplation, and inner knowledge, and therefore material images, which directly affect all the senses, were believed to literally lead the observer to the invisible and unknowable God. With the relationship between image and word, seeing and reading, representation and reality, we arrive at the original principle of interpretation of what we call the eikon/imago or image, which operates in Christian visual culture from the early Christian period onward. [1] Being mystical, the theme of heaven lies at the core of Christian teaching. It was often presented visually, and from the early Christian period it was placed in the very foundations as an axial determinant of the overall Christian visual culture. It seems that only in recent decades, researchers have developed a greater interest in different types of visualization on this topic, which, despite all the significant historiographical contributions, still remains an open question.

1. Id., Turning a Blind Eye: *Medieval Art and the Dynamics of Contemplation*, in: The mind's eye: art and theological argument in the Middle Ages, Princeton University Press 2006, 413-439; R. M. Jensen, Living Water: *Images, Symbols, and Setting of Early Christian Baptism*, Leiden: Brill 2011. See more. P. Brown, *Image as a Substitute for Writing*, 15-34; E. Bevan, *Holy Images, Allen and Unwin* 1940, 13-19; T. Lanfer, Allusion to and Expansion of the Tree of Life and Garden of Eden in Biblical and Pseudepigraphical Literature, in: *Early Christian Literature and Intertextuality*, Vol.1, ed. C. A. Evans, D. Zacharias, London 2009, 97.

In the ***Book of the Prophet Isaiah (51,3)*** we read: ***"The LORD will surely comfort Zion and will look with compassion on all her ruins; he will make her deserts like Eden, her wastelands like the garden of the LORD. Joy and gladness will be found in her, thanksgiving and the sound of singing."*** Descriptions of the Garden of Eden can be found in the ***Book of the Prophet Ezekiel (28:12-16),*** who addresses the king of Tire as the so-called mythological fallen angel. This has led many exegetes to identify the *"Holy Mountain of God"* with the New Jerusalem or Temple, [2] a vision that is consistent with the idea of St. Ephrem the Syrian (ܡܪܝ ܐܦܪܝܡ ܣܘܪܝܝܐ, *Mor Afrêm Sûryāyâ*), who was a Syrian deacon and Christian theologian from the 4th century.

Another prophecy of Ezekiel *(Heb. 47:12 ,יְחֶזְקֵאל),* gives the exiled Jews in Babylon light, vision, and confidence in the restored temple from which the new river will flow "(...) because its water flows from the sanctuary;

therefore, their fruit shall be for food, and their herbs for medicine." In other words, the prophet Ezekiel used the iconography of the Garden of Eden from the book of *Genesis*, which describes the tree of life [3], which bears fruit in the midst of a watered garden that is abundant vegetation. [4] Therefore, we can conclude that a constituent element of the earthly paradise has existed since the 6th century BC. [5] Later, the image of the cosmic mountain in which Ezekiel places the Garden of Eden with precious stones will be used in the description of John's *"Apocalypse"* and Messianic Jerusalem. This New Jerusalem will shine like jasper and crystal, and the foundations will be decorated with "every precious stone: the first foundation is of jasper, the second of sapphire, the third of chalcedony, a fourth of emerald" *(Rev. 22, 11-33)*. From the heavenly throne of the "Lamb of God" will flow "the water of life clear as crystal" *(Rev. 22,1-2)*. Namely, the walled garden, water, rich vegetation, light, eternal spring, sweet and intoxicating smells and animals, in other words *hortus deliciarum*, according to **Isidore of Seville** *(lat. Isidorus Hispalensis, ca. 560 – 636),* who perfected and shaped it medieval thought, [6] became the standard and direct association of heaven, the Garden of Eden, and therefore heaven is an appropriate place where it would be high in the mountains or somewhere far away where the human race cannot live *(ante-mortem)*.

2. In Hebrew tradition, the "Mountain of God" is Sinai, but with the growing importance of Jerusalem, Mount Zion practically takes over its function and importance, Ps. 48: 1-2; E. Noort, *Gan-Eden in the Hebrew Bible*, 27.

3. In the prophecy of Ezekiel 31, the Tree of Life, whose beauty surpasses the other envied cedar trees, is compared to Egypt, "comprising all the three regions of the world, as an *imago mundi* to represent the world as a whole in all his majesty." The tree, as well as Egypt, are fed by water that springs from the depths of the earth, gives shelter; E. Noort, *Gan-Eden in the Hebrew Bible*, 34.

4. S. S. Tuell, *The Rivers of Paradise*: Ezekiel 47: 1-12 and Genesis 2: 10-14, 171-189.

5. J. Delumeau, *History of Paradise*, 44.

6. Ibis. 44

"The image of the heavenly mountain reaching the heavenly heights suggests the continuity of Eden's existence on earth as a separate and alternative reality that exists despite God's punishment of humanity, expulsion from paradise and the flood." [7]

A depiction of the four heavenly rivers. From a twelfth-century book in the monastery of Zwiefalten, Germany. Stuttgart WLB Libellus capitulorum cod. brev. 128. Central medallion with the mystical Lamb of God (Agnus Dei)

Namely, if we rely on the comments of **Ephrem the Syrian** about the source of the four heavenly rivers *(potamos, ποταμος)* in the fountain located in the heart of the Garden of Eden, which has also been the subject of numerous discussions in history, we will see that the idea of self-sprouting arose in the heights, that is, in the mountains. Therefore, the rivers that flow through the mountain, enter the sea as an aqueduct and leave the land to find their way in the mentioned areas. [8] This view is found in **Philo of Alexandria** *(Φίλων ὁ Ἀλεξανδρεύς, lat. Philo Alexandrinus, also known as Philo Judaeus 20 BC - ca. 50 AD)* and **Hippolytus** *(Ἱππόλυτος)*. In other words, according to their interpretation, rivers are located underground from where they spring and branch out to the four corners of the world. Probably for this reason, the exegetes of the same name preferred to identify the Geon and Phison rivers with the present-day Ganges and Nile rivers, rather than with the Danube. [9] The idea that rivers are underground is based on the study of the famous Tigris and Euphrates rivers.

7. A. Scafi, *Mapping Paradise, 50.*

8. J. Delumeau, *History of Paradise,* 40; E. Noort, Gan-Eden in the *Hebrew Bible,* 27.

9. Loc.cit.

Terms used by John the Theologian in descriptions of the kingdom of heaven come from parts of the book of *Genesis (2-3),* the **Book of the prophet Ezekiel** (47) and **Zechariah** (14). Namely, the throne of God and the Lamb of God *(Agnus Dei)* are located in the heart of the city where the rivers of life flow. [10] They form a unity and a whole in the form of the temple of the *"Heavenly Jerusalem" (21:22).* The *"Tree of Life"* also found its place, located on both sides of the river *(22:2)* and bears twelve fruits a year, whose leaves help heal people. [11] Of course, the thread we follow through the *book of Genesis* and the vision of the prophet Ezekiel consists first of all of the image of a tree, which not only opens chapters

40 and 42, but also serves as an integral building material. Namely, in visual art we will see that the *"Tree of Life"* becomes an integral part of the image of the paradise settlement, and it is the connection between the Old and the New Testament, it is the beginning and the end. The tree connects Eden, Zion, and the temple along with the rivers of Paradise. [12] Namely, the water flowing from the Lord's throne irrigates the *"Tree of Life"*, through which the entire human race is nourished and healed. Together they form a whole that cannot be broken, much less seen separately. The blessed life enjoyed by the inhabitants of the *"Heavenly Jerusalem"* was created and "nourished" by God's action and providence and was made possible by Christ's sacrifice on the altar, as stated in the prophet *Ezekiel (47:1),* who emphasizes the nature of his sacrifice through death.

10. G. Macaskill, *Paradise in the New Testament*, 74-76; A. Scafi, *Epilogue*: a heaven on earth, passim. I. S. Gilhus, *Animals, Gods and Humans, Changing Attitudes to Animals in Greek, Roman and Early Christian Ideas*, London-New York 2006, 176-180.

11. For Christians, the "new" Tree of Life also represents the crucified Christ. see A. Scafi, Epilogue: a heaven on earth, 211; see later in the text for the *Tree of Life* chapter p. 161.

12. S. Tuell, *The Rivers of Paradise*: Ezekiel 47: 1-12 and Genesis 2: 10-14, 171-189, especially p. 175-176.

In the 6th century, ***Cosmas Indicopleustes*** (Κόσμας Ἰνδικοπλεύστης) of Alexandria in the ***"Christian Topography"*** (Χριστιανικὴ Τοπογραφία) [13] presented the idea that the Tabernacle of the Covenant that God showed Moses on Mount Sinai was actually the image of the world. Based on the preserved illuminated manuscripts of the ***"Christian Topography"*** from the 9th century, it can be seen that the world is represented in the form of a quadrangle with clearly marked heavenly rivers that water and the ocean that surrounds the human part of ecumenism.

Further east, there is heaven. It is presented in the far-right corner of the full-page thumbnail, in a rectangular section on a white background with a row of trees, grass with flowers and four rivers of paradise. So, the rivers flow from the Garden of Eden, flow under the ocean, and rise again in the inhabited world. Namely, after the original sin, according to Cosmas

Indicopolus, Adam and his descendants still lived in paradise, but outside the gates of the garden of paradise, which were sealed for them and on which the cherub stood as a guard at the entrance to the garden of God. The place where Adam found himself was hard to cultivate, desolate and inhabited by wild animals. The first generations of mankind lived there until the flood. It took Noah and his saved descendants one hundred and fifty days to cross the ocean from that place and reach the land where they would settle, the land of today's man. ***Cosmas Indicopleustes*** continues his comments and says: ***"Since then it is impossible to cross the ocean, just as it is impossible to ascend to the sky while we are mortal."***

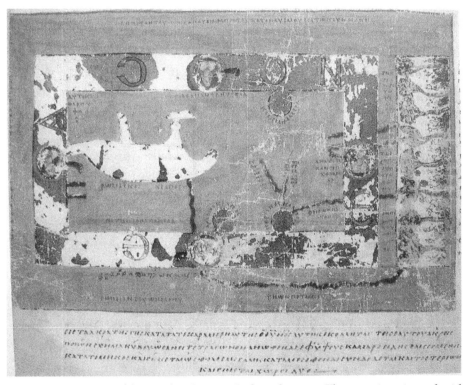

CΟKEANOC, *World map, by Cosmas Indicopleustes. The map is oriented with north to the top. 6th century - "Les Sciences au Moyen-Age","Pour la Science"*

13. Maguire, Paradise Withdrawn, 24. According to new research, a manuscript now heard in the Vatican (Biblioteca Apostolica) is attributed to Constantine of Antioch, see H. L. Kessler, Gazing at the Future: The Parousia Miniature in Vatican gr. 699, in: Byzantine East, Latine West: Art Historical Studies in Honor of Kurt Weitzmann, Princeton 1995, 365; H. L. Kessler, *The Codex Barbarus Scaligeri,* the *Christian*

Topography, and the *Question of Jewish Models of Early Christian Art, in: In Between Judaism and Christianity.* Pictorials Playing on Mutual Grounds: Essays in Honor of Prof. Elisabeth (Elisheva) Revel-Neher, Leiden: Brill 2008, 139-40, for the idea of paradise see p. 141; H. G. Saradi, Space in Byzantium, in: Architecture as Icon, Perception and Representation of Architecture in the Byzantine World, ed. S. Ćurčić, E. Hadjitryphonos, Princeton University Art Museum, Yale University Press, New Haven, London 2010, 89-90. Kozma Indikoplov, an educated and learned merchant, with a deep knowledge of Greek, Latin and Eastern culture and language, designed and developed cosmological systems related to Christology, covering both physical and spiritual space. This is a metaphysical dimension, because the world / universe is divided into two worlds: visible (terrestrial) and invisible (spiritual, eternal, heavenly), and rests on a tabernacle, see W. Wolske, *La Topographie Chrétienne de Cosmas Indicopleustés, Theologie et Science au VIesiècle,* Presses Universitaires de France 1962.

The Coptic Apocalypse presents *Paul* as described in the **Second Epistle to the Corinthians** *(12:1-4),* where he ascends to the third heaven. While climbing he encounters various scenes, e.g. in the fourth heaven he sees the soul being punished, in the sixth heaven he meets the tax collector (a common name for the watchman figure), but Paul only asks for permission to enter. In the seventh heaven he meets the old man Dan, who asks him where he went and where he came from (very similar to the conversation about the soul in the Gospel according to Mary). The spirit encourages him and shows the Elder the sign he wears. In chapter 45, the angel shows him the four rivers of Paradise: *Phison* in Havilland, *Geon* in Egypt and Ethiopia, *Tigris* in Assyria and *Euphrates* in Mesopotamia, and when he entered the Garden of Eden he saw a tree (the Tree of Knowledge of Good and Evil) from which roots flow these rivers. The Holy Spirit rested on that tree and moved the rivers with his breath. And then he saw the *"Tree of Life"* in the middle of Eden. For *Paul,* the city of God is the *"Heavenly Jerusalem"* and is located in the mystical regions beyond the river Ocean *(Okeanos);* the city is heavenly in character, but is on earth. [14]

14. For example, the discussion see A. Golitzin, *Earthly Angels and Heavenly Men: the Old Testament Pseudoepigraphia,* Niketas Stethatos, and *the Tradition of "Interiorized Apocalyptic" in: Eastern Christian Ascetical and Mystical Literature,* DOP LV 2001, 125-131; H. Maguire, *Paradise Withdrawn,* 27-31.

In the Hebrew, **Old Testament** culture, Jerusalem (Mount Moriah to be more precise) represented the *umbiculus mundi* and the axial Tree was a picture of the kingdom *(Dan. 4:10-14; Ezek. 17:22-24).* [15] The link connecting the *Tree of Life* to the center of the world can be seen in *Psalms (1:3),* and on Judgment Day it will be in the middle of the garden (earth / heaven) on the right side of the new temple, in near the life-giving rivers, as described in *Ezekiel (47: 1, 12).* Thus, the Hebrew alphabet and legend unite the Near Eastern myth of the cosmic tree with the messianic hope of a return to heaven. These ideas were expressed by the writer of the *Apocalypse* in the culminating vision of the *Heavenly Jerusalem,* where the *Tree of Life* is located by the river that flows from the throne of the *"Lamb of God" (Rev. 22:1-2).* Examples of art accompanying the literary pattern can be seen in several churches from 12th- and 13th-century in and around Rome, which are painted in the manner of early Christian sacred church painting.

15. *Jews and Muslims*, c. *Psalms 1:3, Ezek. 47: 12.* O Jerusalem and the tree of life c. J. Erdeljan, PhD Dissertation; id., Studenica. All Things Constantinopolitan, 95-97; id., Selected Places. *Construction of New Jerusalem code of Orthodox Slavs*, Belgrade 2013.

One of the most significant examples of the *Tree of Life* is the apsidal space of the Church of San Clemente in Rome, reconstructed in the 12th century on the basis of a probably 5th or 6th century template, indicating an assimilation of the Middle Eastern image of the *Tree of Life.* [16] Stylized acanthus, which spreads through the earthly and heavenly space of the apse in the form of a vine, carries in its center the image of the crucified Christ, under whose feet four rivers of paradise flow with deer which, like the souls of the *dead (Ps. 42:1),* they feed on water. Namely, the sacramental symbolism of baptism represented by water at the base of the cross (tree) took the form of four heavenly rivers flowing from Eden. Under the whole composition is the *Lamb of God.* Namely, at a certain historical moment, the *Heavenly Jerusalem* with Golgotha in the middle and the crucified Christ emerged in the form of one image, and the eternal cosmological tree of life that comes out of Eden and reaches its eternal glory in the sky of the New Jerusalem testifies to that. When it comes to the liturgical context, it is important to emphasize that here are presented the fruits of the tree, which are always available to the faithful, during the act of the Eucharist, which is happening right under the mosaic representation, under the altar space. This example not only testifies to the importance and iconography of the image of paradise, represented by the image of the *"Tree of Life"*, but also indicates the important correspondence and relationship between the architectural solution and the symbolism of the building, as well as its mosaic, decoration. On the other hand, the complex role of architecture and architectural models in the iconography of the paradise settlement, and especially the scenes related to the baptism, developed separately from the scenes and images related to the *"Tree of Life",* although numerous Eastern Christian representations of sources of life *(fons vitae)* they still bear the distinctive image of two smaller trees bordered by trees commonly associated with *lignum vitae*. The *"Tree of Life"* can often be seen represented in the classical Middle Eastern tradition when it is symmetrically surrounded by birds and animals. In this case, which we can safely say is the most common, the sacred nature of the fruit as water flows, beyond a tree-trunk showing that the whole scene takes place in a paradise settlement. In such scenes, it is important to note the liturgical meaning, context and function of the artistic solutions that are in service and constitute an integral part of the iconography of the early Christian period.

John Chrysostom (Ιωάννης ὁ Χρυσόστομος, Jovan Zlatoust, c. 347 – 14 September 407) and *Theodore of Mopsuestia (Θεόδωρος Μοψουεστίας, c. 350 – 428)* are members of the group of early exegetes who advocated a literal interpretation, i.e. reading the Holy Scriptures, which implies that heaven is on earth, while *John Chrysostom* went so far as to he cursed all who were not adherents of this idea. [17] According to him, Moses was inspired by the Holy Spirit when he wrote the *Pentateuch*, and God did create a place of eternal bliss in the east. [18], We have previously given a logical explanation of how confusion arises in the establishment of Paradise in the East. *Epiphanius of Salamis (Ἐπιφάνιος)* in the 4th century is perhaps the most famous opponent of the allegorical interpretation of Scripture since in 394 he sent a letter to *Bishop John of Jerusalem* pointing out the doctrinal errors attributed to Origen. According to him, Adam and Eve existed and were expelled from heaven after sin, but not "from heaven to earth", but lived east of Eden because the cherubim guarded its gates in the east. The rivers of Eden flow from Eden and do not descend because, as *Epiphanius of Salamis* adds, *"rivers could not fall from heaven because the earth would not withstand such a blow." St. Augustine* (Aurelius Augustinus 354 -430 A.D.) clearly indicates in his writings that he accepts both the allegorical and the literal existence of paradise, which led to a clear distinction between the physical paradise of Adam and the heavenly paradise belonging to the saints.

16. P. Allen, W. Mayer, John Chrysostom, in: The Early Christian World, 1128-1150; Documents on Early Christian Thought, M. Wiles, M. Santer, Cambridge University Press 1975, 120-122, 251-257.

17. A. Scafi, Mapping Paradise, 39-40.

18. A. Scafi, Epilogue: a heaven on earth, in: Paradise in Antiquity, cmp 212.

Theologians, Christian and Jewish, have in all ages differed, and irreconcilably differed, as to the location of the cradle of the human race. The evidence of this are so well known, or so easily accessible to every intelligent reader, that they need not be adduced in this place. [19] The fathers and theologians of the Early Church and of the Middle Ages held many curious and conflicting opinions upon the subject. Some, following the allegorizing method of *Philo*, interpreted the whole narrative in *Genesis* as a parable setting forth spiritual things. Eden was not a place, but a state of spiritual blessedness. The four rivers were not rivers, but the four cardinal virtues, etc. The majority, however, held to the historic character of the narrative, and to the strictly geographical reality of Eden. To the question of its location, numberless were the answers. Often it was in the far East, beyond all lands inhabited by men. Sometimes it was thought of as perhaps within, or under, the earth, in the regions of the dead. Sometimes it was neither on nor below the earth, but high above it, in the third heaven, or some way associated with the lunar orbit. Again, it would be stated that there are two paradises, a celestial and a terrestrial one, the one in heaven, the other on the earth. *Tertullian (Quintus Septimius Florens Tertullianus; c. 155 AD – c. 220 AD)*, conceiving of the torrid zone as the flaming sword, which turned every way to keep the way of the tree of life *(Gen. iii. 24)*, placed Eden beyond it, in the southern hemisphere. Now it was at the bottom of the sea; [20] or again it held a position mid-way between earth and heaven. *Anon*, it was on the summit of a miraculous mountain, which rose to the height of the moon. Of this mountain only the base was washed, when by the waters of the Deluge all other mountains were covered. It was conceived of as rising in three gigantic stages to its stupendous height. All kinds of marvelous plants and precious metals and gems adorned it, but its supreme adornment was a divine river, which, starting from the *Throne of God* in the highest heaven, descended to the holy garden on the mountain s head, and thence parting into four, after watering and beautifying the whole mountain in its descent, gradually lost more and more of its celestial taste and vivifying virtues, and became the water system of the habitable globe.

19. See McClintock and Strong, *Cyclopedia of Biblical, Theological, and Ecclesiastical Literature*, Arts. "Eden" and "Paradise."

20. "In some legends Eden was submerged by the earliest deluge that covered the Mount. The happy garden was believed to be lying at the bottom of Lake Van, in Armenia." Gerald Massey, *The Natural Genesis,* vol. ii., p. 231

Sometimes the location of this mountain was described as in some distant portion of the earth, "where the sea, or earth, and the sky meet." Impatient of such contradictions, **Luther**, in his own brusque way, rejected all attempts to locate the primeval garden, declaring that the Deluge had so changed the face of the earth and the course of its original rivers that all search was fruitless. **Calvin**, on the contrary, confidently affirmed that the writer of the *Genesis* narrative must be understood as locating the Garden of Eden near the mouths of the Euphrates. Soon this original diversity of Protestant teaching upon the subject became aggravated by new theories, some of them suggested by orthodox ingenuity, some introduced by rationalistic conceptions of the semi-mythical character of the Bible, until at the present time the state of the ontological teaching respecting Eden is, if possible, a worse Babel than in any preceding age. For a partial illustration of the confusion, one has only to turn to the most recent and authoritative biblical, theological, and religious encyclopedias. In **McClintock and Strong's**, the writer on Eden inclines to locate it in Armenia. In **Smith's "Bible Dictionary"** the problem is abandoned as probably insoluble. In the **Great German Encyclopaedia** of **Herzog** it is declared necessary to deny to the story of Eden a strictly historical character; it is *"a bit of mythical geography."* In the supplement, however, **Pressel** makes an elaborate argument of many pages in favor of the location at the junction of the Tigris and Euphrates. ***Dillmann***, in Schenkel's ***"Bibel - Lexicon"*** places it in the Himalayas, north of India. In the chief Roman Catholic ***Cyclopaedia***, ***Wetzel*** and ***Welte's "Kirchen – Lexicon"*** the writer vacillates between Eastern Asia, taken in a vague and undefined sense, and an equally undefined North. In ***Lichtenberg's "Encyclopédic des Sciences Religieuses"*** the whole story in *Genesis ii.* is declared a "philosophic myth." ***Professor Brown***, of New York, in his work edited by ***Dr. Schaff,*** on the basis of ***Herzog***, enumerates a variety of opinions advocated by others but refrains from expressing any opinion of his own. Such is all the light which contemporary theology seems able to throw upon our problem. But here some plain reader of the Bible opens at the second chapter of *Genesis*, and reads, ***"And the Lord God planted a garden eastward in Eden, and there he put the man whom he had formed."*** And the plain reader asks how a believer in the Bible can doubt that this passage fixes the location of the garden somewhere to the East of Palestine. But, looking a little more critically, our inquirer himself quickly sees that the verse does not necessarily affirm anything as to the direction of the garden from the writer. It may naturally mean that the garden was planted in the eastern part of the land of Eden, wherever that was; and turning to the most careful and orthodox commentators, he finds that not a few take this view of it. Moreover, *Miqqedem* here translated "eastward" may be otherwise translated, as it is in ***King James's Version*** (modern KJV Bible), in the passages *Ps. lxxiv. 12, lxxvii. 6,* and elsewhere. In fact, in the ***Vulgate*** (Latin Bible) it is here translated, *principio*, ***"in or from the beginning."*** Among the early Greek translators, ***Symmachus***, ***Theodotion***, and ***Aquila*** understand the term in the same way. Hence, nearly two hundred years ago, the learned ***Thomas Burnet*** wrote as follows: ***"Some have thought that the word Miqqedem, Gen. ii. 8, was to be rendered in the East, or Eastward, as we read it, and therefore determined the site of Paradise; but t is only the Septuagint translate it so; all the other Greek versions, and St. Jerome, the Vulgate, the Chaldee Paraphrase, and the Syriak, render it from the beginning, or in the beginning, or to that effect. And we that do not believe the Septuagint to have been infallible or inspired have no reason to prefer their single authority above all the rest."*** [21] The same writer says again, ***"We may safely say that none of the Christian Fathers, Latin or Greek, ever placed Paradise in***

Mesopotamia; that is a conceit and innovation of some modern authors, which hath been much encouraged of late, because it gave more ease and rest as to further inquiries in an argument they could not well manage." [22] As to the new source of evidence opened by the decipherment of the Cuneiform inscriptions, **Lenormant** says, that in none of these, so far as yet deciphered, has anything been found indicating that the Chaldaeo-Babylonians believed that their country was the cradle of the human race. [23] *"But the four rivers"* says our inquirer, and he reads verses *10-14: "And a river went out of Eden to water the garden; and from thence it was parted and became into four heads. The name of the first is Pison. . . . And the name of the second river is Gihon. . . . And the name of the third river is Hiddekel, . . . and the fourth river is Euphrates."*

21. *Sacred Theory of the Earth.* London, 2d ed., 1691: p. 252.

22. Ibid., p. 253.

23. *Les Origines de l'Histoire.* Paris, 1882: tom. ii. I, p. 120.

"Surely here in the fourth river, we have one undeniable landmark. However impossible it may be satisfactorily to identify all four of the primitive rivers of Eden, the mention of the Euphrates at least restricts the location of the garden to some part of the region drained by that river." Consulting the theologians, however, our investigator finds a great variety of serious objections urged against this short and easy method of settling the controversy.

First, he is told that some Biblical critics have expressed doubt as to the genuineness of the verses and that as earnest a defender of the Bible as **Mr. Granville Penn** considered the whole passage an interpolation.

Secondly, he learns that *Perath* or *Phrath*, the Hebrew name of the river, is from the older form *Buratti* or *Purattu*, a word believed to signify "the broad" or "the deep." [24] Of course, such a descriptive term may well have been the name of more than one ancient river, just as "Broad Brook" is the name of many an American stream. Indeed, in his learned work *"Le Berceau de l'Espece Humaine"*, **Obry** shows that in ancient times *Phrat*, or Euphrates, was the name of one, or possibly two, of the rivers of Persia. [25]

24. Delitzsch, *Wo lag das Paradies?* p. 169. Grill, *Die Erzväter der Menschheit*, Bd. i., p. 230. In Old Persian it is Ufratu, "the fair flowing." F. Finzi, *Antichitá Assira*, Turin, 1872: p. 112.

25. See pp. 95, 136, 140.

One of these in **Pliny's** time still bore the name in the hardly changed form *Ophradus*. **Lenormant** says he does not hesitate to consider the *Phrath* of the **Khorda-Avesta** identical with the Persian river *Helmend*. [26] Africa also had its sacred Euphrates. [27] If therefore the passage in *Genesis* is genuine, and Moses wrote of the *Phrath*, it is not absolutely certain what "broad" or "abounding" river he had in mind. Moreover, in any case, the Euphrates of Mesopotamia is not one of four equal offshoots into which the one "river" proceeding "out of Eden" divided itself according to the statement of the text. Its source is not from another river at all, but from ordinary mountain springs.

Thirdly, it must not be forgotten, our friend is told, that all peoples coming into a new country love to name their new rivers and towns after the loved and sacred ones they have left in the elder home. The Thames of New England perpetuates the memory of the Thames of Old England. *"It is very seldom indeed"* says a late writer, *"that a river has no namesakes."* [28] Very possibly, therefore, the *Phrath* of Mesopotamia may have been named for some elder river of the antediluvian world, wherever that may have been. That it was so is the firm belief of various learned writers. [29]

26. Origines de l'Histoire, tom. ii. I, p. 99.

27. "Also there is a very sacred river in Hwida called the Euphrates or Eufrates." Gerald Massey, *The Natural Genesis*. London, 1883: vol. ii., p. 165.

28. "There is no improbability in supposing that there may have been in Britain two rivers named Trisanton. On the contrary, it is very seldom indeed that a river has no namesakes" Henry Bradley, in *The Academy,* April 28, 1883, p. 206.

29. See Grill, *Die Erzväter der Menschheit*, Bd. i., pp. 239, 242.

Fourthly, continue the theologians, the language of *Ezekiel xxviii. 13-19*, and of *Proverbs iii. 18; xi. 30*, etc., shows that poetic and symbolical applications of the name and images of Eden were common. And if the Hebrews named one of the water-courses at Jerusalem Gihon, in commemoration of one of the four Paradise rivers, [30] it is not irrational to suppose that the inhabitants of Mesopotamia may have called their chief stream in honor of another of the four. ***Lenormant, Grill, Obry***, and others support this view. They might have rendered the probability still stronger by calling attention to the fact that the oldest name of Babylon, *Tin-tir-ki*, was of the same commemorative or symbolical character, and signified ***"the place of the Tree of Life."*** [31] Finally, pursuing these curious investigations further, our plain reader finds mention in ***Pausanias***, *ii. 5, (Παυσανίας; c. 110 – c. 180)* of a strange belief of the ancients, according to which the Euphrates, after disappearing in a marsh and flowing a long distance underground, rises again beyond Ethiopia, and flows through Egypt as the Nile. This reminds him of the language of ***Josephus***, according to which the Ganges, the Tigris, the Euphrates, and the Nile are all but parts ***of "one river which ran round about the whole earth"*** the *Okeanos-river* of the Greeks. [32] And he wonders whether the old Semitic term from which the modern Euphrates is derived was not originally a name of the general water system of the world, a name of that Ocean-river which ***Aristotle*** describes as rising in the upper heavens, descending in rain upon the earth, feeding, as ***Homer*** tells us, all fountains and rivers and every sea, flowing through all these water courses down into the great and "broad" equatorial ocean-current which girdles the world in its embrace, thence branching out from the further shore into the rivers of the Underworld, to be at last fire-purged and sublimated, and returned in purity to the upper heavens to recommence its round. [33]

30. Ewald, *Geschichte des Volkes Israel*, 2d ed., Bd. Hi., pp. 321-328

31. Lenormant, Origines de l'Histoire, vol. i., p. 76. English version, p. 85. See also Rev. O. D. Miller, "The Symbolical Geography of the Ancients" in the *American Antiquarian and Oriental Journal,* Chicago, July, 1881.

32. Compare Rev. ix. 14.

33. Paradise Found: The Cradle of the Human Race at the North Pole, William Fairfield Warren, 1885 "The Quadrifurcate River." Part V., chapter 5.

And just as he is wondering over the question, he finds that some of the Assyriologists, in their investigation of pre-Babylonian Akkadian mythology, have found reason to believe this surmise correct, and to say that in that mythology the term Euphrates was applied to *"the rope of the world"*, *"the encircling river of the snake god of the tree of life"*, *"the heavenly river which surrounds the earth."* [34] Furthermore, as he turns back to the pages of **Hyginus** *(Gaius Julius Hyginus c. 64 BC-AD 17)*, and **Manilius** *(Marcus Manilius, fl. 1st century AD),* and **Lucius Ampelius**, and reads of the fall of the *"World-Egg"* at the beginning "into the river Euphrates" he perceives that he is in a mythologic, and not a historic region. [35] And when he lights upon a mutilated fragment of an ancient Assyrian inscription, in which descriptions of the visible and invisible world are mixed up together, and in which the river *"of the life of the world"* is designated by the name "Euphrates" [36] he quickly concludes that it will not do to take the term Phrath, or *Eu-frata*, as always and everywhere referring to the historic river of Mesopotamia. Hitherto, then, the "results" of the theologians as to the location of Eden are purely negative and mutually destructive. "It would be difficult," says one of their number, "to find any subject in the whole history of opinion which has so invited and at the same time so completely baffled conjecture as this. Theory after theory has been advanced, but none has been found that satisfies the required conditions. The site of Eden will ever rank, with the quadrature of the circle and the interpretation of unfulfilled prophecy, among those unsolved and perhaps insoluble problems which possess so strange a fascination." [37]

34. The Rev. A. H. Sayce in *The Academy*. London, Oct. 7, 1882: p. 263. "Professor Sayce, after recently observing that in early Akkadian mythology the mouth of the Euphrates was identified with the River of Death, adds, The Okeanos of Homer had, I believe, its origin in this Akkadian river which coiled itself around the world. " Robert Brown, Jun., F. R. S., *The Myth of Kirké* London. 1883: p. 33.

35. Bryant, *Analysis of Ancient Myths,* vol. Hi., pp. 160-162.

36. *Records of the Past*, x., p. 149.

37. William A. Wright, of Trinity College, Cambridge, in Smith's *Dictionary of the Bible,* Art. "Eden".

End of the Volume I

Made in the USA
Las Vegas, NV
29 December 2024

15510323R00249